Summer Haven

The Catskills, the Holocaust,
and the Literary Imagination

Jews of Russia and Eastern Europe and Their Legacy

Summer Haven

The Catskills, the Holocaust, and the Literary Imagination

Edited by
Holli Levitsky
and
Phil Brown

BOSTON
2016

Library of Congress Cataloging-in-Publication Data:
A catalog record for this book as available
from the Library of Congress.

ISBN 978-1-61811-418-1 (hardback)

ISBN 978-1-61811-419-8 (electronic)

ISBN 978-1-61811-516-4 (paperback)

Cover design by Ivan Grave.

Published by Academic Studies Press in 2015, paperback 2016.
28 Montfern Avenue
Brighton, MA 02135, USA
press@academicstudiespress.com
www.academicstudiespress.com

Table of Contents

Table of Contents

Acknowledgments

We would like first to thank Michael Berenbaum, whose insight, guidance, and friendship helped make this project possible.

At Loyola Marymount University, Nadia Pandolfo and Sarah Markowitz have been wonderful research assistants, helping with permissions, editing, research, manuscript assembly, and many important details. They kept us on track in all the ways we needed to enable us to bring this book to completion. Naomi Cahn also assisted with some important tasks.

Our contest for fiction and non-fiction original writings on the Catskills and the Holocaust was an important part of this book project. We offer thanks to the entrants, and of course the winners, whose works are published here. The contest was sponsored by the Catskills Institute, the Jewish Studies Program at Loyola Marymount University, Jewish Book Council, the "1939" Club, the Sigi Ziering Institute at American Jewish University, Brown University Judaic Studies Program, the Jewish American and Holocaust Literature Symposium, AskAbigail. com, and The Four Seasons Lodge film group. We are grateful to our distinguished contest judges, who read many entries and gave us their expertise in selecting the winners. Hasia Diner, Deborah Dash Moore, and Jonathan Sarna served as judges for the non-fiction contest, and Eileen Pollack, Thane Rosenbaum, and Yale Strom served as judges for the fiction contest.

Funding to assist in the production of this book came from the Office of the Dean in the Bellarmine College of Liberal Arts at Loyola Marymount University, and from Northeastern University's Jewish Studies Program, Humanities Center of the College of Social Sciences and Humanities, and the Department of Sociology and Anthropology.

The living relatives and writers represented in this book gave so much of themselves in letting their work be reprinted and in providing reflections on the selections. They are the ones who made the literature of the Holocaust-era Catskills so vivid and significant. We especially acknowledge Naima Prevots, daughter of Reuben Wallenrod, who continually helped us uncover more of the legacy of her father's foundational writing that inspired this book. She was a magnet for scholars who appreciated Wallenrod's work, and she provided us with many invaluable theses, dissertations, and studies.

So too did we get deep inspiration from our involvement with *The Four Seasons Lodge* film, especially director Andrew Jacobs and producer Matthew Lavine. The lodgers who ran that amazing bungalow colony gave us a legacy to draw on. In particular, Charles Swietarski, who spoke along with Andrew Jacobs at the 13th Annual History of the Catskills Conference, helped us understand the importance of the Four Seasons Lodge as a prompt to our book.

Conversations with colleagues, relatives, and friends added more ideas and support for this project, and we thank Jill Aizenstein, Stephen Katz, and Jeff Wallen. A lengthy interview with Sylvia Levitsky, and additional conversations with Louise Cohen Uzan, and Evelyn Cohen, added essential details. Some of the material in this book was presented at the Jewish American and Holocaust Literature Symposium, the conference for the Association for Jewish Studies and the Western Jewish Studies Association, and at "Absorbing Encounters: Constructing American Jewry in the Post-Holocaust Decades."

The Catskills Institute has been the beacon for over two decades of historical and archival work to preserve the amazing century of Jewish life in the Catskills. The executive committee, advisory board members, regular members, and conference attendees provided a milieu in which the work in the book could develop.

Sharona Vedol, our editor at Academic Studies Press until her recent departure just before we finalized the manuscript, gave us continual encouragement and help as we moved through this process. Meghan Vicks, our current editor, was very helpful as we finalized the manuscript and moved into the production process. Finally, Maxim Shrayer offered additional layers of material that enhanced the overall production. We owe him many thanks.

Our spouses and children listened to many conversations on this subject over the years, and offered consistent support for our work. We thank Ronnie Littenberg, Michael Littenberg-Brown, and Liza Littenberg-Tobias; and Mark Weitz, Sofya Levitsky-Weitz, and Jake Weitz. It is to them that we dedicate this book.

Sources and Permissions

Framing
and
History

Introduction

Phil Brown and Holli Levitsky

We provide here for the first time a collection of the most important writing that explores the stories and struggles of Holocaust survivors in the Catskills, as well as the experience of those already living in the United States who were in the Catskills during the Holocaust and the immediate years following. We present new and existing works of fiction and memoir by writers who spent their youth as part of the Jewish resort culture. Through these primary works, we explore how vacationers, resort owners, and workers dealt with a horrific contradiction—the pleasure of their summer haven against the mass extermination of Jews throughout Europe. We also examine the character of Holocaust survivors in the Catskills: in what ways did these people find connection, resolution to conflict, and avenues to come together, despite their experiences that set them apart? We took the opportunity to conduct more original research on the Holocaust and the immediate after-period in the Catskills. And we asked each author whose work is reprinted here in whole or part to reflect on the significance of their work in hindsight. Most of these reflections are written by the authors themselves, except in three cases where a wife, a daughter, or a scholar of the deceased writer provided the reflection, and one case where the author could not do so.

How We Conceived of This Project

Two main phenomena fostered our collaboration on this book. First, we were both involved in the film *Four Seasons Lodge*, a beautiful documentary of a bungalow colony collectively owned and run by Holocaust survivors. Phil was on the advisory board, having been asked to help because of his long-standing work in preserving the Jewish Catskills legacy via the Catskills Institute, and having written one book and edited another on the subject. At the thirteenth annual History of the Catskills Conference, he brought director Andrew Jacobs and two colony leaders to speak about their home and to show rushes from the film. Holli was involved in an associated project that did not come to fruition: a photo exhibition and book created from the same material as the film. The strength and creativity of the "lodgers" captivated us, as we came to see them as a unique contribution to Catskills history, and more broadly to Holocaust studies. Andrew Jacobs' essay in this book gives a full picture of the Four Seasons Lodge story, so we will not dwell on it here.

The second factor leading to our collaboration was a deep, shared appreciation of Reuben Wallenrod's novel, *Dusk in the Catskills*. Once we began to talk about how people in the Catskills lived during the Holocaust, we understood that Wallenrod portrayed this experience in a fashion unparalleled by others. Certainly Wallenrod's eloquent juxtaposition of genocide and pleasure made for a jarring, yet necessary, understanding. But more than that, Wallenrod told his story over the entire season of the Rosenblatt Hotel, from pre-season preparation all the way to post-season closing down. In the process, he recorded the life not just of a hotel, but of a people. We were glad to have had many years of contact with Wallenrod's daughter, Naima Prevots, who provides us with a reflection on her father's work. That contact gave us much more insight into this central work of Catskills Holocaust history, as we engaged with Naima's own interactions with students and scholars who were writing about Wallenrod's literary contributions. In *Catskill Culture: A Mountain Rat's Memory of the Great Jewish Resort Area*, Phil had already explored Wallenrod's fiction, as well as the work of other authors whom we include here. The present book was a welcome opportunity to expand Phil's earlier work, adding new historical research and Holli's knowledge of literary and Holocaust studies. In the second essay in this book, we explore *Dusk in the Catskills* in detail.

Our research on Reuben Wallenrod did uncover a literary prize that his family, upon his death and in partnership with the Hebrew Writers Association in Israel, established in his name.[1] The discovery of the Wallenrod family prize came after we had already taken the opportunity to run a pair of essay contests—one for fiction and one for nonfiction—that would produce original writing on the Catskills Holocaust experience. We are pleased to include the winners in this volume. Bonnie Shusterman Eizikovitz is co-winner of the fiction contest for "Catskill Dreams and Pumpernickel," a short story about a girl given the nickname Pumpernickel by a woman bungalow colony resident, a Holocaust survivor who is a parent figure for the youngster. The woman and her husband, despite his mechanical assistance to whomever asks a favor, are still outsiders because of their unique experience, while young Pumpernickel berates her own parents for their derision of these "greeners." Memories of the smuggled *shofar* in the concentration camp mingle with the current holiday in America.

Rita Calderon is the other fiction co-winner for "Your Dovid," a short story centered in 1938 on a girl and her family's effort to bring her father's brother to the Catskills hotels where her mother is the chef. Uncle Dovid arrives, but alone, since visas were denied to the rest of his family. Memories of other brothers punctuate the conversations, and we see the juxtaposition of Catskills' pleasures with Europe's horrors. Through these lenses, family secrets are revealed, while Dovid returns to France to try to get his family out.

Michael Kirschenbaum won the nonfiction contest for "Forgiving God in the Catskills," a chapter from his forthcoming memoir, *Not to Believe*. "Forgiving God in the Catskills" focuses on a Holocaust survivor

---

1 Benjamin Andrew Lerner, "A Portrait of the Hebraist as a Multifaceted Man: Using Reuben Wallenrod's Be'ein Dor to Examine American Hebraism." BA Thesis, Harvard University (2011), 23.

and his sons' visit to Kutsher's Country Club in the Catskills to celebrate *Rosh Hashanah*. Memories of the Holocaust punctuate the holiday services, as the Catskills are themselves memorialized as the places where "The *greeneh* were happy to mingle with the others who still embraced a Jewish culture with European roots."

It was a delight to be able to recruit new writing on this subject, and to add to the genre of "Catskills Studies" that has proliferated quite remarkably since the 1990s, and has engaged some of the top talent in Jewish literature.

A Brief History of the Jewish Catskills

The history of the Jewish Catskills begins with the farmlands of Ulster, Sullivan, southern Greene, and a tiny sliver of southeastern Delaware Counties. The year-round Jewish population of chicken and dairy farmers had a hard time making a living on the poor soil there, and began taking in boarders. Eventually many made that into their main enterprise. Some boarding houses became *kuchalayns* ("cook for yourself"), where rooms were rented in a boarding house in which kitchen and dining room were shared. These facilities housed ten to forty guests. *Kuchalayns* frequently developed into bungalow colonies, in which individual small cottages complete with kitchens were rented out. Some *kuchalayns* later turned into hotels. *Kuchalayns* and bungalow colonies provided a familial milieu: people were together the entire summer, forming very close connections.

By the 1950s few *kuchalayns* remained, all but replaced by bungalow colonies and hotels. The small- (50-250 guests) and medium-sized (250-500 guests) hotels retained the *kuchalayns*' intimacy. The owners, often a pair of in-law couples, were always present. They mingled with guests, many of whom were relatives and friends. Even in large hotels (500-1,000 guests), owners, guests, and staff often knew each other. Smaller hotels frequently employed "solicitors" to recruit guests from their city neighborhoods, and hotels acquired a local culture that continued into the rest of the year. Guests returned year after year, and often from generation to generation—a child in the day camp might later be a junior counselor, later he or she might work as a busboy or waiter in the dining room, and then return once again as a guest with a spouse and children. Guests developed a loyalty to the hotel and its owners, based on family, friendship, and on participating in a miniature society where relationships were amplified by the proximity. Many of the workers developed close bonds with each other, with the owners, and with longstanding guests, and many friendships lasted past the summer. Staff-guest romances were also not uncommon.

Guests made frequent visits to delis and shops in nearby towns, strolled past other resorts, and visited friends and relatives in other hotels and bungalow colonies. Bungalow dwellers were always sneaking into hotel casinos (which were social halls and night clubs, not gambling casinos), guests at small hotels were doing the same in larger hotels, and staff were perpetually visiting other hotels for romance. The Catskills Institute's research has located 863 bungalow colonies and 1,172 hotels that operated in the Catskills. At any given time in the golden era of the 1950s and 1960s, there were about 500 colonies and 550 hotels operating. An estimated one-half million people vacationed there annually in that period. No matter where you went in the Catskills, you were never far from a hotel or colony.

Catskills hotelkeepers pioneered the idea of the all-inclusive vacation, with three meals plus a nighttime tea-room, nightly entertainment, many sports and activities, and eventually day camps for children. During many decades when Gentile hotels barred Jews, the Catskills offered a vacation with kosher food, Yiddish conversation, and Jewish comedy and music as entertainment. Offering a range of prices, the resorts housed people of all classes and occupations. Even the more expensive resorts were still affordable to the average family for a weekend or a short stay.

In terms of origins, the Catskills were largely a bastion of Russian and Eastern European Jews. The Northern Catskills (Northern Ulster County and part of Greene County) in the area of Fleischmanns, Hunter, and Tannersville were largely German and Hungarian, though some Eastern Europeans were there as well. As Abraham Cahan's *The Rise of David Levinsky* records, German was commonly spoken in that northern area, and Yiddish was disparaged. The "Yekkies" of German descent commonly looked down on the poorer, more recent immigrants—an oft-told tale of American Jewish history. The vast majority of what we know of as the Catskills were in Sullivan and lower, western Ulster County, and the area had a decidedly Yiddishkeit culture. Yiddish was the first language for many hotel owners and guests in the pre-WWII era, and even after that Yiddish was commonly spoken. In 1913, Jewish farmers started the nation's first fire insurance cooperative, the Associated Cooperative Fire Insurance Company, since they faced problems of anti-Semitism and high rates. Business in the insurance co-op was conducted in Yiddish, including the meetings and minutes; the policies were written in Yiddish and then translated for legal purposes. Into the 1950s Hotelmen's Association meetings were full of people speaking Yiddish.

Some hotels and bungalow colonies were thoroughly Yiddishist, even into the sixties. The best known was the Grine Felder (Green Fields) literary colony in Woodridge, a major center of Yiddish writers, including Isaac Bashevis Singer. Merging both socialist and Yiddishist traditions, Grine Felder had bungalows named Emma Goldman, Karl Marx, and Mendele Sforim. Singer's Catskills background and interest shows through in his writings, including *Enemies, A Love Story*[2] and the short story "The Yearning Heifer"[3] that features the traditional small farmer putting up boarders from the city. His experience with the Catskills began in 1938—just three years after immigrating to New York from Poland. The visit was an opportunity to join his young friend and budding theater director Zygmunt Salkin at the Woodridge, NY bungalow colony, where he would oversee the rehearsal in English of I. L. Peretz's *At Night in the Old Marketplace*. Grine Felder was pioneered (and staffed) by a number of notable Yiddishists, including David Pinski, Mendl Elkin, Nahum Stutchkoff, Samuel Charney, Peretz Hirshbein, Jules Fainberg, Lazar Weiner, and Moishe Rudinow. The community also included prominent Zionists and socialists such as Joseph Schlossberg, and Polish and Russian refugee poets, writers, dramatists,

---

2   Isaac Bashevis Singer, *Enemies, A Love Story* (New York: Farrar, Straus and Giroux, 1988).
3   Isaac Bashevis Singer, "The Yearning Heifer," in *The Collected Stories of Isaac Bashevis Singer* (New York: Farrar, Straus and Giroux, 1983).

directors, producers, and critics such as Maurice Schwartz, Alexzander Mukdoiny, Abraham Shiffrin, Sidor Belarsky, and Rosina Fernhoff (whose father, Dr. William Fernhoff, was an Austrian-Jewish immigrant who made house calls in the Catskills to colonies such as Grine Felder). Much of the artistic material was produced in Yiddish, a common language among the immigrants. The persistence of Yiddish speaking, of Yiddish-English patois, and of Yiddish jokes in the Catskills after the Holocaust was a form of resistance against the Nazi attempt to destroy Jewish life. Most of the murdered Jews were Yiddish speakers, and the daily use of the language nearly died except for the Hassidic revival in the latter twentieth century and a smaller revival by secular Yiddishists.

A Glimpse into the Origin of the Jewish Catskills

There is a surprising number of *beshert* (destined) discoveries about the Catskills—finding connections with people and events that seem impossible. Indeed, Phil's years of running the Catskills Institute have yielded innumerable requests for connections to people from many decades ago, connections that were often found. We began this project with a strong focus on the significance of Reuben Wallenrod's *Dusk in the Catskills* as the emblematic examination of how the Holocaust was experienced in the Catskills. Wallenrod's vantage point as a writer-in-residence at Rosenblatt's Hotel (during the mid 1940s) is the underpinning of the very real basis for his work.

Rosenblatt's later was called the Coronet, and then the Empress, as we learned from John Conway, the Sullivan County Historian. Caryl Ehrlich wrote to the Catskills Institute in 2008 that her father, who had leased and owned other hotels, bought the Empress. It's another example of the endless connections that bring us into this web of Rosenblatt's and early Catskills history. As it turns out, the village of Glen Wild, Rosenblatt's location, is linked to even more important Catskills history. In particular, it has long been known that the first Jewish resort was started there in 1899, as advertised in the Ontario and Western Railroads' *Summer Homes*, the primary listing for Catskills resorts, which were only Gentile up till then. John Gerson has been considered the first

Rosenblatt's Hotel. Courtesy of the Catskills Institute.

The lake at Rosenblatt's Hotel. Courtesy of the Catskills Institute.

Jewish farmer, arriving in 1892.[4] I (Phil) had the great fortune to interview Gerson's granddaughter, Sylvia Ader, born in 1916. Yana (later changed to John) Gerson arrived in New York in the 1880s and worked in a bakery, which he didn't like. Having been a farmer near Vilna, and already running a small farm on Pitkin Avenue in Brooklyn, he followed that legacy and bought a farm in Glen Wild.[5] His doctor asked if he would take in a patient who needed the healing mountain air, and he did so. The doctor kept sending people up but John didn't charge them anything until the doctor pressured him into that. Fairly soon there were enough paying boarders to put up a new building, which sadly burned just before the scheduled opening.

4   Abraham D. Lavender and Clarence B. Steinberg, *Jewish Farmers of the Catskills: A Century of Survival* (Gainesville, FL: University Press of Florida, 1995), 31-33.

5   Lavender and Steinberg, *Jewish Farmers of the Catskills*, 31-33.

Gerson's resort was called the Rock Hill Jewish Boarding House, as Rock Hill was the next and more significant settlement, slightly to the west along the Glen Wild Road. The *Summer Homes* ad indicated that Gerson's had room for forty people at $6 per week for adults and half that for children.[6]

Gerson provided land for the Glen Wild *shul*,[7] and had to know Louis Rosenblatt, whose hotel hosted Wallenrod, since Rosenblatt was a charter member of Congregation Anshe Glen Wild (the name of the Glen Wild *shul*). The *shul* construction started in 1912 and took two years to finish. Louis Rosenblatt

Glen Wild *shul*. Courtesy of the Catskills Institute.

donated funds in 1955 to build a rear wing, used as a social hall.[8] When I (Phil) interviewed Abe and Dave Jaffe in 1993, they spoke about how proud they were to have had two *Torahs* in their house for services, for ten years until the Glen Wild *shul* was built across the road from them. They still treasured the *shul*'s huge ledger-size minutes book that they kept in their house.

Abe's daughter Naomi Jaffe still owns the farm in Glen Wild (as of 2014) that her grandfather Simon Jaffe bought in 1919 (he arrived in Glen Wild in 1904). It is right across the road from Gerson's property, though Naomi thought she remembered that Jaffe's is actually on the site of John Gerson's boarding house. From the twenties through the late fifties or early sixties, it was the Jaffe House Hotel and later *kuchalayn*, though they called it a bungalow colony and rooming house. On the premises they had a chicken farm from the thirties through the

---

6   Lavender and Steinberg, *Jewish Farmers of the Catskills*, 32.

7   Sylvia Ader interview (2004).

8   Kathleen LaFrank, "National Register of Historic Places Nomination, Anshei Glen Wild Synagogue," New York State Office of Parks, Recreation and Historic Preservation (October 1998). Retrieved April 29, 2009.

Jaffe House. Courtesy of Naomi Jaffe.

Glen Wild Honor Roll at Rosenblatt's Hotel. Courtesy of Naomi Jaffe.

seventies. Naomi Jaffe gave us a 1944 photo of the Glen Wild Honor Roll plaque of the Glen Wild men who served in World War II, with the women of the Glen Wild Women's Club standing and sitting in front of it. It is on the front lawn of Rosenblatt's Hotel, clearly visible in the background.

After the fire mentioned above destroyed the new building, Gerson became a partner with others in building South Fallsburg's New Prospect House, later to be renamed the New Prospect Hotel, and finally the Levitt. They gave away land to Jewish merchants so that there would be a butcher and baker, which helped build the Jewish community and also made it unnecessary to travel to New York City for kosher meat. Later they cut the original building in half and moved it to become two annexes, and in 1928 put up a new building with terrazzo floors and even some private baths, a rarity then. Perhaps the cost of that expansion was

Levitt Hotel. Courtesy of the Catskills Institute.

Levitt Hotel advertisement. Courtesy of the
Catskills Institute.

Pool at the Levitt Hotel. Courtesy of
the Catskills Institute.

Levitt Hotel casino. Courtesy of the
Catskills Institute.

prohibitive, since in 1935 the hotel was taken for unpaid taxes.[9] That was also the year Gerson died.

So, it is exciting to have identified Rosenblatt's and Wallenrod's Glen Wild as a central connection to the historical hub for the Jewish Catskills overall.

Jerusalem on the Neversink

Having a place with land aplenty and the freedom to live on it—that was a long-standing Jewish dream. *Eretz Yisrael*, the Land of Israel, was in the Jewish heart, liturgy, literature, and folklife for millennia. There are parallels between the return to Israel and the move to the Catskills. *Kibbutzniks* and others would make the desert bloom and grow the food to support themselves and their whole society. Jewish farmers moving to the Catskills would try to do something similar, though not being as successful beyond milk and eggs. Jewish philanthropist Baron de Hirsch provided funds and training for Jewish farmers to settle in Argentina, New Jersey, the Dakotas, Canadian Midwest provinces, and the Catskills, thinking that the land-driven productivity would make Jews acceptable to their larger societies.

The Jewish farmers, at least in the Catskills, in fact did something different, by building a very strong Jewish-centered culture from the 1890s onward. The extensive Catskills Jewish culture briefly described above in the "Brief History" section, and more completely recounted in Phil Brown's *Catskill Culture*, Irwin Richman's *Borscht Belt Bungalows*, and Abraham Lavender and Clarence Steinberg's *Jewish Farmers of the Catskills*, situates a context of hundreds of square miles of extensively Jewish territory. The thousands of resorts were served by synagogues, Jewish schools, Jewish tradespeople and merchants, Jewish cultural institutions like the Workmen's Circle, the Jewish Agricultural Society, the Farmers' Coop, and the Insurance Coop. The Jews in the Catskills created their own sort of Promised Land.

I (Phil) wrote five short stories about the Catskills, one of which is included in this book. Another, "The Boss's Visitor," recounts the

---

9 Sylvia Ader interview (2004).

relationship between a distressed hotel owner and his unexpected guest who ultimately shows him that his hotel/home/family/land is the Jerusalem of his heart. My intent was to locate this realization in his heart, but in retrospect I think the symbolism of return to Jerusalem is about the whole land of the Catskills. After the masses of immigrants came between the 1890s and 1920s, and when the survivors came in the 1940s, they built in the United States the largest Jerusalem outside of Israel. And they built their mini-Jerusalem in the Catskills.

Stemming from strong radical traditions of many Eastern European Jews, the Catskills also became a location for leftists of varying types, some preparing to return to *Eretz Yisrael,* and others seeking to build different visionary societies. For those who wanted to build the Promised Land, Hashomer Hatzair's Camp Shomria, Camp Hemshekh, and other labor Zionist and socialist Zionist groups set up training camps in the Catskills to recruit and prepare Jews for *aliyah* to Israel. Vladimir Jabotinsky, the Zionist-Revisionist leader, died of a heart attack while visiting Camp Betar near Hunter, NY in August 1940. The campers were members of the Zionist-Revisionist youth organization known as Brith Trumpeldor.[10] Some hotels were pointedly leftist. At Maud's Summer Ray, most guests were leftists in the pre-World War II era, ecumenically composed of socialists, communists, and Trotskyists. At Chester's Zunbarg radicalism met fine entertainment, and shows featured Pete Seeger, the Weavers, Woody Guthrie, Paul Robeson, Leon Bibb, Ossie Davis, and Rubie Dee. Arrowhead Lodge in Ellenville was very closely affiliated with the Communist Party and its adult education Jefferson School, an adult non-credit school in New York City. The radical Furrier's Union even built the Fur Worker's Resort, later called White Lake Lodge, started in 1949, but selling to a Jewish camp only six years later. Paul Robeson was a regular singer and speaker, and novelist Howard Fast was among the eminent lecturers there. Green Acres Hotel, owned by socialist New York State Assemblyman Elmer Rosenberg, sponsored

---

10 "Vladimir Jabotinsky Dies of Heart Attack at 59; Was Visiting Youth Camp," *The Global Jewish News Source* (August 5, 1940). http://www.jta.org/1940/08/05/archive/vladimir-jabotinsky-dies-of-heart-attack-at-59-was-visiting-youth-camp.

local socialist activities, and hired blacklisted show business figures like Zero Mostel.

Woodridge, a town whose year-round population had a Jewish majority, bought an ambulance to send to the Spanish loyalists in the Civil War. Workmen's Circle chapters were founded in several towns, with their combination of socialism, union organizing, Yiddishist culture, and benevolent associations. In the 1930s when some Jews supported the Soviet Union's plans for a Birobidjan homeland for the Jews, camps in the Catskills trained people for that failed effort. Late 1940s and 1950s Catskills activism included local efforts on the progressive 1948 Henry Wallace campaign for president, as well as going across the Hudson to Peekskill to the famous 1949 Paul Robeson concert where the singer and his audience were stoned while state and local police looked on with encouragement, and then arrested the victims.

Another kind of return has occurred in recent decades: Soviet Jews, whose modern-day, large-scale migration to the United States began in the 1970s,[11] made their way to the Catskills even as the area had begun to fade as a major resort destination. Sergei Dovlatov, the Jewish-Russian writer widely considered among the most talented and influential of "third wave" Russian émigrés, in 1988 purchased a bungalow in Monticello (borrowing the location for his thinly fiction-alized novel, *A Foreign Woman*). Already in the mid-to-late 1980s there are hotels—formerly Jewish resorts in the Catskills—that either cater to or are owned by Soviet Jewish émigrés. Among the contributions of this new group is the revival of two abandoned hotels: the Grand Mountain in Greenfield Park and the Rainbow (formerly the Alpine) in Ulster Heights. Tenderly coaxed from near ruined status, these hotels, which had never been modernized and hence retained their 1920s phys-ical character, still look so authentic that they could be movie sets for a film about that era. The Catskills Institute included them on a bus tour at one of its History of the Catskills Conferences, to show the proud revival of beautiful small hotels that epitomized that legacy. Somewhat

---

11 Maxim D. Shrayer, *An Anthology of Jewish-Russian Literature: Two Centuries of Dual Identity in Prose and Poetry, Volume 2: 1953-2001* (Armonk: M. E. Sharpe, Inc., 2007). http://fmwww.bc.edu/sl-v/ShrayerNEH2013Selection.pdf.

differently, the 100-year old Campbell Inn in Roscoe, until recently owned by Russian Jews, will soon be demolished and rebuilt as The Campbell Chateau Resort and Health Spa. The $80 million, eleven-story hotel, which once catered to primarily Jewish vacationers, would not be affordable to the Soviet immigrants who found their way there in the 1980s and 1990s.[12] For several years, younger Russian and other Eastern European immigrants have been retreating in droves to campgrounds in the Catskills for weekend-long music and cultural festivals.

The Order of the Book

To round out the "Framing and History" section, our first essay after this Introduction is a detailed analysis of Reuben Wallenrod's novel *Dusk in the Catskills* and its central role in Catskills Holocaust history. As the premier literary representation of the Catskills Holocaust experience, Wallenrod's work takes center stage for us. Our second section "Memoirs and Conversations" includes memoirs by each of the two co-authors, as well as by Jewish literature scholar Sandor Goodhart and Michael Berenbaum, eminent Holocaust scholar who was responsible for the design of the United States Holocaust Memorial Museum's exhibits. Phil's and Holli's memoirs situate their Catskills experiences as a way to understand the importance of the Holocaust era. Goodhart's memoir links testimonial, literary, and Jewish values, while Berenbaum's memoir addresses the tasks in and role of memorializing the Holocaust in various manners. In the third section, "Imaginings and Re-imaginings," we present short stories and excerpts from novels and memoirs, accompanied by the authors' or others' reflections on what those works meant for understanding the Catskills Holocaust experience. In keeping with our focus on Wallenrod, his work leads off this section. It is followed by Isaac Bashevis Singer's *Enemies, A Love Story,* Harvey Jacobs' *Summer on a Mountain of Spices,* Martin Boris' *Woodridge 1946,* Art Spiegelman's *Maus II,* Eileen Pollack's *Paradise,*

---

12 In an email interview with Jewish-Russian author Maxim Shrayer, he reflected on a discovery-filled August 1988 visit to the Campbell Inn during his second American summer in the United States. A fictional memoir, based on that nine-day experience, is nearly completed. (Interview with Maxim Shrayer, 2015).

New York, Thane Rosenbaum's "Bingo by the Bungalow," Phil Brown's "A Catskills' Muse," Joseph Berger's *Displaced Persons: Growing Up American After the Holocaust*, Jake Ehrenreich's *A Jew Grows in Brooklyn*, and Ezra Cappell's *Dreaming in the Ninth*. In our section "New Imaginings and Last Days" we feature an essay by Andrew Jacobs about the making and reception of the film *The Four Seasons Lodge*. Finally, we include the three contest-winning essays that we described above.

Themes

Each selection in our book was chosen because the author writes about an element of the Holocaust or immediate after-period that takes place in the Catskills. The Catskills as a new Jerusalem is prominent in each of these selections. For the survivors who populate the Catskills stories, it was enough to have a safe retreat with others like themselves—a haven—to consider it a new Jerusalem. But we also observed a particular set of themes emerging, themes that both highlight the idea of the Catskills as a haven, and extensively draw out the well-known features of Catskills life. Considered together, the stories weave a mosaic of characters. Their words and feelings convey a longing to recapture the pre-Holocaust past, an incapacity to measure the immense loss caused by the Holocaust, a willingness to laugh and cry simultaneously, and an understanding of the human need for love and connection even after such full-scale loss. These themes also surface frequently in Holocaust literature, but examined against the backdrop of the Jewish Catskills, they can be seen to embody both the Jewish literary imagination and the deeply felt Jewish connection to the Catskills. Thus the primary themes we identify in these literary works—nostalgia, loss, humor, and sexuality—also bind that literature to more established literary genres (the Holocaust, the Catskills) while serving the need to define the borders of this new genre of writing. In examining these themes, we find a language peculiar to survivors and the Jewish Catskills dwellers, both of whom were seeking a new Jerusalem in the mountains. Our main focus is on two questions: When the knowledge about the atrocities against the Jews in Europe began to emerge, what did Jews in the mountains say and do? How did the Catskills landscape provide a haven for the refugees and survivors who made their way to the mountains? Each story in this collection uniquely addresses these questions, and the answers to them add up to a kind of grammar, one that borrows heavily from the vernacular of the Jewish Catskills. The stories articulate how survivors approached their new Jerusalem in the mountains, detailing moments both unique to the survivors and familiar to the many other visitors to the Catskills.

In the next chapter, we investigate in detail the literary imagination of Reuben Wallenrod, whose 1957 novel, *Dusk in the Catskills,* plays a central role in Catskills Holocaust history. The novel's focus on the inner life of hotelkeeper Leo Halper helps to create a sharp tension between the stories of violence and destruction coming from Europe and the Jewish immigrant's comfort in the calming, panoramic Catskills landscape. In keeping us in both linear, chronological time and the cyclical time of seasons and associative memories, our reading experience is directed by Halper's thoughts but also by the larger story of Catskills resort life and Halper's—and likely Wallenrod's—own memories of his childhood village in Poland. Halper can neither imagine what has been lost in Europe nor what that loss will mean to him, personally, in his haven. But he suffers deeply from his concern.

I. B. Singer's 1972 novel, *Enemies, A Love Story* (directed as a 1989 film by Paul Mazursky), similarly addresses the incapacity to imagine the extent of the Holocaust. In this story, we learn about the impossibility of life returning to normal for survivors after the Holocaust. And yet, even with the knowledge of such loss, and in the face of fractured lives, there is humor, love, sexuality, and, always, the search for a haven from that knowledge. For some, life can go on, but not without serious cost. Similarly, Harvey Jacobs' 1975 novel, *Summer on a Mountain of Spices* romps through the lives of the owners and guests at a small family hotel in the Catskills during the final two weeks of World War II. The characters' longings and desires are played out amid an abundance of sexual activity and humor, and as a haven against the war (fortunately raging to an end). The lustiness and earthiness of the landscape builds to a climactic end on the day the war ends. In the final chapter, the main character, now an adult with a family of his own, returns with a burning nostalgia to seek out his original Catskills homeland.

Loss is the central theme in Martin Boris' novel *Woodridge 1946* and in Art Spiegelman's graphic memoir *Maus II*. Apart from sharing this central theme, the two books could not be more different in shape and in content, and their juxtaposition highlights the diversity of texts about the Catskills and the Holocaust. In the former, soldiers are returning home from the war; what they witnessed there altered their worldview, dwarfing their own concerns as they contemplate the massive loss of European Jewry. The love story at the center of the novel moves from passion to revenge in the face of one returning soldier's "psychic paralysis." In the graphic memoir, the second written by Spiegelman about his father's experiences in the Holocaust and after, we see the ongoing effects of Vladek Spiegelman's ordeal—over four decades later. For Vladek, the Catskills are a retreat *from* as much as a retreat *to*; the mountains are a calming distraction from the constant traumatic memories he carries like a second skin (French survivor Charlotte Delbo writes that "Auschwitz is there, unalterable, precise, but enveloped in the skin of memory, an impermeable skin that isolates it from my present self"[13]). His home in the Catskills gives him some level of autonomy over his increasingly chaotic life.

Later authors continued to mine their own personal histories while imagining life in the mountains. Eileen Pollack's novel, *Paradise, New York*, artfully and sympathetically uses humor and nostalgia to call into question the "new" new Jerusalem. The best of the Catskills was full of earthiness, humor, and community—her story asks if a new Catskills can offer a similar refuge for the exiled. As the original Catskills *Yiddishkeit* world dies off, can modern anthropologists keep it alive as a place to let people experience the old Catskills resorts while studying that world? The short story, "Bingo by the Bungalow," by Thane Rosenbaum, shows us that communal world as it might look if inhabited only by Holocaust survivors. The story creates a universe in which the deafening, clashing, and completely unsuitable topic of the Holocaust is so mainstream that

---

13 Charlotte Delbo, *Days and Memory*, Trans. by R. Lamont (Evanston: Northwestern University Press, 2001), xvii.

its existence provides a case for Holocaust renewal (or at least Holocaust refuge). In "A Catskills' Muse," Phil Brown turns to the imagination to find the right voice for his own sentimental journey through the Catskills, stopping to consider how he can use that nostalgia for the past to further preserve Holocaust memories for all time. Drawing on the power of nostalgia to assist the imagination in creating whole worlds becomes a kind of alchemy, in much the same way that good literature transforms experience and imagination into art.

Joe Berger's *Displaced Persons: Growing Up American After the Holocaust,* is a love story to his survivor-parents. They experienced immeasurable loss, working tirelessly after the war to re-establish a home and family life. While he chronicles the immense loss suffered by his parents and others, he also honors the refuge in the mountains that offered an opportunity for survivors to carve out new lives for themselves and their children. Similarly, Jake Ehrenreich's coming-of-age story and theatrical stage piece, *A Jew Grows in Brooklyn,* transforms his Holocaust survivor family's challenges into a positive message, as a mission to spread healing. For the Ehrenreichs, as for others, the Catskills was a place to experience fresh air, wide-open spaces, and the healing power of laughter. Our final selection, a chapter from Ezra Cappell's unpublished novel *Dreaming in the Ninth,* captures the excruciating moment when a boy hears the ineffable story of his grandfather's suffering. Even the exquisite sound of the Kaaterskill Falls cannot drown out his new knowledge, and the reader suspects that for the boy, everything has changed.

Now, we welcome you into this mixture of the old and new worlds from seven decades ago, in which we can find many traces of our identity and history.

Bibliography

Ader, Sylvia. Interview with Phil Brown. 2004.

Aizenstein, Jill. "Engaging America: Immigrant Jews in American Hebrew Literature." Ann Arbor: ProQuest, UMI Dissertation Publishing, 2011.

Berger, Joseph. *Displaced Persons: Growing Up American After the Holocaust*. New York: Washington Square Press, 2001.

Boris, Martin. *Woodridge 1946*. New York: Crown Publisher, 1980.

Brown, Phil. *Catskill Culture: A Mountain Rat's Memories of the Great Jewish Resort Area*. Philadelphia: Temple University Press, 1998.

Brown, Phil, ed. *In the Catskills: A Century Of The Jewish Experience In "The Mountains."* New York: Columbia University Press, 2002.

Cahan, Abraham. *The Rise of David Levinksy*. New York: Harper, 1917.

Cappell, Ezra. *Dreaming in the Ninth*. Unpublished manuscript.

Delbo, Charlotte. *Days and Memory*. Translated by R. Lamont. Evanston: Northwestern University Press, 2001.

Ehrenreich, Jake. *A Jew Grows in Brooklyn*. Deerfield Beach, FL: Health Communications Inc, 2010.

Global Jewish News Source, "Vladimir Jabotinsky Dies of Heart Attack at 59; Was Visiting Youth Camp," *The Global Jewish News Source* (August 5, 1940). http://www.jta.org/1940/08/05/archive/vladimir-jabotinsky-dies-of-heart-attack-at-59 -was-visiting-youth-camp

Jacobs, Harvey. *Summer on a Mountain of Spices*. New York: Harper & Row, 1975.

LaFrank, Kathleen. "National Register of Historic Places nomination, Anshei Glen Wild Synagogue." New York State Office of Parks, Recreation and Historic Preservation (October 1998). Retrieved April 29, 2009.

Lavender, Abraham D. and Clarence B. Steinberg. *Jewish Farmers of the Catskills: A Century of Survival*. Gainesville, FL: University Press of Florida, 1995.

Lerner, Benjamin Andrew. "A Portrait of the Hebraist as a Multifaceted Man: Using Reuben Wallenrod's Be'ein Dor to Examine American Hebraism." BA Thesis, Harvard University, 2011.

Ontario and Western Railroads. *Summer Homes*. Various Years.

Pollack, Eileen. *Paradise, New York*. Philadelphia: Temple University Press, 1998.

Richman, Irwin. *Borscht Belt Bungalows: Memories of Catskill Summers*. Philadelphia: Temple University Press, 1997.

Rosenbaum, Thane. "Bingo by the Bungalow." In *Elijah Visible.* New York: St. Martin's Press, 1996.

Shrayer, Maxim D. *An Anthology of Jewish-Russian Literature: Two Centuries of Dual Identity in Prose and Poetry, Volume 2: 1953-2001.* Armonk: M. E. Sharpe, Inc., 2007. http://fmwww.bc.edu/sl-v/ShrayerNEH2013Selection.pdf

Shrayer, Maxim, Interview with Phil Brown. 2015.

Singer, Isaac Bashevis. *Enemies, A Love Story.* New York: Farrar, Straus and Giroux, 1972.

Singer, Isaac Bashevis, "The Yearning Heifer." In *The Collected Stories of Isaac Bashevis Singer.* New York: Farrar, Straus and Giroux, 1983.

Spiegelman, Art. *Maus: A Survivor's Tale, II: And Here My Troubles Began.* New York: Random House, 1992.

Wallenrod, Reuben. *Dusk in the Catskills.* New York: Reconstructionist Press, 1957.

Reuben Wallenrod's *Dusk in the Catskills* and its Central Role in Catskills Holocaust History

Holli Levitsky and Phil Brown

American popular culture has long represented Catskills mountain life as offering a home away from home for Jews. Films, novels, plays, and short stories share a common landscape that include many Catskills mountain resorts, hotels large and small, bungalow colonies, and *kuchalayns* (boarding houses with shared kitchens) that were primarily in Ulster and Sullivan Counties, New York. Generations of writers in America have documented, as witnesses and as participants, the life of the Jewish mountain dwellers, while others have poetically reimagined the world as a perfect confluence of people and place, culture and time. In the earlier literature, like Abraham Cahan's 1917 American masterpiece, *The Rise of David Levinsky*, we get a glimpse into that particularly Jewish domain, within which functions an entire range of Jewish society and whose naturalistic borders seem more in line with Theodore Dreiser than Cahan's Yiddish speaking and writing ancestors.

The medium of film has also mined the cultural richness of Catskills life, almost always as an opportunity to tell a larger story about Jews in America. Paul Mazursky's 1989 adaptation of I. B. Singer's *Enemies,*

A Love Story, which takes place in 1949, brings the Holocaust into contact with Jewish-American and Jewish-immigrant life. The 1999 Tony Goldwyn-directed film *Walk on the Moon* takes place against the backdrop of the Woodstock music festival, and Ang Lee's 2009 *Taking Woodstock* reimagines the 1960s zeitgeist in dialogic encounter with that earlier heyday that was the Jewish Catskills.

By the time more contemporary American writers such as Art Spiegelman, Allegra Goodman, Thane Rosenbaum, and others write about the Catskills, in the 1980s and beyond, the genre of Jewish Catskills has identifying characteristics. Its narratives present landscapes upon which reside a deeply connected community of Jews who remain wary of others—mostly gentiles—and segregate themselves from those others. In the stories that take place before the 1960s, segregation from the American mainstream was often a result of anti-Semitic practices barring Jews from other hotels and resorts.

Elinor Lipman takes up this issue of exclusion in a comic fashion in *The Inn at Lake Devine* (1998), where she links the culture of two very different resorts—the large Jewish Halseeyon in the Catskills and the small anti-Semitic Inn at Lake Devine in Vermont. Natalie Marx, incensed at the family's 1962 exclusion from the Inn at Lake Devine, plans revenge. But revenge gets tempered by a later visit when she accompanies Robin, a gentile summer camp friend and her family who just happen to be long-time vacationers at the Inn. Robin is later engaged to one son of the Inn's owners, but dies in a car crash on the way to her wedding at the Inn. Natalie, then a newly graduated chef, stays and helps cook and tend to the mourners, cementing Natalie's attachment to the Vermont hotel. By the book's end, Natalie has married the other son, whom she has fallen for when they formed part of a group visiting the Catskills.

In general, characters in all of the narratives of the more recent writers on the Catskills—including those about communities of religious Jews, socialists, and Holocaust survivors—voluntarily isolate themselves from a world that poses existential threats to their belief systems or frames of reference. Commonly, the desire to be in the mountains also signals an alienation from the city and a Romantic appreciation for the natural world. These characters are drawn away from the metropolis and out into rural, small-town America. The stories present a landscape rich with human contact, in a place culturally and abundantly Jewish. It is nostalgic, to be sure, but nostalgia evokes yearning for a real as much as ideal past. For example, there are extensive descriptions of food purchasing, meal preparation and consumption, exuberant and lusty sexuality, family politics and friendly and not-so-friendly bickering, and the ubiquitous tummlers, or entertainers, and their uniquely humorous ways. All of this abundant life is carried out within a world that is both synchronic and diachronic, deeply present in and upon its own landscape and inescapably pressed into chronological time, affectively clothed as nostalgic.

As each decade of Jewish-American life is woven into these Catskills stories, it becomes increasingly clear that Catskills Jewish life mirrors and reflects the larger state of Jews in American life and the issues they confronted. For example, what became known as "the Borscht Belt" (a term often used by journalists but which veterans of the culture rarely, if ever, used)—the Catskills era from the 1930s until the early 1970s—was in fact crafted out of institutional and tacitly practiced anti-Semitism: discriminatory practices of the twentieth century that kept Jews and other so-called undesirable groups away from housing in certain neighborhoods, membership in country clubs, and mainstream centers of recreation. Later, ultra religious Jewish groups looking for a way to keep their community insular would recreate a kind of *shtetl* life in the mountains. The current flavor of the Catskills is largely influenced by growing numbers of these religious Jews. Socialists, bundists, communists, and others in the Catskills had a way to collectively congregate and practice their beliefs away from more mainstream American Jews—and mainstream America—who at significant points in history did not want to be associated with what seemed like godless and ideologically driven systems.

From this leitmotif of Jewish separateness, we can identify at least three distinct and common themes in Catskills literary writing. The characters are drawn to the small-town, rural life that the Catskills Mountains offers, but remain segregated from the gentile world there.

They are exuberant in their appetites: for food, sexuality, humor, and entertainment. And the setting, though localized, tends to reflect the larger issues facing Jews in America.

The largest issue facing Jews during the Jewish Catskills' heyday was the Holocaust. As Jews in the Catskills mountain resorts, hotels, and bungalow colonies, as well as those living private lives, began learning about the extent of the atrocities against the Jews of Europe, how did they respond? Fortunately, we have a critical mass of literary writings about the war and postwar eras that address the situation of the Jews in Europe. These writings forge a sense of connection between Jews in America and their European coreligionists, identify conflict within the hearts and souls of the Jews in America in their inability to act upon those feelings of connection, and articulate a deep commiseration with their plight. These literary writings have offered the non-observer to these atrocities an opportunity to witness the horror of the time. It is a particular kind of witnessing, active rather than passive, with literature mediating the testimonial experience. The texts we introduce in this project help us understand the complexity of this commemorative space—they offer plots, scenes, characters, and settings that stage connections between Jews in the United States and those trapped in, or survivors of, war-ravaged Europe. The stories create shapes through which to explore internal conflicts that shamed some to silence. And they use these themes to move private memory into public space. These literary acts honor the memory of and serve as a memorial to the murdered Jews of Europe and the destruction of Jewish European life.

Novels, short stories, and memoirs pose this commemorative space. These literary and graphic writings can be seen individually and collectively as lamentations on the theme of life and loss in the Holocaust. We focus here on one novel, the American Hebrew writer Reuben Wallenrod's *Dusk in the Catskills*, which as we noted in the Introduction, was one of the key features that fostered our collaboration. Written in Hebrew between 1941-44 and first published in 1946 as *Ki Fanah Yom* (literally, *Because the Day Turns*), it was translated by the author into English and published by the Reconstructionist Press of Wyncote, PA in 1957. Although no longer well-known, Wallenrod was part of a group of writers known as "Jewish Nationalists," or "Hebraists": Jews whose core identity was neither American nor Jewish American but ardently and nationalistically Jewish. He was an accomplished novelist and literary critic with a number of published books and studies on Hebrew literature.

Dusk in the Catskills follows hotel owner Leo Halper over the course of one full year, from the end of one summer season to the following autumn. During this period, the United States has entered the war in Europe. Leo Halper, like Wallenrod, a Jewish immigrant from Eastern Europe, feels acutely and painfully aware of the atrocities happening to the Jews in Europe. At the same time, he simply and unabashedly loves his little hotel and the beauty of the Catskills landscape. Wallenrod provides a third-person limited narration in order to share Halper's thoughts as they are happening. Thus the book unfolds in real time as Leo experiences it. Further, it is prophetic in its mixing of past, present, and future tenses to unfold the terrible story of the destruction of European Jewry. Wallenrod provides a clue to his prophetic role as writer and witness in the opening epigraph from Jeremiah 6.4: "Woe unto us! For the day declineth, / For the shadows of the evening are stretched out." Interestingly, the epigraph exists only in the English version, written after the war, and seems to send back a warning, announcing the imminent arrival of danger. The idea of warning one's "flock" is a leading feature of the writer's mission to his people and his nation, and to the surrounding world. And this warning was confirmed by time. *Dusk in the Catskills* then stands—with Jeremiah—as a prophet's lamentation at the suffering of his people, even as he sees some expression of divine verdict in their exile. Exiles can still be reached by God.

Who are these exiles? Leo Halper offers his limited and shared point of view on their lives. Safely ensconced in his American mountain retreat, he sees that European Jewish life is disappearing. Most of his associates are other European Jewish immigrants, many of whom had lived in Israel, like him, and most of whom spoke Hebrew. These intellectuals, writers, and artists were the ones who came each summer to his little hotel, who valued the Hebrew language, art, and culture over

English language and American culture. There was an understanding among them that a diasporic and alienated Jewish American public, which was unable or unwilling to learn and read Hebrew, or to know Jewish texts or practice Jewish rituals, would likely not read their works or invest in their intellectual climate. Thus they formed their own culture-in-exile.

Interestingly, this culture-in-exile looks different from the dominant culture-in-exile in the Catskills—the Yiddishist culture that itself was a minority among the generally modernist cultural features of most resorts that favored Broadway shows over classic Yiddish literature and music. Perhaps the most classic of the Yiddishist resorts was the bungalow colony in Woodridge, Grine Felder (Greed Fields), founded in 1936 by largely communist friends dissatisfied with their accommodations at the nearby Mirth Colony. They purchased land from Avon Lodge, a hotel most known for nurturing Sid Caesar's tummler career. Each bungalow was named for a Yiddishist (Sholem Aleichem, I. L. Peretz) or leftist (Rosa Luxemburg, Emma Goldman) leader, and the colony lasted till 1978 (Boris 1998). As Martin Boris, also represented in our book by an excerpt from his *Woodridge 1946*, notes about Grine Felder:

> But this was no ordinary Catskill resort for the families of middle-class Jewish shopkeepers and businessmen who would come for a respite from Manhattan's swelter. When [Zygmunt] Salkin and [Isaac Bashevis] Singer arrived, Grine Felder had been for two years summer home to the most concentrated assemblage of Yiddishist elite anywhere on Earth. While other groups—artists, leftists, Bohemians—organized their own colonies, none equaled the caliber of talent at Grine Felder.

As a small hotel owner, Leo Halper has many bills to pay, and fewer visitors to his little hotel. He worries that he might lose his hotel. He worries that the world of the Jewish Catskills is fading. He worries that the many immigrant writers and artists who depend upon him each summer season will lose that community. These are real concerns that emerge in his conversations with his wife and family. But the larger and more poignant worry that grows within him, hidden from the others, is the trouble in Europe, the horrifying details about which he comes to know more and more during the course of the novel. As he enjoys his family time, community engagement, and verdant surroundings, he simultaneously bemoans what he imagines may be an imminent demise of this domestic serenity. He obsesses over the destruction of European Jewry, roused to an almost feverish state of anxiety over his helplessness. Halper feels existentially connected to his coreligionists in Europe. He remembers fondly his early years on that landscape, a setting not unlike the Catskills where he now lives. He remembers himself as a boy, running in the fields and swimming in the ponds of the old country. Many of his relatives remain there still. While these memories of his youth crowd his mind, he notes with wonder the young people dancing in the hotel casino:

> The heart knows well that there is another great wide, threatening world outside you, but you are afraid to stop your dancing and think of that world. Such knowledge may well break up the charm of the circle, it may well break up your very being, all of you. . . . They come, however, those people and stand before you. You see among them men and women you actually knew. You have known them with your eyes and you have known them in your imagination. (151-2)

> It was bad when they started coming. They crept from outside and from inside, from yourself. They seemed to speak somewhere in your consciousness. (256)

Switching between third-person omniscient and third-person limited omniscient narration, Halper refers both to the others and to himself with the pronoun "you." This carries the tone of either a sermon or a rabbinical blessing or command. Like the leader of a congregation, Halper bears responsibility for his people and believes that they may not know what is best, or how to act, or how to see the deeper catastrophe underlying the Holocaust. In the first passage in particular, he conveys the strength of the connection between all Jews: the younger generation, who cannot help but know about the developing destruction in Europe, joyously dance together in the casino, because that's what young people do, while images of his family and friends in the old country flood his heart and stand before his eyes. He sees their suffering. In the merging of the pronoun in both passages, from the "you" of others to the "you" of himself, all Jews become connected to one another. Whether they came from the old country or were born in the new one no longer matters: the crisis of their suffering emerges from consciousness and has the potential to crack open their world.

In the pages of the novel, we don't always know which particular historical event is being depicted, nor whether this is deliberate, but we learn about general mayhem, and the roundup, torture, deprivation, and murder of the Jews, as Leo reads the *New York Times*, or listens to radio broadcasts from his living room. The characters share this information among themselves, but our point of view is through Leo, and it is Leo who dwells on the terrible details coming from abroad. Among his greatest concern is what to do with the knowledge of the atrocities. There is an ambivalence that he cannot shake. Like other Jews, he donates to the Jewish National Fund and other sources willingly, to help the new Israeli refugees and resettlement. In his many inner monologues, he struggles with feeling satisfaction in being amidst the lakes and the mountains: as soon as he feels grateful to have escaped the bleakness and death, fear and torture, he also feels shame. He is deeply conflicted, and his anxiety breaks down into three main feelings: he is frustrated at not being able to help his family and friends in Europe; he feels shame for being safely away from the atrocities; and he experiences guilt at the feelings of joy his life brings him. He isn't willing to sacrifice his daily comfort. But he has whole memories of a world now being destroyed, and lives in a liminal state between feelings of shame and joy:

> He was gnawed by the thought that he and Lillian were hiding here between the mountains in a sheltered den. There, across the mountains, terrible things were going on. People were being driven with whips in the cold and wind; little children stood helplessly on the side of the road like forsaken sheep, and near them and from above them came fearful shrieks through the storm. And he, Leo Halper, was hiding here between the walls of his house in the Catskill Mountains. It was awesome and shamefully pleasant in the shelter. (24)

Writing this story during the terrible years of 1941-1944, when so many atrocities were being committed against the Jews of Europe, but when the full extent was not yet known, the European born Reuben Wallenrod wrote what he knew then. When he returned to the story, rewriting it in English for a 1957 publication, much more was known, and could be written back into the novel. In both the Hebrew and English versions, Wallenrod bemoans the atrocities so that they are voiced, and thus remembered. Revealed only to the reader, this private form of commemoration is associated with Leo's ambivalence about feeling safe while his coreligionists are dying in Europe. In a novel of almost 300 pages, we are asked to think about the war in Europe and its Jewish victims in every chapter, on almost every page. It is neatly and elegantly drawn into the larger story of the fading Jewish Catskills, but it is a story in its own right. The terrible facts are just surfacing in the 1940s for author Reuben Wallenrod; for narrator, hotel owner, and European Jewish immigrant Leo Halper, they are happening in real time:

> People hid behind frost-covered windows, warmed their hands on iron stoves, and listened to the sounds coming from the radio. The sounds seemed to come in the storm. The window panes trembled, the trees hummed, the voices on the radio told of terrible storms across the mountains and the oceans. There people fled in terror, hid in snow pits; men and women left the houses in which they had lived all their lives and ran like frightened animals. There, across the mountains and the oceans, wild beasts laughed and mocked and threatened, and here a man sat and listened to the radio. (63)

Leo is a character who commands sympathy and respect, and thus his inner monologues about the victims in Europe offer the reader a site of remembrance that is authentic and reliable. His self-reflective nature offers us ongoing access to his inner thoughts so we know this ineffable desire to commemorate the suffering of his coreligionists. We know, and feel, his frustration over the lack of understanding among his gentile neighbors. He wants to reach everyone with his tender feelings, but he is ashamed to feel blessed at the same time.

In remembering those who lived—and died—through his fictional account, Wallenrod's very private narrator presents a public and thus shared memory of the Holocaust. Indeed, the novel operates as a commemoration of the Holocaust in the Catskills, which resonates with new research put forth by historians such as Hasia Diner. This position forcefully rejects the belief that the war years and immediate postwar years were barren of memory and memorialization of the Holocaust. It was unlikely that during those years American Jews deliberately avoided talking or writing about the Holocaust, or bringing the Holocaust into the public sphere. These new studies shift our understanding of that period, as does Wallenrod's novel, and indeed, so does the body of literary and commemorative writings that come from or are about Jews in the Catskills.

We must also note that Halper's personal financial concerns are tied to his fear that the whole Catskills Jewish culture was declining—in fact it was about to enter a two-decade period of bloom. The potential loss of the Jewish Catskills is parallel, though of course not comparable, to the large-scale destruction of Jewish life in Europe. We don't know if Wallenrod intended this, but it certainly appears so. All loss of Jewish life and culture is part of a millennia-old narrative of destruction and exile, and this is definitely a point we must take away from *Dusk*.

It is clear that the Jews of the United States shaped, from the ground up, a memorial culture during the war. They had to: there was no recent Jewish, or American, historical precedent for this sort of commemorative culture. Wallenrod's novel, and others like it in this genre, show that Jews of all traditions made room for the Holocaust in large and small ways, that they "wove the catastrophe deeply into the basic fabric of community life and that they considered what they said and did as monuments to Europe's destroyed Jewish world."[1]

The community life of Jews in the Catskills bears out this thesis. It offers a powerful example of Jews finding ways to release their rising fears and ongoing anxieties during and after the war years by engaging in community life while living beside the disaster. The ubiquitous entertainers—hired to amuse and distract the guests at every large and many small hotels—were as conscious as other Jews about what was happening overseas. Their acts often included jokes about the war. But, as Jake Ehrenreich pointed out in his reflection piece, survivors cried at home and laughed in the Catskills. The social climate of the mountains

---

1   Hasia Diner, "A Place in the Country," *The Jewish Monthly* (September/October 1998): 10-13.

addressed a lighter side of life: an abundance of pleasures in the form of food, sex, dancing, humor. Surrounded by carnality, it would not have been seemly to speak directly and publically about the state of European Jewry. But it was surely within the heart and mind of every Jew.

For the European-born Reuben Wallenrod, such things were even more complex. Wallenrod lost his father, sister, and her two children in the Holocaust. His book honors their memory even as it closely examines, through the loneliness of Leo Halper, the terrible crisis of being removed from one's family as they faced their death. Leo Halper feels fear, joy, and shame all at once. Wallenrod must also have felt that he escaped a fate so many of his dear family and friends did not; as his memories return to those people and his former life "over there," he is tortured by an inability to act. And yet, his memories become a blessing, a monument to those people and places. *Dusk in the Catskills* memorializes the several fields of loss in its beautiful evocation of those worlds. Leo's thoughts are private memory; but the book is shared and public, and openly expresses sorrow and sympathy in its lamentation.

Bibliography

Boris, Martin. "A Place in the Country," *The Jewish Monthly*, September/October 1998: 10-13.

Diner, Hasia. *We Remember With Reverence and Love: American Jews and the Myth of Silence 1945-1962*. New York: NYU Press, 2009.

Ehrenreich, Jake. Performance at the Los Angeles Museum of Tolerance, January 15, 2012.

Lipman, Elinor. *The Inn at Lake Devine*. New York: Random House, 1998.

Memoirs
and
Conversations

A Memoir from Before My Birth

Phil Brown

The year after the war ended, 1946, Holocaust survivors began to arrive in the United States from Displaced Persons camps, while GIs returned from extended tours in occupied Europe. Some settled into jobs in the Catskills. That same year European and Mizrachi Jews (from the Middle East) began to flee to the Yishuv (pre-nation Israeli state apparatus) where they would establish the State of Israel two years later. At the same time, Hashomer Hatzair's (Youth Guard) Camp Shomria and other labor Zionist/socialist groups set up training camps in the Catskills to prepare Jews for *aliyah* (immigration) to Israel.

The year 1946 was also significant because Jews began to vacation without guilt in "The Mountains" (what most New York Jews called the Catskills), opening the floodgates of the "Golden Era" of the 1950s and 1960s when over one and a half thousand hotels and bungalow colonies operated in what was then probably the world's largest resort area.

1946 was the year my parents bought the Royal Hotel in White Lake. With little savings, they tried to enter this world of the "Golden Era," when both business opportunity and *Yiddishkeit* (Jewish culture) leisure seemed to go hand in hand. The hotel would be foreclosed in

Brown's Hotel Royal. Courtesy of the author.

**Author and Father at Brown's Hotel Royal, 1951.
Courtesy of the author.**

only six years, signaling my parents' lifelong series of failures in small business.

But how can there be a memoir before my birth on January 1, 1949? Most simply, the placement of my family in White Lake largely cemented my future. Perhaps their series of business failures was behind my strong desire for a long-term, stable professional position. At any rate, the purchase of the Royal Hotel in White Lake was a pre-history into which I was born and which would mark the origin of my lifelong passion as the Catskills' historian, chronicler, and archivist. More personally, in the inhalation of the Catskills legacy and the legacy of the Jewish people who came before me, it inducted me into an intensely Jewish community. In that complexity I have been channeling history, making connections between people who had been lost to each other, discovering family secrets, unearthing archeological ruins covered over by decades of forest. That channeling is itself boundless and timeless, so I can easily consider my own memoir to begin before my first breath.

I have been well prepared for this life as a Catskills *zichronista* (my term for someone working on preserving memory—*zichron* in Hebrew)—tutored by parents who held a dozen different jobs in dozens of hotels, and who knew so many people in all roles across the Catskills; given remedial courses by the owners I worked for and the staff I labored with; brought into the library stacks and my Catskills Institute archives by the Catskills veterans now clamoring for their own memories that I could facilitate.

Years later, about the age of eighteen, my friend from college came to visit in the summer, and we visited his younger brother at what was probably Camp Shomria—but it could have been another camp of that

Author's mother, Sylvia Brown, chef at   Author's father, William Brown,
Seven Gables Hotel.   maître d' at Normandie Hotel.
Courtesy of the author.   Courtesy of the author.

sort since there were many. And then about six years ago I was contacted by Eco-Practicum, an environmental summer program based at Camp Shomria, to help recruit the environmentalist students I work with to attend there. From pre-birth to young man to professional—everything is connected. The *chalutzim* (pioneers) buzz around me in so many forms and eras.

Was there something wrong with a twelve-year-old Jewish boy, who instead of thinking ahead to college and medical school, yearned for a job in the main dining room of a Catskills hotel? Did that presage a kind of subjugation to the seasonal bondage that Mountain Rats endured, unable to escape the familiar routine? Or did it instead open up a pathway into collecting the postcards, menus, rate cards, signs, silverware, dishes, photos, and memories of the Catskills, so that we could all remember it as a formative element of American Jewish life? Was this bondage in itself life-affirming? Having carried on this effort since 1993, I hope the latter.

My work running the Catskills Institute and holding (now) thirteen Annual History of the Catskills Conferences transformed me, and proved itself as life-affirming. The Institute and the annual conference

Author at Cherry Hill Hotel, 1962, first year as full-time busboy.
Courtesy of the author.

Seven Gables Hotel, postcard. Building at bottom right did not exist.
Courtesy of the author.

brought together all sorts of people, some who had the great pleasure of learning that their relatives had become cult figures for Catskills fans. At one such conference, Jim Landis learned that his father Albert Landis's hotel postcards were the premier postcards for collectors. The 1940s and 1950s pseudo-aerials conveyed a sense of the daily life of the small hotels in exquisite detail and playfulness, writing on top of buildings their names, like "casino" (casinos were entertainment halls, not gambling casinos) or "day camp." Albert Landis also occasionally put in the post-cards buildings that were not there. My own deep understanding of Catskills' history tells me that it was probably because the owner said "We're going to put up another building this coming year, so add it to the new cards." It was always deeply gratifying to know the long history of the Jewish Catskills and to be able to provide shared knowledge.

At one point in the gorgeous film about bungalow colony life, *A Walk on the Moon*, the loudspeaker trumpets, "The knish man is here." Though it doesn't mention Ruby by name, we of the Jewish Catskills know who he is. Ruby the Knishman is such an amazing person because of the role he played during that "Golden Era." He was an iconic reminder of the marriage of business opportunity and *Yiddishkeit* that was at the heart and soul of the Jewish Catskills.

Of all the memories of Ruby that are now circulating, none is so delicious as this email I got in December 1998 from Dara Oshinsky-Deitz, another reminder of my role in bringing people together:

Your Catskills Institute webpage is only the latest of amazing sources of fondness that I have recently uncovered on my father, Ruby the Knishman. It started last summer when my husband was looking for a gift for my aunt and came across *Borsch Belt Bungalows* by Irwin Richman at Amazon.com. Then, a few months later, he was reading his Penn State Alumni Magazine and found a review of the book, and the reviewer mentioned Ruby the Knishman. No sooner than a few days later, my neighbor, who grew up in the same neighborhood of Canarsie, Brooklyn that I did, told me that my father has his own Webpage in the "Official Canarsie" Webpage, where the author has asked people to send him stories of their memories of my dad. Now, I discover when doing a net search for "Ruby the Knishman" on America on Line, that Arthur Tanney's memoirs come up, and he dedicates almost his entire Chapter 8 to his memories of my dad. It is now clear to me and my family that my father touched the lives of thousands of people. His family misses him terribly. I appreciate your response and your devotion to the memories we all cherish.

Indeed, at the 2004 conference, now-departed essayist of the bungalow world, Arthur Tanney, read his paean to Ruby, which can be found on the Catskills Institute website. I convinced Dara to come to the Fifth Annual History of the Catskills Conference in 1999. I told the audience in my welcome: "What can it mean that Ruby the Knishman is such an amazing person to remember? *A toizint taamen fun di pedlers* [a thousand good

Ruby the Knishman. Courtesy of the Catskills Institute.

tastes from the peddlers], each and every one bringing something special to eat, but none so delicious as the fresh knish from Ruby." I read her letter, introduced her, and had her stand out to prolonged applause from the attendees, some of who exclaimed their past experience buying knishes from Ruby.

My passion took me into our earliest Catskills Jewish history: John Gerson started the first Jewish boarding house in the Catskills, an event that is a cornerstone of Catskills history articles and books. His granddaughter, then ninety, came to my talk at the International Association of Jewish Genealogical Societies in 2006, following some recent contact I had with her son and daughter-in-law. Subsequently I got to interview her and learn more about this important starting point.

Catskills Jewish history connected me personally to the landscape and to the people. In 1999 a woman emailed me, saying that the 5th Annual Catskills Conference announcement was interesting, though she couldn't make it. Perhaps, though, I could help her with a family tree problem. It seems that one of her Snyder family married a Brown who owned a Catskills hotel. I wrote back saying that it sounded like my mother marrying my father, and indeed it was. This woman is my mother's first cousin, though I never knew she existed. Through her I located a bunch of other relatives as well, one of who was even a graduate student at Brown University, where I taught at the time. And the weekend before that year's conference we had a family reunion. Such is the miracle of the Catskills.

Channeling Catskills history meant helping people find long-lost connections—one of many I brokered is the subject of the following:

I just spent the last thirty minutes listening to my dad tell me the joy he had visiting with the gentleman who used to own the Apollo Hotel. You had sent me his name and number and my dad went to visit with him this past weekend. The owner used to put my dad to bed and they spent quite some time going down memory lane. I could hear the joy in my dad's voice as he talked about walking over the property where he had so many boyhood memories. Thank you so much for giving my dad such a great day and a chance to relive a time of his life that still brings a smile to his face.

In brokering these connections, in helping people find their lost Catskills relationships, I was to some extent using these actions as a way to reconnect myself to that time and place. Every new link was part of my overall mosaic of Catskills life, and the more of those I could foster, the more I would be at home.

For me, the Catskills became the center of the world, from which all forms of consciousness emerged. It started early, before my birth, and it gets stronger with time. In practice this meant simple things like meeting Marc Zalkin in junior high school, and upon learning his last name, asking him "So, your family had Zalkin's Birchwood Lodge?" Or meeting the new gym teacher in that same school, Miss Zeiger, to whom I queried, "You're from Zeiger's Eldorado, right?" I was not alone in this hotel-centered universe, as witnessed in this story Helene Kenvin wrote me in 2005 and I read in my welcome at the History of the Catskills Conference that year:

> Dear Professor Brown,
>
> As a former resident of Esopus and someone who wintered every year in the 1950s at the Flagler's and Pines hotels, I have followed with interest the news about your institute. I just learned (from a posting on the jewishgen email list) that your family owned Brown's Hotel [she meant Brown's Hotel Royal, not the large and better known Charles and Lillian Brown's Hotel in Loch Sheldrake] in the Catskills, so I want to share with you a true story that has become legendary in my family, which may amuse you.
>
> I graduated magna cum laude from Brown University in 1962 and was elected to Phi Beta Kappa. The summer after my graduation, this conversation was overheard between my maternal grandmother and a friend of hers:
>
> Grandma Ida: "My grenddaughter just greduated from Brown's."
>
> Friend: "No joke!" (My informant remarks here: There is no doubt that the friend thought it was Brown's Hotel and was somewhat confused as to why my grandmother was so proud.)
>
> Grandma Ida: "And she greduated hi-fi mit loudness!"
>
> Friend: "Good for her!"

This entire universe of Jewish life—not just the summer guests and staff, but the year-round populations with their *shuls*, Workmen's Circle chapters, Jewish Agricultural Society, egg-marketing and fire insurance cooperatives, and philanthropies—was the creation of a place of safety. Like the whole "goldene medina" of the United States, the Catskills would be a place where the Nazis could never threaten Jews again. No wonder there were Zionist training camps to prepare people for making *aliyah* to Israel—the safety of the Catskills helped shape the safety of the post-Holocaust State of Israel.

As a child and teenager I saw this vacation diaspora as endless and timeless—it seemed like it would always be there as an immense presence. To grow into adulthood and watch it disappear was a great loss, though that loss is what propelled me to become its chronicler. I suppose I should have expected the decline and disappearance, since others seemed worried. Indeed, Reuben Wallenrod's *Dusk in the Catskills*, a central facet of this book you hold in your hands, has hotel owner Leo Halper constantly fearful of the decline of the Catskills, even though it was about to enter the greatest growth era for two decades. But the fullness of this life in "The Mountains" was too powerful to entertain its loss.

Beyond the many joys of my memories of this fabled land, there is also a deep sorrow for its passing—a passing not just of a resort area but of a whole world of Jewish culture. Reuben Wallenrod's epigraph from *Lamentations* sets the stage for his book: "Woe unto us! For the day declineth. For the shadows of the evening are stretched out." For hotel-keeper Leo Halper this was the fear of the end of his hotel ownership and, writ larger, of the whole Catskills—the latter which was just not ready to happen that early. We can look further, and remember that *Lamentations* is Jeremiah's mourning poetry about the destruction of the Temple:

> How doth the city sit solitary that was full of people!
> How is she become as a widow!
> She that was great among the nations,
> And princess among the provinces,
> How is she become tributary!

She weepeth sore in the night,
And her tears are on her cheeks;
She hath none to comfort her
Among all her lovers;
All her friends have dealt treacherously with her,
They are become her enemies.[1]

After the Temple is destroyed comes exile, and always the age-old hope for return. The Catskills is part of our repatriation, as I and others memorialize its legacy, photograph its ruins and remnants, collect its mementos, and mine the memories of its players. I rejoice in this return.

---

1   Lamentations 1:1. *The Holy Scriptures*. Philadelphia: Philadelphia Jewish Publication Society, 1917.

The Holocaust, the Catskills, and the Creative Power of Loss

Holli Levitsky

I.

My parents took their honeymoon in 1946, at the Nevele Country Club in Sullivan County, New York. The Catskills beckoned the young couple, as they had welcomed tens of thousands of Jews, young and old, American and immigrant, families and singles, for decades. Like my mother and her family, the Jews vacationing in the Catskill Mountains came primarily from New York City. In this city, and this America, it was expected that my mother's friends' parents—like her own—had thick foreign accents, spoke fluent Yiddish at home, and worked hard to succeed. One sign of success was the ability to take a summer holiday in the Catskill Mountains. Families and close friends or neighbors might share the cost of a rented van for the two-hour ride from Brooklyn to Sullivan County, and then rent rooms or cabins at the same bungalow colony or *kuchalayn* (boarding house). My mother remembers her first *kuchalayn*, in Ellenville, as a large farm with chickens and hayrides, and her father—like the other fathers—coming up only on weekends.

The American and immigrant Jews, who had made the many hotels, bungalow colonies, and farms of Ulster and Sullivan Counties

The author's mother, Sylvia
Levitsky, with her brother in
1931 at a *kuchalayn* in
Sullivan County.

their summer retreats year after year, were always looking for family, for *landsman-shaftn* (society of immigrants from the same town or region), for a home away from home. As a second home to generations of Jews, the Catskill Mountains became a place where a Jewish family could bond *as* a Jewish family—that is, they could practice the culture of Judaism without the pressure to assimilate. Families spending summers together with other Jews could anticipate recreating— and recreating with—these Jewish friends year after year. The Jewish threads of their winter lives might seem to be slowly unraveling through their increasingly secular lives, but the Catskills remained essentially a subculture that they renewed each year, as yet another summer of Jews were beckoned there. Because the Catskill Mountains summoned one with the promise of prolonged engagement and deeply felt connections—replacing the congestion of the city for the wide open spaces of the mountains— children and adults mingled in acts of *community*: feeling *nachis* as the children paraded their gifts through the weekend talent shows, cooking meals together in the common kitchen of the *kuchalayn*, meeting for card games every evening. For the parents, each day must have been another rare and wonderful moment when time stands still amid the deep well of family love, safely netted by a sense of community so complete it seemed impossible to find elsewhere.

By the time my mother's modern Orthodox family took their summer holidays in Ellenville, or Monticello, or Woodridge, staying at chicken farms or rooming houses, it was already a segregated world. Lost was the innocence of the Founding Fathers' declaration that "All men are created equal." Jews were restricted from participating fully in American society in a number of ways—they experienced professional

bias and discrimination by hotels, country clubs, and resorts; neighborhoods and cities limited or denied access to Jews hoping to purchase
houses or land. Influential Americans, such as Henry Ford, were publicly
denouncing Jews as either international financiers intent on world domi-
nation or godless Bolsheviks who undermined American policy and
morality. Americans tuning into their radios during the 1930s might hear
Father Coughlin's weekly anti-Semitic broadcasts from his Detroit
pulpit; they might open their *Dearborn Independent* and read "Mr. Ford's
Page" with its anti-Semitic commentary.[1] Those Jews who returned each
year to the Catskill Mountains—primarily from New York, but also from
Detroit, Philadelphia, or Baltimore—were seeking escape not just from
the thick heat of another urban summer; they were hoping to escape
from the darkening forces of the era's anti-Semitic proscriptions.

II.

A new kind of Jewish immigrant community was born from and after
World War II, and they, too, purchased or leased colonies together. They,
too, were looking for family and a home away from home. They, too,
shared a past—but their past was in a lost and now vanished world. They
were stressed not only from the terrifying and exhausting act of losing
their homes and families; they were traumatized from experiences that
defied comprehension. For the most part, each survivor had undergone
uniquely horrifying traumatic experiences during the war years. They
may have survived in concentration or work camps, or in hiding—either
literally or with an Aryan identity—in ghettos; they may have escaped to
a safer city or country. But wherever they were, they were hunted by
Nazis or their collaborators, marked for death because they were Jews.
This community lost everything, yet citizens of that community survived.
Where were they to go? What would they do with their lives?

Survivors of the Holocaust asked themselves these questions. When
the war ended, they were young. But they were also alone. Where were
they to go? Germany and Poland offered little more than bad memories

---

1   Jeffrey Schandler, *While America Watches: Televising the Holocaust* (New York: Oxford
    University Press, 1999), xx.

and remnants of anti-Semitism. When the fugitives and survivors from Hitler's mass murder of European Jews began to come to America, they were confronted with a number of challenges; they did not know what to expect. Why was it so difficult for this wave of refugees to settle into their new lives in the United States? Why was assimilation into American Jewish life so complex for Holocaust survivors? Just as earlier Jewish immigrants held widely divergent views about Jewish practice, ritual, faith, and culture, and certainly about the issue of assimilation versus separatism, the views held by these refugees also spanned the spectrum of Jewish belief and practice. And although the US was never free of its own nativist attitudes, and anti-Semitism often followed on the crest of such waves of new-Jewish immigration, the post-WWII surge of Jewish DPs (they were first called Displaced Persons) immigration posed special problems.

In the first years after the war, 140,000 European Jews immigrated to America. Where they settled was usually not their choice, as special agencies had been created to deal with the onslaught of new refugees, or DPs, and their housing and employment needs. The Truman Directive facilitated certain shifts in procedures for dealing with this enormous surge in immigration, such as allowing organizations, in addition to

Sylvia Levitsky and friend in 1939 in the Catskills.

individuals, the right to provide affidavits for DPs. The American Jewish community created the United Service for New Americans (USNA), a national agency, and the New York Association for New Americans (NYANA) in New York City, to direct the resettlement process. So, in addition to quotas and other restrictions imposed upon the immigrants, they had to deal with newly developed agencies whose workers, although well-intentioned, had no experience treating such monumental financial, legal, emotional, and physical needs.

Where did these 140,000 new immigrants (they were not called "survivors" until the 1960s) settle? What was this resettlement process like? Were they happy in their new homes? Public perception was that, in fact, the new refugees were happy to be given a second chance and adjusted relatively easily to American life. But accounts by survivors themselves, and case studies from the early years of their new lives by social workers and others, suggest otherwise. Holocaust survivors tried to adjust to what might be considered "normal" family life, but attempts were colored by the intensity of the trauma, which did not disappear with the end of the war and the liberation of the camps.[2] Although more than half of the refugees settled in New York City—which already hosted the majority of American Jews—over 40 percent settled elsewhere in the US, either voluntarily or more likely because of the mandate of the Displaced Persons Act, which hoped to avoid a large concentration of refugees in major urban areas.[3] Within the Jewish community itself, there were tensions between the established American Jewish popula-tion and the new displaced persons. Years earlier, American Jews worried about the large influx of Eastern European Jews and their "greenhorn" ways; these new immigrants posed similar problems with language, clothing, food, and other "old country" habits. American Jews felt sympathy and compassion for their brethren, but feared that too many Jews would provoke more anti-Semitism. Thus, it was with ambivalence

---

2   Beth Cohen, *Case Closed: Holocaust Survivors in Postwar America* (New Brunswick: Rutgers University Press, 2007), 173.
3   Cohen, *Case Closed*, 174.

Sylvia Levitsky in 1945 in the Catskills.

that many American Jews hoped the displaced persons would settle else-where, perhaps in Palestine.[4]

Many survivors characterize the tension between survivors and American Jews in this way: they know, as the French writer Charlotte Delbo wrote, that "Auschwitz is so deeply etched in my memory that I cannot forget one moment of it."[5] They have no choice but to return to the war years, watching conversations meander to that place time and again, feeling the loss each and every time. They could tell horrific stories of those years as if they were commonplace, as if escaping death was a trip to the corner store for milk. Who could better understand the need to talk about the terrors than those who also still lived with those terrors?

By their very act of living, survivors tell us that they survived. "All of us are born," they say, "but we survived." When you lose your family, you make friends with those who are like family, who have experienced the same loss and seek the same comfort. Survivors are a culture, a people who share a deep sense of gratefulness without forgetting for one second all that they have lost. The pleasure in being with other survivors was to be able to feel the loss and then to speak it and share it, and in some ways, to revel in their difference from the others.

4   Cohen, *Case Closed*, 175
5   Charlotte Delbo, *Days and Memory* (Evanston, IL: Marlboro Press, 1990), xiv.

Still, the public face of the postwar immigration surge has long shown the happy state of refugees settling in the US after their terrifying experiences. Americans, in general, were under the impression that bringing these displaced European refugees to our democratic republic was enough, and that once settled here, they could quickly return to being father, mother, wife, husband, son, daughter. But this attitude sadly contradicts the reality of life for most, if not all, of these survivors. For they were survivors, and being survivors meant they had had to leave their many dead, mostly murdered relatives, friends, and neighbors behind—graveless, and without mourners. They had witnessed the worst atrocities humans were capable of committing. And then they had to go on living.

Survivor Ruth Klüger, author of the 2001 memoir *Still Alive: A Holocaust Girlhood Remembered*, writes that when she first came to the US as a displaced person, her American aunt told her, "You have to erase from your memory everything that happened in Europe. You have to make a new beginning. You have to forget what they did to you. Wipe it off like chalk from a blackboard."[6] Klüger rejected that invitation to forget, as evidenced by her widely successful memoir, published first in German as *weiter leben: Eine Jugend* (1992), and selling over 250,000 copies in Europe before being rewritten by the author in English for a specifically American audience. The widespread belief was that survivors were better off leaving the past behind—neither thinking nor talking about what happened in Europe. It would also be better for Americans—Jews in particular—to have the Jewish refugees start over as Americans, leaving the baggage of the European disaster at the door of importation.

But even as family, friends, caseworkers, and others urged the survivors to forget the past and what was lost, we know now that it was not possible for victims of such trauma to simply leave everything behind and start over. Survivors tried to tell their stories to fellow Jews, but found little sympathy and little interest among them in hearing about the atrocities, which some found too gruesome and others simply could not believe.

---

6   Ruth Klüger, *Still Alive: A Holocaust Girlhood Remembered* (New York: The Feminist Press, 2003), 177.

Perhaps even more startling were the social workers, psychiatrists, and psychologists who treated the survivors' traumatic experiences and symptoms as if they were within the normal range of human experience. There were a number of reasons why people in the helping professions didn't or couldn't address the particular mental and physical health issues of survivors, and why the American Jewish public was equally resistant to offer the kind of help they needed. Among the reasons were: 1) guilt over being safe in America while the Jews of Europe were being murdered; 2) the first workers' responses in the displaced persons camps indicated a triumphant physical survival of even the most war-torn individuals—but without regard to these survivors' emotional fitness; 3) the professional norms of the time in the healing professions were Freudian in nature—which meant any mental health diagnosis was filtered through the patient's childhood developmental difficulties, and thus treatment would include the analysis of concepts pertaining to the survivor's prewar personality—and absurd in retrospect; and 4) an inability to confront the depths of the Holocaust's destruction. All of these reasons facilitated a gulf between the American Jewish community and its professionals and the survivors.

Moreover, countless studies have shown that the massive physical and emotional disruption in the lives of Holocaust survivors have continued to affect them to the end of their lives. Holocaust scholar Lawrence Langer refers to their present lives as "a life after 'death' called survival, and a life within death for which we have no name, only the assurance of witnesses. . . ."[7] Clearly, the trauma of the Holocaust caused an irreparable rupture in the memories of survivors and became the focal point for their identities.

III.

The gulf continued to widen over time, as survivors tried to tell their stories but found little sympathy and little interest in hearing about the Holocaust. And so, for several decades after the war ended and the refugees had settled into their new homes, they looked for ways to replace

7   Lawrence L. Langer, *Holocaust Testimonies: The Ruins of Memory* (New Haven, CT: Yale University Press, 1991), 35.

what was lost. They turned to American culture, which seemed so successfully to shape identity, to *tell them* how to become more part of the American victory, and less part of Jewish victimhood. If they tuned in to their televisions on May 27, 1953, they might have seen survivor Hanna Block Kohner unveiled as the honoree on one of the most popular entertainment programs of the 1950s: *This Is Your Life*. They would have heard the host, legendary Ralph Edwards, muse that Hanna seemed more like a "young American girl just out of college, not at all like a survivor of Hitler's cruel purge of German Jews." She was an American hero, washed clean of any Jewish particularism. They might also have watched their televisions with great interest in 1961, as the Eichmann trial unfolded in Israel, preparing to hear the totality of the final solution against the Jews emerge, story by story. Instead, when they opened their *New York Times* or watched the CBS Evening News, the American press coverage presented the Holocaust as a universal tragedy, using the trial to raise, in a general way, moral questions about responsibility and the nature of evil.

How did they replace what was lost and essentially irreplaceable? How did they go on with their lives, in the face of this vacuum? For the survivors of Hitler's Europe, there was no way to replace all that had been taken from them. Indeed, in trying to recover their lives in this new land, they faced misunderstanding and frustration. The American and earlier immigrant Jews had a difficult time understanding the extent of

The author with other children at play outside the bungalows, Sullivan County, late 1950s, early 1960s.

the survivors' loss, since they either didn't know the world of Jewish Eastern Europe before the war, or left before it became a graveyard. How could the survivors' friends and neighbors, Jew or gentile, understand what it had been like to survive under those circumstances? In the lives of postwar American Jews, who were fearful of calling attention to themselves as Jews, conformity became the new religion. If assimilation cost them their identities, it was worth it not to stand out and face tacit, overt, and even deadly forms of anti-Semitism that the Jews had faced in Europe.

Even if they were not religious, conformity to American national identity—whatever it looked like at any given time—did not comfort the survivors. Each survivor had a harrowing and unique story about what they lost. And although what was lost differed from person to person, the imperative to tell the tale of that loss was common to most survivors. Reclaiming their lives meant seeking a community within which they would find affirmation and comfort, and some found that community in the Catskill Mountains, where together with other survivors, they could retreat from the (sometimes creepy) postwar cultural patriotism of their American brethren. They could be with those who were like family, friends who shared the worst moments of their lives together, in the same concentration camps, resistance units, and hiding places. They had escaped death and were still escaping, taking these summer holidays together as a way to elude the stares and questions and silence that surrounded them when their summer clothing revealed the tattoos, or when the past was inevitably brought up for conversation and the war traumas were massaged again and again as they needed to be. Sometimes, even in such a bucolic setting, comfort came only when the like-minded were together, mulling over their shared pasts in complete understanding. What would they lose if they agreed to silence their cries? To dismiss the past as if it hadn't broken them? They knew they were cracked and broken. They still heard screams and cries for help they could not answer. They feared dogs, uniforms, the German language. They wandered around the open fleshy landscape, so similar to the mountains of their homeland, wielding their flashlights like weapons. And in the card games, bridge tournaments, and daily games

The author's parents, Sylvia and Louis Levitsky, dancing in the Nevele Hotel during their honeymoon, 1946.

of chess and checkers, over endless retellings of their stories, they found family, and home. The Catskills offered many Jewish European survivors of the Holocaust a world of their own within a larger world, for them, without home.

On the East Coast, the Catskills' resorts that catered to survivors were destinations that might have mirrored the holidays of their former lives, save their stories of suffering and loss. They might have escaped the Nazis with nothing or almost nothing of their former life intact, but their prewar lives had been rich with family, friendships, religion, culture, school, work, and holidays. If they had lived in Poland (not unlikely, since Poland's prewar Jewish population of 3.3 million was the second highest in the world), they might have taken summer holidays in the quaint village of Kazimierz Dolny on the Visla, or winter trips for mountain hiking and skiing to Zakopane in the Tatra Mountains.

Together in the ghettos, camps, and in hiding, survivors shared innumerable experiences that made them what one might call intimate strangers. They shared the hardships of hunger, thirst, disease, infestation, horrifying and cruel living situations, torture, the witnessing of atrocities towards others including loved ones, random selections for death or loss of liberty and uncertain future, and for most, loss of family, home, belongings, hair, clothing, and for the younger survivors, loss of childhood as well. In the bedlam of that world, tightly bonded friendships formed. It is not surprising that the survivors who survived together, or who were from similar areas, pursued life together afterwards.

How can those of us who were not there imagine the complicated and ongoing effects of the trauma on the postwar life of Holocaust survivors? From their early days as misunderstood DPs, the survivors found comfort in one another's shared experiences. The impulse to be together in the Catskill Mountains—or in social groups or *landsmanshaftn*— came from the same desire for comfort.

Together, survivors talked about the past, sharing their darkest moments in the camps or in hiding, but also sharing details of their prewar lives. Other survivors would know what it meant to have been born in the Polish towns of Bilgorai or Lututov or the big cities of Lodz or Warsaw, and that their lives did not begin as Jewish victims of Hitler, but as human beings who were loved and wanted.

IV.

A survivor from Krakow, the cultural center of Poland, might have had something of a life not terribly unlike my mother's. Perhaps this survivor's European surroundings were a little more elegant, her friends more diverse, her interests and travels more sophisticated than my mother's first-generation American Jewish upbringing. Still, she would have watched Loretta Young and Greta Garbo at the movies and read *Gone With the Wind*. Her mother might have been glamorous—not old-fashioned, like my maternal grandmother. Like my mother, she might have had a sister and a brother, though her childhood might have been more privileged, with well-educated, modern parents, not immigrants who could barely speak the language and were superstitious. This survivor would have had housekeepers who cooked and cleaned for the family, beautiful clothing, holidays in the Tatra Mountains. My grandmother would have spent all day in the family's small kitchen, preparing gefilte fish and baking *mohn* cookies or *mandelbrot*, like her many neighbors, and then taken their holidays together at a chicken farm in Sullivan County.

What was the survivor thinking as she moved from the ghetto to Plazsow and then to Auschwitz and Bergen-Belsen, losing her family, friends, and home, and growing from child to young woman? The long days of swimming, hiking, and tennis, and the winters of ice-skating, skiing, and sledding were replaced by endless days of inconceivable hunger, thirst, exhaustion, and the fear of random beatings or death. She might have witnessed a girl her own age in unimaginable torment, as her mother was shot by camp commandant Amon Goeth. She might have watched her sister, naked and shorn, begging for her life from Dr. Mengele. She might have been on the same train to Bergen-Belsen as Anne Frank. Neither privilege nor youth kept this survivor out of harm's way. Her "coming of age" experiences were loss, humiliation, and the totem she shared with other Auschwitz survivors: the numbered arm tattoo.

One can only imagine the complicated and ongoing effects of this trauma on the postwar life of such survivors. Still, the natural vitality of the Catskills has always been presented as so forceful that it has the power to calm even a fevered soul. Cradled by the setting in the Catskills—their dramas and resolutions, their war and prewar lives— are played out on its landscape; its boundaries—geographically but also emotionally—safely cushion the ride. You know you are safe because of those boundaries. In this bungalow colony, or lodge, or hotel, with these friends beside you, you can stretch yourself a little further, dance a little harder than usual. And you may return to your house and neighborhood the same person, but you will always have these friends in your heart—they will be your lost father's wide arms, your murdered husband's loving embrace. And, in time, family becomes a place in your heart that you carry with you always, even when the end comes. Even when you're on the other side, and the photographs are a postcard from a ghost story you once knew. Even when the rituals remain only in memory, revealing a place no longer there.

The year 1946 was a popular year for weddings, and the Nevelle was filled to capacity with newlyweds that post-WWII April. My parents moved west to my father's native Detroit, but during magical summers of my childhood, we drove in our borrowed station wagon to meet my Brooklyn cousins and aunts and uncles who continued to rent a bungalow each year. Our extended family would take meals together at a resort nearby. Always, there would be daylong activities for the kids and long lazy days for the grownups. Mothers would sit by the lake or the pool with their hair tied up in *shmatas,* smoking Kents and playing Canasta or Spite and Malice or Michigan rummy, and fathers might take their sons out fishing, or more likely, take a long, hard summer nap. It was a world that seemed as if it would continue forever, a landscape larger than life itself. On that canvas sat the Yiddish-speaking *alte cockers,* the family tummlers, the smarty-pants cousins, all real then, all ghosts now. The clear, quiet lakes upon which rowboats held the promise of young love—or lost virginity. The elderly couples helping each other walk carefully to the next card game. In my mind, this multi-generational, self-enclosed Jewish subculture, full of loving, abundant, exuberant life, should have continued forever. Yet it no longer exists. It was, after all, another world. Was that era a flash point, always signaling its own demise? Perhaps it was.

The wealth and breadth of testimonial and imaginative responses to Jewish life and culture in the Catskills stand as a testament to the power of nurturing such worlds in memory. These shared memories offer lessons about the challenge of aging, the comfort of old friends, the power of memory, and the importance of embracing joy even in the face of mortality. This legacy is also the broader Catskills legacy and gives us an opportunity to dwell in that world again. In *All's Well That Ends Well,* Shakespeare identified the need we all have to hold in memory that which was loved and lost: "Praising what is lost / Makes the remembrance dear," even as that loss is absolute and all consuming.[8]

Bibliography

Cohen, Beth B. *Case Closed: Holocaust Survivors in Postwar America.* New Brunswick: Rutgers University Press, 2007.

---

8   Shakespeare, *All's Well That Ends Well,* in *The Complete Works of Shakespeare,* edited by William Aldis Wright (New York: Doubleday, 1936), V, iii, 20.

Delbo, Charlotte. *Days and Memory.* Evanston, IL: Marlboro Press, 1990.

Klüger, Ruth. *Still Alive: A Holocaust Girlhood Remembered.* New York: The Feminist Press, 2003.

Langer, Lawrence L. *Holocaust Testimonies: The Ruins of Memory.* New Haven, CT: Yale University Press, 1991.

Schandler, Jeffrey. *While America Watches: Televising the Holocaust.* New York: Oxford University Press, 1999.

Shakespeare, William. *All's Well That Ends Well.* In *The Complete Works of Shakespeare,* edited by William Aldis Wright. New York: Doubleday, 1936.

Catskill Reflections: Testimonial, Literary, and Jewish Values in Singer's Novel

Sandor Goodhart

I have an image of my grandfather standing on the porch of one of the bungalows in a plain white tank top, the kind made famous in American consciousness by Marlon Brando in the film version of *A Streetcar Named Desire* (Warner Brothers, 1951). The memory is unique for me because it is one of the only times I remember seeing him relaxing. My grandfather had a job of some importance in the city of Philadelphia. He was a "higher up" in the Republican Party, the "go-to" man as we would say today for fixing things that went wrong in people's lives of a legal or civic nature, and in later years became the "head of taxes" in city government. As the oldest of four children of an immigrant Jewish family that had come to America from Russia (as so many others did) around the turn of the century—no doubt to escape the pogroms that had begun threatening the Jewish communities of Odessa—he was considered successful. And when I would visit him and my grandmother (along with my mother and father) in their three-story Fairmount Avenue row house (near Marshall Street in the Jewish section of Philadelphia)—as we did on almost a weekly basis—I never saw him "dress down." He was always wearing something approaching formal slacks, a clean white shirt, and often a necktie that he had untied, having recently returned from his center city Philadelphia office. The bungalow image was an anomaly.

It was unique as well for other reasons. My parents seemed to be slightly uncomfortable in the bungalow setting. On the particular occasion I recall, I remember that we drove up late morning, met my grandparents and their friends around noon, and returned from the mountain community sometime later that afternoon. I vaguely recall that we came there to transport someone (my grandmother? an aunt or friend of my grandparents?), and we returned within a few hours of accomplishing our task. My parents were not adorned in the leisurely garb that my grandparents wore, and I have no memory of having a meal at the camp or of staying there overnight. Nor had I ever before (or again) met the people we met there that day and who seemed to be on relatively close terms with my grandparents. I remember asking my mother who these people were and learning from her that they were my grandparents' "friends"—as foreign to my mother, in other words, as they were to me, accustomed as we all were for the most part to greeting only other members of our extended family as opposed to my grandparents' personal acquaintances. These were people who seemed to know my grandparents outside of the ways in which we knew them, who perhaps met them only in the summer weeks that my grandparents would annually stay at this or that summer camp resort, and perhaps for that reason (or others) shared with them a bond from which my parents and I were more or less excluded.

But there must have been more to the situation. Years later, when I saw Richard Dreyfus in movies like *The Apprenticeship of Duddy Kravitz* (Paramount Pictures, 1974), or Woody Allen's *Radio Days* (Orion, 1987), or Andrew Jacobs' documentary *The Four Seasons Lodge* (First Run Features, 2008), or learned about the "Borscht Belt," or played piano myself in a band for a few weeks in a mountain resort in upper New York State, I recognized a kinship with these communities and felt an immediate authenticity about them with regard to the Jewish life of my parents and that was still alive in my childhood. And when I read the chapters of Singer's book on the camps, I felt as if knew the scene.

These communities were undoubtedly a kind of escape, a "retreat" as we would say in today's parlance, a break from the daily routine of Jewish life in the big city. But they seemed also to have a positive dimension to them and not play exclusively the negative role of a summertime getaway.

What dimension? It was a way for them—to put it simply—to breathe more freely. For my parents, who were both born in this country, it was a strange and unsettling experience. Like my mother, my father was born of two Yiddish-speaking immigrant parents. My father's family emigrated around the turn of the century (probably for similar reasons to my mother's family) from the city of Stryj in the area of Eastern Europe known as Galicia. The region was previously part of the Austrian-Hungarian Empire. Then in the latter half of the nineteenth century it became a part of Poland. After World War II, the same region became part of Ukraine by which governmental authority it remains administered today. Born at the end of the second decade of the twentieth century, my father (along with his family of six older brothers and sisters and two parents) lived first in New York City and later in the Strawberry Mansion section of Philadelphia. They were constitutionally shy individuals. My grandfather spoke a little English (as well as Yiddish) and worked for an insurance company as a door-to-door salesman to support his family when he was not officiating in one capacity or another at the local synagogue, while his children attended public school and made their way on the streets of Philadelphia.

Summer camp in the mountain resorts of Pennsylvania or New York State did not fit in. My father (the only one of the seven to gain a college education) became a teacher in the public school system, and, when he was not teaching, drove a taxicab for a living to make ends meet. My aunts and uncles took less professional jobs, selling insurance like my grandfather, working in clothing factories, or managing a family novelty store. Their work kept them too busy and without sufficient resources for such summer outings even if they had been so inclined (which they were not). If my parents were in attendance at all at the summer gathering on the day I remember, it was undoubtedly because of my mother's affiliation with her family and some special task that had been asked of them.

For my maternal grandfather, on the other hand, in the memory I have of him, the release value was evident and primary. Here he did not need to be "on" all the time. Here he could breathe. What was he thinking about as he stood there? It was not a question I could ask, then or now. He stood on the porch in his tank top undershirt, surveying the wooded area surrounding the small row of cabins, inhaling the cooler country air, while his wife sat next to him in the worn shoddily painted wooden rocker, chatting away with friends and neighbors, and his daughter and her husband, standing aside of the cabin, took in with uncertain glance the unfamiliar and slightly disconcerting rustic environment.

$$\longrightarrow\hspace-0.5em\partial\hspace-0.3em\xi\hspace-0.5em\longleftarrow$$

For Isaac Bashevis Singer, the camp environment he imagined in the Catskills in his novel was no less disconcerting, although, I suspect, for entirely different reasons. If I were called upon to respond to the question (and I have been) "What did Singer really think of these mountain side retreats?" I would say, with all of the literary critical expertise I could muster, "I haven't the foggiest idea." And even if we found a document in Singer's hand stating "here is what I think of the Jewish adult mountain side camp communities that formed in America in the Catskills, the Adirondacks, the Poconos, or elsewhere in the wake of the war," and the document was signed "I. B. Singer," I would still say the same thing. What Singer thought of the camps is expressed in what in fact we already have before us: the two chapters at the center of *Enemies, A Love Story* and the multifarious attitudes towards the camps represented in those chapters by its participants, not the least important of which is Tamara's, Masha's, or Herman's.

Herman's view is probably the most negative, as I tried to indicate in my essay on the novel (in this book), qualifying the experience as he does at varying moments as ostentatious, vulgar, and an odious and shameful denial of what had just taken place in Europe to the Jewish community, an insult, in short, in his view, to creation. Undoubtedly, I. B. Singer owns a piece of this negative assessment. But when Singer wants to present himself in his own figure, I also suggested, he does so as the mysterious and nosy Nathan Pesheles, whose intervention into the two relatively isolated worlds in which Herman functions is sine qua non of narrative progress. Without their confrontation—which Pesheles's presence and behavior in both worlds insures—the book might not have moved forward. And so if we are willing to identify Singer with one character at one point, we should probably be ready to identify him with another elsewhere in the narrative.

$$\rightarrow\!\!\!\mathcal{E}\!\!-$$

Is there virtue to discussing the literary and/or Jewish value of the camp scenes in his novel? Again, as I tried to suggest, the scenes on the mountain operate as the book's structural center. The chapters before it set the stage. The first four chapters describe in detail Herman's relation with his current wife, Yadwiga; his relation with his mistress, Masha (and her mother, Shifrah Puah); his relation with his resurrected first wife, Tamara; and the consequences following from their unexpected encounter. Chapters five and six are largely devoted to the meetings in the Adirondacks (with Masha) and the Catskills (with Tamara).

And the final four chapters describe the attempted (and failed) solutions to the complications occasioned in the wake of these scenes along with accidental happenings engineered by the novelist: the re-entrance of Tamara into Herman's marriage with Yadwiga; the sudden and pesky appearance of Nathan Pesheles to the unsuspecting groups; the gathering at Rabbi Lempert's house (and the Rabbi's sudden fascination with Masha); Masha's sudden renewed interest in Herman; Shifrah Puah's unexpected death; the mortal (and thwarted) pact that Herman and Masha undertake; Masha's suicide; Tamara's sudden inheritance of the house in which she has been living along with the bookstore formerly owned by her former landlord; and Herman's disappearance.

But there is another level on which the central scenes also function. The camps are for the world of the novel as "America" is for Europe: namely, an escape that is also an intensification of the strains one is leaving; a "declaration of independence" and move toward freedom that is also steeped in a dependence upon European origins and obsessions.

And finally there is a third level. Singer's very body of work plays just such a role, just such an escape-as-intensification for his American colleagues. Singer's writing, and especially this novel—which is the only one of his set entirely in America—may be characterized as something like the "camp scene" of Jewish American fiction writers. Given his fascination with the marginalia of Jewish folklore (the plethora of figures hovering around Talmudic reading in the Eastern European eighteenth century), Singer's writing played the role for these postwar writers of the fantastic. As such, it came to serve as something of a mirror for other writers of the so-called "gang of four" (which includes Roth, Malamud, and Bellow, along with Singer) in which by contrast their writing may also be reflected. Think for example of the differences between the way the camps function in Singer's work and the way summer camps function in Philip Roth's *The Plot against America* (Vintage, 2005), or the European camps in Saul Bellow's novella *The Bellarosa Connection* (Penguin, 1989), or in Bernard Malamud's short story "The Lady of the Lake" from *The Magic Barrel* (Farrar, Straus and Giroux, 1958).

Or the way they functioned in Europe. If there is a specifically "Jewish" value at work in these operations and at these levels, it is the dimensions of the historical realm in which they are conceived. The Holocaust is the shadow that looms in the background of every page of this novel both within and without. Literary writing after the war for Jewish writing in America is the "writing of the disaster" to use Maurice Blanchot's phrase, the repetition and extension of the traumas in Europe from which that community was barely emerging, their "Lazarean" resurrection in its wake which is not unlike that of the Holocaust survivors in their midst. The distinctly "posthumous" nature of writing by authors of Jewish origin in America after the war (whether identifying and "charging" that origin or not) constitutes in my view their veritable modus operandi, their way ironically of assuring their continued existence in a world that in effect would like to see them dead.

But to develop these ideas further is to repeat what I will show in my critical essay to follow; so it is to my essay that I now must direct your continued attention.

Legacy

Michael Berenbaum

Old age is not for cowards.

—Rhea Berenbaum

Don't believe anything I said about old age before I turned 85.

—Erik Erikson, lecturing to a seminar at Harvard School of Education[1]

Do not send us into old age, when our strength wanes, do not abandon us.

—The beginning of the Confessional on Yom Kippur

Permit me to begin with a personal word: I registered for Medicare this week, a certain milestone in life that seems to indicate that I am becoming a "Senior Citizen," that there are more yesterdays than tomorrows, and that despite the blessing of good health, I will soon be needing medical care. One hears that "50 is the new 40," and "65 the new 50." Surely I am younger than my father was at this age, much younger than

---

1   As related to the author by his former wife, Dr. Linda Bayer, who was a student in Erikson's seminar at Harvard University in the mid 1980s.

my grandfathers and theirs before them. But I am cognizant of aging, no matter how young I feel.

I first saw Andrew Jacobs' film, *The Four Seasons Lodge,* in the comfort of my home, late at night and alone, and found the film more haunting than moving and more about old age than it was about the Holocaust. The Holocaust is the backstory, adding poignancy and power to everything that we saw, to each achievement and to each loss, but perhaps not quite essential to the story the film has to tell. In the words of one survivor, "it is always there, especially at night."

I saw it again as I was writing this essay in the comfort of my office, and found it more moving than haunting and cherished the residents of The Four Seasons Lodge as wise, accepting of life in ways that only those who have averted death can accept the vicissitudes of life, with its tragedy and triumph, with its losses and joys. They reminded me of so many survivors I knew and of so many that I had lost.

On my first viewing I noticed the sadness, the sense of impending loss. On my second screening I also saw the joy. Joy—I am always surprised by how much joy survivors have in each other's company. Their joy is perhaps their sweetest revenge. At weddings they dance. Certainly there is sadness. They notice not only those who are present, but most especially those who are absent; but still they dance. Often one hears the phrase, which is so much better in Yiddish than in English, "He lies in *drerd*—the ground, meaning in shit—and I am dancing." "He" is always Hitler, and the dance such wonderful revenge.

They had a sense of confidence: "We survived!"

Some words about the Catskills: before air conditioning, New York City was uninhabitable during the summer. Hot and humid, the city's pavements were burning and its denizens were struggling for air. Those who could afford it and even many who could not fled to the mountains to escape the oppression of city life. At the turn of the twentieth century and throughout its first decades, Jews could not afford to go elsewhere. They came by bus; only a few had cars; those who did would fill them with family and friends, with luggage and foods, the steep climbs on mountain roads strained the cars' engines.

Single Jews would go up to the mountains for a week or so to find their *bashert* or for romantic liaisons. Read Herman Wouk's *Marjorie Morningstar* for one such depiction, but there are many others in American Jewish literature. And even as postwar affluence took hold, accommodations improved, hotels became luxurious or what was considered luxurious at the time: golf courses, swimming pools (some even indoors), tennis courts, and abundant—overabundant—food. Almost all resorts were kosher or at least kosher-style. Women and children might stay up for the entire summer or at least for a month. Men would join them on the weekend and return to work on Sunday evening and Monday morning.

Many families—my own included—remember fondly the trip up the mountains. The better the car we drove, the easier the climb. Some even remember when Route 17 opened as a four-lane expressway without lights and without tolls and suddenly the resorts were two hours away, not three or four. There was a traditional stop along the way at the Red Apple Rest that suddenly was bypassed by the expressway, and we would stop at the charmless rest stop along the New York State Throughway. It was there that we could eat our first *chametz* (bread or leavened foods) immediately after Passover.

Grossingers, one of the grandest, could serve more than 1,000 at a time. The Concord was even larger. Jewish conferences were held there, assemblies of rabbis and cantors, regional and national meetings of *Hadassah*. Many Jewish comedians began their careers in the Borsht Belt: Jerry Lewis was associated with Browns; other began at Kutshers. Eddie Cantor and Eddie Fisher were frequent entertainers at Grossingers, which billed top name talent before Las Vegas took hold. For Passover these hotels became a place for Jews who found the ordeal of Passover preparations too burdensome and entire families would come year in and year out. There was a sense of community and continuity.

For the less affluent there were bungalow colonies, rented by the season. The cabins contained the bare necessities of life. Some were improved over time with heating for year-round use and after awhile some were equipped with air conditioning. As equal accommodation laws allowed Jews to travel freely, as airplane travel became more accessible, and as air conditioning allowed one to remain in the city, Jews went to more exotic places for their vacations. Instead of returning to the same place at virtually the same time with the same people year after year, Jews went to different places each year. Some travelled alone, husband and wife; others were joined by friends. But few travelled with an entire community transplanted. Much was gained with the new freedoms that Americans enjoyed, but these gains were not without losses. There is a price to freedom. Cities are not *shtetls*, Club Med is not a community, and some might say the tight-knit leisure communities of the Catskills took their biggest hit at this point.

Haredi Jews, the fervently pious, still require community: synagogue services and kosher accommodations, a *minyan*, a quorum of men to read the *Torah* and recite prayers. They prefer to live with one another and can find a community that meets their needs even on vacation.

The Four Seasons Lodge was one of the last of such colonies for the non-ultra Orthodox Jews. One senses throughout the film the magnitude of their collective achievement as a colony, an achievement so very rare, perhaps even antithetical to the dynamism of American life: community and continuity. As the film attests—the portraits of weathered but vital faces, the communal landscapes, the still lifes capturing a culture alive but on the edge of extinction—virtually every frame speaks to a community created out of both tradition and the willful collective survivorship that allowed them to last while those around them decayed. These survivors came back to the same place at the same time to live with the very same people, year after year after year.

I think that the survival of this colony had something to do with the very make up of survivors. Survivors know each other. They understand some code words: "camp," "there," "ghetto." They speak many languages and can move easily from one to another. They can laugh and cry together, laugh and cry at the same time, and because many came here as orphans without parents and without siblings, they sought to create families, not just in isolation as nuclear, but extended families through communities of fellow survivors. They understand how precious such a sense of community is, precious and so very precarious, and, therefore, they struggled to preserve their "very special community" for as long as it was possible.

These people took life's journey together. Once they were young and raised their families at the Lodge, kids coming up with their parents and staying together. They enjoyed the freedom to roam virtually unsupervised, the safety of the Lodge and also the many explorations that it permitted. When they went off to college, they never returned for the summer; at best, they visited for a weekend. Still later, these children of the Lodgers might drop off their own kids and enjoy the freedoms that young couples enjoy when they are without their children. But as we encounter these shrinking denizens of the Lodge, they are the parents not only of grown children, but of grown grandchildren, even great grandchildren. They have each other and the community that is achieved among retirees. Aging takes its toll; illness is a burden. Tomorrow will offer less than yesterday.

As the owners and the inhabitants of the Lodge grew older, each task that was routinely performed summer after summer became all the more difficult; ordinary maintenance became a burden, and non-routine repairs a drain on scarce resources. The Lodge was not profitable enough to permit one to outsource repairs and the difference between being in the black and being hopelessly in the red was how much the owner could do on his own.

The documentary focuses on one chapter of the survivors' lives, but survivors' lives are generally divided into three distinct chapters: *Before*, *During*, and *After*.

Before the Holocaust, they lived elsewhere and imagined their life otherwise. They could not have imagined what was about to take place. The *Before* chapter of life's journey had an abrupt ending. For some German Jews it was January 30, 1933. For Austrian survivors, it was March 1938; for Sudetenland survivors it was September 1938; and Czech survivors March 1939. Most of the survivors who were part of The Four Seasons Lodge community were Polish and for them the end of the life they knew came swiftly on September 1, 1939.

During was the experience of what we now call the Holocaust, or what the Germans aptly called the "Final Solution"—systematic murder is all too final—and what the Jews themselves called the *Churban*, the great destruction, echoing the historic destruction of the First and Second Temples and the exile of the Jewish people.

Once, differences in Holocaust experiences divided the survivors. Death camp survivors stressed the gap between what they endured and what those who hid on the Aryan side had to undergo. But over time, survivors had shared experiences—both in their rootedness in European Jewish life and in the trauma and the triumph of their adjustment to American life. *After* transcended their different experiences of *During* the *Shoah*.

The survivors at the Lodge were solicitous of each other's experience; they understood the differences between life in death camps or on death marches and life in hiding, but these paled in comparison to their sense of camaraderie. Having been through so much, they understood each other.

Looking at the faces and the ages of these survivors in the film's images, we can understand a bit of the demographics of survival: as a rule, only the young survived. At Auschwitz the old and the infirm, young children, and women with children were sent to their deaths immediately. Only the young and the able-bodied were *selekted* to work.

Even then, those who could not endure the hardships of concentration camp life—arduous work, limited nutrition, Polish winters, and the physical and the psychological assault on their humanity—soon succumbed to despair; death inevitably followed.

So most of those who survived were between 18 and 40—today the youngest of those are in their early eighties and the oldest are now past one hundred. The last survivors will be child survivors of the Holocaust, who most often avoided the camps and found refuge in hiding either openly by pretending to be a non-Jew, or in secret in attics, basements, and barns, most in conditions that made Anne Frank's seem enviable. They will be around for another twenty years, but their direct memories will be more limited as they experienced the events known as the Holocaust as very young children.

Once they were young, vibrant, and vital; they struggled to piece together their new lives after the rupture of the wartime years. They experienced the joys and burdens of young children, *bar mitzvahs*—perhaps *bat mitzvahs*—and weddings. There was a time when survivors were worried about making a living in their new homes and they could share those burdens and those achievements together. They needed to say so little because they had shared so much. They understood one another as only survivors could.

As they adjusted to American life, they spoke to their children in English and later to one another in English, but they could switch to Yiddish on a moment's notice with its familiarity, warmth, and even joy.

And they drank. Drinking was a natural part of East European life. The pious would go to synagogue in the morning and then drink *l'chaim*, lifting up their cup of wine or whiskey together, before they set out to work in the cold Polish winters. One would drink after synagogue on Shabbat morning. The Kiddush club is not an invention of contemporary Modern Orthodox Yuppies. Of course Eastern European Jews did not drink $100-a-bottle aged Scotch, but vodka was plentiful, herring and a *kichel* or a bowtie. I still remember my *Zeide's shul*. One drank in synagogue more often than in bars, but the bar at Saturday evening events was a natural. The quantities of liquor plentiful not only for joy but to drown sorrow, numb painful memories, overcome death by *maching*—making—a *l'chaim*. Surely, in today's society drinking is the prerogative of the young; in old age one drinks moderately and slowly, not wanting to strain the body, but one still drinks. So the survivors bemoan their own enforced moderation.

Religious observance was a natural part of Jewish life in Eastern Europe. It pulsated throughout the society. Homes were naturally Kosher, a *Mezzuzah* on the right doorpost, and even for those no longer pious, Sabbath evening was a time to gather and celebrate, most often at home. Many of the Catskills hotels had synagogues as did many of the colonies. It was not a place for daily prayer but for Friday evening and *Shabbes* morning. Candles were lit in the home and the men, primarily the men, went to synagogue.

There is a story that the pre-Holocaust American immigrant generation told and retold that may be apt to describe the religious life of this community: Cohen was a believer and he went to synagogue. Shapiro was a socialist, a known atheist, a proclaimed non-believer; yet he too went to synagogue. When pressed, Shapiro would describe his attendance: "Cohen goes to synagogue to speak with God; I go to synagogue to speak with Cohen." For religious Jews, the synagogue is about God; for others, or dare I say for many more, the synagogue is about community and friendship. If God is present, it is only at a distance.

Old age is also about loss; survivors are familiar with loss. Many had lost parents and siblings; some had lost spouses and worst of all children. All had lost their childhood or their youth, their home and their community. They had lost it abruptly, suddenly, completely. Now they are experiencing loss again, slowly, ever so slowly. And for the Lodgers depicted in this film, the loss is twofold in the loss of this community they built from the ground up. During the Holocaust they had no opportunity to mourn; if the truth be told, they became numb to loss, they could not permit themselves to feel. So for survivors the loss that they experience in old age, the natural loss that they now feel, is a special type of loss. It is natural and normal, ordinary, calm rather than violent. And they can bury the dead and grieve, sit *shiva* and say *Kaddish*.

In *The Four Seasons Lodge* one hears and sees the wisdom of their grief, their triumph even in loss. Listen to the words; heed the wisdom:

One blind and semi-deaf survivor—he has selective hearing, hearing what was necessary, disregarding the rest: "I am 91 years old and last night I danced."

A woman said of her husband: "Like everyone else he's going to live until he dies."

A former soccer champion said of his aging: "Last year I thought I could play soccer and today I can hardly move."

Another said: "Every good thing comes to an end. Nothing is forever. I made it to 85. Many other people never made it."

The work Jacobs created around this community demonstrates that the clock is indeed ticking—there are four seasons: spring and summer, autumn and winter. And just as surely as the leaves begin to change the denizens of The Four Seasons Lodge are well into the autumn of their lives; still there is one more summer—together.

One survivor said what the entire film proves: "Life can be beautiful even when it is not so easy."

These are not clichés but rather important lessons that the journey of life has to offer us, lessons absorbed and exemplified by these survivors, made more poignant when the Holocaust is the "back story."

An immigrant's life is always tough even in the expanding prosperous America of the 1950s and 1960s. It is good to be reminded of those difficulties especially at a time when immigrant bashing is in vogue and immigrants are being blamed for all the ills of society, and when Jews in particular are forgetting their immigrant roots or romanticizing the past.

What was the glue that bound these survivors together? With no one left from the past, friends had to become extended family, to substitute for the uncles and the aunts, the cousins and even the grandparents the children would never know.

The Four Seasons Lodge focuses on the achievements of the community that made the lodge its home. But there is a larger achievement of survivors that hangs in the background. First and foremost, they rebuilt their lives. They did not give death the final word; they began again with the knowledge and despite the most intimate knowledge that life is fragile, that all we have and almost all we are could be taken away all at once.

Survivors created and recreated lives; they brought children into the world. They did not give up on the Jewish people because they raised these children as Jews. Many survivors went to Israel; escaping one war, they went to fight another to found the Jewish state, a haven for all Jews.

In subsequent years, they took on a public mission. Under the leadership of survivors:

- The *Shoah* has been moved into the forefront of contemporary political and ethical consciousness. It has become the negative absolute, a cornerstone for consideration of values.
- Museums and memorials teaching and commemorating the Holocaust have been created throughout the world.
- Holocaust remembrance has become a basic part of the Jewish calendar and increasingly a part of the calendars of many nations affected by the Holocaust, including the United States, Germany, Poland, and Great Britain—as well as the United Nations.

Because of Holocaust denial and anti-Semitism, these countries have intensified the emphasis on Holocaust commemoration.

- Testimony has been gathered on an unprecedented scale, in the most contemporary technologies. In addition, many memoirs have been written. Both of these forms will provide living voices of their witness far beyond their lifetimes. Their stories will form the basis for scholarship, films, and educational programs for generations.

Individually and as a collective group, survivors have also been essential to Holocaust education:

- They have served as volunteers, guides, and teachers at every Holocaust institution in the United States. Each memorial or museum can point to a number of survivor volunteers who have become an essential, irreplaceable part of their staff.
- Survivors have been a major part of the funding of Holocaust institutions. They could not have created these institutions alone; nor could these institutions have been created without their monetary support.
- Their monetary contributions have been significant and their ability to appeal to others to support these institutions irreplaceable. One suspects that many descendants of Holocaust survivors will continue to donate funds, albeit with less urgency than their parents and often more out of a sense of obligation than of mission. The Claims Conference is now the major supporter of Holocaust education, memorialization, scholarship and exhibitions. There is an 80/20 allocation of funds between assisting survivors and Holocaust education and scholarship and also a 60/40 division between Israel and the Diaspora. So as the last survivor passes, as the number of survivors diminishes, support for these programs will be severely cut.
- Holocaust survivors were once perceived as victims, refugees, the newest arrivals in America. Increasingly, they have become symbols of resilience and of people's ability to overcome the catastrophes of life and to rebuild their lives with dignity and

decency. In classrooms throughout the United States and even in other countries of the world, students look to them for confidence to understand that not every defeat need be final, that one can overcome even the most horrific of circumstances, and that one can come back from near death. The survivors describe weakness and humiliation. Students see strength and fortitude.

Survivors have a unique moral authority. Elie Wiesel once wrote: "only those who were there will ever know and those who were there can never tell."[2] The abundance of Holocaust testimony has demonstrated that those who were there *can tell*—if not everything, then many things. And those of us who work in the field of Holocaust Studies have come to give special recognition to survivors' testimony, not to the exclusion of other evidence nor even to determine historically what happened, but for a feel for the inner conditions of the ghetto and the camps, for the human dimension of their interaction with a historical experience.

Such authority will not automatically transfer to their descendants. Such authority will have to be earned by scholars who work through this material, by writers, filmmakers, and creative artists like Jacobs and the authors of the literary writing in this book who wrestle with the Holocaust and create in its aftermath, and by children of survivors to the degree—and only to the degree—that they embrace the experience of their parents and create from it. Many children of survivors have kept a certain distance from this experience, a distance necessary for them not to live in the shadow of their parents and to achieve their own identity. Their children, the third generation, has less need for distance but a much greater distance to travel to bridge the understandings of one generation to another.

It is also fair to note, as Peter Novick did in his controversial book *The Holocaust in American Life*, that authority in this field will transfer to institutions that are the guardians of memory such as Yad Vashem, the United States Holocaust Memorial Museum, and many others; but institutional charisma is different than the charisma of experience or

---

2   Walter Laqueur, ed., *Encyclopedia of the Holocaust* (New Haven and London: Yale University Press, 2001), 208.

individual charisma. And if in the future these institutions are handed over to managers who embrace the mission rather than embody it, much will be lost.

When the last survivor is gone, the Holocaust will become about the past and recede into the past; whether it can still retain its current status is unknown but perhaps not unknowable. It is clear that courses will be taught on the Holocaust and genocide, but just months ago a college renamed its Center for the Study of the Holocaust, Genocide and Human Rights to The Center for the Study of Human Rights. A college, which started a program in Holocaust Studies and then in Holocaust and Genocide Studies, now has but one course in Holocaust Studies and many in other genocides. This renaming and rebranding will happen more often and with much less opposition in the future.

In my view, the survivors' most important achievement is almost biblical.

Let me explain: They transformed victimization into witness, dehumanization into a plea to deepen our humanity. Holocaust survivors responded to survival in the most biblical of ways possible: by remembering evil and suffering to deepen conscience, to enlarge memory and broaden responsibility. They have made a most particular story universal. It is thus that the Ancient Israelites responded to slavery and the Exodus. It is thus that its survivors responded to the *Shoah*.

The survivors leave the rest of us who are not survivors or descendants of survivors with an important legacy with significant responsibilities.

We were not witnesses. We have lived in the presence of witnesses. Future generations will not even be able to say that.

But alas: there are four seasons.

Ecclesiastes taught:

There is a time for everything, for all things under the sun.

A time to be born and a time to die;

A time to laugh and a time to weep

A time to dance and a time to mourn

A time to seek and a time to lose;

A time to forget and a time to remember.

Nature swallowed up much of the land of the Catskills. Nature will claim The Four Seasons Lodge and its inhabitants who will return to the earth from whence they came. That too will be a triumph for those they left behind in the camps and the ghettos, who had no burial place, certainly no individual burial place to mark their lives. And time will also all too soon claim the last survivor.

But how these survivors lived—and what they shared together for a time—must endure. Theirs is a time to remember.

Imaginings
and
Re-imaginings

From *Dusk in the Catskills*

Reuben Wallenrod

In the evening the casino becomes the center of Leo Halpa's hotel in Brookville. The band plays, the young people dance, and the joyous sounds fill the grounds and the road. The casino hall is flooded with light and men and women seek one another, draw close to one another. The drum beats out the rhythm definitely, urgently; the violin doubts and prays, the saxophone sounds pour forth with vehemence and joy; and the piano sounds run beside them like little animals down the hill . . . Men and women dance, separate for a short while and come close again; men and women are dancing in narrow circles: you and I; he and she; let us rush down together; what *else* is there besides our narrow circles? All these two or three hundred people, men and women dancing in one of the casinos in the Catskill mountains, these two or three hundred lives are nothing but little narrow circles, dancing their own dance, desiring only their own little desires, living their own little lives.

The heart knows well that there is another great wide, threatening world outside you, but you are afraid to stop your dancing and think of that world. Such knowledge may well break up the charm of the circle, it may well break up your very being, all of you. Outside there are lakes and woods and the moon is pouring soft light on the frightful distances, but your heart is afraid to look at all that.

Tomorrow you will go out of your circle and buy your newspaper, and you will read in it before eating your roast chicken about one hundred Jews that have died a frightful death. You will read about thirty girls who have been thrown into whorehouses, about towns full of memories that have been erased and are no more. If you let this news enter you, become a part of you, you will become insane. You will be no more, you will become one of them. Don't! For your own sake. Don't! Don't go out of your little circle. While in New York you keep away those terrible sounds and visions. You keep them away with the sounds of your machines, of your typewriters, with your bargaining, your laughter, your quarrelling. Now you have escaped to the Catskill mountains, try to keep those sounds away, through your rush for enjoyment, an excited nervous enjoyment. Close yourself up in your narrow circle, listen to the sounds of the band, to the sounds of the dancing people. Let all those terrible sounds and visions become just numbers; let the one hundred, the thirty become a mere statistical, visionless number, and you will not see the contorted faces of your tortured brethren, of the women dragged into whorehouses, of their strangled children.

They come, however, those people and stand before you. You see among them men and women you actually knew. You have known them with your eyes and you have known them in your imagination. And then they come separately, and distinctly, and at times they rush towards you as one terrible face, a frightened face.

Chase away all these visions and repeat to yourself that hundreds, that *thousands* of men and women were killed and are dead. Numbers will dispel your fear. Death also dispels fear.

The finality of death and the indifference of numbers will relieve you. Your calculation will reassure you and cheer you. The calculation is simple: so many Nazis in the world, so many people who are against the Nazis, and of course, "those bastards, those gangsters will be exterminated." Even your curses reassure you somewhat. That is, you feel now that you have done your part, you have cursed them. And now you may again return to your circle and follow the music. Again you hear the wild

Reuben Wallenrod

84

pommeling of the big drum and little drums, the triumphant tones and sudden passionate impatient ecstasy of the saxophone, the heavy self-satisfaction of the bass, and the little rushing broken sounds of the piano. But you can't run away. The visions and sounds blended into one terrible contorted face will beckon to you and admonish you.

The youngsters dance their new steps like young heifers with joyous jumping and animal enthusiasm, but fear is creeping into the hearts of their elders.

Leo Halper stands near the entrance to the casino. He comes from time to time to check up on the cleanliness of the hall, on the playing of the band, and to show the guests and the musicians that there is an eye that sees them. Besides, it is also necessary to keep an eye from time to time on the conduct of the various men and women who come to the hotel. Not that he wants to be a watchdog for their morals. He knows that people come to have a good time in the Catskills, otherwise they would not come here. Still, let them know that Halper sees. He knows what is going on in other hotels, and he will not allow that in Brookville. Not while he is here.

And while he is standing and watching, various thoughts come crowding each other. Here they are, Jewish boys and girls, dancing and enjoying themselves. And he is angry at his previous anger and resentment at them. Aren't the youngsters entitled to a little happiness? Are there many places left in the world where a Jewish boy and girl could have a bit of joy? Let them dance! Who knows what the morrow will bring?

Halper stands at the entrance to his casino and mumbles within himself: "Dance, youngsters, dance," but he knows that someone within him is protesting, and a sharp pain is awakened. It seems that every passing moment is strained and tense like those strings of the violin, that another moment and it may tear apart, and then all these boys and girls will suddenly stop their dancing, and their faces will blend in that terrible face of those that are far away.

Halper leaves the entrance to his casino and the sounds follow him into the summer night.

Dusk in the Catskills:
My Father, the Holocaust, Memories, and Reflections

Naima (Wallenrod) Prevots

Memories came flooding back, re-reading *Dusk in the Catskills*. Growing up, the Holocaust was physically distant, but emotionally close. I was born in 1935, and remember my father telling me often about Nazis murdering thousands of Jews and trying to conquer the world. Growing up, my father would talk about anti-Semitism, and his fears for Jewish life in America. He also spoke often about Yiddish as language of the past, and Hebrew as language of the present and future, and always, the vulnerability of Jews in the world, and the urgent need for a Jewish state in Israel.

The memories began to take on more coherence as I tried to piece together highlights of my father's life and understand his thoughts and influences surrounding *Dusk in the Catskills*. For smoother reading, from this point on I will refer to him as Reuben, as I journey backwards and then forward. Born in 1899, in the small town of Vizna (population then 1,600), his father was a successful shopkeeper. Hebrew and Zionism held fascinations for him when he was young, as he recounts in his last book, *Bayit Bakfar* (Hebrew, 1965), a semi-autobiographical account of around two years spent with grandparents after his mother died, when he was about 15-16 years old. An important later milestone was his acceptance into the boy's classical gymnasium in nearby Slutsk, where tight quotas mandated a very small Jewish acceptance rate. This was a rigorous intellectual secular environment, and provided him with strong academic background. His sister Myriam, three years younger, attended the girl's gymnasium, and while Reuben's transcripts do not exist, I have the record of her attendance and courses during 1918-1919 as follows: Russian, Polish, Latin, mathematics, history, geography, physics, geometry. It is safe to assume the boy's gymnasium had a similar curriculum. The town of Slutsk (population then around 15,000), was a center at that time of Zionist activity.

The Bolshevik Revolution and outbreak of World War I brought chaos to Russia. Myriam and Reuben emigrated to Palestine, arriving there in 1920, leaving behind their father, brothers, and sisters. Myriam worked as a practical nurse at Hadassah, and Reuben worked with *Gedud Haavodah* in the Galil and Jezreal Valley, drying swamps and paving roads. According to my mother, he left Palestine in 1921, because he became ill with malaria working in the swamps. His next stop was Paris, where he stayed around two years, working odd jobs. There is documentation that he arrived in America on July 1, 1923, on a boat from Cherbourg, France, with $25 in his pocket. He initially stayed with an uncle, and worked in a garment factory owned by a relative, and this was followed by assorted other jobs, including time as a Western Union messenger.

Reuben received his BA from NYU in 1929, and his MA from Columbia Teacher's College in 1930, with degrees in education and French. He began his career as a teacher in the late 1920s, working at Herzliah Hebrew School and at the religious Zionist Mizrahi Talmud Torah, and briefly at the Yeshiva of Flatbush. He hated teaching children and adolescents, and it was clear to him that he wanted to set his sights higher and study for a PhD. A close friend, Winograd, wanted to be a doctor, and found it impossible to enter medical school in the United States because of quotas. Reuben convinced my mother Rae, whom he married in 1927, that they should move to Paris with Winograd, where he would attend the Sorbonne for his PhD studies. His dissertation *John*

Dewey, Educateur was completed and published in 1932, and Reuben kept a handwritten note from John Dewey thanking him for his work.

My mother stayed with him in Paris through 1931, and then went to Palestine to be with her sister Lifsha, who had married and emigrated from Poland in the late 1920s. Reuben joined her there after completion of his dissertation, and the plan was for him to find work so they could stay. Nothing materialized and they returned to the United States. He began teaching in a variety of places, among them Jewish/Hebrew day schools, teacher's institutes, and the Jewish Theological Seminary. He also began writing, contributing to *Ha'Aretz*, Hebrew journals in Palestine, Europe, and America. A major breakthrough was publication of his short stories in 1937, *Badeyotah Hashelishit*. In 1939 he began teaching at Brooklyn College, where he was known and beloved for his teaching of Hebrew language and literature. He was a strong presence on the faculty until his retirement in 1963, due to onset of Alzheimer's. He published significantly during the 1940s and 50s, and his work includes numerous articles and several books, covering a wide arena of fiction and non-fiction.

Dusk in the Catskills was first published in 1946, in Hebrew. Most likely it was begun in 1941, and finished in 1943 or 1944. In the 1957 English translation page 36, we read: "The topic of the conversation was the latest news about Pearl Harbor. Bill spoke with assurance: 'I say we'll break those Japs into pieces. Our boys will get to Tokyo and will repay them for their treachery.'" On page 234, we read: "To Halper this was also the end of another summer in his life, the fifty-second year of his life, the end of the third year of the Second World War." These two quotations could be seen as a discrepancy in the writing, as the novel's action is designed to take place over the period of one year, and yet the two quotations indicate different time periods. My sense is when he began writing, Pearl Harbor was a recent event. As the writing and overseas atrocities continued, he placed events further into the war. What follows is exploration of his life and thought during the years he wrote the book: his relationship to the Catskills; his views on ever increasing horrors of the Holocaust; his deep involvement in Hebrew; and feelings about the future of Jewish immigrant life in the United States.

The setting for *Dusk in the Catskills* was Hotel Rosenblatt in Glen Wild, called Hotel Brookville in the novel. I remembered spending one summer there as a very young child, and it is not clear when Reuben was there. Inquiries with two relatives clarified family history, although there are still uncertainties. Rosenblatt was originally from Poland and grew up with extended family of my mother. When he established his hotel, various family members and friends living in New York were invited to work there during the summers, starting in the late 1920s. My cousin Saul Isserow, now 91, remembered his mother's stories about her first summer working at the hotel in 1930, when she supervised the chambermaids and her sister (Reuben's wife and my mother) worked as a bookkeeper. Reuben completed his undergraduate degree in 1929, and his graduate work in 1930, and it is unlikely he spent those summers at Rosenblatt's, except perhaps for brief visits. Cousin Saul also remembers that my mother's friends who had emigrated from Warsaw, the Rom sisters, worked during summer 1930 as waitresses. I knew the Rom sisters very well, and they became prominent in New York as dance teachers. Saul also remembered that Rosenblatt saw himself as an "intellectual" and was proud he was a "registered socialist."

When my parents returned from Paris and Palestine in 1932, it is possible my mother worked at Rosenblatt's once again. I remember stories about her unpleasant experiences in the kitchen and as a waitress, where people demanded certain kinds of eggs (soft boiled, hard boiled) and she always managed to cook the wrong thing. Here again, it is likely Reuben stayed and worked in New York during that summer. Another cousin, Miriam Herscher, told me her mother Sylvia was at Rosenblatt's for two summers. In 1933 she was at the front desk checking in guests, and in 1934 she ran the dining room. Saul is very clear about working at Rosenblatt's from 1939 through 1942, first as a bus boy and then as a waiter. His sister Minnie also worked there during those years, first as a tea girl, and then as a waitress. Saul remembers that when he worked there, Rosenblatt's had around 250 or 300 guests. It is most likely Reuben was at Rosenblatt's for a whole summer in 1939, and then in 1941. I have a strong memory of all three of us at the hotel when I was around four, and Reuben telling me at some point that he spent his time there as "writer in residence." I also remember attending Camp Kindervelt at age five in 1940, when my parents spent the summer travelling. It seems possible the three of us were there again in 1941. After that, my summers were spent at Camp Massad in the Poconos, and my parents spent their summers travelling and taking short stays near my camp.

During the 1940s, the increasing devastation of the Holocaust was closely intertwined in our household conversations with Reuben's concerns about the future of American Jews and his passion for Hebrew language and literature. His choice of the Catskills as a setting for the book seems to me a commentary on his views of identity and survival. For Reuben, as transmitted to me, it was essential to preserve Jewish identity not through religion or Yiddish, but by encompassing Hebrew as a living language, thus forging a bond with an historical tradition and with a future homeland in Palestine. We were secular Zionist Jews. Growing up, I thought there were huge numbers of Jews in New York just like us. Reuben had a close circle of friends who were Hebraists and Zionists. All the children knew Hebrew. Many of us went to the Yeshivah of Flatbush, which at the time was a secular school with a double English/Hebrew curriculum. Many of us went to Camp Massad during the summers for eight weeks. We spoke Hebrew, learned about Jewish history, and were surrounded by Zionist ideals.

It is hard for many in 2013 to capture the Hebraist/Zionist environment that existed in New York for Reuben, my mother Rae, and myself. Several scholars and writers interested in Reuben's work and in the Hebraists of the 1940s-50s have corresponded with me over the last few years. As I look back now, we certainly did not constitute a majority of the Jewish community in terms of way of life, thoughts, and ideas. Most of Reuben's friends were writers and teachers, and the term "intellectuals" would probably be a good fit. Many of them had emigrated from Russia, at various times. They all hoped Palestine would become a home for the Jews. They all spoke and wrote Hebrew, and passed this on to their children. They all looked down on Yiddish as a past language in terms of speaking it themselves and teaching it to their children, although they valued its cultural and historical heritage. They all were worried about anti-Semitism, assimilation and inter-marriage in America. The Holocaust was terrifying and constant in their thoughts.

Reuben's portrayal of Rosenblatt's Hotel, the guests, and the surrounding community takes up all these themes. In re-reading the book, and thinking about my growing up, many new connections and insights surfaced. I can sense Reuben's pain in several areas. Why is Halper the only one who thinks about the Holocaust, the Nazis, the destruction of villages, cities, families, loved ones? Why do the guests think they can escape the issues of their identity? Why does Emily persist in singing old Yiddish songs and thinking of an imagined and faulty past? What will happen when the younger generation of non-Jews who own the land and run the Catskills take full power? Why does Toozin fool himself with his marriage to Emily and his materialistic preoccupation with powerful cars, both of which eventually kill him: physically and emotionally? Why does Raymond distance himself from his parents and his roots and what does that mean for the next generations? Why is Hymie presented as a sympathetic artist figure, possibly reflecting Reuben's perceived role as a writer and artist, and often society's looking down on the artist? Why does Reuben foresee on page 264 that "All those who used to gather here would not be here again." Why does the title "Dusk in the Catskills" and the Jeremiah quote have such a powerful resonance for him and for us?

I have asked these questions to highlight Reuben's concerns in the novel, which were also his concerns in life. I have been asked by current scholars if he was involved in nostalgia for the past. I would say this was not his orientation. He was more involved in thinking about the future, and hence the above questions. He was an intense man, with a quiet passion about life. It was not always an easy household, as there were convictions so deeply held, and fears so profound, that going against them was problematic. There were times when I did not want to learn or speak Hebrew, and this occasioned arguments. I did end up with fluency and interest, and even took two of his courses my last two years at Brooklyn College. At one point my parents wanted me to spend some time in Israel, and I wanted to move ahead as dancer and choreographer, and this occasioned conflict. I eventually ended up with close ties to some of our family in Israel, and to the worlds of dance and education through my consulting work there over the years.

It is not clear to me when my father found out about the Nazi murder of his beloved sister, her children, and his father, all of whom lived in Slutsk. But the fact remains that on a constant basis his thoughts were with those who were being murdered and displaced by the Nazis, based on all the reports during the period 1941-44. His emphasis on Hebrew language and literature, and his desire for a Jewish state in Palestine were his solutions to the creation of a strong presence and identity for Jews in America and in the world. He was terrified that the Jewish community in America would disappear through assimilation and intermarriage. He was terrified that the young people would forget and let go of their heritage, and this would be disastrous for his people and for parents and grandparents, and he notes on page 133: "The young are cruel to the old." This was an emotional, historical, and cultural cruelty. Reuben, in his book, is concerned about a void at Rosenblatt's. He is concerned about escape from reality. He wants a more spiritual context for Jewish life, and his fears of the Holocaust are closely tied with his secular/Zionist/Hebraist thrust. He also had a loathing for the Bolsheviks, for Stalin and his murders and dictatorship, and for communist ideology.

For Reuben Wallenrod, writing *Dusk in the Catskills* may have been a reflection and a catharsis. He was a Hebrew writer, with a perspective on Jewish life in America, and the catastrophe we eventually called the Holocaust. It seems now in retrospect that he felt there was an element of escapism at the Catskills resorts that led people to ignore what was happening and to some degree who they were. He was unhappy about the nostalgia implied in the Yiddish songs, poetry, references. He was not happy about the loose sexuality implied with some of the resort life, as he felt it meant a loss of values and spirituality. He saw some humor in how people came to the Catskills, expecting to experience moments/hours of release from more difficult experiences and lives in New York. He had no sympathy for those who were nostalgic for Russia or the old country. His hatred of the Bolsheviks was loud and clear, and his fears of ironclad ideologies were palpable.

There is a story behind the English translation of *Dusk in the Catskills* and its publication in 1957. My mother's cousin, Sylvia Herscher, was married to Seymour, and they both had met at Rosenblatt's in 1933, and married in 1935. Sylvia and Seymour were producers, managers, and dramaturgs in the Broadway arena. In 1955 Herman Wouk published *Marjorie Morningstar*, first a successful novel and then a movie in 1958. I remember discussions about Reuben's portrayal of the Catksills, and the value of his work in contrast to Wouk's. The translation took place around 1955, and although there are no credits given, I know my mother was involved, as was cousin Seymour. Published by The Reconstructionist Press in 1957, there was serious consideration of making it into a Broadway play. Herman Wouk's novel centers around the rebellion of Marjorie Morningstar (née Morgenstern) against her family's traditional expectations of her future life as Jewish wife and mother. She awakens to love and sexuality in the fictional South Wind adult camp in the Catskills, where she falls in love with Noel Airman, (née Ehrmann). If my memory is correct, there was a push to transform *Dusk in the Catskills* into a "sexier" presentation, and Reuben was not willing to make any changes. It was unusual for him to try and reach an English speaking public, as his aim was to write for those who knew and loved Hebrew, both in the United States and in Palestine. It is worth noting that the English translation is of greater interest to a wider public now, as it captures a past era with delicacy and insight.

Reuben's world has vanished but the questions raised in his book remain. There are still schools such as Ramaz, the Yeshivah of Flatbush, and Jewish day schools with bi-lingual curricula or Hebrew language instruction, although the older emphasis on *Ivrit b'Ivrit* (Hebrew in Hebrew) is mostly gone. All the major Hebrew journals published in the United States have gone under. The hardcore Hebraists are no longer a strong, elite group of intellectuals. Yiddish has achieved a status as an important facet of Jewish life, as witnessed by the growth and success of the Yiddish Institute at Hampshire College. Jewish life in America has taken many forms, but there are still concerns about inter-marriage and cultural continuity. There is an increase in religious Judaism, and a reduction in the number of secular Jews who maintain a strong affinity to language and tradition. Reuben raised questions about our memories and relationship to the Holocaust, to Jewish life in America, to spiritual as opposed to material existence.

The Holocaust was not a strong preoccupation with the American Jewish community when Reuben published his book in 1946. The creation of the State of Israel was a dream for a small number of Zionists here in America. The State of Israel now exists, but it is no longer the idealistic environment he and his cohorts imagined. I look back on my secular/Zionist/Hebraist environment and find it rich. But I look at issues in Israel now, the settlements, the rise of religious groups, the horrors of occupation, and views of the Holocaust that preclude moving forward for a secular, democratic environment. At first, I did not want to write this essay. I am not nostalgic, and tend to change and move on with my life. But this has been immensely important. Reuben and my mother, Rae, gave me a strong heritage in Hebrew and Jewish values. *Dusk in the Catskills* seems an even stronger statement now than in 1946, about the importance of spirituality and awareness in Jewish life. My belief in the State of Israel is still strong, in the hopes that reactionary voices there will be silenced, and leadership will be provided for peace, end of occupation, and a two state solution. That would be very much in keeping with Reuben's passion for a State of Israel.

I am grateful to Phil and Holli for asking me to contribute to this volume. It is my hope that memories of growing up and of my father help illuminate his writing. As I re-read *Dusk in the Catskills* it seemed even more important now than when first written. Reuben Wallenrod wrote about Jewish immigrants in New York and he was angry. He was angry at the lack of values surrounding him: money, sex, entertainment, but no concern for fellow Jews suffering in concentration camps and gas chambers. The request from Phil and Holli to write about his Catskills book has led me to re-read some of his other writings. His was certainly a complicated relationship to American Judaism: love of the possibilities afforded by a new world, but fear of losing old and important values and connections. There is much sadness in many of his stories about Jewish immigrants in his writings of the 1930s through the 1950s. They are portrayed as having a very hard time adjusting to their new lives. They are often lonely, poor, lost, homesick, confused. These are not immigrants who found an easy life in America, and perhaps they were so involved in adjusting and finding their way in this new country that focusing on what was happening with the Jews they left behind was difficult. Perhaps the contemporary importance of *Dusk in the Catskills* is the dilemma it presents for us: ordinary people with ordinary lives and concerns, who cannot comprehend or encompass the evils of the Holocaust.

From *Enemies, A Love Story*

Isaac Bashevis Singer

The rabbi had apparently prepared a new set of jokes for the evening meal; his store of anecdotes seemed inexhaustible. The women giggled. The student-waiters served the food noisily. Sleepy children didn't want to eat and their mothers slapped them on the hands. One woman, a recent arrival in America, sent back her serving and the waiter asked, "By Hitler you ate better?"

Afterward they all gathered in the casino, a remodeled barn. The Yiddish poet gave a speech, lauding Stalin, and recited proletarian poetry. An actress did impersonations of celebrities. She cried, laughed, screamed, and made faces. An actor who had played in a Yiddish vaudeville theater in New York told bawdy jokes about a betrayed husband, whose wife had hidden a Cossack under her bed, and about a rabbi who had come to preach to a loose woman and had left her house with his fly open. The women and young girls doubled over with laughter. "Why is it all so painful to me?" Herman asked himself. The vulgarity in this casino denied the sense of creation. It shamed the agony of the Holocaust. Some of the guests were refugees from Nazi terror. Moths flew in through the open door, attracted by the bright lights, deceived by a false day.

They fluttered about awhile and fell dead, having beaten themselves against the wall, or singed themselves on the lightbulbs.

Herman glanced around and saw that Masha was dancing with an enormous man in a plaid shirt and green shorts that exposed his hairy thighs. He held Masha by the waist; she barely reached his shoulder with her hand. One of the waiters was blowing a trumpet and another was banging a drum. A third blew on a home-made instrument that looked like a pot with holes in it.

Since Herman had left New York with Masha, he had had little chance to be alone. After some hesitation, he walked out without letting Masha see him leave. The night was moonless and chilly. Herman passed by a farm. A calf stood in a pen. It gazed into the night with the bewilderment of a mute creature. Its large eyes seemed to ask: Who am I? What am I here for? Cool breezes blew from the mountains. Meteors streaked across the sky. The casino grew smaller in the distance and lay down below like a firefly. With all her negativism, Masha had retained the normal instincts. She wanted a husband, children, a household. She loved music, the theater, and laughed at the actors' jokes. But in Herman there resided a sorrow that could not be assuaged. He was not a victim of Hitler. He had been a victim long before Hitler's day.

He came to the shell of a burned-out house and stopped. Attracted by the pungent smell, the holes that had been windows, the sooty entrance, the black chimney, he went inside. If demons did exist, they would be at home in this ruin. Since he could not stand humans, perhaps ghosts were his natural companions. Could he remain in this rubble for the rest of his life? He stood among the charred walls, inhaling the smell of the long extinguished fire. Herman could hear the night breathing. He even imagined that it snored in its sleep. The silence rang in his ears. He stepped on coals and ashes. No, he could not be a part of all that acting, laughing, singing, dancing. Through a hole that had once been a window, he could see the dark sky—a heavenly papyrus filled with hieroglyphics. Herman's gaze fixed upon three stars whose formation resembled the Hebrew vowel "segul." He was looking at three suns, each probably with its planets, comets. How strange that a bit of muscle fitted into a skull should be capable of seeing such distant objects. How peculiar that a panful of brains should be constantly wondering and not able to arrive at any conclusion! They were all silent: God, the stars, the dead. The creatures who *did* speak revealed nothing . . .

He turned back toward the casino, which by now was dark. The building, so recently filled with noise, was quiet and abandoned, sunk in the self-absorption of all inanimate objects. Herman started to look for his bungalow, but he knew he would have difficulty finding it. He got lost wherever he went—in cities, in the country, on ships, in hotels. A single light was burning at the entrance of the house where the office was located, but there was no one there.

The thought ran through Herman's mind: perhaps Masha had gone to bed with that dancer in the green shorts. It was unlikely, but anything was possible among modern people stripped of all faith. What did civilization consist of if not murder and fornication? Masha must have recognized his footsteps. A door opened and he heard her voice.

$\rightarrow\!\!\ell\!\!\ell$

Masha took a sleeping pill and fell asleep, but Herman remained awake. First he waged his usual war with the Nazis, bombed them with atomic bombs, blasted their armies with mysterious missiles, lifted their fleet out of the ocean and placed it on land near Hitler's villa in Berchtesgaden. Try as he might, he could not stop his thoughts. His mind worked like a machine out of control. He was again drinking that potion which enabled him to fathom time, space, "the thing in itself." His pondering always brought him to the same conclusion: God (or whatever He may be) was certainly wise, but there was no sign of His mercy. If a God of mercy did exist in the heavenly hierarchy, then he was only a helpless godlet, a kind of heavenly Jew among the heavenly Nazis. As long as one does not have the courage to leave this world, one can only hide and try to get by, with the help of alcohol, opium, a hayloft in Lipsk, or a small room at Shifrah Puah's.

He fell asleep and dreamed of an eclipse of the sun and funeral processions. They followed one after another, long catafalques, pulled by black horses, ridden by giants. They were both the dead and the mourners.

"How can this be?" he asked himself in his dream. "Can a condemned tribe lead itself to its own burial?" They carried torches and sang a dirge of unearthly melancholy. Their robes dragged along the ground, the spikes of their helmets reached into the clouds.

Herman started and the rusty springs of the bed jangled. He awoke frightened and perspiring. His stomach was distended and his bladder full. The pillow under his head was wet and twisted like a piece of wrung-out washing. How long had he slept? One hour? Six? The bungalow was pitch black and wintery cold. Masha was sitting up in bed, her pale face like a spot of light in the dark. "Herman. I'm afraid of an operation!" she cried out hoarsely, her voice not unlike Shifrah Puah's. It was a few moments before Herman realized what she was talking about.

"Well, all right."

"Perhaps Leon will divorce me. I'll speak frankly to him. If he won't divorce me, the child will bear his name."

"I can't divorce Yadwiga."

Masha fell into a rage. "You can't!" she shouted. "When the king of England wanted to marry the woman he loved, he gave up his throne, and you can't get rid of a stupid peasant! There's no law that can force you to live with her. The worst that can happen is that you'll have to pay alimony. I'll pay the alimony. I'll work overtime and pay!"

"You know that a divorce would kill Yadwiga."

"I know nothing of the sort. Tell me, were you married to the bitch by a rabbi?"

"By a rabbi? No."

"How then?"

"A civil marriage."

"That's not worth a thing according to Jewish law. Marry me in a Jewish ceremony. I don't need their Gentile papers."

"No rabbi will perform a marriage without a license. This is America, not Poland."

"I'll find a rabbi who will."

"It would still be bigamy—worse, polygamy."

"No one will ever know. Only my mother and I. We'll move out of the house and you can use whatever name you like. If your peasant is so dear to you that you can't live without her, then go spend one day a week with her. I'll make my peace with that."

"Sooner or later, they'll arrest me and deport me."

"As long as there is no marriage certificate, no one can prove that we're man and wife. You can burn the ketuba right after the wedding ceremony."

"You have to register a child."

"We'll work something out. It's enough that I'm prepared to share you with such an idiot. Let me finish." Masha changed her tone. "I've been sitting here and thinking a full hour. If you won't agree, you can leave this minute and not come back. I'll find a doctor who will perform the operation, but don't you ever show your face to me again. I'll give you one minute to answer. If it's no, get dressed and get out. I don't want you here another second."

"You're asking me to break the law. I'll be afraid of every policeman in the street."

"You're afraid anyhow. Answer me!"

"Yes."

Masha was silent for a long time.

"Are you just saying that?" she said finally. "Or will I have to start all over again tomorrow?"

"No, it's settled."

"It takes an ultimatum to get you to decide anything. First thing tomorrow morning I'll telephone Leon and tell him he must give me a divorce. If he won't, I'll destroy him."

"What will you do? Shoot him?"

"I'm capable of doing that too, but I have other ways of getting at him. Legally he's as unkosher as pork. If I wanted to report him, he could be deported tomorrow."

"According to Jewish law, our baby will be a bastard anyhow. It was conceived before the divorce."

"Jewish law and all the other laws mean as much to me as last year's frost. I'm only doing it for my mother, only for her."

Masha got out of bed and moved about in the dark. A rooster crowed; other roosters answered him. A bluish light shone in through the window. The summer night was over. The birds started chirping and whistling all at the same time. Herman could no longer stay in bed. He got up, put on his trousers and shoes, opened the door.

The outdoors was occupied with its early-morning tasks. The rising sun had executed a childish painting on the night sky—spots, smears, a mess of colors. Dew had settled on the grass and a milky-white mist hung over the lake. Three young birds perched on the branch of a tree near the bungalow, kept their soft beaks wide open while the mother bird fed them little bits of stems and worms from her beak. She flew back and forth, with the single-minded diligence of those who know their duties. The sun rose behind the lake. Flames ignited the water. A pine cone fell, ready to fructify the earth, to bring forth a new pine.

Masha went out barefoot in her long nightgown, a cigarette between her lips.

"I've wanted your child since the day we met."

⤙⤚

Herman was again getting ready for one of his trips. He had invented a new lie about going on the road to sell the Encyclopedia Britannica, and had told Yadwiga that he would have to spend a whole week in the Middle West. Since Yadwiga hardly knew the difference between one book and another, the lie was superfluous. But Herman had got into the habit of making up stories. Besides, lies wore thin and had to be repaired constantly, and recently Yadwiga had been grumbling about him. He was away the first day of Rosh Hashanah and half of the second. She had prepared carp's head, apple and honey, and had baked the special New Year challah exactly as her neighbor had taught her to, but apparently Herman sold books even on Rosh Hashanah.

The women in the house were now trying to convince Yadwiga—speaking half in Yiddish, half in Polish—that her husband must have a mistress somewhere. One old woman had advised her to consult a lawyer, get a divorce from Herman, and demand alimony. Another had taken her to the synagogue to hear the blowing of the ram's horn. She stood among the wives and at the horn's first wailing sound had burst into tears. It had reminded her of Lipsk, of the war, of her father's death.

Now after only a few days with her, Herman was leaving again, to join not Masha but Tamara, who had rented a bungalow in the Catskill Mountains. He had had to lie to Masha too. He had told her that he was going with Rabbi Lampert to Atlantic City to attend a two-day rabbinical conference.

It was a lame excuse. Even Reformed rabbis did not hold conferences during the Days of Awe. But Masha, who had succeeded in getting Leon Tortshiner to give her a divorce and expected to marry Herman when the ninety-day waiting period was over, had stopped making jealous scenes. The divorce and her pregnancy seemed to have changed her outlook. She behaved toward Herman as a wife. And she showed more devotion than ever to her mother. Masha had found a rabbi, a refugee, who had agreed to perform the wedding ceremony without a license.

When Herman told her that he would be back from Atlantic City before Yom Kippur, she didn't question him. He also told her that the rabbi would pay him a fee of fifty dollars—and they needed the money.

The entire adventure was fraught with danger. He had promised to phone Masha and he knew that the long-distance operator might mention where the call was coming from. Masha might decide to phone Rabbi Lampert's office and discover that the rabbi was in New York. But since Masha had not called Reb Abraham Nissen Yaroslaver to check on him, she probably would not call Rabbi Lampert. One additional danger did not make that much difference. He had two wives and was about to marry a third. Even though he feared the consequences of his actions and the scandal that would follow, some part of him enjoyed the thrill of being faced with ever-threatening catastrophe. He both planned his actions and improvised. The "Unconscious," as von Hartmann called it, never made a mistake. Herman's words seemed to issue from his mouth of their own accord and only later would he realize what stratagems and subterfuges he had managed to invent. Behind this mad hodgepodge of emotions, a calculating gambler throve on daily risk.

Herman could easily free himself from Tamara. She had said several times that if he needed a divorce, she would give him one. But this divorce would not be of much help to him. There was probably little difference in the eyes of the law between a bigamist and a polygamist. Furthermore, a divorce would cost money and Herman would have to produce his papers. But there was something more: Herman saw in Tamara's return a symbol of his mystical beliefs. Whenever he was with her, he re-experienced the miracle of resurrection. Sometimes, as she spoke to him, he had the feeling he was at a séance at which her spirit had materialized. He had even played with the thought that Tamara wasn't really among the living, but that her phantom had returned to him.

Herman had been interested in occultism even before the war. Here in New York, when he could spare the time, he would go to the public library on Forty-second Street and look up books on mind-reading, clairvoyance, dybbuks, poltergeists—anything pertaining to parapsychology. Since formal religion was as good as bankrupt and philosophy had lost all meaning, occultism was a valid subject for those who still sought the truth. But souls existed on various levels. Tamara behaved—at least on the surface—like a living person. The refugee organization gave her a monthly allowance, and her uncle, Reb Abraham Nissen Yaroslaver, helped her as well. She had rented a bungalow at a Jewish hotel in Mountaindale. She didn't want to stay in the main building and eat in the dining room. The proprietor, a Jew from Poland, had agreed to have two meals a day brought to her bungalow. Her two weeks were almost over and Herman had not yet kept his promise to spend a few days with her. He had received a letter from her at his Brooklyn address chiding him for not keeping his word. She said at the end, "Make believe I'm still dead and come to visit my grave."

Before he left, Herman accounted for all eventualities. He gave money to Yadwiga; he paid the rent in the Bronx; he bought a gift for Tamara. He also put into his suitcase one of Rabbi Lampert's manuscripts to work on.

Herman arrived at the terminal too early and sat on a bench, his suitcase at his feet, waiting for the Mountaindale bus to be announced. It would not take him directly to where Tamara was stopping and he would have to change at some point along the route.

He had bought a Yiddish newspaper, but read only the headlines. The sum total of the news was always the same: Germany was being rebuilt; the Nazis' crimes were being forgiven by both the Allies and the Soviets. Each time Herman read such news, it awakened in him fantasies of vengeance in which he discovered methods for destroying whole armies, for ruining industries. He managed to bring to trial all those who had been involved in the annihilation of the Jews. He was ashamed of these reveries, which filled his mind at the slightest provocation, but they persisted with childish stubbornness.

He heard them call out Mountaindale and hurried to the exit where the buses were waiting. He lifted his suitcase up onto the rack and for the moment felt lighthearted. He was barely aware of the other passengers who had boarded the bus. They were speaking Yiddish and carrying packages wrapped in Yiddish newspapers. The bus started, and after a while a breeze smelling of grass, trees, and gasoline blew in through the partially opened window.

The ride to Mountaindale, which should have taken five hours, took almost a whole day. The bus halted at some terminal where they had to wait for another bus. It was still summery weather outside, but the days were already growing shorter. After sunset, a quarter moon came out and soon disappeared behind clouds. The sky became dark and starry. The driver of the second bus had to shut off the inside lights, because they disturbed his vision on the narrow, winding road. They drove through woods and suddenly a brightly lighted hotel materialized. On the veranda, men and women were playing cards. It had the insubstantiality of a mirage as they drove quickly by.

Gradually the other passengers got off at various stops and vanished into the night. Herman remained alone on the bus. He sat with his face pressed against the windowpane and tried to memorize each tree, shrub, stone along the way, as if America were destined for the same destruction as Poland, and he must etch every detail on his memory. Would not the entire planet disintegrate sooner or later? Herman had read that the whole universe was expanding, and was actually in the process of exploding. A nocturnal melancholy descended from the heavens. The stars gleamed like memorial candles in some cosmic synagogue.

The lights in the bus went on as it pulled up in front of the Hotel Palace, where Herman was to get off. It was exactly like the one they had already passed: the same veranda, the same chairs, tables, men, women, the same absorption in cards. "Had the bus been traveling in a circle?" he wondered. His legs felt stiff from having sat for so long, but he bounded up the wide steps of the hotel with vigor.

Suddenly Tamara appeared, wearing a white blouse, dark skirt, and white shoes. She looked tanned and younger. She had combed her hair differently. She ran toward him, took his suitcase, and introduced him to some women at a card table. One woman, who was wearing a bathing suit, with a jacket over her shoulders, threw a quick glance at her cards before saying in a hoarse voice, "How can a man leave such a pretty wife alone for such a long time? The men buzz around her like flies around honey."

"Why did it take so long?" Tamara asked, and her words, her Polish-Yiddish accent, the familiar intonations, shattered all his occult fantasies. This was no specter from the other world. She had put on some weight.

"Are you hungry?" she asked. "They've kept supper for you." She took him by the arm and led him into the dining room, where a single light was burning. The tables were already set for breakfast. Someone was still puttering about in the kitchen and the sound of running water could be heard. Tamara went into the kitchen and returned with a young man who carried Herman's supper on a tray: a half melon, soup with noodles, chicken with carrots, compote and a slice of honey cake. Tamara joked with the man and he answered her familiarly. Herman noticed that he had a blue number tattooed on his arm.

The waiter left and Tamara became silent. The youthfulness and even the suntan Herman had noticed upon his arrival seemed to fade. Shadows and the hints of pouches appeared under her eyes.

"Did you see that boy?" she said. "He was at the very doors of the ovens. In another minute, he would have been a heap of ashes."

※

Tamara lay in her bed and Herman rested on the rollaway cot that had been brought into the bungalow for him, but neither of them could sleep.

Herman had dozed off for a moment, but awakened with a start. The cot creaked under him.

"You aren't sleeping?" Tamara said.

"Oh, I'll fall asleep."

"I have some sleeping pills. If you like, I'll give you one. I take them, but I stay wide awake. And if I do fall asleep, it really isn't a sleep at all, but a sinking into emptiness.
I'll get you a pill."

"No, Tamara, I'll get along without one."

"Why should you toss and turn all night?"

"If I were lying with you, I would sleep."

Tamara didn't speak for a time.

"What's the sense of it? You have a wife. I'm a corpse, Herman, and one doesn't sleep with a corpse."

"And what am I?"

"I thought you were faithful to Yadwiga, at least."

"I told you the whole story."

"Yes, you did tell me. It used to be that when someone told me something, I knew exactly what he was talking about. Now I hear the words clearly, but they don't seem to get through to me. They roll off me like water on oilcloth. If you aren't comfortable in your bed, come into mine."

"Yes."

Herman got out of the cot in the dark. He crawled under the covers and felt the warmth of Tamara's body and something he had forgotten over the years of separation, something both maternal and utterly strange. Tamara lay on her back, motionless. Herman lay on his side with his face toward her. He didn't touch her, but he noticed the fullness of her breasts. He lay still, as embarrassed as a bridegroom on his wedding night. The years separated them as effectively as a partition. The blanket was tightly tucked under the mattress, and Herman wanted to ask Tamara to loosen it, but he hesitated.

Tamara said, "How long has it been since we've lain together? It seems like a hundred years to me."

"It's less than ten."

"Really? To me it's been an eternity. Only God can cram so much into such a short time."

"I thought you didn't believe in God."

"After what happened to the children, I stopped believing. Where was I on Yom Kippur in 1940? I was in Russia. In Minsk. I sewed burlap sacks in a factory and somehow earned my ration of bread. I lived in the suburbs with Gentiles. When Yom Kippur came, I decided I was going to eat. What was the sense of fasting there? Also, it wasn't wise to show the neighbors you were religious. But when evening came and I realized that somewhere Jews were reciting *Kal Nidre,* the food wouldn't go down."

"You said that little David and Yocheved come to you."

Herman regretted his words immediately, Tamara didn't move, but the bed itself started to groan as if it had been shocked by his words. Tamara waited for the scraping sounds to stop before she said, "You won't believe me. I'd better not say anything."

"I believe you. Those who doubt everything are also capable of believing everything."

"Even if I wanted, I couldn't tell you. There's only one way to explain it—that I'm crazy. But even insanity has to have an origin."

"When do they come? In your dreams?"

"I don't know. I told you, I don't sleep but sink into an abyss. I fall and fall and never reach bottom. Then I hang suspended. That's only one example. I experience so many things I can neither remember nor tell anyone about. I get through the days all right, but my nights are filled with terror. Perhaps I should go to a psychiatrist, but how can he help me? All he can do is give these things a Latin name. When I do go to a doctor, it's for only one thing: a prescription for sleeping pills. The children—yes, they come. Sometimes they visit till morning."

"What do they say?"

"Oh, they talk all night, but when I wake up, I don't remember any of it. Even if I do remember a few words, I soon forget them. But a feeling remains: that they exist somewhere and want to be in contact with me. Sometimes I go with them or I fly, I'm not sure which. I also hear music, but it's a kind of music without sound. We come to a border and I can't cross. They tear themselves away from me and float over to the other side. I can't remember what it is—a hill, some barrier. Sometimes I imagine I see stairs and someone is coming to meet them—a saint or a spirit. Whatever I say, Herman, it won't be accurate because there are no words to describe it. Naturally, if I'm mad, then it's all part of my madness."

"You aren't mad, Tamara."

"Well, that's nice to hear. Does anyone really know what madness is? Since you're here, why don't you move a bit closer? It's all right. For years I've lived with the conviction that you were no longer among the living, and one has different accounts to settle with the dead. When I found out you were alive, it was too late to change my attitude."

"The children never talk about me?"

"I think they do, but I'm not sure."

For a moment the silence was total. Even the crickets grew still. Then Herman heard the gushing sound of water like a running brook, or was it a drainpipe? A stomach rumbled, but he wasn't sure whether it was his or Tamara's. He felt an itch and had the urge to scratch, but restrained himself. He wasn't exactly thinking. Nevertheless, some thought process was going on in his brain. Suddenly he said, "Tamara, I want to ask you something." Even as he spoke, he didn't know what he was going to ask.

"What?"

"Why did you remain alone?"

Tamara didn't answer. He thought she might have dozed off, but then she spoke, wide-awake and clearly. "I've already told you that I don't consider love a sport."

"What does that mean?"

"I can't have to do with a man I'm not in love with. It's as simple as that."

"Does that mean you still love me?"

"I didn't say that."

"During all these years you've never had one single man?" Herman asked with a tremor in his voice, ashamed of his own words and the agitation they evoked in him.

"Supposing there had been someone? Would you jump out of bed and walk back to New York?"

"No, Tamara. I wouldn't even consider it wrong. You may be perfectly honest with me."

"And later you'll call me names."

"No. As long as you didn't know I was alive, how could I demand anything? The most devout widows remarry."

"Yes, you're right."

"Then what is your answer?"

"Why are you shaking? You haven't changed one bit."

"Answer me!"

"Yes, I did have someone."

Tamara spoke almost angrily. She turned on her side, with her face toward him, thereby moving somewhat closer to him. In the dark he saw the glint of her eyes. As she turned, Tamara touched Herman's knee.

"When?"

"In Russia. Everything happened there."

"Who was it?"

"A man, not a woman."

There was suppressed laughter in Tamara's reply, mixed with resentment. Herman's throat tightened. "One? Several?"

Tamara sighed impatiently. "You don't have to know every detail."

"If you've told me this much, you might as well tell me everything."

"Well—several."

"How many?"

"Really, Herman, this isn't necessary."

"Tell me how many!"

It was quiet. Tamara seemed to be counting to herself. Herman became filled with grief and lust, amazed by the caprices of the body. One part of him mourned for something irrevocably lost: this betrayal, no matter how trivial compared to the world's iniquity, was a blot forever. Another part of him yearned to plunge himself into this treachery, to wallow in its degradation. He heard Tamara say, "Three."

"Three men?"

"I didn't know you were alive. You had been cruel to me. You made me suffer all those years. I knew that if you were alive, you would do the same. In fact, you married your mother's servant."

"You know why."

"There were 'whys' in my case, too."

"Well, you're a whore!"

Tamara made a sound like a laugh. "Didn't I tell you."

And she stretched out her arms to him.

⟿⟾

Herman had fallen into a deep sleep, out of which someone was waking him. He opened his eyes in the dark and didn't know where he was. Yadwiga? Masha? "Have I gone off with another woman?" he wondered. But his confusion lasted only a few seconds. Of course it was Tamara. "What is it?" he asked.

"I want you to know the truth." Tamara spoke with the trembling voice of a woman barely holding back her tears.

"What truth?"

"The truth is that I had no one—not three men, not one, not even half a man. No one so much as touched me with his little finger. That is God's truth."

Tamara was sitting up, and in the dark he sensed her intensity, her determination not to let him go to sleep again until he heard her out.

"You're lying," he said.

"I'm not lying. I told you the truth the very first time when you asked me. But you seemed disappointed. What's wrong with you—are you perverse?"

"I'm not perverse."

"I'm sorry, Herman, I'm as pure as the day you married me. I say I'm sorry because, if I had known that you would feel so cheated, I might have tried to accommodate you. There was certainly no lack of men who wanted me."

"Since you talk out of both sides of your mouth so easily, I'll never be able to believe you again."

"Well, then, don't believe me. I told you the truth when we met in my uncle's house. Perhaps you'd like me to describe some imaginary lovers just to satisfy you. Unfortunately, my imagination isn't good enough. Herman, you know how sacred the memory of our children is to me. I would sooner cut out my tongue than desecrate their memories. I swear by Yocheved and David that no other man has touched me. Don't think it was such an easy thing to accomplish. We slept on floors, in barns. Women gave themselves to men they hardly knew. But when someone tried to get close to me, I pushed him away. I always saw the faces of our children before me. I swear by God, by our children, by the blessed souls of my parents, that no man so much as kissed me all those years! If you don't believe me now, then I beg you to leave me alone. God himself couldn't force a stronger vow from me."

"I believe you."

"I told you—it could have happened, but something didn't allow it. What it was I don't know. Though reason told me that there wasn't a trace left of your bones, I felt that you existed somewhere. How can one understand it?"

"It isn't necessary to understand it."

"Herman, there is something else I want to say to you."

"What?"

"I beg you, don't interrupt me. Before I came here, the American doctor at the consulate examined me and told me that I was in perfect health. I had survived everything—the hunger, the epidemics. I worked hard in Russia. I sawed logs, dug ditches, dragged wheelbarrows filled with rocks. At night, instead of sleeping, I often had to tend the sick who lay near me on planks. I never knew that I possessed so much strength. I'll soon get a job here, and no matter how hard it may be, it will be easier than what I had to do there. I don't want to go on accepting money from the 'Joint,' and I want to return the few dollars my uncle insisted on giving me. I'm telling you this so that you will know that I won't, God forbid, have to come to you for help. When you told me that you made your living by writing books for some rabbi who published them under his own name, I understood your situation. That's no way to live, Herman. You're destroying yourself!"

"I'm not destroying myself, Tamara. I've been a ruin for a long time."

"What will become of me? I shouldn't say this, but I can't ever be with anyone else. I know it as surely as know that it's night now."

Herman didn't answer. He closed his eyes as if to get another moment of sleep.

"Herman, I have nothing to live for any more. I've wasted almost two weeks, eating, strolling, bathing, talking with all kinds of people. And all the while I've been saying to myself: 'Why am I doing this?' I try to read, but the books have no appeal for me. The women keep making suggestions about what I should do with myself, but I change the subject with jokes and meaningless banter. Herman, there's no other way out for me—I must die."

Herman sat up. "What do you want to do? Hang yourself?"

"If a piece of rope would make an end of it, then God bless the rope-maker. Over there I still had some hope. Actually, I had planned to settle in Israel, but when I found out you were alive, everything changed. Now I'm entirely without hope, and one dies of that more quickly than of cancer. I've observed it many times. I saw the opposite too. A woman in Jambul was lying on her deathbed. Then she received a letter from abroad and a package of food. She sat up and instantly became well. The doctor wrote a report about it and sent it to Moscow."

"And she's still alive?"

"She died of dysentery a year later."

"Tamara, I too am without hope. My only prospects are imprisonment and deportation."

"Why should you be imprisoned? You haven't robbed anyone."

"I have two wives and soon I'll have a third."

"Who is the third one?" Tamara asked.

"Masha, the woman I told you about."

"You said she already had a husband."

"He divorced her. She's pregnant."

Herman didn't know why he was revealing this to Tamara. But apparently he needed to confide in her, perhaps to shock her with his entanglements.

"Well, congratulations. You're going to be a father again."

"I'm going crazy, that's the bitter truth."

"Yes, you can't be in your right mind. Tell me, what sense does it make?"

"She's afraid of an abortion. When it comes to such things, a person can't be forced. She doesn't want the child to be illegitimate. Her mother is pious."

"Well, I must promise myself never to be surprised again. I'll give you a divorce. We can go to the rabbi tomorrow. You shouldn't have come to me under these circumstances, but talking consistency to you is like discussing colors with a blind man. Were you always like this? Or did the war do it? I don't really remember what kind of human being you used to be. I told you there are periods of my life about which I've forgotten almost everything. And you? Are you just frivolous, or is it that you enjoy suffering?"

"I'm caught in a vise and can't free myself."

"You'll soon be free of me. You can also get rid of Yadwiga. Give her her fare and send her home to Poland. She sits there alone in the apartment. A peasant has to work, have children, go out into the fields in the morning, not stay cooped up like an animal in a cage. She can go out of her mind that way, and if, God forbid, you are arrested, what will become of her?"

"Tamara, she saved my life."

"Is that why you want to destroy her?"

Herman didn't reply. It had begun to grow light. He could make out Tamara's face. It was taking shape out of the darkness—a patch here, a patch there, like a portrait in the process of being painted. Her eyes stared at him wide open. On the wall opposite the window, the sunlight suddenly cast a spot that resembled a scarlet mouse. Herman became aware of how cold it was in the room. "Lie down. You'll catch your death," he said to Tamara.

"The devil isn't taking me away so soon."

Nevertheless, she lay down again and Herman covered them both with the blanket. He embraced Tamara and she didn't resist him. They lay together without speaking, overcome by both the complexities and the contradictory demands of the body.

The fiery mouse on the wall grew paler, lost its tail, and soon vanished altogether. For a while, night returned.

The Holocaust, Three Women, One Man, and a Rabbi: Posthumous Reading in Isaac Bashevis Singer's *Enemies, A Love Story*

Sandor Goodhart

> This hysterical woman . . . had risen from the dead.
>
> —I. B. Singer[1]

Herman Broder lives in a world dominated by the trauma of the Holocaust. When the Nazis invade his hometown in Poland, and his wife and children are taken away from him (and presumably murdered), he moves in with the family of his parents' serving girl, who hides him for the remainder of the war in a hayloft on her family farm.

After the war, a sense of life-saving obligation compels him to take the girl, Yadwiga, to America, to New York City, to live together as husband and wife in a small Coney Island apartment. But he finds that infinite gratitude is not sufficient to fuel a romantic relationship between them and quickly discovers himself visiting, and then playing house with, another survivor, a Jewish woman, Masha, who lives with her mother, Shifrah Puah, in the Bronx, on the other side of town.

---

1   Isaac Bashevis Singer, *Enemies, A Love Story* (New York: Farrar, Straus, and Giroux, 1972), 62.

For a while the "double life" works. He gets paid by a local rabbi, Rabbi Milton Lambert, in exchange for ghost writing speeches for him. When he lives with Masha and her mother in the Bronx, he tells his Polish Gentile wife that he is out of town on bookselling trips to Phila-delphia or Chicago. And when he lives with Yadwiga in Brooklyn, he informs his Jewish girlfriend of his infinite obligation to this "peasant serving girl" in Coney Island. His relationship with Yadwiga satisfies his sense of obligation, although the relationship is not a sanctified one within Judaism since Yadwiga is not Jewish. And his relationship with Masha satisfies his desire for comfort and pleasure, although that union is not sanctified either, since whatever else stands in the way of a conventional relationship with Masha, Masha remains married to Leon Trotshiner.

Then the unexpected occurs. Herman's first wife, Tamara, shows up alive. Although their children were in fact killed and she was indeed shot (as an eye-witness reported the incident to him), she survived the shooting and has been living since in Russia and Sweden. He informs her that he has married Yadwiga (whom she also knew as their house servant), and that he now visits a mistress, Masha. Although Tamara is more or less content, given the extraordinary circumstances of their lives (in which she was presumed dead), to remain something of a third wheel to the two other women, a crisis occurs when Masha (who knows only of Yadwiga but not of Tamara) announces that she is pregnant, and demands that Herman divorce Yadwiga and marry her (once she obtains a divorce, of course, from her former spouse, Leon). And that difficulty is in fact compounded when Herman realizes (on a trip to the Catskills and a conjugal visit with the mother of his deceased children) that he also still loves his first wife, Tamara, and when shortly afterward Yadwiga announces her conversion and her pregnancy.

The entirety of the second half of the novel is given over to the series of failed attempts to resolve the burgeoning problems that now accrue as a result of this potentially polygamous entanglement. At first, Masha's former husband, Leon, offers Herman what appears to be an easy way out. He contacts Herman. They meet. And he exposes Masha as an unfaithful partner throughout their marriage. Herman now becomes determined to leave her. He avoids her phone calls, denounces her when she finally does get through to him, and endeavors to become a pious Talmudic scholar living in marital union with Yadwiga. But Masha vigorously denies the accusation. He eventually marries her by a Rabbi, and returns to Yadwiga and to his old life of shuttling back and forth between the two households largely unchanged. Yadwiga, on the other hand, has her own ideas about moving on. Under the influence of her Jewish neighbors, she has now converted to Judaism, and will soon bear him another Jewish child. "Yadwiga's pregnancy," he reflects, "was a new catastrophe" (177).

Then one day, another interruption alters things once again. Tamara suddenly shows up at their doorstep in Brooklyn and Herman is forced to acknowledge the existence of his former wife to his current one by civil law. Yadwiga thinks she sees a ghost—the consequence in her mind of living with her mistress' husband—and Tamara attempts to calm her down: "I am not here to take your husband or punish you," she says in effect. And from this point on, unexpected occurrences abound. As the three of them are dealing with the newness of the discovery of Herman's pre-Holocaust wife, they are visited by a neighbor who introduces them to a nosy Mr. Nathan Pesheles (who, while professing an interest in helping Herman with his bookselling enterprises, expresses a distinct interest in Tamara). In the midst of this turmoil, Herman receives a call from Masha's mother, Shifrah Puah, who informs him that Masha is dangerously ill. Nearly overwhelmed by the complications of the situation, Herman arrives at her Bronx apartment to find a doctor who determines that she is not really pregnant after all, and Herman decides he will have to try and maintain all three relationships.

That attempt is no less doomed than his previous attempts to contain the chaos. The rabbi (for whom he works) learns his Bronx phone number and address, and invites the couple to an elegant party where Masha encounters an old flame, the actor Yasha Kotik, while Herman meets up again with the devious Nathan Pesheles who now cannot help but publicly reveal the existence of Herman's other two wives—for which Herman fears imprisonment and deportation. Masha decides that Herman has been unfaithful to her with other women besides Yadwiga (despite Herman's protestations that Tamara is his first wife), and announces she is accepting the rabbi's job offer and is leaving Herman for good.

Herman returns to Yadwiga and Tamara, and for a while stability is regained. Yadwiga will keep house for the three of them (plus the baby), and Herman and Tamara will run a bookstore from the volumes owned by the couple at whose home Tamara is staying (and who have decided for the moment to relocate to Israel). The stability is breached, however, shortly after that, just before Yadwiga is due to give birth to a child, when Herman is contacted by Masha. She informs him that although Rabbi Lampert has declared his love for her (and situated both her and her mother comfortably in a home for the elderly that he administers in Florida), she still loves Herman and would like to live with him. She demands from him an immediate response. He realizes that he, too, still loves her, and agrees to the sudden departure. They plan to flee together to Florida or California.

That decision similarly collapses when Shifrah Puah turns out to be of exceedingly frail health, and when other potential dangers of life in the big American city intervene. In the course of their errands before undertaking their planned elopement, Masha discovers that her apartment has been robbed. Shifrah Puah suddenly becomes seriously ill and dies on the way to the hospital. And when it seems clear to both that the situation has become intolerable ("I can't leave my mother even if she is dead," Masha admits), they make a joint suicide pact. In a last minute attempt to clear the air, Herman asks that they both confess their deceptions with regard to each other. Have you been with anyone other than me since the beginning of our relationship? He wants to know. When he learns that as he slept with his first wife Tamara in the Catskills, so Masha slept with her ex-husband, Leon, when she sought a divorce from him (although she had vigorously denied it when confronted about it after Herman's meeting with Leon), Herman feels he can no longer go through with the plan. He leaves her apartment feeling betrayed and abandoned, and with nowhere to go. An epilogue to the book informs us that Masha kills herself shortly after Herman's departure, that Tamara continues living with Yadwiga and the newborn child (a girl they decide to name "Masha"), and that neither of them hears further from Herman, who they surmise is either dead or living in another American version of his Polish hayloft existence.

What are we to make of this story? As Singer's first novel set entirely in America, the book constitutes something of a departure for the Yiddish-speaking Polish born writer. Known largely for writing tales about the pre-war *shtetls* of Eastern European Jewry—tales derived from eighteenth-century midrashic stories of *golems, dybbuks*, demons, goblins, and other ghostly figures from the supernatural fringes of Jewish belief—Singer's entrée into the American fictional mainstream with this account of post-Holocaust Jewish immigration to New York City offers us an early appreciation of Jewish modernity. As in his previous writing, the demonic and the superstitious dominate this narrative. But within this realistic setting, it is human desire rather than the supernatural that governs motivation.

If one were to read this sequence psychologically, other insights become possible. At least the first part of the story reads like something of an allegory of dissociative personality disorder. A trauma has occurred and a single personality is no longer capable of registering its full dimensions. So the registry mechanism subdivides and the parts independently develop into three or four separable personality structures frequented by a single consistent host agency. A personality capable of satisfying social obligations and gratitude is presented to the world. But this personality eliminates most traces of Jewish life and personal desires, and so another, formed on the basis of personal desires and a relation to Judaism, is constructed. But as these two personality structures develop in their separate realms, a third based upon history and the original world historical marriage enters the picture. Herman is in effect "married" to all three personalities and moves fairly freely among them, although the arrangement is unavoidably labor intensive. A fourth dimension related to the mainstream of Judaism via the local rabbi enables communication with the outside world. As a commentary on the effects of the Holocaust, the arrangement may represent something like Singer's view of life after the disaster, the multiple personalities into which Judaism as a group (if not Jews as individuals) is drawn.

But in the real world there are real consequences. The arrangement is temporary and cannot hold long-term. Babies are born. People want to get married and shore up more temporary arrangements. The difficulties of maintaining separate existences become simply too difficult. Nosy neighbors, rabbinical authorities, changing technology inevitably and decisively intervene. At the center of the intervention in this book is the trip to the Adirondacks and Catskill mountains.

The central scenes of the novel in the Adirondacks and the Catskills tell it all—both structurally and metaphysically. Structurally, the remainder of the novel could not occur without them. While the time away for Herman reminds him of the death camps ("somewhere on this lovely summer morning, fowl were being slaughtered; Treblinka was everywhere" [117]), for Masha the "vacation" from the cares of city life inspires different emotions. Although the prospect of marriage to Herman (presuming, of course, his divorce from Yadwiga and hers from Leon) has always hovered around the edge of their relationship, the trip renews that dream's intensity. Her announcement that she is pregnant only augments that position. And when, concomitantly, Herman decides to visit Tamara during the last few days of her visit to the Catskills, a similar desire is aroused in him—in this case, for his former wife.

More than a simple break from the city, in other words, the mountain escape functions to encourage a regrouping of the community, as if the trauma founding that community had not already occurred. Masha wants marriage to Herman, and Herman wants reunion with Tamara. If Masha had allowed things to remain as before, the entrance of a third significant other into Herman's already fragile arrangement might have worked. Herman would now have to lie to Masha (much as he lied before to Yadwiga), but at least the structure could be maintained. Tamara was offering divorce. Masha was not demanding marriage (although she desired it), and Yadwiga was content to tolerate Herman's regular weekly "bookselling" exits as a means of holding things together. Even with the intensification and Masha's marital demand in the midst of their bungalow escapade, Herman might have survived the fray. But Herman's newly discovered desire for Tamara is the straw that breaks the camel's back. He can divorce the Gentile Yadwiga, divorce his first

Jewish wife Tamara, and marry the newly-divorced Jewish Masha. But how can he remarry Tamara? He can "re-domesticate" Yadwiga perhaps, encourage her to assume once again her former status as servant to the marital pair, but how could he explain to Masha that he has re-married Tamara?

Masha's former husband offers the prospect of an excuse. Denouncing his former wife, Leon grants Herman the opportunity to do the same. Herman declares his intention to leave her, and catastrophe once again would appear temporarily averted. But then Masha's return to Herman (and Herman's return to her) emotionally, undoes even that potential solution. Could not Herman then choose Masha and reject marriage with both Yadwiga and Tamara? He resolves for a while to do just that. But then the triangulation of his sense of infinite obligation to Yadwiga, of an ineluctable history with Tamara, and of an unquenchable desire with Masha would appear to thwart that possibility. Upon the sudden death of Masha's true living partner, her mother, Shifrah Puah, Herman resolves at Masha's prompting to put an end to all of it: death with Masha in an act of double suicide. The conclusion is averted only when Herman reveals to Masha his days in the mountains with Tamara, and Masha similarly reveals her fleeting sexual reunion with Leon.

Reigniting old desires for closeness, the weeks away in the mountains function in other words for its participants to exacerbate the already fragile existing arrangements. Placed literally in the novel's narrative center, the episodes reflect what has occurred and influence decisively what will occur. The first four chapters of the book describe in sequence Herman's relation with Yadwiga (chapter one), with Masha and Shifrah Puah (chapter two), with Tamara (chapter three), and their aftermath (chapter four). Chapters five and six largely describe the encounters in the Adirondacks (with Masha) and the Catskills (with Tamara). And chapters seven through ten elaborate the attempted (and failed) solutions to the complications brought about in their wake as described above: the appearance in Coney Island of Tamara, the entrance through a neighbor of Nathan Pesheles, the party at Rabbi Lempert's house, Rabbi Lempert's sudden interest in Masha, Masha's renewed interest in Herman, the death of Shifrah Puah, Herman and

Masha's thwarted suicide pact, Masha's independent suicide, Tamara's inheritance of the bookstore and the house of Rabbi Nissen, and Herman's disappearance.

But the central passages function metaphysically as well. They offer us an account of Jewish modernity. The following passage exemplifies the new outlook they present:

> A row of bungalows belonging to the hotel fronted a lake. Women and men in bathing costumes were playing cards outdoors. On a tennis court a rabbi, wearing a skullcap and shorts, played tennis with his wife, who was wearing the wig of an orthodox woman. In a hammock between two pine trees lay a young boy and girl, giggling incessantly. The boy had a high forehead, a head of disheveled hair, and a hairy narrow chest. The girl wore a tight bathing suit and a Star of David around her neck.
>
> The proprietress had told Herman that the kitchen was "strictly kosher" and that the guests were all "one happy family." She escorted him and Masha to a bungalow with unpainted walls and a bare-beamed ceiling. The guests ate together at long tables in the hotel dining room. At lunchtime scantily clad mothers stuffed food into their children's mouths, determined to bring up tall Americans, six-footers. The little ones cried, gagged, and spat up the vegetables that had been forced down. Herman imagined that their angry eyes were saying "We refuse to suffer just to satisfy your vain ambitions." The tennis-playing rabbi poured forth witticisms. The waiters—college or yeshiva students—joked with the older women and flirted with the girls. They immediately started questioning Masha as to where she came from and showered her with insinuating compliments. Herman's throat tightened. He could swallow neither the chopped liver and onions, the kreplach, the fatty piece of meat, nor the stuffed derma. The women at the table complained "What kind of man is he? He doesn't eat."
>
> Since his stay in Yadwiga's hayloft, in the DP camp in Germany and in the years of struggle in America, Herman had lost contact with this kind of modern Jewry. But here they were again. (115-116)

Here they were again. The Jews of before, of the DP camp in Germany, of the Polish *shtetl* before his stay in the hayloft. This was Jewish life untouched by the Holocaust. In its wake, in the shadow of its misery and suffering, something was fundamentally wrong with this picture.

What? Here is another passage in which the criticism becomes perhaps more explicit and perhaps through Herman's criticism, so does Singer's:

The rabbi had apparently prepared a new set of jokes for the evening meal; his store of anecdotes seemed inexhaustible. The women giggled. The student-waiters served the food noisily. Sleepy children didn't want to eat and their mothers slapped them on the hands. One woman, a recent arrival in America, sent back her serving and the waiter asked, "By Hitler you ate better?"

Afterward they all gathered in the casino, a remodeled barn. The Yiddish poet gave a speech, lauding Stalin, and recited proletarian poetry. An actress did impersonations of celebrities. She cried, laughed, screamed, and made faces. An actor who had played in a Yiddish vaudeville theater in New York told bawdy jokes about a betrayed husband, whose wife had hidden a Cossack under her bed, and about a rabbi who had come to preach to a loose woman and had left her house with his fly open. The women and young girls doubled over with laughter. "Why is it all so painful to me?" Herman asked himself. The vulgarity in this casino denied the sense of creation. It shamed the agony of the holocaust. Some of the guests were refugees from Nazi terror. Moths flew in from the open door, attracted by the bright lights, deceived by a false day. They fluttered about awhile and fell dead, having beaten themselves against the wall, or singed themselves on the light bulbs. (120-121)

The Jews of the bungalows, Singer appears to be saying, flattering and fluttering and flirting with the guests, constitute a denial of creation rather than its celebration, a shaming of the agony experienced by the victims, some of whom may even be in the audience. "Why is it so painful to me?" Herman wonders. And in the lines that follow we have undoubtedly Herman's thoughts. But perhaps we also have Singer's as well. Attracted by the light, deceived by a false day, and then finally dead, having beaten themselves against the wall, Jews in the modern world are like moths before the flames.

Can we take these passages as Singer's account of Judaism in postwar America? As an example of Jewish assimilation within the new country, these words would appear for Singer at least summarized by Herman's bus trip. What should have been five hours turned out to be an entire day, and during that ride he seems to have been circulating around the same trees and landscape several times. And as such, they constituted in Herman's mind an undeterred ride in America, as once before in Poland, to destruction.

Is there a relation between these two levels, between the structural function of the bungalow colonies in the center of the novel and their metaphysical status as a criticism in Singer's thought about modern Jewry? Perhaps there is one final theme we need to address before concluding. Singer died in 1991, ten years before two planes slammed into the World trade center in New York City incinerating instantly some three thousand people in its wake. In the thirteen years since that event, a shift has taken place in Holocaust studies in this country, in the paradigms of Holocaust historiography, a change in the perspectives or theoretical frameworks through which we now view these events, a change that may be summarized somewhat simplistically perhaps as a shift from memory to shadow.

There is no place here to outline the dimensions of this shift. Suffice it to say that it has occasioned a new interest in what has come to be called the posthumous. "You are looking at a different woman," Tamara says to Herman. "Tamara who left her murdered children and fled to Skiba—that's the name of the village—is another Tamara. I am dead" although "it's true, this body of mine is still dragging itself about" (77). And at times, others feel the same way about her. "Sometimes as she spoke to him he had the feeling he was at a séance at which her spirit had materialized. He had even played with the thought that Tamara wasn't really among the living, but that her phantom had returned to him" (131). The return from the dead, the necessity of a "Lazarean" reading after the Holocaust, the sense that only if I acknowledge my own death as a starting point can any genuine authenticity be achieved on my part, has come to dominate the discussion.

In its purview, all major writings are being re-examined. Singer's novel is among them. One aspect of the discussion is the increasingly indelible nature of the events. For example, with regard to Masha and her mother, the narrator observes, "Other refugees used to say that with time one forgets, but neither Shifrah Puah nor Masha would ever forget. On the contrary, the further removed they were from the Holocaust, the closer it seemed to become" (43). Or, speaking of the death of her children, Tamara remarks, "Everyone tried to console me by telling me that time heals. It's been just the opposite: the further away it is, the more the wound festers" (102).

Another is the extent to which all characters in the book who have survived the Holocaust (and not just those who remark upon it) have effectively risen from the dead. Tamara says to him at one point, "My mother, blessed be her memory, once told me a story about dead people who don't know they've died. They eat, drink, and even get married" (239). The Lazarean sense of one's existence after a disaster of such proportions may be summarized in the formula "I died; therefore, I am"; or in the French (with a nod to Descartes), *Je suis mort; donc, je suis.*

How does that idea apply to this novel? To the extent that modern Jewry—as displayed in the bungalow colonies of the Eastern American mountain resorts—would seem bent upon enacting a Judaism of the past, one that may or may not have existed prior to the Holocaust, such enactments exhibit one more example of the Lazarean. To live amidst such "vulgarity" (to use the language Singer assigns to Herman), amidst such "denial of the sense of creation," such "shaming" of "the agony of the holocaust," is to live as self-annihilating moths that incinerate themselves in their contact with the false light, "deceived by a false day."

And Singer's work itself represents something of that colony within the larger sphere of Jewish American writing. If Singer's work, with its goblins and *golems* and *dybbuks* and demons, has come to constitute itself among modern American Jewish writers as something of a nostalgic orientation (by comparison, say, with Malamud, Bellow, and Philip Roth), it is not a perspective pursued, I have tried to suggest, unselfconsciously or without an awareness in the post-Holocaust age of its own limitations. Not unlike the resort communities he describes in the book's center, with their own evocation of past associations, Singer's body of writing may also afford us some reflection upon the circularity of the trip. "The ride to Mountaindale, which should have taken five hours, took almost a whole day" (133). As "the bus . . . pulled up in front of the Hotel Palace, where Herman was to get off," the narrator observes that "it was exactly like the one they had already passed: the same veranda, the same chairs, tables, men, women, the same absorption in cards. 'Had the bus been traveling in a circle?' he wondered" (133). And the question compels us to reexamine an earlier observation Herman made about an earlier repetition in the bus ride along the way, a repetition or circularity which raises the possibility that the universe has already ended and that we are in fact already engaged in some process of cosmic mourning, some act of Lazarean or posthumous reading:

> He sat with his face pressed against the window-pane and tried to memorize each tree, shrub, stone along the way, as if America were destined for the same destruction as Poland, and he must etch each detail on his memory. Would not the entire planet disintegrate sooner or later? Herman had read that the whole universe was expanding, and was actually in the process of exploding. A nocturnal melancholy descended from the heavens. The stars gleamed like memorial candles in some cosmic synagogue. (133)

Constituting itself as an extension of that explosion, as a writing of and a writing from the disaster, as a performance of that cosmic mourning ritual, Singer's work invites us to share the dimensions of that nocturnal posthumous reading, of a reading that takes place at once just after its departure from the big city and just before its arrival in the mountain resort where the traveler will find food and welcome from his arduous journey, in a no-man's land in which one has already died and yet "miraculously" returned from the flames to speak as their messenger or witness. "Did you see that boy?" Tamara says to Herman as he sits down to his meal in the dining hall, referring to the young man who brought his food on a tray. "He was at the very doors of the ovens. In another minute, he would have been a heap of ashes" (134).

But Tamara is also herself another version of that boy. Having been denied "the privilege of going through the Hitler holocaust" as he puts it in the "Author's Note" that stands in the place of a preface to the book, Singer will construct for us (and perhaps for himself) the Lazarean perspective of those who did, a perspective embodied most faithfully perhaps in this book in the figure of Tamara, who saw her children die, and who was shot herself and yet returned from the dead.[2] And she of course has a second "double" in Singer's world, a second "another

---

2   Ibid. "Author's Note," v.

Tamara," a scriptural counterpart in a text with which Singer would undoubtedly be familiar. To her biblical namesake Tamar, her father-in-law, Yehuda, remarks (after recognizing in her hand the "seal and cords and staff" that he gave her, having grossly misrecognized the wife of his deceased child earlier, items that render her a messenger from and witness to another time and place), "she is in-the-right more than I!" (38:26).[3] Not unlike the "rabbi who had come to preach to a loose woman and had left her house with his fly open," Yehuda is forced to own his own implication in the affair he would attribute entirely to the other. It is to this renewed emphasis upon the happening of the impossible, the posthumous predicament in which we find ourselves, and the new and legitimate and authentic perspective that it constructs for us—in which a return from the dead describes the ground of interpretation of the Holocaust rather than its absurdity—that Singer's novel invites us, I would suggest, to turn our own undivided attention.

Bibliography

Fox, Everett. *The Five Books of Moses*. New York: Schocken, 1997.

Singer, Isaac Bashevis. *Enemies, A Love Story*. New York: Farrar, Straus and Giroux, 1972.

---

3   Everett Fox, *The Five Books of Moses* (New York: Schocken, 1997).

From *Summer on a Mountain of Spices*

Harvey Jacobs

In the year 1942, Harry Craft reported his mother for hoarding cans of Bumble Bee salmon. It was on a day in the first spring of the young war. The lady who heard his report sat in the decorated gym of P.S. 63 in Manhattan. She was taking applications for ration books.

Harry Craft's mother, Betty Craft, began laughing. The ration book lady laughed too since only five cans of Bumble Bee were involved. Still, she tore stamps from the Craft book.

The story of how Harry made his mother declare her cans to the last can became a family classic. It was told and retold as example of Harry's seriousness, deep-rooted honesty and patriotism. Fear was never mentioned, though it was the major part of Harry's motivation.

The same Harry Craft gave his lead soldiers to the neighborhood scrap drive. He sacrificed an expensive army, navy and air force to the effort.

Assuming that his father, Dr. Lawrence Craft, oral surgeon, was wrong and the collector didn't "take them home for his own kids," they had long since been melted into bullets that flew in Europe and Asia.

Harry often speculated on the fate of those bullets. Did they find fleshy homes or did they lodge in trees or bounce off rocks or just bury themselves in the earth? If there were only a way to mark such gifts and know their ultimate history.

Now it was the summer of 1945. The war in Europe was over. Pictures were being released of broken cities and Germans with dead eyes, of liberated skeletons and Americans playing with alien children, of diplomats and generals, of smashed armor and piled bones, of flags in the mud, of proud flags flying.

A vast armada waited off the coast of Japan. Each night Tokyo was broiled with firebombs. The United Nations Charter had been drafted. The victory banners that hung between tenements on most of the Lower East Side streets were torn and blotchy. Some had already been taken down by the wind. The threat of death from the air was gone from the city. Harry Craft's brother, Hyman Craft, was stationed at Mitchel Field on Long Island, New York. Victory was assured. The Allies toyed with the Empire of the Rising Sun. Banzai.

Sweet suspense.

A sudden fresh energy moved like electric through the purged world. The Lord was praised, the ammunition passed. Bluebirds flew over the white cliffs of Dover. All things were possible and coming to pass.

Millions died in the war's fire. They had no voices. They lost their faces. Even the face and sound of Dave Lemkin, Hy's best buddy, killed in France, was sucked back into a mouth of shadows. Harry Craft could think sadly of the dead, but he celebrated the time he was born to, the crisis of battle, the tension of counterattack, the newspaper maps with thick ink arrows tracing the blitz, the eruption of history. Harry Craft liked living on dates they would teach forever in schools not yet built. They jibed with his own throbbing history.

On the night of the Battle of Midway, Harry Craft jerked off for the first time. On the day Hitler died in Berlin he touched his first tit. United nations on the march with flags unfurled. Harry moved too.

The fetal faces of Dachau, Buchenwald, Bergen-Belsen looked out through barbed wire. Harry looked back. Was it his fault that his testicles were full? Was it his fault that he had plans? Was it his fault that the morning was beautiful?

The Pharaohs of Egypt filled tombs with food and jewels to buy their way through Paradise. The citizens of Willow Spring, having gotten the message from their former employers, filled their insides with nourishment enough to carry them over the ocean of sleep and back again in time for breakfast. The last social act, included in the bill, was a snack in the kitchen.

A genuine Berman was always present to watch over the oral epilogue that ended the day. Service was do-it-yourself from a tray of sponge cake, honey cake, mohn cake and assorted cookies. Coffee and tea simmered on the stove. Milk came from a large enamel bucket, ladled by dipper into glasses or warming pans. The snacking went on until no appetites were left unsatisfied.

The kitchen was democracy. Hired help were welcomed to the last *nosh*. They fraternized boldly with paying guests, sipping, nibbling, swapping stories, comparing bargains, lamenting losses, commenting on the news. The rich sat down with the poor. Generations mingled.

Talk was of subjects close to the heart, the daily universals. Each subject got equal time and equal weight. None was considered more important than another—diapers, the cost of living, Betty Grable, the Emperor of Japan.

Politics and the war were the big items. Old socialists and communists, even a Trotskyite or two, speculated on the role of the USSR in the new order of things while capitalists yelled bullshit they're all the same. No Berman or Ferinsky ever participated in political diatribe. It was a rule. Both families once marched in the May Day parade carrying signs of hot protest. Now, because they ran the Willow Spring with iron gloves, battering down complaining help, they were too vulnerable, at least during the season. The guests heard daily shrieks from the kitchen when Shlomo Ferinsky, sometimes with Ida Berman beside him, stood off an attack by the laborers, especially the heat-crazed cooks, who sometimes threw pots and cleavers.

When Joe Kamin was in form, or a guest with vocal cords volunteered, there would be singing. Songs in Yiddish about Hungary, Galicia, Palestine, Russia, came from fleshy jukeboxes fed by pastry, not nickels.

In those moments of song the old left their sons and daughters behind. Even if they could speak the language they could not sing of a Cossack lusting for the rabbi's wife with proper emphasis. They didn't even try. They tapped the table and hummed in the background, forced to the inarticulate future. Talk of the Nazis, of the death camps, was rare. That horror was too close, the vines of guilt sprouting and tangling too quickly. New ghosts sang when the old songs were done and the present snapped back like a spring whipping the singers. Most had lost contact with someone, a brother, a sister, a cousin, an uncle or aunt, someone. The faces they saw in the centerfold of the *News*, the *Mirror*, the *Journal*, *Life* magazine, the *Forward*, the *Day* were anonymous zombies, dreams of death, but not their relations, not yet.

It was too soon to talk of the holocaust, of the graves of babies. So the old songs followed each other with little space between. Few shadows had time to penetrate such thin cracks in the sound. It was summer, vacation, the war was ending and these were winners in a time of triumph.

The honey of victory is rare and sweet.

On Friday the kitchen filled early with parents and kiddies hopped up by their performance. Ice cream waited in round bowls. Trays of glasses warm from their wash in the giant sink ringed the milk bucket.

City bulls careful to humor their women measured their own heat against the time it would take to get the brats to sleep. Wives who went five days without *kvetching* stood quietly smiling beside husbands who took shit from the boss without pissing or moaning, holding back the marital urge to punish, anticipating the welcome release of a *Shabbos* screw.

The Wandering Jew

JOE: WANDERING! WANDERING! WANDERING!

Wandering from dawn to night, hot, cold, thirsty, hungry. WHY? WHY?

Oh, my creator, giver of the Commandments, the Torah, the Talmud, why do you decree such suffering to this old and broken body? I hear my own bones shake. God of Israel, give me an answer, one GOOD REASON.

I walk over continents. I wait, I am persecuted, hit, beaten, burned, killed. Why? I have no home. No promised land. Why? Why do I go with my soul in my hand? Why? Why when I sit down to rest and eat something they throw things? Why?

I AM IN PAIN. AGONY. I CANNOT FIND MY WIFE OR MY BABIES.

Every step my legs throb. My back is sprained. Why do I live like this, wandering, wandering in all kind of weathers, taking abuse?

WHAT DID I DO TO MAKE YOU MAD? TELL ME. LET MY SUFFERING END.

No. I wouldn't die. I wouldn't lay down. I will go where I have to go until my tribulation, MY TRIBULATION, GOD, I WILL GO UNTIL IT ENDS. I will wake up under the stars and sing praises. I will wander as far as the MOON if you tell me.

WANDERING . . . WANDERING . . . WANDERING . . .
GOD, O MY GOD, GOD OF MY FATHERS, WHY?

Joe Kamin waves his stick and kicks out his leg. A light bulb smashes at the base of the stage. Glass flies. His screams echo in the casino.

Curtain.

Across the Old Liberty Mrs. Kar's dog barks.

Not a sound in the casino after that.

✦

Somewhere in the world there are two tribes of hunters who go to war with each other so they can enjoy the day their war ends. On that day winners and losers roast pigs. They do not roast pigs any other day. It is the only day of peace they trust. Twenty-four hours must pass before another war is even considered. A firm rule.

The Willow Spring tribesmen began to feel a lifting of anxiety on the afternoon of August 14, 1945. Invisible cement shells fell away, cracked by blades of grass that began to grow on quiet battlefields. Natives who knew that if you relax too much you're surprised by your own death agreed that this day celebration was surely in order.

Shlomo Ferinsky, caught on Victory's tide, took it on himself to announce a midnight supper.

The midnight supper belonged only to Labor Day. But in that summer of extraordinary endings and beginnings, even the calendar could be changed. Al and Ida Berman agreed.

While the PA played military hymns and songs of glad tidings, Shlomo Ferinsky headed for town to do some shopping. The midnight supper was his domain. Nobody meddled. He sat in the house car making plans. Shlomo built blueprints in lettuce, tomatoes, celery, onions, green pepper. He built with cold cuts, salmon, herring. He moved olives and pickles, cheese and crackers. He dreamed in chopped liver, meatballs and sliced eggs.

Every year Shlomo Ferinsky created miracles with food. Every year blind tongues and Philistine teeth ate his art while the band of music played in the dining room.

Nobody took time to browse and appreciate the nourishing museum.

This midnight supper was going to be different. While Jack drove the car, singing "Give My Regards to Broadway," Shlomo planned obstacles for his guests. If he could slow them down for even a minute their eyes would be forced to see.

He heard Sarah say, "Shlomo, it's gorgeous. You made that?"

Chomp.

—❧❦—

Dr. Noah Radish came out of his father's office. Dr. Father and Dr. Son had a glass of *schnapps* together. Dr. Moses Radish had attended the autopsy of six wars. He couldn't get too excited. Dr. Noah heard sounds of public pleasure. From the window of his examining room he saw a parade being formed at the firehouse. The parade was led by five gold star mothers. They wore silk armbands and carried flags.

A call to the Willow Spring told him Renee Clepper quit cold. They didn't know where she went. It was predictable. Flight in the face of cure. Or maybe it was the coming of peace that made her escape.

Peace is bad for the disturbed, worse than war. In war the enemy is defined. In peace his face is disguised. He wears ordinary expressions. When cannons grew legs and became civilians, when grenades became piggy banks and bombs became vases, hatred of self replaced hatred of nations.

Dr. Noah thought that maybe he should have warned the girl of the dangers of peace.

The gold star mothers got flowers. The parade moved. After the parade the mothers would go home to look at pictures in patriotic frames. Dead boys littered the world. Now they spoke one language.

Dr. Noah wondered about the statistics of mortality. A life is saved by ministration and taken by violence. Often it is the same life. No wonder Dr. Moses Radish shrugged even when he drank to the good guys.

The gold star mothers marched. Dr. Noah considered the smiles of justified sacrifice on their proud hick faces. Then he cried for their mindless dead, for the unborn children of their fallen sons, he cried for the winners and the losers, for the young and the old, the rich and the poor. He cried for war and peace and for doctors in love with soft crazy chambermaids they never would *shtup*.

⤙❦⤚

Manya Moskol put Davey on the phone.

"You come back," Davey said.

She took back the receiver.

"There. You heard. Come up, Howie honey."

"I'm taking inventory. You know that. This is the worst time of the summer for me."

"Please. I'm very lonesome."

"I'll ask Miltie if he can take over. I'll call you back."

"Howard it's very important to me."

"You know what traffic will be tonight? They're carrying on all over the streets."

"Don't come. Is that what you want me to say?"

"I'll come. I don't know how late."

"Tell Davey. He'll be happy."

"You tell Davey. I got to get back to my customers."

"They're having a midnight supper."

"Tell Davey I got him a toy. Wait until you see it. Dolls of a family. When you take off their clothes it shows the real stuff. Even hair. This salesman from a new company came in with the line. It's educational."

"Dolls?"

"They have no faces. The idea is for the kid to imagine in the faces. No moving parts. You can throw them around."

"You'll show him when you get here."

"He'll be sleeping when I get there, won't he?"

"He'll be sleeping. He'll see the dolls in the morning," Manya said.

"Good. Save me a dessert," Howard Moskol said.

⤙❦⤚

Al Berman fed the PA rumbas, horas, semi-classics, swing, songs of combat, the music of Betty Coed, an eclectic selection of the rhythms that stirred Willow Spring hearts.

In late afternoon Harry Craft and Arnie Berman came back from Monticello with cases of whiskey, vodka and gin for the midnight supper. Harry saw Essie Poritz leaping over the lawn followed by jumping-jack children.

"The kids look like they're already juiced," Harry said.

"They should be. They got it made," Arnie said.

"Tits and toys for girls and boys," Harry sang. He had a glass of beer with Arnie in town. The brew went to his head.

While Harry and Arnie pulled into the parking lot, the PA music changed to a fox-trot. Essie Poritz danced her sprites around Ray Stein, who stood with her hands together, the model of a contented *bubba*. They made a friendly picture, a cover for the *Saturday Evening Post*, fitting for the hour when the lights went on again all over the world.

When the music changed again, Essie grouped the children around her. She showed them a box of Outstanding Camper Buttons.

Ordinarily only one button was awarded each week, a coveted prize. Today Essie felt high. She had a hundred buttons left, enough for a decade of Willow Spring summers. To commemorate the capitulation of Japan she decided to give each Willow Spring camper a button to cherish.

Marvin Katz and Charlie Mandel helped her pin one button on every little shirt. There were still multitudes of buttons left. So Essie gave seconds to all.

"What the hell," Marvin Katz said. "You only live once."

He pulled Jerry Tomato out of the ranks and began pinning Outstanding Camper Buttons all over him. Jerry laughed. The kids laughed. Essie laughed. Together they pinned buttons on Jerry Tomato's cap, shirt, pants, socks and even his hair. Outstanding Camper Buttons filled all his available space. They kept pinning the buttons on until only a fistful were left in the box.

The decorators stepped back. The most Outstanding Camper in history stood crying.

"He's bawling," Charlie Mandel said. "Why you crying, Jerry?"

"What's the matter, kid?" Marvin Katz said.

"The thing is," Essie Poritz said, "the thing we forgot is that he takes them *seriously.*"

Essie cradled the most decorated camper in her arms.

─☙❧─

Charlie Mandel watched Shlomo Ferinsky finish a bust of Franklin D. Roosevelt. He put it near the Winston Churchill.

"No Truman? No Stalin?"

"I don't feel like it," Shlomo said.

"Where did you learn how to do that?"

"I learned. I had the talent."

"Could I try something?"

"Don't bother me now, Charlie."

Charlie Mandel looked into the tub of chopped liver. It was like clay.

"You could sell those," Charlie said.

"To who? The Museum of Art?"

The busts rested on a long table, the result of joining four tables together. Near them was Shlomo's famous display of vegetable flags, a Star of David, a likeness of the Willow Spring Main House in cucumbers, olives, anchovies and pimento against an egg salad sky.

"Did you tie up the door?" Shlomo said.

"It's tied. Only the one from the kitchen works."

"Good. Now put chairs by the rope. I want the door absolutely shut."

Charlie dragged two chairs to the door and propped them under the rope.

The Schneitzels and Boulaks came in and out of the dining room clearing away supper dishes and replacing them with fresh items. Vinnie Berman brought paper hats and noisemakers for each place. Shirley Berman hung bunting on the walls. Barry Guerfin decorated the piano with candles and crepe. Harry Craft poured ice in the portable box that served drinks to the dining room.

Ida Berman came to inspect.

"Looks good. Who put chairs and ropes on the door? Take them off."

"I put," Shlomo said. "Let them stay."

"Why?"

"To keep out."

"To keep who out? To keep out guests?"

"Let me alone," Shlomo said.

"Take away the ropes," Ida said.

"Don't touch the ropes. Don't touch the chairs," Shlomo said.

"We don't need the door closed."

"Get out. Get out. I'm warning you."

"Idiot. Take off the ropes and chairs. What is this, a prison?"

Shlomo slammed a ladle on the floor.

"Out. Out. Everybody."

They left. Charlie Mandel stayed.

When Shlomo Ferinsky calmed down, he checked his creations.

"I got enough left for a Truman," Shlomo said. "I'll do a little one. I suppose he deserves."

⇀↽

Al Berman stood on the porch looking up at the evening sky.

"Gorgeous," Mrs. Rifkin said.

"They should wait for the dark," Al said.

"It's dark enough," Mr. Rifkin said.

Fireworks blasted from the general direction of Wishninskiwitz Park.

"Beautiful. There is nothing like firecrackers," Joe Kamin said.

"It's a fire hazard," Al Berman said. "Trees, houses, barns like tinderboxes."

Rockets broke into bubbles of light. Roman candles sent up lazy globes of color. Bombs burst in air. A low boom boom boom came to the Willow Spring soon after the magnificent splashes.

"That display must cost a fortune," Zalik Boulak said.

"What fortune? It don't cost a fortune," Al Berman said.

"Look. Marvelous," Zalik said.

Al Berman considered calling the Monticello Fire Department. The whole thing was illegal. Where did Wishninskiwitz Park get such fireworks?

"You know, I don't think it's coming from their grounds," Zalik Boulak said. "I think they got them down by our lake."

Al Berman got a gas pain.

Boom boom.

$$\rightarrow\!\!\in$$

Elaine Fish told Harry Craft she would pick him up in a car.

A car?

Harry waited on the Old Liberty watching Wishninskiwitz fireworks scatter their transient atoms.

"Fireworks are the jelly apples of light. Jelly apples are the fireworks of food," he said to the road.

Whose car?

A red Ford came driven by the answer. In front sat Elaine and Malcom Wishninskiwitz. In back sat Gilda Glutzman. It was the back door that opened for Harry Craft.

Malcom Wishninskiwitz?

Harry got into the car next to a perfumed Gilda. Malcom offered him a bottle of bourbon. He unscrewed the cap and took some. Why was he in the wrong seat?

"It's glorious," Elaine said. "Peace. Peace."

"Victory," Malcom said.

"Unconditional surrender," Gilda said. "That sounds terrific."

"There's good news tonight," Harry said.

Harry had another drink. The car moved, jerking into gear. Where were they going? When would the people change places? He reached over and stroked Elaine's hair.

"Um. That feels good," Elaine said.

"What feels good?" Malcom said.

"Drive. None of your business," Elaine said.

They drove ten miles. Malcom Wishninskiwitz stopped his Ford in the woods on a dirt road.

"A great thirst burns in my throat," he said. "To peace, health and a good life for all."

The bottle was passed.

While Gilda Glutzman sipped bourbon and Harry Craft prepared to open his door and change places, Malcom dumped Elaine on the front seat like a commando. Her legs came up over the upholstery. She *ummmed.*

Harry Craft took a look over the seat. It was Elaine Fish, no question. Wishninskiwitz was all over her. Her hands were busy holding on. She was making soft music. Harry sat back. Gilda kept her eyes on the window. There was no view. It was too dark even to see leaves. Harry tapped her shoulder. Gilda turned. With his peculiar expression Harry asked what was going on. Gilda moved her head up and down.

Yes?

"How long?" Harry whispered.

"By the time I got up here is all I know," Gilda said. "They're pretty thick."

A shoe came off Elaine. It fell in back. She wore no stockings over her sweet young legs.

"*Malc, Malc, Malc,*" Elaine said.

"So here we are," Gilda said.

Harry Craft closed his eyes but his ears wouldn't quit.

"*Malc, Malc, Malc.*"

In front of her girlfriend? In front of him? A spawn of the *koch alayn* reverted to type.

"What are we supposed to do, the cat's cradle?" Gilda said.

Harry put his arm around Gilda's back. She had hard shoulders and a stiff neck.

"I do not believe when in Rome a person has to do as the Romans do when it comes to sex," she said.

"Neither do I," Harry said. He took his arm back.

"You can keep your arm there but that's it. Let's face it, Harry. We hardly know each other, right?"

Harry put his arm back.

"So, you think this is the last war?" Gilda said.

"No."

"You're cynical."

"*Malc. Malc.*"

Harry found the bourbon and drank.

"Do you think Eisenhower planned better than, say, Alexander the Great?"

"I don't know."

"You must have some opinion. From the viewpoint of tactics. Considering the problems."

"*Malc. Now, Malc.*"

"You want to walk outside," Gilda said.

"I can't," Harry said. "I can't move."

"This isn't very stimulating."

"I feel paralyzed."

"So we'll sit," Gilda said. "Like good little chaperones."

"Gilda," Harry whispered. "Take a look. Are they going the whole way?"

"That's vile of you."

"Take a look. Please."

"No. I will not."

Malcom Wishninskiwitz growled. Elaine was clearly out of control.

A grabber.

Now Harry Craft heard crickets and other sounds of bug joy.

"I wish this car had a radio," Gilda said.

"This car doesn't even have a radio?" Harry said.

"My heart is melted in the midst of my bowels," Elaine said.

"That's from the Psalms."

Harry heaved his supper.

—⊰⊱—

"He won't let us in there," Red Toritz of the truncated Willow Spring band said to Al Berman. "We got to set up."

"Shlomo, let the band in."

"Wait."

"Now."

"They can come in through the kitchen."

Red Toritz, Morty Popkin and Danny Abrams stood on the porch. The dining room door was roped at the knob. Al Berman stood with the band of music demanding entry.

In the dining room Shlomo Ferinsky finished Harry Truman. He gathered up his tools.

"Every year for twenty-two years the musicians come this way," Al Berman said. "Not through the kitchen."

"Let them in, Charlie," Shlomo said.

Charlie opened slipknots. Al Berman entered with the entertainment.

"Put back the cord," Shlomo said.

Charlie complied.

Ida Berman looked in through the kitchen door.

"We open in five minutes. They're all outside."

Shlomo went to the window. The guests were clustered on the porch. Ready. Hungry.

"They just ate," Shlomo said. "They just had a full-course meal."

"Should I move the chairs?" Charlie Mandel said.

"No, do like I told you."

Shlomo Ferinsky designed a corridor of chairs, a simple maze, to slow the advance on his buffet tables.

"What is that? Stop it," Ida Berman said. "We'll get sued. Somebody will trip and get a hernia."

Ida came into the dining room and moved the guardian chairs. Shlomo watched. Red Toritz And His Boys played "Star Dust."

Charlie Mandel looked over the table. Easily a masterpiece.

"You should take pictures of that," he said.

"Pictures?" Shlomo said. "For what?"

Ida pushed away the chairs but forgot the ropes on the door.

"Let us in, it's the nice wolf," Zalik Boulak yelled from outside. "We wouldn't huff and puff and blow the house down. Open up, the *chozzers* are waiting, yoo-hoo, little pigs."

Shlomo looked at the door.

"Anybody home?" Zalik said. "It's the Fuller Brush man."

"Open," Ida Berman said.

"Not yet," Shlomo said.

"Why?" Ida said. "Give a reason."

No answer.

"Play a song," Ida said.

The band played a song.

"I'm opening the door," Ida said.

Shlomo Ferinsky stood by his table with his arms stretched out.

The door bent back with a bang. Zalik Boulak, propelled by rear pressure, came through first. Charlie Mandel punched him in the belly.

"What's the matter with the boy?" Zalik said.

"Charlie," Shlomo said. "Stop it."

Roosevelt went first, then Churchill, then Truman. Then the flags and the Willow Spring. Five minutes later the buffet table was a grave-yard of leftovers.

Music played. Guests danced. Arnie Berman poured drinks on the house.

Shlomo Ferinsky still wore his apron. Charlie Mandel stood with him, his face a smear.

"Every year," Shlomo said. "The same thing."

"The bastards. The fucks," Charlie said.

"What are you talking about? Wash your mouth with soap," Shlomo said.

Ida Berman came down in a fresh dress.

"Everybody is having a good time," she said.

"Why not?"

"Go and put on a shirt, Shlomo. Dress up."

"I'm going to sleep," Shlomo said. "You'll tell me the story in the morning."

꒰ ꒱

The Mummy Walks.

Harry Craft came up the Old Liberty in peculiar condition.

He waved the bourbon bottle at the tail of Malcom Wishninskiwitz's perky red Ford.

"You spare a drink, friend?" said a voice from the dark.

"Absolutely," said Harry.

Jack the handyman drained Harry's bourbon. He gave back the empty bottle. Harry threw it at a rock.

"Plenty fucking tonight," Jack said. "Every country. Germans. Japs. Don't worry."

"Tell me something," Harry Craft said. "Tell me honestly. Tell me the truth now, do you believe that Vera Hruba Ralston is getting it right now?"

"Yeah. Sure. From the Mad Russian."

Jack headed toward Monticello.

Lindy barked. Harry barked back. He looked for fireworks but the sky was black blank.

There were lights on in the Main House. Harry headed toward them. On the way he met Arnie Berman sitting on the porch steps.

"Happy end of war," Harry said. "And congratulations."

"Beat it," Arnie said. "Screw off."

Radio sounds came from the lobby. *Squeak. Scratch.*

He found the radio alone in the card room.

Squee. Blurt. Oowiee.

Harry patted the radio. He left it alive and went up the steps toward a vague destination.

All they could do was kill him. The last tin soldier.

Harry went holding the walls. He passed the room his parents had, he passed his mother's mother's room. Good old mother's mother.

Harry stopped at Leslie Quint's door.

They could cut out his guts organ by organ and throw them in Chinese food. No more than that, though.

Harry banged with two fists.

"Please open up," he said. "This is urgent."

Leslie Quint opened. She was in pajama tops.

"It's the pope," Harry said. "But I'm not here in my official capacity. I am here as a drunken youth."

Harry put his hands on Leslie's cheeks.

"I covet you. Please put out for me," he said. "We don't have much time."

"Thanks anyhow," Leslie said.

"Wait," Harry said. "Did you understand what I said? I said I covet you. It's almost morning. It's almost Postwar."

Leslie giggled.

"Don't laugh at me," Harry said.

"Why not?"

"Because I want to covet with you and coveting is not funny. Fucking is serious."

"Wrong. Fucking is funny," Leslie said. "Most of the time."

"You're kidding," Harry said.

"No," Leslie said. "I'm not kidding."

"Boy, that is some news," Harry said. "That comes as a shock. If the word gets around it could change the condition of life on Earth. Be very careful with that information, Leslie. Promise me."

"Come in," Leslie said.

"I'll come in," Harry said. "But I'm warning you. I have a very strange penis. It goeth up and down. Up and down goeth it. What I mean is I don't know if I love you with all my heart and soul, in sickness and health and the gloom of night. But I covet you tremendously."

"Come in."

"Wait," Harry said. "In the matter of protection. I have two fairly recent Trojans. Condoms. Contraceptives. The Trojan brand is supposed to be good because they have reservoir tips. The name is peculiar. It sounds like when the device gets inside little sperms come out and take the city."

"Oh yeah?" Leslie said.

"I have practiced their use," Harry said. "But they have this weird tendency to roll up like window shades. I find that inhibiting."

"We'll work something out," Leslie said.

"Now in the matter of possible offspring. Raise it in the church if you want so long as some sense of ethics is communicated to it."

"Harry, if you don't want to go through with this . . ."

"I do. I do. In the matter of my death . . ."

"Your death?"

"If Moe Rubin executes me for penetrating you I do not want to be cremated or buried. I want to be stuffed by an eminent taxidermist and hung in the casino near my concession."

"Anything else?"

"Do you accept my conditions? Maybe you want to think it over."

"I'll call my lawyer in the morning," Leslie said. "Come in, hungry boy."

"Hungry boy? Is that how you see me?"

Leslie Quint took Harry Craft's hand.

"I don't care what they do to me," Harry said. "You see? It's not even courage. It's just what it is. You see?"

"Be quiet, Harry. You'll wake the dead."

"There's a thought," Harry said. "All right, what do we do first? Don't pull any punches. I want the facts."

"Hold me," Leslie said.

"That's all? Hold me?"

"That's all we do first," Leslie said.

"This is fantastic," Harry said. "This is easy."

"The best-kept secret of the war," Leslie said.

—⊱⊰—

When Harry Craft came down to the lobby, dawn's blue fingers reached in through the screen door and stretched toward his feet. He stood just beyond the fingertips of light, teasing the future.

"You should have told me they took it. It had my name on it."

Harry heard Mendel Berman's voice from the office.

"What was the use to tell you?" Al Berman said. "It would only leave you upset."

"So now I'm upset."

Harry found Al and Mendel Berman, Zalik Boulak and Red Toritz standing near the Mosler.

"Lookie, lookie, here comes cookie," Zalik said. "Harry, what's the shit-eating grin about?"

Harry tried to stop smiling. He shrugged.

"What's missing?" he said.

"My shofar. With the silver. They stole it. They should choke on it," Mendel said.

"Have a little *schnapps*," Zalik said.

"He had enough," Al said.

Mendel took a bottle of Calvert's and gulped a drink. The bottle went around. When it came to Harry he swallowed quickly. The whiskey tasted like Malcom Wishninskiwitz's Ford.

"Look at smiley. I thought you drank sodas," Zalik said.

Harry had another drink.

"Take it easy," Al Berman said.

Hannah Craft, carrying a glass of hot water and lemon, pushed into the office.

"Good morning, Mama," Al Berman said. "You're up early."

Hannah turned on the PA switch. Static crackled. She stood looking at the microphone.

"People are sleeping," Al said. "Please, Mama, you shouldn't play with that."

Al clicked off the switch.

"She's OK. She's in good shape, right?" Mendel Berman said.

"She won't make no more trouble, right?"

Harry Craft followed his Uncle Al, Mendel, Red and Zalik outside to the fresh morning. They met Vinnie and Shirley Berman on the lawn. Barry Guerfin and Irwin Lapides came from peeing behind the bungalows.

At the casino, Red Toritz went to get his horn. He blew reveille on the casino steps.

Roosters answered from Mrs. Kar's chicken coop.

"It's light," Harry Craft said.

"You'll remember this night," Mendel Berman said. "The older you get the better you'll remember. Take my case. I'm just beginning to dance at my wedding."

"If we were in Europe we would all be dead," Harry said.

"It's true," Mendel said. "We survive for many. We are like pregnant women. But still people, still fools. You would think a survivor would light and burn like a candle. No. Still people, still fools, pregnant with the living and pregnant with the dead. It's no new story."

"Does it make any sense to you?" Harry said.

"Ask me next year. Maybe I'll give an answer."

Zalik Boulak stood beside the bandleader. He cupped his hands around his mouth. A blast of sound came from him.

"Listen to that," Al Berman said. "You would swear it was the *shofar bleusen.*"

Zalik blew again.

The sound of the ram's horn. News of treaties and alarms.

Blah. Blah.

Zalik blew a duet with Red Toritz.

The PA speaker crackled.

"Hannah," Al Berman said, heading for the Main House.

The Willow Spring PA, an electric ventriloquist, played the sounds of Hannah's breath.

The sun came up, a cap on the skull of the planet.

Harry Craft sat on the damp casino steps considering the journey of atoms.

Reflections on *Summer on a Mountain of Spices*

Harvey Jacobs

The title *of Summer on a Mountain of Spices* derives from the "Song of Solomon." The novel is based on life at The Spring Lake House, a small family hotel, in the summer of 1945 during the last week of World War II. Spring Lake was a mile from Monticello, the summit of the "Jewish Alps." It catered to refugees from the garment center and an occasional professional (a lawyer, a dentist) escaping Manhattan's brutal heat for a few weeks, and allowed wives and children the chance to breathe some fresh air, feast on incredible Jewish dishes, and polish skills such as tennis, baseball, swimming, mah jongg, poker, pinochle, even dancing to a four-piece band in the "casino."

Guests at the modest hotel were financial mosquitoes compared with the wealthy at enclaves like Grossinger's and The Concord where, my father would say, "people walk on cement, not grass"; however they still considered themselves superior to families that rented bungalows in colonies we called *kuchalains* where you had to do your own cooking and cleaning.

Spring Lake was owned and operated by my aunts and uncles. My summer job, at age fifteen, was running the "concession" under a banner that read "WHY STARVE? YELL HARV!" and sold cigarettes, cigars, sodas from the Nu Icy bottling plant, candy bars and other essentials of the "good life." That same summer I was hammered by three gigantic events: the discovery of girls and browsing the mysteries of sex; the unthinkable horror of the Holocaust revealed in the press and on the radio; the dawn of the atomic age that signaled both the end of the war and possibly the world. Those huge revelations took root beside my own self-centered fantasies about my future. It was these three events of 1945 that still swirled within me and were my inspiration to write *Summer on a Mountain of Spices* in 1973.

Despite the bloody tally of the war and the crushing acceptance of the Holocaust, I wanted my own turn at life, and I told my story like it was, a mix of pain and humor, the amalgam that's part of every Jew's heartbeat. Curiously, that summer while there was the sense of impending elation over victory on the battlefields, there was hardly any talk about the Holocaust. Perhaps the subject was too overwhelming and the sense of survivor's guilt too strong. We were forced to face the truth that if it hadn't been for the courage of parents and grandparents who came to America with no money, no language, nothing much but hope, we would all be ashes blowing through history.

I wondered, and still do, why as children growing up we had heard nothing of the "final solution" even though the truth about the death camps was known by many, including President Roosevelt, who we all adored. Why were there no cries of rage? Were my parents ignorant of the horrors that allowed for an Auschwitz, or had they purposely kept those facts from the children? In those days, Jews were careful not to attract too much attention to themselves, even in America. Their own sons were fighting and dying, but anti-Semitism was a frightening fact of life.

I had trouble forgiving my parents for what I perceived as their indifference to and my ignorance of the brutal facts. By 1973 I had already met several Holocaust survivors, had traveled to Germany on business, and had sensed that no Jew would ever walk again without a ghost beside him or her. In 1945, at our hotel, denial was the rule of the day and our joy in America's victory over the enemy prevailed over our sense of grief. I became suddenly aware of the heroics of my ancestors who left their homes and came to America without knowing the language or having much money or even a trade. Why had America welcomed my ancestors and turned away others like the passengers of the oceanliner St. Louis, who were refused permission to dock and in effect sent back to the roaring ovens of the death camps in Europe? Why hadn't I turned to ashes and instead been left to speculate on some enormous questions?

The Holocaust was, as I said, hardly talked about in depth at Spring Lake during my teenage years, for whatever reasons, and I had no sense of contributing much to the impact of the revelations of human degradation with my text. I must have recoiled from the depth of that knowledge back then and the novel honestly reflects my lack of reaction to the toxicity of such a painful event. At the hotel most of the guests were more insistent on feeling good about their sons who were fighting the war and who were no longer in harm's way. The same reaction was true about the use of the A-bomb to end the carnage in the Pacific. God was thanked for those who had survived and was seldom cursed for the millions who had been shattered or killed. People work in mysterious ways.

When I wrote *Summer* my object was to preserve the events and emotions I'd experienced some thirty-five years earlier. I thought members of my family who were still alive (both of my parents had died by then) would be pleased at the attempt to preserve our legacy of memory. The novel is fiction but family members looked for characters that were closely based upon them and which maybe revealed too many of their little foibles and secrets. Many were outraged instead of pleased at what I thought was a warm, loving, and funny memorial.

The critical reception was very positive and resulted in a Broadway and film option that, alas, never came to anything. I was told by my agent that one reason involved a well-known and powerful figure who complained that the book was a *shonda* since it made too joyful a noise, which he thought could harm the image of Jews. I never understood his perspective, but I was later told that the nay-sayer was probably protecting the territory of one of his own clients who planned to write about "the Borscht Belt." I can't confirm that story, and I prefer not to name names. For me, it was devastating that *Summer* did not, in the end, gain the wider exposure a film or a Broadway show could have offered it. In any case, my memory of a long-ago summer remains alive and well.

Others, like Alan King, optioned the novel for film. King wanted me to make the narrator a boy from the Midwest, not a New York Jew, who ends up in the oval office as the first Jewish President, to be played by guess who. . . . I refused that offer. Films like *Walk on the Moon* produced by Dustin Hoffman have helped stir curiosity about the nostalgia of the Catskills or "The Jewish Alps," as they were called.

Humor has always been hugely important to me—the way I look at life when the joke is on somebody else. To me, there is nothing that is too sacred for becoming the subject of some kind of joke, even if it is often bittersweet. Sometimes a large chunk of time must separate the bad stuff from the laugh, but the time does eventually pass. One of the best things about Americans has been their ability, even eagerness, to smile or laugh at themselves and events. America created P. T. Barnum and Mark Twain along with George Carlin, Richard Pryor, Woody Allen, Mel Brooks, W. C. Fields and a host of other "comics" and *tumlers* who are revered and who have performed a vital public (and private) service reminding us all of our shared humanity—we have all stared into the void of an indifferent universe. What worries me is that our ability to laugh is vanishing, that wit is now often being replaced by confrontation, that stupidity has become a surrogate for comedy.

Humor as well as subjects like sexuality, nostalgia, and loss are key motivators in my writing. *Summer on a Mountain of Spices* was my first novel, and it was not easy to write. Many of the dear people I wrote about are now gone as are the innocence of that time and the pain and delight of the playground. Time and tide . . .

The novel tries to honestly reflect my feelings and reactions as they were in 1945. I did not censor any of my feelings; though now I wince just thinking about what was going on in Europe at the time while I was trying to get to second base with giddy girls, playing ball, juggling ideas about truth, lies and beliefs, i.e., doing the things we now call what teenagers do. Back then, there were no teenagers, only young adults. Now those years have become the subject for bad sitcoms, vital years regarded as jokes, no more than footnotes in a file marked Nostalgia 101.

I do not think of my novel as making any significant contribution to the body of work about the Holocaust. It does reveal and preserve a bit of the climate in those days of transition that catapulted every Jew, if not every person capable of compassion, into a very new vision of a world, which, at that fleeting hour, seemed on the verge of achieving welcome pride and sanity. All in all, I wanted the book to make a joyful noise even in the face of tragic loss. *Summer on a Mountain of Spices* is about, discovery, love, tears, sacrifice, and honoring the past, while at the same time laughing at our clumsy attempts at grace and the fun of watching us all trip on the banana peel we call reality during the summertime voyage from somewhere to somewhere before the snow falls.

From *Woodridge 1946*

Martin Boris

Douglas soaked, scrubbed, then polished the glasses until they shone brilliantly when stacked against the ceiling-to-floor window. The clear glasses caught the sun. He smiled at the sparkle and shine.

Andy had come in before him. In his favorite spot opposite the register, at his favorite angle, hovering over a cup of coffee the way Douglas was told he did over bourbon and soda at the Red Cat in Monticello before the war. A sip, a look out the window, up the street toward the bank and down where the sidewalk ended at the City Hall, then a puzzled stare into the cup, as if searching for something he might have dropped. Followed by the ritual of smoking. First a fresh pack of Luckies, square and white, with a red circle in the center. He tore a thin ribbon of cellophane around the top, ripped the corner off the roof, then coaxed out a cigarette by hammering the pack against his hand. He removed the cylinder, and tapped the loose cuts of tobacco into place against the tabletop. Next the magic of transferring the dormant fire in the match to a smoldering in the cigarette tip. He inhaled deeply while the smoke infused his blood, his lungs, his brain, then exhaled through funneled lips. Douglas wondered how much of a man's life was surrendered to the near-religious act of lighting a cigarette, start to finish, without even assessing the years stolen because of the poisons it contained. If George Seldes's newsletter *In Fact* were fact about the link between smoking and cancer.

Douglas remembered that the pre-Pearl Harbor Andy was a study in restless energy failing to be confined within the boundaries of a chicken farm. Despite a mother and a father to whom work was a religion Andy had spent endless hours foraging the countryside for attractive, easy women. Douglas admired that wild free look in Andy's eyes, that Lord Byron look, as he sped by in his Ford pickup truck going to or coming from some fabulous adventure. Andy was small and stringy, with a curly head a little too large for his bantam-rooster body. When he stood straight his legs bowed as if bent by the weight of that oversized head. Harry, never one to judge a man out in the open, said to Douglas at the time that he thought Andy had gone over the edge with Jed Parker's wife. Amelia Dooley, twenty-one, had married Jed, twice her age. Fear was the match-maker. She wasn't pretty, she had no prospects and Jed worried himself into an ulcer about leaving the farm to the county, there being no more Parkers left. After a week of courtship he had married Amelia. During the next five childless years they had increasingly little to say to each other. Then one day Amelia moved into Monticello, leaving Jed a short businesslike note devoid of feeling or recrimination. She took a job in Warren Senstacker's hardware store where Andy found her, ripe for picking. Some said she knew Andy before that, but Harry wasn't sure.

Douglas heard that Andy and Amelia entertained each other at her place, sometimes until four in the morning. Since no law was broken, neighbors in town could only express concern and indignation. Another time that would have been enough to send her scurrying back to the farm, but small-town censure had lost its bite by then and they were merely a gossip item for three months. Then Amelia upped and moved east someplace. Harry liked Jed Parker and blamed Andy for not returning her to the farm when the flame died.

Andy finally stirred his coffee. Without lifting his head he knew that he was being observed, scrutinized, judged by Douglas. The Strong kid with his distant yet worshipful eyes was waiting for him to do something spectacular. Andy felt the burden of being someone's idol. War had taught him that there were no idols, both captains and corporals had run like hell when the shrapnel exploded. He had once seen a major general vomit all over himself after a particularly bloody battle. He'd like to tell that to Douglas and sink his obvious case of hero worship. Dumb kid.

Andy looked at Douglas, who was freshening up the chicken salad with mayonnaise. He suddenly felt the need to say something to the boy.

"Do you remember how my grandfather used to walk, Douglas? Those short baby steps? As if each one was a small miracle?"

Douglas nodded.

"You know, sometimes a week goes by and it's like he never was, then sometimes he's so real that I could swear he's in the next room."

There were moments, too, when Douglas's memories of Zaida captured his present. Andy's summoning up of the old man stirred as well the sweet heavy scent of apple blossoms. In the air-conditioned luncheonette Douglas could swear he smelled apple blossoms. It was happening all over again and he could not believe how vivid the memories were.

A warm April afternoon long ago that hinted of abundant life and growth. All the trees sprouted green tips that became, on close examination, tight little fists of leaves. Douglas remembered wondering then why the dead couldn't also return to life every year, for a little while. His mother's death still cut like a thin knife when he thought of it. He remembered that times were bad and they couldn't even *give* the eggs away, then.

He recalled firing strikes at the apple trees with pebbles when Harry had come to tell him that it was time that he became a Jew.

"What do you mean become a Jew? I already am a Jew."

"You still have to become one."

"Even if I am one?"

"Even if."

"Would you explain that?"

"No. Nothing to explain."

"But I have baseball practice. The team needs me. It's an obligation."

Douglas had him there. As he learned both new words and Harry, he tried mixing intelligences. Harry was big on duty, morality, obligation.

"No," his father said.

Harry was short on explanation. The shorter the explanation the shorter the next argument.

"That's not right, Harry. I went to *shul* with you last Yom Kippur. Doesn't that make me a Jew?"

Harry walked toward him with one of his here-we-go-again looks.

"Yom Kippur wasn't for you. It was for me. My sins. You haven't been around long enough to have your own. Except for when you play these . . . games, but that's small potatoes."

"C'mon, Harry, what kind of sins could you have?"

But it wasn't all sham. It had never occurred to him that his father was composed of the same inferior material as the rest of mankind. Douglas continued to stare at his father, surprised at his own surprise. Thomas Jefferson owned slaves; Babe Ruth could be traded to Boston when the Yankees decided that he was of no further use. It was that level of disenchantment.

"Do I have to become an American, too?"

"Not the same thing."

"Why? Tell me why."

"I got something else to do."

"Isn't this important, too? Just because you don't make any money from it . . ."

"You know, you're giving me a headache with this damn rube routine of yours. I'm too busy for games. Case closed. Personally it doesn't matter to me one way or the other, but I promised Stella, I promised your mother to have you bar mitzvahed. That should be enough. For both of us. You're going and you're going to do it with the least amount of noise. With *no* noise. From now on no discussion and no having fun at my expense. You want to resist, do it passively, like Mahatma Gandhi."

"Do I go there or does he come here?"

"You'll go there."

"Where is there?" Douglas asked. Now it was about ninety percent question and ten percent mosquito biting.

"Starting Monday and every day until it's over, except Saturday, you'll go up the road to the Foremans'. Go into the kitchen and ask for Ben's father-in-law. His name is Mr. Baum. Ask civilly, now, none of your intellectual card tricks. You'll also make sure you've washed up. I don't want you touching the books with dirty hands. You'll sit down with Zaida, that's what everyone calls him, and you do what he tells you. Simple. No fuss, no noise. Easy as cracking an egg. You do it until August and I won't bother you. About that."

"What about my chores?"

"You idiot, if I take you away from your chores then I *intend* to have them done for you. Give me credit for some intelligence."

Harry had an immobile gray face with gray eyes that could convince you that you just didn't exist and jet-black hair combed straight back in a no-nonsense fashion. A policeman's face or a bill collector's. When provoked it rubberized and became animated, unused blood vessels suddenly swelled and ran red. Douglas knew how to bring life to Harry's face but only at the risk of triggering his tongue. He hated his father the most when that happened.

Times like those he felt defeated, alone, worthless. It made him wonder if the sharp edges they faced each other with would have been rubbed smooth by now if his mother were the buffer between. They needed a translator and Stella spoke both their languages. Harry had been changed by her death. Douglas did not remember if Stella could move Harry. Maybe she might have convinced him that their son wasn't just another day laborer on the farm.

Genuinely surprised, he remembered saying to Harry, "I didn't know the old man was a rabbi."

"He's not."

"He's not? Then I guess he's a teacher of bar mitzvahs, if there's such a thing."

"No, he's not a teacher of anything. Just an old man, a very religious old man who happens to be handy. That's credentials enough for me."

Harry walked Douglas up the steep hill to the Foreman place. It was raining that day. Douglas was not prepared to begin. He needed sunshine to start new things. Harry wouldn't listen.

"So you're finally joining the flock," Ben said with a broad peasant grin that always infuriated Andy. "*Mazel tov.*"

Douglas looked at him vacantly.

"The Jewish people, the Jewish people, *boychik.*" Ben added. He's been with his chickens too long, Douglas thought, talking about flocks. And he wasn't joining anything, just submitting to Fascist pressure like the Czechs.

The house was old, older than anyone who was living in it, and like the elderly it had begun to bend into itself. The porch sagged in the middle and little puddles of water had formed there. The roof had buckled, too. In the rear, behind the parlor, was a large old-fashioned kitchen with the highest ceiling Douglas had ever seen. An enormous woodburning stove, like a metal dragon, covered the back wall. It breathed fire and belched smoke intermittently. He heard hissing and crackling noises escape from its bowels. Something strange and delicious was cooking on it.

The long wooden table and six chairs near the stove were simple and rough. Hanging from a fuzzy white cord, thumbtacked into a ceiling beam, was a circular staircase of flypaper. It, too, was in poor condition due to exposure to light, heat and the rigors of the previous winter.

Old Mr. Baum sat in the far corner of the room on a small bench that was bleached of all color. He was slumped over a nondescript table, his head supported by an arm, reading the Torah, his lips moving with an uneven regularity. The presence of visitors meant little to Zaida. Douglas looked out the window at the steady, perpendicular rain and knew that there would be difficulties.

"Zaida," his son-in-law called, the way you do to someone you wish to awaken without frightening. The old man turned up his hand like a traffic cop to silence yet hold Ben while he finished the page. Then he closed the book and looked at them. Douglas swore that the old man actually looked through, and past them as if they were clear glass statues of no particular merit.

He was short and shaped like a barrel. Possibly if he arched his back he could manage five feet. A yellowish shredded-wheat beard hung from his face like a shade on a window. Above it was a pair of eyes unlike anyone's he had ever seen before. Maybe once. His mother had taken him, long ago, to the Bronx Zoo, where he had watched a sick old elephant who had great difficulty in rising. An attendant told them that the animal was to be destroyed soon. She told Douglas that someday he might meet people who had eyes like the elephant and carried the pain of the world in them. He now looked into Zaida's eyes and knew what she meant. Zaida finally stood up and seemed no taller. He and Ben spoke in a strange language Douglas thought was Yiddish.

"He says he'll be ready in a few minutes, he's got to take a leak," Ben said. "You should be so kind and wait."

"Would you ask him please if he might speak English," Douglas said when Zaida had managed a slow, laborious exit.

Ben shrugged. "Zaida speaks some nine languages. Can you imagine that, nine languages? Hebrew and Yiddish and Polish and Russian and German. A little Hungarian, too. I forget the rest, but English ain't one of them. I figured you knew."

Douglas thought he caught Harry looking a little puzzled for a second, the way the first American Indian might have looked when he felt the first Caucasian's bullet. No matter, Harry had quickly readjusted.

"No big deal," he said. "You're not here for polite conversation. Just get started and stick with it. That's how things get done."

Without looking, Zaida motioned him to sit down next to him with a short, flyswatting slap. Douglas complied cautiously, uncomfortably. The old man smelled of musty wood and mildewed rooms, of dried tobacco and deeply ingrained sweat. His beard had indistinct particles trapped in its mesh. Under a maroon sweater that had begun unraveling a long time ago at the cuffs he wore suspenders. Douglas saw the outline of the buckles on each side like tiny square breasts.

Shifting his weight to one side Zaida dug an amputated stub of a pencil from his pocket. It was pointless and withered with age like the crap he's going to make me learn, Douglas thought. As if unused to writing, Zaida smothered the pencil with stumpy, nicotined fingers. He turned to the end of the book which was its beginning and fell on a small group of mysterious symbols that bore no relationship to any of the twenty-six letters in Douglas's alphabet.

"*Baruch*," Zaida growled, and it could have come from some wounded animal deep within its lair.

"Pardon me?"

The old man repeated the growl and tapped impatiently waiting for its echo.

"*Baruch*?" Douglas replied, disoriented. He couldn't see how the old man could get *that* sound from *those* symbols.

Zaida advanced to the next cluster, showing neither satisfaction nor disappointment in his pupil. Showing nothing.

"*Attoy*."

"*Attoy*," Douglas repeated shakily. He lifted his head when something flew across the comer of his eye.

Andy strode into the kitchen without the basic salutations and sat in a rocking chair next to the stove. He opened a book of crossword puzzles, then got up to fill his Parker pen from a hexagonal bottle of ink in the cupboard. After finding the right puzzle he settled back comfortably in the rocker and threw a nod in Douglas's direction, which Douglas quickly snapped up and returned.

"*Baruch*," Zaida grunted when those symbols reappeared again, which Douglas failed to recognize and felt stupid about.

"*Baruch*—that's a six-letter word meaning blessing, which the next few months ain't going to be," Andy volunteered from his place by the fire. He chuckled and reburied himself in the puzzle.

The old man ignored the chuckler. He continued to point and growl—sometimes waiting a second for Douglas to return the growl, sometimes not. But the pattern was clearly established that first day. Either Douglas would follow closely or he would fall hopelessly behind.

The first session depressed Douglas. His eyes thumped and he had a nauseous headache. It was education by echo, religion by rote. It was neither education nor religion, but it elated him, too, because Andy was there to witness the stupidity of it all even though he expressed his opinions to no particular audience. They were brothers, now, so to speak.

As one day dissolved into the next Douglas repeated the words of Moses and Solomon, Joseph and Isaac, not knowing what they meant or who had said them. And forgot even the simplest of phrases. Yet Zaida plowed on unaffected by his student's gross failures or small successes, when, at last, a few did come. He never turned back to look.

Andy snickered, hooted and peppered with buckshot every chance he could from across the huge kitchen. Unruffled, with four thousand years of patience, Zaida moved his pencil across the pages that were on the verge of disintegration through age and use. Douglas remembered wondering, that last spring before the war, why the old man kept silent, as Andy's steady barrage of abuse grew more intense, its dispenser more animated, more involved. It took little intelligence to realize that it was no mere coincidence that Andy was in the rocker while Douglas studied with Zaida. And if Douglas knew, then surely the old man must know that his grandson was not sending him bouquets even if he spoke none of Zaida's nine languages. But it never varied, those two hours a day, listening to Andy's undirected atheism, watching Zaida's indifference.

"God, and I use the word the way I use 'shit,' is this boring! How can anyone stand it? And from *him*? How do you drill it into his thick head that there is no God? God is a cartoon character the capitalists invented to entertain and police the masses. At least those idiot Reds are right about that. Now look at this damned fool. He pissed his whole life away on a book of fairy tales. Just like they expect me to piss away my whole life on a two-by-nothing chicken farm. I'll be goddamned if I will. First chance I get it's up and out. Anyplace, anywhere but here."

Douglas decided that it was exciting to watch and see how much the old man could take before he would finally react. He was constantly braced for a clap of thunder or a bolt of lightning from a God they both denied since Zaida refused to defend himself or how he spent his life.

Nothing happened. It was all so strange. Yet something was occurring that he did not understand, like a card game in which he was the dummy. Neither of them spoke to him, but barmitzvah lesson aside, he was providing some twisted, arcane line of communication between a bearded lunatic and a ranting, raving maniac. And after August the two of them would probably never sit in the same room again. If that blessed month ever arrived.

The lessons continued, however, in the same manner, day after day. April and May vanished easily enough, but June was tough on Douglas.

So many things to do. Yet, despite the lack of time and weeks of wet weather he had perfected a curve ball that would give Ted Williams nightmares. Douglas was anxious to hold the stitching and slice down hard, then watch the ball act crazy as it nicked the strike zone of the makeshift batters' cage he had set up behind the coal shed. Zaida would never understand why he fidgeted on the smooth bench, suffering each minute away from the pitcher's mound.

"*Boray, p'ree, ha-gofen,*" Zaida said, completing the prayer over wine.

And that triggered Andy. He threw his Parker against the stove, the writing tool separating into its component parts. The tubular rubber well sizzled on the iron monster that raged even though it was June. First the odor of burning rubber, then the hiss of the ink as it evaporated in little puffs of blue smoke. The words flew from Andy's mouth as if someone were inside throwing them out.

"What a dumb old man. Not just dumb, stupid. Dumb you can outgrow. Stupid is for life. To sit and read that damned gibberish all day and smoke those stinking cigars after. And where the hell does it get him? A moron, a nitwit. Oh, God, if anyone is up there, strike me dead right now if this is what I've got to look forward to. Even hell is better than stealing eggs from under chickens' asses."

Andy stood up from his chair and choked the thin arms of the rocker, a little more bowlegged than usual. He looked as if he felt awkward, like standing in a crowd while everyone else was seated. He sat down, too, and stared at the stove.

And that triggered Douglas, that and the airless, heated kitchen, compounded by Zaida's gruff monotone.

"Goddamn you, old man, let me alone. Stop torturing me. I can't wait until you're the hell out of my life."

After Douglas had finished he realized that he was doing the shouting and not Andy. He grew dizzy, glanced at Zaida's face and tried to read it as he never had during Andy's wildest assaults. The old man looked at him with elephant eyes, narrowing one of them. It happened so fast that it almost didn't happen at all. Zaida quickly returned to the page.

Instead of returning there, too, Douglas looked at Andy. He expected a big-brotherly smile, a secret signal of acceptance in their exclusive society of atheists and shakers of authority's rotten foundation. It shook Douglas when Andy rose slowly, was about to say something, hesitated and walked to them. Looking concerned, Andy placed his hand on Zaida's shoulder. Without glancing up the old man patted Andy's hand and continued the lesson. The boy, confused, sought answers in Andy's face.

"Kid, you ever do that again and I'll kick your ass out of here so fast it'll take a week for the rest of you to catch up."

Andy's jaw looked as if it had been nailed shut and his eyes raked Douglas with the kind of intensity that might melt cast iron. There were no further outbursts from either end of the room for the rest of the summer.

Arlene took her seat on the high wooden chair close to the register. She sent Douglas a cold-fish stare that evaporated his reverie. He grew busier. Eggshells he had saved were the first thing he threw into a fresh coffee urn. They absorbed the fusel oil that gave coffee its bitter taste. It was one of Phil's secrets that he shared with his protégé.

This time Andy took a prune danish with a fresh cup from the fresh urn, and traded glances with Arlene, slowly, carefully. She looked for Douglas's eyes before submitting to Andy's. Slowly she crossed and uncrossed her legs while sending the tip of her tongue along her upper lip. Douglas ignored everything while Andy, drinking her all in, missed nothing.

It became busy in the store but Andy was oblivious to the afternoon crowd. He had retreated into the sanctuary of himself.

It was almost nostalgic for Andy to sort things out, to piece together internal and external history and remember how it was politically in Sullivan County before the Japs attacked. A time of clean and simple issues. Capitalism was corrupt and in an advanced state of decay; labor was saintly. Every liberal worth the price of the *Nation* knew that the South was one big lynch mob and only the Soviet Union held high the beacon of freedom and democracy in the world. It was so deceptively simple then that he must have been simple-minded not to doubt it. Politics and simplicities—they never really go hand in hand.

He remembered how his across-the-road neighbors, the Ostermans, had shaped his thoughts at the beginning of the forties. Nice people, most thought. Lilly and Paul Osterman raised eggs, like everyone else, to survive, but they practiced Marxism to live. Country Marxists are different from city Marxists, Andy soon learned. The urban variety were sharp-tongued, strident. They moved at a rapid pace. They were always having meetings, strike committees, protests, fund-raising rallies; they had little time for nonsense. Their country cousins, Lil and Paul, were the friendly smile, sit-awhile-and-have-a-cup-of-coffee, what-do-you-think-of-the rotten-weather kind of Marxists. They oozed friendliness the way maple trees exude sap in the spring. And they caught flies by the droves—himself, Douglas, and the top ten percent of the high school graduating class. Meetings at their house were always large, noisy affairs. Glasses clinking, a fire eating up pine knots, voices warm and friendly. Hayseed politics. Who's who in Sullivan County and nobody important queuing up for Lilly's deep-dish apple pie which was always prelude to supporting the Abraham Lincoln Brigade—those American idealists who fought the Fascists in Spain—or the setting up of a committee to organize the steam laundry or the hotel workers, or some other neglected group.

The Ostermans probably thought they had struck oil with him. He remembered brooding, being noticeably dissatisfied. And he was already going out with DeWah O'Brien, one of the colored girls who emptied the giant tumblers at the laundry. It was a baby step in Lilly's lithe and seductive mind from sleeping with DeWah to the struggle for racial equality.

They stuffed him with literature as if he were a Sunday roaster. The Ostermans had Moscow-leaning pamphlets on every conceivable subject: *Farm Cooperatives in the Soviet Union, Sex—The Leninist View, Hollywood and Fascism, The Hoax of the New Deal, The Capitalist Exploitation of Motherhood.* Andy wondered if there was a Marxist-Leninist way to move his bowels.

One Friday night, after a most difficult soiree, during which the patently simple had suddenly grown complex, hosts and guest mutually decided to give each other up. With malice and forethought Andy asked the smiling, well-fed, well-liquored audience of doctors, students,

Negroes and housewives the definition of an act whereby two countries agree to divvy a third one situated between them. Before being
shouted down he asked if they saw Comrade Molotov of the USSR
shaking hands with Von Ribbentrop, Hitler's Foreign Minister, in this
morning's *Times,* both grinning like well-fed wolves.

"Obstructionist," Paul screamed, spilling good Scotch on the couch,
when he realized that Andy was rubbing their noses in the Russo-German
Pact of 1939 that made a doormat of Poland.

"Opportunist," a young woman shouted, whom Andy remembered
from a Sunday picnic where she had openly nursed a baby.

Those two words were among the harshest in the Marxist lexicon,
Andy knew, signaling his expulsion from a society in which he had
never felt comfortable, anyway. He would just have to find something
else to do with his Friday nights. A shame, he was making excellent
progress with Lilly's sister, a ravishing brunette he felt had been especially conscripted to keep his interest in socialism high. But they were
so smug, so sure that they had all the answers, so willing to bend when
the breezes from Moscow blew. He just had to tweak noses. Looking
back Andy realized that that night was the high point and the end of his
political life.

Afterward he still signed petitions and donated small amounts,
selectively, to Lilly, who took with a seductive smile. But he also bought
Girl Scout cookies without feeling committed to their cause either.

From the enormous distance of the four war years Andy realized
that after the Ostermans he had narrowed his sights. He had given up
searching for large, powerful enemies in Washington, in corporate
boardrooms, in foreign capitals, and settled for three at arm's reach.
Until the day he was drafted he believed that all that was wrong with
the world lived in his father, his mother and his grandfather. There was
plenty of evidence. His father, Ben, an elfish man who gave Andy his
size and shape, had a blindly cheerful disposition that condemned him.

"So what? A hunnert years from now it won't mean borscht."

Translated that meant let it all pass: your life, your mind, your ambition. The hell with bettering yourself, getting the chickenshit off your
shoes. Stay and get buried alive.

And Momma. The cow, he called her. She always wore her hair in a bun that came to a point. One of two answers to anything. Often chosen at random. Both totally unacceptable.

"It'll be all right. You'll see, you'll see."

Her second answer was performed in pantomime, a shrug of the shoulders with eyes closed, that infuriating thousand-year-old *shtetl* answer of resignation to whatever happened. To starvation and the sweep of a Cossack's sword. To the torch of the Inquisition and fixed quotas for Jews in medical schools. She alternated dumb optimism with stupid body motions. Andy wanted more than that. This was 1941, the Fascists owned half the world; the other portion was in an uproar and he wanted more than one-night stands and discontented wives in awkward places.

But Zaida, his grandfather, received the most abuse in Andy's post-Osterman days. Zaida was the triumph of religion over life, of the past over the present. He was the supreme example of what happens when one fraction of human experience rises up to smother all the others. Like the Bolsheviks in Russia, like the Catholic Church during the Dark Ages. Zaida had a long beard, wore dirty clothes and carried an Old Testament that appeared to be more an extension of his left hand than an artifact. Saints breed more misery than sinners, which is probably why many of them are martyred. Andy was unable then to forgive Zaida his saintliness.

As exorcism, when Zaida walked the two miles to a *shul* that he often prayed in alone, Andy recalled racing up and down the road with Delilah in the truck and waving vigorously to the old man. Zaida had ignored them as he inched home. When he had finally reached the farm and sat on the porch reading the *Rambam,* a cube of sugar between his molars, sipping hot tea from a glass, Andy had forty-miled it up the driveway, slammed on the brakes and leaped out of the cab like a lunatic, and bolted the steps to his room to change his perfectly clean shirt. While Zaida read and calmly sipped his steaming tea.

Then Delilah would honk three or four times and Andy would perform the same act again down the steps and off the porch. Both he and Delilah laughed when he popped into the cab of the truck, rocketed out of the driveway and disappeared in a cloud of dust and smoke. While Zaida had never taken his eyes off the page or spilled a drop.

Andy went to war the first week of the new year. The Selective Service Board, composed of a group of townspeople too old to fight, decreed that the farm could carry on without him. Andy was overjoyed. This answered prayers for a way out. He had a clear picture in his mind of mock-saluting Douglas from the bus and grinning at him before they pulled out for Fort Dix. Almost four years later he returned, wondering why he had been so anxious to go. It was hardly worth the trip, personally, except for liberating the concentration camps. That made the difference. That was the part of the war that changed him.

Zaida died while he was in England practicing for D-Day, Momma the week his platoon broke out of a German trap at Saint-Lô and Ben when they marched into Aachen. He attended none of the funerals, there being greater need for his presence elsewhere.

By 1946 his restlessness and anger were gone the way some allergies disappear by adolescence. Andy did not attach a label to it. Seeing men die in combat and fleeing civilians cut down in terror were explainable things, but Bergen-Belsen and Buchenwald were something else. A whole race, his, scientifically blueprinted for extermination because of some mad theory of inferiority. Contemplating that dwarfed all his ambitions, his drive, his restlessness. A general contentment to leave things as they were replaced it. Psychic paralysis, a clever friend said. He returned home and was glad to be there, happy to raise chickens and watch the seasons change. He often thought of Zaida and had his regrets. Those were his bad days. He wore the old man's sweater with the protruding suspender marks when it was cold and didn't mind the winds at all.

Andy was low on cigarettes and that gave him the excuse to approach the register without being obvious. Arlene saw him on his collision course with her and with birdlike glances quickly took measure of the store to see where Douglas and Phil stood and if they were watching.

"Something you want?" she asked him.

"How can YOU say that with a straight face?" he asked.

"I mean now," she said, suppressing the urge to smile.

"Now, yesterday, tomorrow—the answer's the same."

"You're making it difficult for me. Andy," she said.

"That's the *last* thing I want to do. Give me a pack of Luckies," he sighed, "and I'll get out of your hair."

"Don't go too far," she answered and handed him his change.

"Not to Know the Past is to Diminish the Future": Reflections on *Woodridge 1946*

Gloria Boris

Martin never wrote about the Holocaust directly, but his writings bore its influence. During the war—before I knew him—he lived on the family farm and read about three books a week. After the war they converted their farm to a bungalow colony by redoing the chicken coops, building more bungalows. They built a main house, a casino, and a pool. As Martin learned from conversations, many of the renters were survivors. He talked to them and learned first-hand of the impact on their lives. Martin had many occasions to speak with them but he never incorporated this in his novels.

He couldn't get enough information about WWII and the Holocaust and absorbed everything. In *Woodridge 1946* the towns were bustling, and it showed in his works. I know that he made it a point to enlighten our children, who had not much discussion about WWII in their classes. We made them aware by spending a weekend at a convention of survivors at a Manhattan auditorium, sponsored by the Anti-Defamation League and led by Abraham Foxman and Eli Wiesel, the latter whom he ultimately got to know and kept in touch with.

At the convention he didn't learn anything he didn't already know, but he met people who were subjects of the Nazi criminality, and he listened attentively to the tales of people's conditions. He thought, "Not to know the past is to diminish the future."

After his novels he went on to write for magazines, especially *Lifestyle*, interviewing celebrities—mainly Jews, including Seymour Rexite, Leonard Nimoy, and Lillian Lux. He wrote much about the Jewish theater and became quite friendly with survivors who were actors. In his travels he met many Jewish theater people who were stars of the Second Avenue Theater. His relationship with them flourished and in the course of studying Jewish actors he became very interested in Maurice Schwartz, founder of the Yiddish Art Theater, established in 1918 and often called "the John Barrymore of the Jewish stage," at which point Martin embarked on a project to write Schwartz's biography. Martin also wrote an article for the *Jewish Weekly* on the Grine Felder bungalow colony in Woodridge, which was a Yiddishist colony full of artists, musicians, and actors.

Martin met I. B. Singer sitting on a bench on the Upper West Side. Martin enjoyed writing, using every venue to write a weekly column, magazines, newspapers. Writing was a joy, and he did it well. However busy Martin was he always had time for the philanthropies—he gave so much to our community and people who needed help—because not to know the past is to diminish the future.

This man was a gift to society, and the greatest and most endearing gift to me and my family.

From *Maus:*
A Survivor's Tale, II:
And Here My Troubles Began

Art Spiegelman

SUCH A SUNNY DAY AND STILL YOU'RE BOTH SLEEPING?!
WHU? WHATIME IZZIT?
IT'S ALMOST 8:00, AND ALREADY I'VE MADE FOR A HALF HOUR ON THE PORCH MY GYMNASTICS. SINCE I WAS A BOY I'VE MADE EVERY DAY MY EXERCISES...
UNH?
AT FIRST THE NEIGHBORS TRIED TO MAKE EXERCISES WITH ME, BUT THEY COULDN'T KEEP UP... SO NOW ONLY THEY WATCH!
IS THERE ANY COFFEE?
MALA HAD HERE SOME INSTANT COFFEE... TOMORROW WE'LL EXERCISE TOGETHER.
WHA? MY ONLY EXERCISE IS WALKING OUT FOR CIGARETTES! ...INSTANT COFFEE'LL HAVE TO DO.
YOU HAVE TO HURRY NOW TO GET READY... TODAY I NEED YOU'LL HELP ME TO PREPARE MY BANK AND TAX PAPERS- MALA LEFT THEM IN A MESS, YOU CAN'T IMAGINE!
?
YAH-HERE I HAVE IT. IT'S THE CAFFEINE-FREE KIND OF COFFEE.
GROAN.
UM. HAVE YOU SEEN MY PANTS?
ALL YOUR THINGS I PUT ALREADY IN ORDER IN THE BUREAU, THERE.
WELL... THANKS FOR NOT THROWING THEM OUT.
WAKE UP, HONEY. I'VE GOT BAD NEWS. THE ONLY COFFEE HERE IS SANKA!
UNF? I BROUGHT OUR COFFEE AND OUR POT. LOOK IN MY BAG.
ACH!

A few tense hours later...

What We Didn't Know

Hilene Flanzbaum

In *Maus II*, Art visits the Catskills in order to tend his elderly father, Vladek, after his second wife, Mala, leaves him. It is a difficult visit for Art since he finds being with his father, a Holocaust survivor, intolerable. Yet he goes—not only out of a sense of filial duty—but because this physical proximity facilitates the task he has undertaken: chronicling the complete story of his father's ordeal during World War II. This mission, to get the whole story, obsesses Art. And yet, living with Vladek and watching how he conducts his life drives him crazy.

It is not unusual for a child to be mortified by the actions of his parents, yet Vladek's peculiarities would make anyone squirm. In fact, Spiegelman encourages the reader to sympathize with the wife who has fled Vladek. To demand repayment from your wife *for a* hairbrush or a bar of soap certainly crosses acceptable standards for husbandly behavior. Yet, because Spiegelman intersperses Vladek's present with the reimagined story of his past, the author skillfully illustrates the double-edge of the survivor's insufferable stinginess. What is now a curse was once a blessing: Vladek's compulsion to save everything and spend nothing (a trait that may or may not have been with him pre-concentration camp life) can easily be labeled resourcefulness when it helps him survive Auschwitz. In the camp, Vladek had cleverly collected scraps of paper to use as barter for more important things—food and favors. In the book's present, however—in Vladek's small bungalow in Catskills—it seems more than absurd, when he leaves the gas lit on the stove all day so he doesn't have to "waste" another match (even more so since he is stealing the matches from the lobby of the Pines hotel anyway).

The writer of the book, Spiegelman, knows that Vladek's miserliness contributed to his survival; Artie, the *character* inside the text, however, has little patience for it, noting to his wife, Francoise, "But lots of people up here are survivors . . . if they're whacked up, it's in a different way from Vladek." The pinnacle of Art's humiliation occurs in the dreadful scene where Vladek returns groceries to the store, already half-eaten. Artie thinks his father will be thrown out of the store, but Vladek is successful getting "six dollars of groceries for one," because as he explains, the manager helped him "as soon as I explained to him, my health, how Mala left me and how it was in the camps."

"We can never return to that store," Art tells Francoise, and the reader too senses the inappropriateness, or even absurdity, of what Vladek has accomplished. On a larger scale, however, Vladek's "deal" raises other questions: could it be that Vladek telling the store manager that he has been in the camps is premeditated? And that he has exploited his own "survivor" status to get free groceries? And if this is the case, how does that work exactly? How does telling anyone in the Catskills in 1986 that he is a survivor gain him favors?

The brilliance of *Maus* is precisely in these vignettes in which Spiegelman can relate an entire zeitgeist of a time and a place in one small graphic. First, that Vladek has learned to exploit the sympathy of Americans for his own financial gain is more evidence of his resourcefulness. Vladek cares little, perhaps, for the public's sympathy, but has calculated to use it to his own advantage. Second, when the manager of the supermarket does as Vladek predicts he will, Spiegelman cogently illustrates the attitudes of Americans towards survivors of the Holocaust *at that time*. This manager epitomizes all of the sympathetic and guilt-stricken

Americans that by the mid-eighties have been thoroughly schooled in the horrors of the Holocaust and who now feel eager to make reparations, even if it is in the most trivial of ways.

Twenty years earlier, when my family vacationed in the Catskills, no such transaction could likely have taken place: obliquely making reference to the camps or even straightforwardly announcing that you had survived the Holocaust would have probably gotten you nowhere, gained you nothing—even if you were brave or foolish enough to say it aloud. If we know anything now, we know that Americans' relationship to the Holocaust and its survivors has not been static. In the sixties, being a survivor was something to be hidden not only from one's children, but from other non-survivors, Jewish or not. This would change. Many scholars have labeled 1978 as a turning point in Holocaust Studies; in this year the television mini-series *Holocaust* aired and President Carter established a commission to look into building a national museum. In his book, *On Listening to Survivors*, Hank Greenspan has documented how attitudes towards survivors shifted along with the increasing awareness of the Holocaust. By the late seventies, Greenspan tells us that Jewish Americans began their romance with survivors, a cultural trend that intensifies, and reaches its height in the nineties when *appreciation* of the survivor's ordeal becomes *celebration*. Survivors become national celebrities or local folk heroes. Elie Wiesel threw the first pitch at the Mets game at the 1986 World Series; and a documentary about the survivor, Gerda Klein, won both an Emmy and an Oscar in 1996. High school teachers invited survivors to talk to their classes and synagogues honored survivors at their annual *Yom Ha Shoah* ceremonies. Director Steven Spielberg's Video Archive was firmly established. The twenty years between 1986 (when *Maus II* was published) and 1965 (when I lived in the Catskills) is a lifetime in the development of Holocaust Studies.

I grew up in the decades of silence and suburbanization, unfettered by any threat of persecution or danger. If my own parents are an example, second-generation Jewish Americans (who were not survivors), they acted as if the Holocaust had nothing to do with them. And of course, on some level, it hadn't. Yet when the silence began to break, and the seventies produced a climate where many Americans began to investigate their "roots," second and third generation Jewish Americans—over 90 percent of whom had descended from Eastern Europeans—could almost too easily find a connection to this terrible history.

My father's mother, Sabina, was not a Holocaust survivor. She was not even in Europe during World War II. Sent away from her family in Rodin, a large town near Poland, in 1922 to marry a "rich American cousin" (actually a ne'er do well *schmattes* salesman), she did not particularly care for her husband, nor was she happy about immigrating. In Poland, her family had servants and private tutors, and she wore jewelry and furs. But she had made the mistake of falling in love with her tutor—a Gentile—and for this crime her father decided she would be better off in America. For the first decade that she lived in New York she was convinced she had gotten the short end of the stick. But in 1932, her father would be exiled to Siberia and he and one of her brothers died of the tuberculosis they caught there. Her father's dying words, "Get out of Poland," were closely heeded by his wife—who, both shrewder and wealthier than many other Polish Jews—spent most of their fortune paying smugglers to escort her and her six children out of Poland and into France.

History tells us that my great-grandmother did not make a perfect choice; but undoubtedly, her family fared better in France than they would have in Poland where over 90 percent of the Jews perished. Half of my grandmother's immediate family survived—an outcome that was consistent with statistics of the entire population of immigrant Jews in France. 50 percent of immigrant Jews (or stateless Jews, as the French labeled them) survived the War; 75 percent of French Jews did. How these losses affected my grandmother I can only guess for she had the finest manners and must have viewed speaking of such a dreadful occurrence, to her children or grandchildren, as an egregious breach of etiquette. As for the eight *yahrtzeit* candles that burned on her kitchen counter during the high holy days, I had no explanation.

My father must have known some of her history—but any knowledge he consciously acquired he brushed away like a pesky housefly. Who of his generation wanted to, or thought they should know, more? Even Spiegelman is thirty years old before he begins to look at his past.

As a second-generation American Jew it was convenient to believe this had nothing to do with you—even though you knew, you *knew* differently. I remember what my father said when I asked him if he would see the movie *Schindler's List*. "No," he replied wryly, "I already know the story." And he did know—had somehow always known, sensing the tragedy around him as certain animals can intuit the weather. The knowledge of his own connection to what had happened to the Jews of Europe may never have been fully acknowledged but it lay beneath him like the wobbly stanchions of a bridge.

He does remember that his mother was desperate to get news of her family. He can recall her long ordeal with HIAS, the agency that worked to help Americans find members of their families, and then finally the news—not until 1947—that she had lost her mother, three of her siblings, a brother-in-law, three nephews and nieces. But he explains his inattention to such matters this way, "I didn't know these people, I was a kid." He remembers nothing, but then I did not begin asking questions until he was in his sixties when the unexpressed anxieties of his youth had long been forgotten or buried so deeply that they cannot be extricated from the defense mechanisms that we call personality. Still, the old aphorism holds true: what the second generation tries to forget, the third generation tries to remember. That is me, the third generation, trying to remember. And yet, had it not been for the "French relatives," as we called them, I might never have known any of this history.

I took for granted this unusual recurring event in my childhood— when at least half a dozen times, a French relative appeared from behind the swinging doors of Customs, and temporarily at least, became a member of the family. Every other year or so, one of my grandmother's siblings, or nieces, or cousins arrived. They were all fabulous—in the original sense of the word—as if descended from fables: Frances, my grandmother's nephew, with his impeccable European suit and hearty laugh; cousin Rosette so tiny with her size four feet and dark red hair; my Uncle Shem with his crisp white shirts and elegant Gauloises. Two or three times, my grandmother went to Europe, by ship, which added to the storybook quality of these voyages. In those days, passengers enjoyed big parties before the boat set sail and their guests came aboard to say bon voyage, to drink champagne and to dance to a twelve-piece orchestra. Corks popped, confetti flew, a twelve-piece orchestra played, and I danced on my grandfather's shoes. When the bells rang, we scurried to get off before the boat sailed. After that, we stood on the pier in New York City, listening to the deep foghorns blast, waving good-bye frantically—just like in the movies. Why would anyone ruin these times by telling me what had happened to these "French relatives"?

When you are a child, everything is as it should be. Nothing is unusual. And so it was. All of my father's relatives lived in France. And they visited sometimes. They were all beautiful and smelled like roses or evergreen, and during their visits, we dined in Manhattan at fancy restaurants and ordered expensive bottles of wine because they insisted. If these people's lives had contained anything unpleasant—if perhaps, they had lived through the most hideous moments of world history, certainly, I knew nothing about it. If the adults talked about it—in Yiddish, perhaps, behind closed doors—my father does not remember. Instead we ate a lot and drank a lot and visited the Empire State Building and the Statue of Liberty.

I can recall many of these visits, but none was more memorable than the visit of my father's first cousin, Jacqueline, who arrived in New York City in 1965, and who was quickly shepherded by her aunt (my grandmother) to the Catskills bungalow colony where her son and his young family were spending the summer.

Jacqueline spent a week at Anawana Beach Colony in our very small bungalow. Anyone who has ever spent time in one of these bungalows knows the adjective "small" is a euphemism—in fact, Vladek's living quarters in *Maus* seem luxurious—a living room with a fold-out couch—compared to ours: two bedrooms, a small kitchen, and a bath. The colony sat on the same lake as Anawana Sleep-Away Camp and Kutshers Hotel, the fancy resort that still stands and was only a short walk away, through the woods on a marked trail. As residents of the bungalow colony, I understood even then that we were the poor relations. An avid golfer, my father always wished he could play Kutsher's, but it way too expensive. Vladek too is not willing to pay the price for visiting his nearby luxury hotel, the Pines. He is willing, though, to take those pleasures without paying. He tells Art that he sneaks past the guards because "it's pretty there to sit on the patio." Sometimes, he even gets free dancing lessons and uses the gym and the steam room. His father would like Art to join him in his stolen pleasures, but Art "does not want to be caught trespassing," which is a fate that holds little threat for Vladek who obviously has endured much worse perils.

As a child, I too tried to steal some pleasures. For some high-stakes entertainment, the kids sometimes followed the trail in order to watch the golfers—as if we were glimpsing the lives of the rich and famous. For this we were always scolded. On very, *very* special occasions, our parents took us to Kutsher's snack bar to have ice cream sodas at their fountain. Although I idly wished that we could stay there, my days at Anawana were pretty terrific. I went to day camp; I learned to swim and passed the deep-water test in Anawana Lake; I watched *Bye Bye Birdie* there in the rec hall, and hummed "One Last Kiss" for a week. I sang "Zippity Doo-Dah" in a talent show. Into this little slice of heaven walked Jacqueline, my father's beautiful first cousin who only seemed to make life more blissful. She was a Holocaust survivor—but of course, I knew nothing about that.

The most dazzling visitor the shores of Anawana had surely ever quartered, Jacqueline arrived in a cloud of mystery and Chanel No. 5. Wearing white slacks, a nautically-striped blue and white polo shirt, and a red silk scarf tied self-confidently around her neck that matched the dark red shade of her lipstick, she was a much better looking (and better-dressed) version of my father. They shared the high cheekbones, aquiline nose, full lips. She had tiny ankles, and a tiny waist. When I look at photographs of her today, I think she looks like a twenty-year old dark-haired Meryl Streep. My grandmother arrived at Anawana with her; and she too might be called beautiful. Often mistaken for Marlene Dietrich, she was blonde and buxom—and her three pack-a-day habit gave her voice a compelling throatiness.

By the time the pair of them arrived in the Catskills, however, they were already at odds. Never used to playing second-fiddle to any woman, my grandmother told us that Jacqueline was "too demanding." My mother told me, twenty years after, that my grandmother had brought Jacqueline to the mountains because she was convinced that her niece was after her husband, my step-grandfather Bill. This unseemly conclusion was no doubt buoyed by the knowledge that Jacqueline had come to America to find a husband—as one of her cousins had successfully done: Francoise who had come two years before had met and married a Jewish orthodontist and then left Brooklyn for Marin County.

At Anawana Beach Colony, there were no available men—in fact, during the week, there were no men at all—(most husbands vanished to their jobs in the city) so Jacqueline satisfied herself with flirting with other people's husbands on the weekend, a behavior that endeared her to no one. She never helped with meals, or clean-up, and she spent way too long in our tiny shower stall. On weekdays, though, she did all the women's hair and showed them how to use make-up to their best advantage. A compulsive liar, Jacqueline told everyone that she modeled professionally in France. She styled my sister's hair into a puffy flip that made her look like Sally Field in *Gidget*, a television program that was very close to our hearts. Although my grandmother and mother grumbled throughout the entire week, my sister and I thought Jacqueline was the greatest thing that had ever happened to us.

This is what I did not know about Jacqueline in the summer of 1965.

Jacqueline's family had survived the war in France (after escaping Poland) in Alsace Lorraine where her father Georges fought in the resistance. In 1941, Georges was captured—not as a Jew—but as a French soldier during the brief period when France fought Germany. Thus, he was not sent to a concentration camp but to a German POW camp very close to the French-German border. Courage, and perhaps a touch of insanity, led him to simply walk out of the camp one evening. He walked all the way back to the French-German border and was back on native soil just a month after he had been captured. From Alsace, he sent for his wife Bella and the two children they then had—Monique, who was then three, and her brother Gerard (one year old). For two and a half years, the four of them lived in hiding in a basement in Alsace. Jacqueline's older sister, Monique, can still recall her tiny perch by the one window where once a day she was permitted to look out. Georges was rarely with his family: he was conspiring with the mayor, also a member of the resistance, who helped to support their family. Jacqueline was born in 1944 just before France was liberated and perhaps would have borne less of a scar than her siblings had if her parents—my great aunt and uncle—had not gone mad at the end of the war. Repatriation for that family of five would be almost fatal.

My great-uncle George became notorious for sending a letter to the mayor that threatened to blow up City Hall (Hotel de Ville) if their apartment in the fourth arrondissement was not returned to him. Of course, it was not returned to him, nor did any of the survivors have much, if anything, returned to them. France was not kind to the Jews that came home; my family's story is not unique for that reason—though my great-uncle was perhaps one of a select few that sent a letter to the mayor threatening to detonate a bomb. The gendarmes hurriedly snatched Georges from the streets of Paris. So after imprisonment in POW camp, living in hiding for three and a half years, and upon resurfacing, learning that his entire family of origin had been killed, my great-uncle had the pleasure of spending five years in prison—all courtesy of the French government.

What happened to Bella, Jacqueline's mother and my grandmother's younger sister, after the war is less clear. Monique's husband intimated to me that she went to prison with Georges, though he stopped short of saying it loudly enough for his wife to hear: there are certain defenses he does not wish to shatter. Monique says her mother just "wandered the streets like a crazy woman." This is an expression that has enduring currency in my family; my aunt Madeline, who lost her first family to the camps, was said to have wandered the streets of Paris like a crazy woman too. Whatever the case, it is clear that neither Georges nor Bella—nor any of the surviving aunts or uncles—was able to care for their three children, then the ages of seven, five and one. It has been difficult to twist the various narratives into a single thread. Even Art, who has the benefit of only one narrator, can find discrepancies between his father's story and others he has heard. "I just read about the camp orchestra that played as you marched out the gate," Art tells his father. "Orchestra?" his father replies. Vladek heard no music, only "the guards shouting."

As for my own extended family, where there is so much guilt to go around, psychological defense mechanisms render irreconcilable narratives. The sister who survived by marrying a French Catholic policeman who had hidden her in the local prison during *les rafles* would no longer be considered a member of the family, for Bella and my grandmother believed that it was she who tipped off the Nazis about where the rest of the family was in hiding (it was not she, but her husband who "accidentally" told a policeman friend—but that is another story). Bella's brother Sam had survived by fleeing to Corsica after his wife and daughter were captured and killed during the *Vel D'Hiv*, but he was also without a home or any means of support. Another of Bella's sisters had survived two years in Bergen-Belson, but was in no shape to raise children—nor would she ever be. Her oldest surviving sister, my grandmother, was much too far away to be useful. So Bella left the children at an orphanage in Paris that had been set up to take care of Jewish children who had lost their parents during the war. These children were not orphans, but the deception had to be maintained in order for them to receive food and shelter. Thus, for the five years between 1945 and 1950, Jacqueline and her two siblings saw virtually nothing of their parents.

It seems as if my grandmother must have known some of this; on the other hand, her sister was never very forthcoming or honest about anything. My father insists to this day that he did not know. In any case, when Jacqueline arrived in the Catskills, she was magically free of her past—a condition that Americans seem to demand, and that Americans seem to aspire to. Perhaps she believed that in America everyone is happy, upwardly mobile and not scarred or driven mad by persecution. In America, one can imagine that the past ceases to exist. Like Vladek who burns the diaries of Artie's mother because the past is something to flee, perhaps Jacqueline too believed that the past could disappear without a trace. In the Catskills, the forgetting got easier. As Art, the character, says to Francoise in *Maus*, "It's so peaceful here; it's hard to believe that Auschwitz ever happened." Art, the artist, however never lets us forget: in the text, this pastoral panel is followed by another that features a cloud of bug spray. "These damn bugs are eating me alive," Art complains. The reader, however, is not left thinking about bugs but rather the image of poisonous gas that explodes on the page.

For what seems like a long time for those of us that lived through it, but is actually only a blip in history, many Jewish Americans believed that if they did not look at the Holocaust, its shadow might be avoided. Such repressions are always harmful, even deadly, as Spiegelman makes clear. In *Maus I*, the reader learns that Art has spent several years in psychiatric hospitals; as a successful artist, he remains depressed. In the brilliant panel that begins section two of Volume II, Art sits at his drawing table, his head in his hands, while beneath him lie dozens of naked dead bodies, positioned to suggest that they are the foundational structure of his work and life. The cause of his depression is all too clear: he is the second-generation, inheritor of a history that can no longer be repressed.

At seventy, Jacqueline has been married five times, calls herself Clara, and refuses to see me when I am in France. Her brother Gerard is dead—a schizophrenic and an alcoholic, his heart failed him when he was in his fifties. The oldest sister Monique has lived a long life with a wonderful husband and productive children, though she is plagued by anxiety and depression. In her seventies, she desperately wants the world to hear her story. I met her for the first time eight years ago and have seen her several times since; she has helped me learn the story of my extended family.

At Anawana Beach Colony, the summer Jacqueline was there, two other survivors—a couple—lived there. I knew they were *survivors*, but had only the vaguest idea what that meant—just that it was a label that seemed to come in tandem with erratic behavior. I knew just enough to be terrified by the bluish tattoo on the fleshy side of a forearm. The woman that lived in an apartment in my grandmother's building, Mrs. Wasserman, had one. She baked cookies for my sister and me and watched us play, but we thought her strange because she never wore anything but a bathrobe. I tried very hard not to look at her arm. One of my friend's mothers was also a survivor. She yelled a lot whenever we made a mess. She was, my mother said, a neat-freak; she was, my mother said, "nuts." In the sixties, my mother did not cut her any slack for being a survivor.

I do not remember when I learned what it was that *survivors* survived. I do remember that when I realized what it was, I was shaken—not only by the enormity of it, but also by the fact that *we* had let it happen. "But why didn't America save them?" I wanted to know. After all, I lived in Brooklyn, where everyone was Jewish and where that ethnic identity automatically seemed to confer power. My parents answered the question—simultaneously—but differently: "We didn't know," replied my mother, the elementary school teacher; "It's complicated," said my father, the high school history teacher—and in their divergence lay a heavy tale about what Americans knew and when they knew it.

The Catskill Mountains has been a second home to Jewish Americans for almost a century. Fancy hotels, communal boarding houses, and small bungalows offered refuge from noise and concrete and crowds—but also provided a place where Jews could be together, although what it meant to be Jewish had vastly different vectors. About the Holocaust: there were those that knew and those that didn't; those who had actually lived through it, like Vladek, and those that had been five thousand miles away; those who lived in its shadow but would not face it, and even those who had not yet been born when it happened. Just a few miles up the road from Anawana Beach Colony stood bungalow colonies that housed only survivors—but for what I knew then, it might as well have been a million miles. For a week, in our tiny bungalow, I slept side by side with Jacqueline and still knew nothing. And even though my personal connection to the Holocaust seems tenuous—merely grandchild to a woman that lost her family—I have spent the last twenty years of my life trying to know as much about that family as I can. In this, I am like Art who, throughout *Maus II*, portrays himself following his father around with a tape recorder. Unlike Art, however, I cannot claim that my psychological health depends upon me knowing that story. And yet, sometimes when I look at my father, I feel that it does.

From *Paradise, New York*

Eileen Pollack

My only hope that old age needn't be frightening came from the Feidels. Each afternoon they appeared at the pool, Shirley in a trim maroon one-piece, Nathan in trunks neither baggy nor too tight. Shirley had the figure of a much younger woman, with smooth skin and long white hair, which she wore in a bun. Nathan had a thick square-cute silver mustache, a cleft chin and a nose that came straight from his brow. He and his wife would step down the ladders on opposite sides of the pool and, without hesitation, even on the chilliest day, slip into the water and swim toward one another, pass and keep swimming, twenty laps in counterpoint, strong rhythmic strokes, as the numbers on their wrists, written in an ink that never washed off, rose from the water again and again.

When they finished their swim, Nathan and Shirley climbed from the pool. Nathan draped his wife's shoulders with a thick purple towel they must have brought from home since the towels at the Eden were threadbare and white. Then Nat kissed his wife. No parts of their bodies touched except their lips, but I felt so unsettled that after they had gone I was attracted more strongly than ever to the waiters sunning on the deck.

"That's her, over there."

The man whistled. "She must have been some beauty. So what's her name, Fiddle?"

"Feidel," I said. "Her name is Shirley Feidel."

I felt like a stoolie, though the man to whom I had revealed Shirley's identity wasn't a cop, just a harmless historian with a thick black mustache and frizzy black eyebrows. He had found out from an uncle that the Eden had been a haven for Holocaust Survivors since my grandfather placed an ad in the *Forward* that all Displaced Persons could stay there half-price. But they hadn't survived very well for Survivors. Unlike the Communists, who lived with their eyes on the future, the Survivors looked back. In the race against death, this weighted them down; they didn't see the dangers just ahead, at their feet. Only a handful still rented rooms at the Eden. I led the historian to each, and I hated to see how reluctant to speak these old people were.

Bringing it up will only give us nightmares.

Who wants to make the gentiles feel guilty? People don't like to feel guilty.

But each Survivor relented. Historians, after all, were God's scribes on Earth, and this one belonged to an institute that bore the name of Anne Frank. A vault of Holocaust stories wouldn't bring the Eden more guests, but I took pride in knowing that my family's hotel would be a footnote to history. I had kept these people alive long enough to deposit their secrets in that vault of recordings at Brandeis.

I introduced the historian to Shirley, then sat in a chair a little way off. The terrors she had been through gave her great dignity. She had witnessed an evil as immense as the Hebrews' captivity in Egypt. But she refused to tell her story. It was possible, she said, to be as vain of one's suffering as of anything else.

"If I can be honest," the historian said, "you won't live forever."

Shirley nodded. This was obvious. The wonder was that she had lived until now, that she was sitting in America on this fresh summer day watching the cottony plume from a jet dissolve to dots and dashes across a sapphire sky.

He ruffled his eyebrows. "But who will tell your story after you're gone?"

At least he hadn't said "dead."

"Story?" she repeated. "What I have lived through is not a story." She had just the breeze of an accent—a sibilant *s*, a thickly rolled *r*. Logically, I knew she had spoken English this way before living in the camps. But her accent seemed a scar, like the numbers on her wrist or whatever the Nazis had done to her womb. "Any words you could say would make it seem . . . small. Something a person could understand if only he read those words enough times. A few familiar phrases. Those same photos, so small and harmless on the page. The naked men in the pit. The skeletons pressing against the fence."

"But I've told you, the book won't be what I say. You'll speak into this." He waved his hand above the slender steel recorder on the broad arm of Shirley's chair. "I'll just transcribe the tape."

"What if I haven't the words?"

"You speak better English than anyone I've interviewed."

Shirley leaned back, flattening her bun against the chair. "Someday they will add a verse to the *Tanach*: 'An enemy rose up and slew the six million. Their ashes and bones cried out to God, and at last He delivered those few who were left.'"

I was struck with awe, as if a chapter of the Bible had been written right there, on the Eden's lawn.

"Great. That's just great." The historian removed his glasses (I expected to see his nose and mustache come off too). "Then the gentiles can doubt the Holocaust really happened, the way they doubt the Jews were ever slaves in Egypt."

Shirley closed her eyes. "Perhaps it's better to test the world's faith than always offer proof."

"Don't you see? This is bigger than the Exodus precisely because we *do* have proof. Most American Jews stopped believing in the Bible a long time ago. They were ready to stop being Jews. Then they found out what was going on in Europe. The world wanted them dead? Ha! They would keep being Jews, out of spite."

"And is spite a good reason to keep alive a religion? Without spite, without being hated, is there really no other reason to go on being a Jew?"

"I would think you wouldn't mind a little spite."

She folded her hands. "Whether it is written or not does not matter. What I have been through is known."

"Maybe it's enough for you that it's written in God's mind how you suffered. Me, I want to leave something my children's children can read."

"What is written in God's mind I cannot know. I meant only my husband. He knows what I have been through. And that must be enough."

Preserving the Catskills: An Exercise in Nostalgia, or Survival?

Eileen Pollack

Growing up, I heard remarkably little about the Holocaust. My grandmother lived in our attic, but until a few years ago, I had no idea that her brother and his family had been wiped out by the Nazis—or by their own Ukrainian neighbors—in a village called Czortkow, in the early 1940s. My parents went out of their way to protect us from any knowledge of what their own parents had endured, or what they themselves had suffered when they were younger—any memory of the pogroms that had driven both sets of grandparents out of Galicia and Lithuania, the rigors of immigration, the grinding poverty of the Depression. My father had grown up in tenements on the Lower East Side and Brooklyn, and then in a cottage at his family's hotel in Ferndale. After he earned his dental degree and served four years in India during World War II, he returned to the United States, married my mother (who had grown up poor in the Bronx), and opened his dental practice in downtown Liberty. But as I describe in my essay "Ranch House," when my parents built their first (and only) new home, they became obsessed with protecting their children not only from poverty and disease, but also history.

And yet, somehow I knew. I sensed at an early age the presence of a danger so terrifying that the grown-ups couldn't bring themselves to mention it, which made it even more frightening than polio, tetanus, or swimming too soon after eating, which, as they ceaselessly warned, might put us in our graves. How else to explain my fascination with finding places I could hide (I remember thinking that if the Nazis came pounding on our door, I could lower myself into the laundry chute and hang on with my fingers) or forcing my friends to play Concentration Camp in my grandmother's bathroom?

Still, it wasn't until I read Anne Frank's diary in the sixth grade that I realized the broken old men we tormented every day when they stood before our classes in Hebrew School must have been survivors of the camps, or maybe they had fled the Nazis, along with many of the guests with funny accents who stayed at my family's hotel. As far as I knew, my grandparents didn't offer survivors a special rate. But in doing the research for my novel, I learned about resorts that went out of their way to welcome Displaced Persons, and I modeled the Eden after them. (I wish I could remember where and what I read, but I started work on *Paradise, New York* in the early 1980s and can no longer find my notes.)

Certainly, in thinking about the relationship between the Holocaust and the Catskills, I wasn't conscious of making any particular contribution to the literature on the subject. There didn't seem to *be* any literature on the subject. When I started *Paradise*, no one was writing anything about the Catskills, which most American Jews my age still regarded with embarrassment. Not until *Dirty Dancing* (Vestron, 1987) came out in 1987 did the Borscht Belt become hip, or, at least, a subject for nostalgia. (You can imagine how delighted I was when I was invited to attend one of the first conferences sponsored by Phil Brown and the Catskills Institute. There, at Sunny Oaks Hotel in Woodridge, I found an enthusiastic audience for my book, along with the very sociologists I had created in my novel, who, as I predicted, were sponsoring a conference at one of the few remaining authentic Borscht Belt hotels so they could study the behavior and language of the few remaining authentic guests.)

That was what my novel was about—the nostalgia I could see coming for a world that my generation of American Jews had been all too ready to repudiate, the sentimentalized equation of Catskills *Yiddishkeit* with Jewishness itself, or, worse, an equation of the Borscht Belt's secondhand *shtetl Yiddishkeit* with Judaism. What I was asking in my book was what, if anything, about the Catskills—and, by extension, Judaism—might be worth trying to keep alive. As Shirley Feidel puts it, if the only reason for remaining a Jew is that Hitler tried to wipe us out, then what does that say about our religion? Without hatred and spite, is there really no reason to be a Jew?

And yet, as I hope the Feidels demonstrate, the Catskills did provide a refuge for what was best about the culture Hitler attempted to destroy. Shirley and Nat exemplify the dignity and grace embodied by those Jews who remained faithful to each other, along with their culture and their religion. Generous, learned, kind, they regard Judaism not as a collection of homey foods, bawdy jokes, and quaint Yiddish phrases, nor as a set of rules defining an intricate game whose mastery sets them apart as chosen or special, but as a theology and a philosophy, a moral code, a way of being. In the hotel's African-American handyman, Thomas Jefferson, they recognize a fellow exile who is attempting to maintain his dignity as a citizen of the world, even as he retains his unique cultural and ethnic history. The Feidels' identity as Jews and their history as survivors only partially define who they are, which means they are able to connect with Mr. Jefferson, for whom being black is only a partial (although very real) identity. The difference is that Mr. Jefferson believes that a person can pick and choose the best of each religion or philosophy and make his way in the world as a sort of universal *mensch* while Nat Feidel argues—from experience—that others will define you according to a much more limited set of criteria.

> "Universal man! You sound like my neighbors in Vienna just before Hitler knocked on their doors."

> "Never said I was trying to pass. Only said that a man can be more than one thing."

"Pah. You think they come with an eyedropper, with a microscope? What they see from a distance, that's what you are."

"Just because a few fanatics see me that way doesn't mean I've got to define—"

"A few! Listen, Jefferson, life isn't a flea market. You can't pick and choose—a wise proverb from Confucius, selections from the *Sayings of the Fathers*, a witty parable from the Sermon on the Mount. You stitch together something like that—a person, a religion, what you call it, a 'project'—a stitched-together thing like that, it's a dead thing, a corpse."

"So if something's not one thing, all the way through, it's dead? You want me to be consistent? I'll tell you who's consistent. Himmler, he was consistent. Eichmann, now there was a consistent thinker. Göring, *he* was consistent."

Nor do the Feidels see material success as a marker of their identity; Shirley is as offended by the idea that an insurance company might pay reparations for her husband's accidental death at the Garden of Eden as she is by the idea that Germany might attempt to reimburse her for what she and Nat suffered in the camps.

I wish I could say that the Feidels are based on real survivors, but I did at least base them on a real couple—my great-aunt Gus and her husband Herman. I only met them twice, and only when I was very young, but they impressed me as having a certain physical beauty and refinement that virtually no other Jews in the Catskills seemed to me to exhibit. Uncle Herman was courtly and distinguished, with silver hair and a silver mustache, while Aunt Gus, delicately boned and finely featured, wore her long, straight, platinum-red hair wrapped up in a bun. Once, she revealed to me that she had been so poor as a little girl that her widowed mother, or maybe her widowed father, had been forced to place her and her brother in an orphanage. Rather than being upset, she had been delighted. Never before had she had her own bed to sleep in, or an entire night table in which to store her belongings, let alone a class in gymnastics and ballet, which, she said, she loved. Sitting in the backyard of my parents' comfortable, serene ranch house in the Catskills, I was shocked by the realization that my aunt had grown up so poor that she considered a bed in an orphanage to be a luxury.

As a writer who had grown up in the Catskills and was writing a novel based largely on the crazy stories my father told at dinner and the bizarre anecdotes that members of my extended family traded and laughed about at holiday gatherings, I had no choice but to work in a comic mode. But writing in a comic mode does not preclude treating serious questions, as I learned from reading the work of such literary heroes as Philip Roth, Bernard Malamud, Grace Paley, Saul Bellow, Lore Segal, and Leonard Michaels (in fact, my initial inspiration for writing my first novel came from reading Roth's *The Professor of Desire*, whose opening chapters are set at the narrator's parents' hotel). In writing *Paradise, New York*, I was attempting to figure out whether my protagonist, Lucy Appelbaum, might be right to preserve her family's hotel, not to bolster her own shaky sense of identity, but to continue to provide a refuge for exiles such as the Feidels and Thomas Jefferson, the way Abraham pleads with God to save Sodom for the sake of the ten truly righteous people who might be living there.

As is true for anything I write, I am never interested in exploring questions whose answers I already know. And yet, by the end of the final draft of a story or novel, I know more than when I started. And in writing about the Catskills, I reached the very tentative, very personal conclusion that if Judaism is to be nothing more than a reification of the Holocaust, or an exercise in nostalgia for a culture that was deeply flawed by ignorance and insularity even when it was authentic, then it might not be worth preserving. But if it retains the earthiness, humor, and communal warmth typified by the Catskills at its best, then it shouldn't be afraid of evolving into something new—something less paranoid and artificial, more spiritual and more inclusive, more Jewish . . . and more American.

Bingo by the Bungalow

Thane Rosenbaum

The woman was eccentric, even for the Catskills. Actually, she was crazy, but that's not the kind of silent confession a child can easily allow about his mother. It takes a measure of distance to appreciate the abnormality. Blind faith in parental credentials is a virtue of childhood, but one day it vanishes. The brittle truce that lies between the gap in generations gives way to new realities, and empathies.

But then the entire colony was filled with crazies. It was a summer loony bin of refugees from the fallen Europe, now resettled in America, spending the months of June through August in Sullivan County—"the country" as they called it. Cohen's Summer Cottages was made up of ten white-boarded bungalows scattered across a lush green field. Small boxy frames with ash roof tiles. Each cottage had a porch and swinging door that clapped firmly against the frame. A stone walkway linking the cottages—a trail for the dispossessed. A lone, rickety shed—home for a lawn mower and washing machine—rested beneath an ancient weeping willow. There was a taut clothesline that stretched from the swings to the slide. On windy afternoons, a United Nations of underwear and brassieres would flap restlessly in the breeze.

"It's over eighty-five degrees today," Hyman Cohen announced, returning from the shed, the first of many daily readings of the mercury stick. "*Ach,* imagine that, eighty-five, like an oven . . . but dry," he said, shaking his head in disbelief, and spitting to the side.

The thermometer always gave the same reading, and he the same response.

Cohen wore an oversized pair of orange cabana shorts with silver crests that trimmed the waistband. His skin was dark and rough; his hair and eyebrows thick and unruly. One of his legs appeared lifeless. He dragged it about as if chained to some burden no one could see.

It was his colony, a piece of real land, paid for in cash to mask the memories from five years before. His tenants shared in his addiction: the need to escape and forget—the smoke, the shaved heads, the ancestral remains. Each a survivor from one camp or another: Bergen-Belsen, Maidanek, Treblinka, Auschwitz. Left behind was a sacred burial ground. The geographic sacrifice. No time, or courage, to place a wreath or a tombstone. Simply too hard to go back.

The music of the colony resonated with the sounds of atonal displacement. Everyone spoke with some mangled, confused accent that had been forced on them in America. English learned in a hurry. Verbs and nouns swallowed without time to digest. Some vowels never made it into the vocabulary, abandoned heedlessly at the docks.

Where better should this horde of runaways, of phantoms, have settled in for the summer? Cohen's was strangely their home. They were safe here—well, as safe as they would ever allow themselves to feel. There was much they could never believe in again. Faith was lost. No god. No humanity. No good places to hide. Cohen's at least offered a refuge of shared cynicism.

And in doing so, it also tolerated a fair amount of dementia. All that insanity added to the atmospheric diversity of the place, like the cool mountain night air and the morning dew. The refugees could swim in Kiamesha Lake. Do as the ancient Indians: purge the sins, cleanse the soul, dive deep into the belly of the water—where it's quiet—hoping to silence the stowaway shrieks that had come along for the ride.

Cohen never liked the word *concentration camp*, preferring instead the German *lager.*

"Why a camp, they should call it? Belsen was no camp, no picnic. In America, camp is where you send the children, or where you learn to be a Communist. We shouldn't call the *lager* a camp." And then, prideful of the haven he offered, he would add: "You want to know from a camp? This is a camp . . . right here. My camp! An American camp, not for children, but for the people like us. We don't march. We play cards all day. We sing, we cry. We look out at the trees. No fences, no wires . . . Now, who wants for pinochle?"

Written on the swinging sign at the foot of the stone road, carved into the wood in seductive script, read:

COHEN'S SUMMER COTTAGES
LEISURE MACHT FREI!

"Keep up with me, you're falling behind," Rosa said. She was wearing a black polka-dot dress with flowing chiffon lace that floated in the air. Moving smartly between branches and twigs, she cut through the woods like an animal beginning its evening hunt.

"I can't walk this fast," a whining voice trailed her brisk pace, "it's too dark. . . . I'm tripping over acorns."

The sky was seared in blackness. A few resilient stars wriggled free of the buried pack. With flashlights, mother and son made their way into the forest. Beams sliced between trees, startling mosquitoes, overexposing fireflies, scattering milky streaks through the bushes.

"We're going to be late for my game," she said. "Do you want your mama to miss her bingo game? Think what we could win."

From behind and stammering: "What can we win?"

"Let's see . . ." she ruminated, pointing the flashlight down against her side, a white mist of light dappling the ground. "They have a blender and a seltzer maker. Ida, next door, tells me there is a bagel slicer; you just put the bagel in a plastic cover, and then slice like regular. No more cutting my hand. Such good prizes, no?"

"We'll never use any of that junk—even if we do win." The child was not easily tempted by convenience, nor fooled by deceit.

"Don't argue with me," she said. "I need to practice for the big game when summer is over—the one at Cohen's. He offers a cash grand prize."

"Why do we have to go? Can't we just stay home tonight? Lucy's on television."

Rosa turned around, lifted the flashlight, and planted a perfect moon over her face. In a possessed voice she said, "What do you think puts food on our table?"

"Bingo?"

"Bingo!"

"How does a bagel slicer put food on our table?"

"Every little bit helps."

"But we went last night. . . ."

"And we go tonight. Tomorrow we will go to Krause's Colony for a movie at their concession. The Three Stooges are playing. We'll have bagels, lox, and cream cheese. That you'll like."

And with that offer she danced through the woods, waving her arms like a sorceress, skipping around each tree; then she turned swiftly to flash a ray of light on her young son, who by now had resigned himself to the night's bingo game.

Two years earlier Rosa's husband had died, suddenly. His heart stopped. Just gave up. They had been two survivors who left much behind in that European graveyard—except death, which must have been lonely, or simply wasn't yet finished with the family. With Morris's parting, the task of raising Adam fell to her, alone.

Rosa Posner, fragile, a thin face with full lips, an unforgetting purple scar molded on her forehead, feared being a widow with child in a new land. Like the other refugees, she stumbled over the language. She did not know the secret handshakes that seemed so natural for immigrants who came before the war. And of course there was the concern over money. *"Ach, geld. Ich brauch mehr geld."* Her money worries never allowed her mind a minute's rest.

"I know from nothing except how to survive," she pondered. In the camps she had been a saboteur, a black-market organizer, an underground operator. It took years to relearn the simple etiquette of life among the living. "Who in this country needs to know from such things?"

They lived in a middle-class section of Brooklyn. Ethnics at every corner. Dark walk-up apartment houses. Trees planted at the foot of the curb, in front of some buildings, but not others. It was a borough built mostly of stone and concrete, not entirely in harmony with nature.

One day, joining a card game in Brooklyn, Rosa learned that she had a knack for recalling numbers, and a certain streakiness with luck that seemed to will the royalty of the deck in her direction.

She became a gambler, a regular shark at the neighborhood tables. During the day she worked in a stationery store off Nostrand Avenue—calendars, magazines, fancy pens, newspapers, especially the *Forward.* She knew them all. But at night, off to a neighborhood game for gin rummy or seven-card poker.

For three weeks each year, during the Christmas season running through the first part of January—the peak time for snowbirds— she would take Adam out of school, board a Greyhound bus, and head down to Florida. It was a long bus ride—almost two days. Adam would sleep for most of the time, or stare down at the pages of a book, or color in a large white pad that Rosa had picked up for him at the stationery store. He never complained about the trip. It was all part of his mother's therapy—he knew it, even then.

Rosa passed the time by staring out the window. She loved the long journey south, chasing the warm weather, anticipating the tropics, breezing through all those unfamiliar towns. "What is this Fayetteville, and Jacksonville? Where are we now?" The motion of the bus rocked her gently, but her eyes never closed as she struggled with all those solicitations posted along the highway. Her lips moved slowly, and then the billboard was gone, already well behind her.

But when the bus reached Miami, Rosa stepped on the warm asphalt on Flagler Street and was immediately reminded of why she had come. There was the dog track on First Street on Miami Beach. And jai alai in Miami. The hotels along Collins Avenue were filled with "pigeons," as she called them—a phrase picked up from late-night movies, the source of much of her English.

"Now you stay in this room until get back," she said, her son lying in bed in his pajamas, shadows from the black-and-white TV flickering off the window. Jackie Gleason droned in the background. "If you need anything, I'll be at the Caribbean Hotel, down the street. I'll come back with lots of money tonight. We'll be rich like Rockefellers. Tomorrow, I'll buy you a stuffed alligator in the souvenir store downstairs, maybe even a painted coconut. Now go to sleep."

In the country, during the summer, the games were fewer, and the stakes lower. But there was bingo, the calling of the numbers—B23, A14, G9—which serenaded her through each night.

—∂ ƒ—

At the top of a road littered with pinecones the forest came to a halt. There was a light that led down to a barn, a long trailerlike edifice where the whole colony gathered for bingo. Once inside, Rosa purchased eight cards.

"You play so many cards, Mrs. Posner," the man at the concession observed. "How do you keep up with all of them?"

"I brought my little helper," she replied.

The room was filled mostly with people from the colony, but there were a few, like Rosa and Adam, who traveled from neighboring villages, playing bingo wherever it could be found. Each colony offered a game a week. For some, that was more than enough.

"You'll play these two, Adam, and I'll play the rest."

They took their seats at a long wooden table with an adjoining bench, and set the cards out in front of them.

"Oh, I like these," Rosa said, uncorking a Magic Marker that had a round sponge for a head. "You see, you just push the marker down on the card like this. Watch me, you don't want to mark the wrong number."

A giant cage filled with wooden balls readied itself for the caller's rumbling spin.

"Our first prize is the bagel slicer," the caller said. "To win you got to have an L in any direction." He let go of the crank. The balls came to a crackling halt. He then opened the cage and released the first of the night's numbers.

"B seven!"

"We got one," Adam said, patting the card with his marker, his small face alternately glowing and serious. "We live in bungalow seven—that's why they called it."

Rosa smiled down at her son but remained earnest in her own vigil. As the numbers dropped from the cage, Rosa was busy blotting her card, checking up and down the rows, hands moving methodically like a spirited conductor.

Several games passed and Rosa gathered her fortune: the bagel slicer, the blender, a summer umbrella, a walking cane, a straw hat, two ashtrays—one made into the shape of a flamingo, the other a fish.

Someone in the front row screamed "Fix!" which drew a wave a laughter from the good-natured folk.

"Who is that lady back there?"

"Check her cards! Read me back her numbers again, will yah?"

"Go back to your own bungalow colony, lady!"

Rosa smiled shyly, but paid little mind to their teasings. With each call of the numbers, her eyes—fixed and hypnotic—would light up like the brightest of moons. Adam concentrated on the pageantry of his mother's luck, the lettering on her forearm raced by him, the branded marks blurred in streaks before his eyes.

His attention faltered. A disapproving Rosa leaned over and blotted in a few of the numbers that her son had missed. "Adam, you are not watching. I cannot depend on you." He, meanwhile, checked his cards once more, trying to see if the hand dealt his mother—the one on her forearm—in any way equaled a winning card. Chasing her movements, he grew sleepy. All that kept him awake was the sound of his mother's calming refrain, the lullaby of his summers:

"Bingo!"

"Bingo!"

"Bingo!"

As the night wore on, Adam dropped off to sleep, stretched out over the bench, beside Rosa. A half-eaten hamburger remained at the table. His cards failed him. So did his stamina. "Bingo!" unaccountably soothed his slumber.

Years earlier, just a few months before Morris's death, a five iron glistened in the sun. Artie was lofting golf balls out into the open blue sky. A scuff of grass, burnished on the blade, mixed with the first moisture of the day. The flight of the ball came into view against the tall green trees that surrounded the colony. On the other side of the forest were other crazies, with their own accents.

"Fore!" he yelled.

The refugees didn't have a whole lot of experience with golf in Poland and Russia, so it took a number of summers for them to realize that the avalanche of dimpled white balls—preceded by the number "four"—was not an air raid, just conspicuous recreation.

The other half of the field was occupied by Abe. He was wearing a pair of white tennis shorts and a white undershirt. At first glance, the features of his face seemed to be getting away from him. He had a fleshy nose, prominent ears, and heavy eyelids.

Abe was holding fast to a spool of cord. A kite flew above him, scattering in the wind, looping in the airy currents.

"Get that kite out of here!" Artie yelled. "I'll punch a hole right through it! Fore!"

The launching of a retaliatory golf ball did not deter Abe.

"How much of the field do you need for that stupid game?" he asked.

Artie paused and contemplated just how valuable breathing room was to everyone at Cohen's Summer Cottages. Once imprisoned, they all now longed for space. Before coming to any conclusions on the matter, Adam, wearing blue short pants with matching suspenders and a striped blue polo shirt, circled up to him. He was pedaling a bright red fire engine, and pulling on a string that sounded a bell.

"Hey kid, come here," Artie said, his tanned face taking on a soft and tender glow.

Adam wore a red helmet that was much too large for his head. It tipped over his face like a catcher's mask.

"How's your dad?"

"He's on the porch," he replied, removing the helmet.

Artie strained his eyes and caught sight of Morris sitting on the porch of the bungalow. Artie liked Morris, considered him a real scholar, a refined and decent man, but emotionally tortured—worse even than the rest. Adam's father had survived two camps, fought in the forest as a partisan, almost died of typhus. And now a heart condition, the poor guy. Artie reached for another club—a wood this time, to satisfy his anger— and before sending the ball into fuming orbit, wondered why a man like Morris, who had suffered so much senseless pain, should not be allowed some kind of immunity from ordinary diseases, at least for a while.

"Is he feeling better?"

"Don't know," Adam said. "He can't come down from the porch."

"What do you mean?"

"Doctor said he's got to stay on the porch, or inside the bungalow. Too many steps to go up and down."

"I see . . . Tell him I'll come by and see him later."

"Okay," and with motoring feet, the red fire engine sped away down the walking path.

Adam was the only child at Cohen's Summer Cottages. One generation removed from the awful legacy, he was their uncorrupted hope, the promise of a life unburdened by nightmare and guilt. Such a delicate compromise they were all forced to accept; all so aware of life's cruelest impulses, and yet they so desperately wanted to trust in the possibility of their renewal. But Adam gave them an alarming sense of the future, Everyone feared that something bad might one day happen to him, forcing them to recast all their hopes and dreams, start all over, amend their expectations.

The men of the colony—most of whom wished someday to have children of their own, or mourned the murdered children they left behind—took it upon themselves to act as surrogates for the Posners. The child was born and lived for most of the year in Brooklyn, but the refugees—many of whom lived in Brooklyn as well—committed themselves to year-round sentry duty. Even before Morris's illness, they undertook a shared communal responsibility to raise the boy.

Adam's actual father was never the kind of man well suited for the task, anyway. All the consolidated anguish of his life left him empty, distant, and cold.

Artie played catch with Adam. He even bought him his first baseball glove—a smooth black leather one with gold stitching and a Mickey Mantle signature. They would go out to the field and toss a pink Spalding back and forth. Artie was patient with some of Adam's erratic throws and his insistence on keeping the mitt sealed.

"Adam, open the glove," Artie would say. "You want to catch it, not knock it down!"

Morris watched from the porch, smiling and nodding occasionally—never once defying his doctor's orders. He had seen so much in his life—a great deal unspeakable and unknowable, particularly for those who existed outside the shared nightmare of Cohen's Summer Cottages. And he had come so far—as a boy in Germany; his early manhood in a concentration camp, and now, a withered and fading creature, unrecognizable to himself, spending his summers in the mountains of upstate New York, recuperating from a lifetime of distress.

Artie also taught Adam not to be afraid coming down on the slide.

"Just kick your legs through and slide."

"It's hot. I'll fall!"

"Come on, son, we've all been through worse than this, you can do it."

The bickering between Artie and Abe always came to a halt on account of Adam. On the days when Abe helped Adam build a kite from brown-paper wrapper, Artie refrained from polluting the otherwise buoyant air with lethal golf balls. In the end it didn't matter. Many a fruitless summer day passed without that reconstituted grocery bag ever getting off the ground.

Even Hyman Cohen himself helped out with the boy from time to time.

"Adam, follow me, *kind,* to the shed," he said, limping about. "We should find out the temperature for everybody."

Only five years of age, but Adam already knew the answer. He followed Cohen, and then obligingly emerged to announce: "It's eighty-five degrees!"

The last time anyone saw Morris was when Adam came running home from Krause's Cottages, crying and blowing on his wrist. Adam had been playing ball with the older boys. But they weren't throwing a soft Spalding. Adam must have been confused by the speed of their throws, or the weight of the ball. Artie's lessons didn't prepare him for life outside the colony. The children from the other edge of the forest didn't care about the *lager*, didn't reserve any special compassion for the boy with the sick father. The ball came too fast. Artie's glove didn't work.

The wrist was badly disfigured. A fleshy spike now occupied the place normally reserved for a pulse check. Panting away at the exposed bone, Adam thought only of how one soothes a burn.

"Phew, phew . . ."

He started to run, away from Krause's, in the direction of the rival colony that was his summer home. Dashing underneath the pines, through the woods, stopping every few steps to blow on the broken bone. As he got closer to the colony, he could make out the sight of his father sitting on the white porch, neat rows of picket columns off to each side. A watchtower connected to a bungalow, the only freedom Morris's doctor would allow.

Morris was sitting on an aqua beach chair, a crumpled German newspaper rested on the floorboards below him. He was perpetually on guard, expecting the worst—even here, so close to the otherwise calming influences of Kiamesha Lake. Adam reached the porch with a face filled with tears. Morris forgot all that his doctor had told him about stairs and the dangers of overexcitement. He pushed off the armrests, grabbed the railing, and then, as though he were a vital, solid man, raced down to his son.

"What happened to you, *mein sohn?*" he said, and hugged the boy as he had never done before. Adam held out his wrist—showing his father—staring down at it as though he had just brought home a wounded bird. "Oh, *mein* Gatt—look at you . . ." And then, reflexively, with immediate regret, he let out, "Where can we be safe?"

Adam's lips trembled, and then, steeling himself, said, "Papa, you shouldn't have come down the stairs."

Morris embraced his son again, sobbing uncontrollably into the boy's small chest.

Moments later, a cavalry of refugees rushed to the Posner bungalow. Card games broke up suddenly. Wet laundry soaked in open baskets. A fishing pole lay dropped by the shore. No alarm had sounded, and yet somehow they knew to come. There was an intuitive sense that something was not right at bungalow 7. A people so sensitive to rescue, and the urgency to protect one of their fragile own.

"What happened?" old man Berman said.

"We came as soon as we saw the others start to run," one of the Jaffe brothers said, heaving desperately for air.

"Who is the sick one here?" Mrs. Kaplan wondered aloud. "Adam or Morris?"

Both father and son were taken to the hospital in Monticello, each in need of medical attention.

For weeks Morris lay in the hospital, connected to all sorts of life-sustaining machinery that couldn't possibly begin to heal what really ailed him. Rosa went off each day to Monticello to visit her husband. Adam, with his powdery white cast, was left in the care of one or several of the refugees, who were more than happy to do their part. There were rules at the hospital about not allowing visits by children. And after his experience with blanking out in that cold place—only to awaken with his arm fully recast in plaster—had his own reservations about returning to the hospital as well. He wished to see his father, but only on the porch.

The bus edged up to the curb near the drugstore on Route 17, across the street from the bowling alley, just down the road from Cohen's. Up the other hill was the Concord Hotel. The door to the bus was open, the engine was running; the driver waited patiently for Rosa to get on.

"You be a good boy," Rosa said, brushing Adam's hair to one side. "Don't throw any more balls."

"I don't throw with my left arm."

"Then don't catch any more balls, and don't cause any more trouble."

She boarded, paid the fare, and slipped into the first seat. She then turned to the window to look back at her son. The bus pulled away. The roar and heavy exhaust seemed to smother the small boy. Adam remained behind, waving his heavy wrist.

With each afternoon return from Monticello, Rosa seemed different. She was edgier, more nervous than usual. Gradually she was saying good-bye to her husband—so unceremoniously, the awful finality so unjust. Each day Morris looked as though more of him had surrendered. There would be no going back to the bungalow.

Rosa would return, but never in the same way again. In sympathy with her husband's deterioration, her sanity began to leave her. She was losing her memory, her sense of place, her essential bearings, her grip on reality. Physically she was still strong, but the psychic toll had now become insurmountable—even for someone so seasoned in survival. Morris was leaving and ghosts were arriving. They took over her mind, ambushed her reason.

In what became an almost daily ritual, Rosa would retrieve her son and take him inside bungalow 7. Then the interrogation would begin:

"What did you tell the neighbors today?"

"I didn't tell them anything."

More forcefully. "What did you tell them?"

"Let go of my arm. . . ."

"Did you tell them about the box?"

"What box?"

"And the bullets?"

"What . . . ?"

"You told them about the bread, didn't you?"

"I don't know what you're talking about! . . . Mama, you're scaring me!"

"Tell me what you told them!"

She slapped Adam, who fell against the kitchen cabinet; the door panel slammed shut by the white cast. The crash caused a loud thud.

The child was too young to understand; the parent too mortified to concede the injury—to both of them.

Overwhelmed with grief, fatigue, and persevering nightmare.

⊰⊱

It seemed like all those living near Kiamesha Lake descended on Cohen's Summer Cottages for the annual Labor Day bingo game. It started off as a bright and cloudless day. The temperature was cooling, fall was a few short weeks away. By then all the refugees would be gone, back to their respective boroughs, grateful that they had lived through another summer. Perhaps by next year, their memories of Europe would grow dimmer. But nobody actually believed that.

The bingo game was held outdoors on the grassy field. Long tables were set out. A sound system was installed to announce the numbers. People who had spent their summer traipsing from colony to colony in search of bingo by now felt fully practiced for the final game of the season—the World Series of bingo, the one with the biggest prizes.

"This is exciting," Adam said, slipping beside his mother in the last row, which was right in front of their bungalow.

Rosa was wearing one of her best dresses—a long beige sleeveless gown with a full-pleated bottom, a garment reserved for very special occasions. She was vastly overdressed—it was still summer, during the middle of the day, and hot—but nobody cared to notice. That's because there was so much else that could not be ignored. She had been given to walking around the colony late at night, howling into the woods like an animal. And, of course, there was her uncontrollable fury. Fortunately, the refugees knew to take care of her son on the days when her anger was directed at him.

"All these people," Adam continued.

Nursing his own two cards, Artie, who had become the closest thing that Adam now had to a father, sat next to him.

"I'd love to wallop a golf ball right into the middle of this place—that would get rid of everybody."

"The more people, the larger the pot," Rosa reminded him. She had instincts for these kinds of observations.

"Welcome to our end of the summer bingo tournament," Hyman announced from the podium with bravado. "The grand prize of two hundred dollars goes to the first person who can fill an entire card."

Rosa had waited all summer for this. She had a treasure trove of household trinkets to show for her preparation; now she was all geared up for the actual cash offerings.

"Mama, I have this card, right?" Adam asked.

"Don't bother me, I'm trying to concentrate."

She worked feverishly, tapping away at her cards.

"O twelve," Hyman's voiced screeched into the microphone.

"I six."

"B thirty."

Rosa blotted the appropriate boxes, scouring the rows for the letters and numbers that would win her the title and bounty she so coveted.

Minutes into the game, Artie offered, "I got nothing. Must be a bum card."

"Shsh . . ." Rosa insisted.

They paid no attention to Adam, who was diligently filling in the boxes of his one card. He feared jinxing the outcome, so he kept the card to himself, hoping that neither Rosa nor Artie would notice the streak he was riding.

Some of the players had gotten up to walk around, moving slowly, mingling, drinking soda pop and eating sandwiches. A sharp, cool wind brushed over the colony, and a faint crackle of thunder echoed in the distance. Birds scattered from trees.

Adam slowly filled in the open spaces of his card—one at a time—as though he were working on a coloring book. Many of the other contestants appeared bored, tapping their fingers, waiting anxiously for a matching bingo ball to drop. Adam never noticed the collective frustration, or even the disappointment on his own mother's face, so uncharacteristic an expression for her to have while caught up in a game of chance.

All but one number had been filled on his card when the rains came. The afternoon summer shower drenched everything. Fortunately the bingo balls, made of wood, could float. As for the cards, streaks of Magic Marker smudged them beyond recognition, making them all indistinguishable. Cohen's Summer Cottages had been transformed into a finger-painting festival.

"This is the best my card is going to look," Artie said. "We should go inside."

"No!" Adam yelled.

"It's raining," Rosa said defeatedly. "We should go in. The game is over." Arms reaching toward the sobbing heavens, "What is wrong with my life! What did I do to deserve all this?"

"I have one number to go!" Adam screamed.

"Come . . ." Artie said.

The rain fell harder. All who had gathered for the afternoon now ran for the cover of the forest, or huddled under the roof of a bungalow, trying to outlast the downpour. Adam remained seated, alone on the bench. He stared at his solitary card, trying to shield it from fading, preserving the record of his unrealized triumph. Deprived of victory at his mother's favorite summer game.

$$\sim\!\!\mathcal{S}\,\mathcal{R}\!\!\sim$$

"Bingo!"

"Bingo!"

"Bingo!"

A man with a thick, silver-speckled beard cried out for his prize, but no one responded.

It was fall in Sullivan County. Brown, red, and purple leaves looked vivid but fragile, about to surrender to the inescapable gravity that comes with autumn. Cohen's Summer Cottages were empty. Not at all unusual for that time of year. Not a living soul ever stayed at the colony past Labor Day. The place looked entirely different, but it wasn't the change in season that made it so.

It had been sold years before—the new name was not really important. The sign at the foot of the road had been replaced by something that had neither the wit, nor historical gumption, of LEISURE MACHT FREI.

He toured the barren grounds. The walking path was overrun with wild weeds and moss, the kind of unkempt, tangled growth that once colonized the former owner's eyebrows. The visitor surveyed the green field. He looked in the direction of the shed, and found nothing. When he got tired, he rested his back against the sinuous spine of that same weeping willow. It was still standing. The swings were gone, as was the slide. The ground was strangely moist, as though the earth had wept, or had never quite gotten used to the change in the landscape.

Looking back toward the bungalow—his old bungalow, 7—he watched as his son stood on an overturned pail. The boy needed a lift to see inside.

"Hey Mory, what are you doing? You'll fall down and hurt yourself! You might break your arm!"

The porch had been dismantled. The entrance was now supported by stilts. Plants uprooted. The entire place had been unearthed, barren, stripped of the emblems that once made it so familiar.

Slowly, Adam walked over to where his son was peering into the kitchen window, hands cupped along the side of his face like blinders.

"You see anything?"

"Not really. Just some old furniture moved up against the wall."

Adam took out his camera and snapped a picture of the boy on the pail. There was a sheriffs warning posted on the door.

AUTHORIZED PERSONS ONLY

"'Authorized'?" Adam wondered. "If not me, who's allowed in then?"

But without the porch, how could you even enter? And once inside, what could you expect to find?

The camera clicked; he took a picture of the front door with the sheriff's sign on it. Ghosts, however, cannot be photographed. Those who he remembered would not sit still for a group picture. Only the sign would survive the eventual processing.

The colony had been transformed into a ghost town, which it had already been in a different way so many years before.

Mory turned around and jumped off the pail. Grabbing his father's hand, he ran off into the lifeless field, leaves crackling underneath each heavy step.

"So this was the place?"

"Sure is."

Looking up at the sky, hoping to pick up the sight of a brown paper kite, or a falling golf ball—some marking, something to pinch the senses and tweak the memories.

Some indication that the boy in the cast had once actually lived there.

"What are you looking for?"

"I don't know."

But he did.

"One number away from the jackpot, huh?"

"Yes. Never got the chance. Game called on account of rain."

"Bummer. Where's Krause's?"

"Over there . . ."

Renewal

Thane Rosenbaum

No two words have ever had less of a right to appear in the same sentence as Holocaust renewal. The first word has become a synonym for the crime of the twentieth century, Jews having earned the ignominious distinction of hitting the jackpot of all genocides ever to plague the earth. The second word is normally associated with the feel-good sensation of a full body massage, a Bikram yoga class, or the spiritual awakening from a Christian tent revival meeting.

Holocaust renewal, stand-ins for mass murder and human transformation, clang up against one another like atonal instruments played by first-timers. Deafening even for the deaf. Clashing colors too disturbing even for the color blind. Together these words have the kind of squirm-producing cognitive dissonance of ill matched opposites, a paradox of word play, impossible to imagine, equally difficult to even say.

Of course, this may have something to do with the fact that at least one of the words is a mouthful no matter what the circumstance. The Holocaust is both a conversation killer as well as a conversation that can never truly end. A mere three syllables, and yet it pulverizes with those hard vowels and consonants that, not surprisingly, sound accosting.

The Holocaust is always the largest elephant in the room—no matter the size of the room; no matter whether there are actual elephants in the room. As a catastrophe it simply expands to fit the occasion, crowding everything else out. There is the sheer fascination with its lurid mystery, its ambitious finality, its godless implications, and the general obscenity of all those naked unburied bodies—that orgy of the Jewish dead—that makes the Holocaust the most improper of all nouns.

From the Greek it means to burn in whole, which accounts for all the ovens and the ash. But it also raises the question of what could have been expected to arise out of those ashes? Surely life itself was impossible. A scorched earth means just that: life is over. Scorched European Jewry would be equally un-replenishable, for sure. With all that ash and ember, could anything ever be renewed again? Two out of three Jews of Europe had been consumed by fire. It would be too cruel to impose a burden on the remaining one-third not only to survive, but to renew and rejuvenate Judaism, as well. Judaism has nothing that mirrors the mythology of the Greek Phoenix, rising from its own ashes, reinvented and stronger still. Reanimating the dead is for sorcerers, not Jews. Even the *golem* started out as mud.

Out of that calamity would come a consolation prize, bizarre as that may sound. The aftermath of Auschwitz left the world with all that mass death and the reality of an even more grotesque mass indifference. The world could reduce its guilt, however, and the Jewish Diaspora could minimize its shame and shore up its ranks, if the renewal of the Jewish people was possible, and especially if Holocaust survivors could lead the way. The evolution of the human species makes us all sensitive to the possibilities for extinction. And Jewish life came very close—indeed, that was the endgame of the Final Solution, interrupted before the Nazis finished the job. We have all heard the battle cries to Save the Whales and the Rain Forest. The clarion call to Save the Jews was always more subtle, less loudly proclaimed, and largely less triumphant.

These were the sentiments behind those who rooted for the creation of the State of Israel. There is, admittedly, a declining audience for those who share those feelings today, what with the moral hypocrisy of a world that singles out Israel for an assortment of sins for which true rogue nations are routinely given a pass. But there was a time—arguably a brief time in world history—when Israel was everyone's favorite underdog and Cinderella story, regarded as that tiny nation with spunk and grit. The Jewish people, no matter where they lived, motivated by their own sense of survival, and as a way to honor the dead, were encouraged to make up for all that was lost during the genocidal sideshow of World War II. After all, a people nearly exterminated did not have the luxury of having preventative sex.

And so the unthinkable happened. The Jewish people actually started over. They rewrote the Book of Genesis, this one manmade, without the patriarchs and the floods, and where the Tree of Knowledge produced not alluring apples but newly minted PhDs. They now even had their own country with sunburned sabras carrying rakes in one hand and grenades in the other, an Uzi machine gun slung over their shoulders as day jobs alternated between defending and farming the nation. They revived a dead language, one that had nothing but liturgical value for 2,000 years. Suddenly you could hear it spoken rather than chanted in falafel shops and discos from Haifa to Tel Aviv.

But the one birth rate that the Jewish world watched most closely and that somehow mattered most was the baby count that belonged to Holocaust survivors. Those with numbers on their arms, oddly enough and against all odds, were now being asked, politely and gently, to increase the number of Jews in the world. Surely if they could somehow rejoin the world of the living the Nazis could not claim an ultimate victory. The Third Reich's scoreboard worked perversely, as one would have expected. In the *Judenrein* contest, they awarded points by subtraction. As long as there were Jews left in the world the game was, theoretically, still in play. In this showdown of absolute numbers the Nazis surely could not be defeated—six million is both a symbolic and a largely insurmountable number. But if those wretched refugees who had already dug themselves out from under all those corpses managed to choose life, and would be inclined or could be convinced to give life, then at least world Jewry could call it a draw.

And so the survivors—absurdly, improbably, instinctively—took the bait. They married—often one another. They had children—healthy ones, but not completely undamaged by a catastrophe they had never actually witnessed firsthand. They joined synagogues and returned to God—but not without bitterness, or a sense of unfinished business with the Almighty. They belonged to AAA and to the PTA—but not because they believed that such memberships could keep them safe on the road or protect their children from harm. Their own parents had joined similar fraternal associations back in Europe and look where that got them. And yet they purchased homes and took out insurance policies and anchored themselves to communities, driving around in station wagons and making pit stops at the local Dairy Queen—just a short surreal decade after Auschwitz.

Neighbors in those days—even Jewish ones, especially Jewish ones—didn't actually wish to know what had happened in those concentration camps. This was not the kind of neutral topic normally shared among polite company. There was nothing polite about it. It was completely unsuitable—for everything. And for their part the survivors didn't particularly wish to share their horrific stories, and surely not with mere strangers—even friendly ones—people who could never truly comprehend what they were being told. It wasn't their fault, after all. How could they understand an event that historians, theologians, and social commentators had already deemed to be unimaginable, ineffable, and unspeakable? Given the natural mental block and glazed eyes of the audience, why speak at all? Why should the survivors put themselves through the daily hell of having to recount their nightly dreams? It was bad enough that they couldn't sleep. Why compound the problem by recalling throughout the day the nightmares that were keeping them up at night? Merely crossing an ocean would not be enough to shake these memories loose. They attached themselves to the survivors like algae and journeyed over to such deceptively placid sounding places like Great Neck, Shaker Heights, the Fairfax district, and, of course, Miami Beach.

Besides, not only wouldn't anyone be able to understand, they wouldn't believe, which would make it all somehow even worse. Perhaps that's why the American relatives and the neighbors didn't want to hear it in the first place. It would be better to ignore the survivors than to kill the messengers. After all, they had only recently crawled back from the dead. They would have to be given some immunity from further death—at least for a short while. In the meantime, the awful truths learned in the death camps and inside the squalid ghettos were not welcome at the dinner tables or the card games, and certainly not in front of the children.

If these refugees spoke, if they casually revealed the true inhuman face of humanity, wouldn't that belie everyone's wish that it was possible for these survivors to start over? How could anyone begin again after something like that? It was already a miracle that these refugees gathered their wits, mustered the courage, and felt secure enough to eat ice cream at Dairy Queen. Now we had audacity, the Jewish *chutzpah* to insist that they convince us that after everything they had witnessed— all that moral failure and mass murder—life wasn't hopeless after all, there were things worth living for, that in the end, good always prevails over the bad.

Actually, it was all simply wish fulfillment—nor theirs, but ours. Maybe the survivors never had to start over. But we did. Perhaps they did it for us all along. Humanity couldn't possibly go on and move forward unless they promised to follow along and act normal. The goal was simply to put a smile on their faces, even if it was just to make us happy.

And, yet, it was surely more than that. Many of the survivors did find happiness—for themselves. Yes, they were traumatized, but not without hope that some future awaited them, a future they might not be able to control but at least a future they could believe in.

The best proof that Holocaust survivors ultimately decided to choose life can be found in the way so many of them chose to spend their summers. Instead of tolerating the sweltering, relentless heat of the cities and suburbs, many survivors retreated to Sullivan and Ulster County, New York, the "country" as it was known, a mere seventy-five miles northwest from New York City. Like so many immigrant inner city Jews in the late 1940s through the 1960s, the refugees of the Holocaust sought refuge in the hamlets and villages that were nestled within the Catskill Mountains.

The air was cooler and, of course, cleaner. The mornings were crisp with early frost as the slippery dew clung to uncut grass. There were wide lakes and rickety rowboats. Dirt country roads led to bungalow colonies in such far-flung places as Swan Lake, Liberty and Livingston Manor, Monticello and South Fallsburg. There were farms with fresh eggs and wild patches of blueberry bushes. There was a bowling alley right on Route 17 down the road from The Concord Hotel. Borscht Belt comics took batting practice in hotels filled with Jewish audiences who were willing to laugh at anything. That's right: to go along with the card games, canasta, and mah-jongg, and the many other summer diversions, there was also laughter.

But what could Holocaust survivors possibly find so funny? How bizarre it all must have seemed. Just a few years earlier they were told that their resettlement from the cities of Europe to the ghettos of Poland was necessary in order to achieve *Lebensraum* for the German people. And yet here, so far away from the Jewish ghettos of Warsaw and Lublin, Krakow and Kovno, Radom and Lodz, and without any true complaints of their own, they were now feeding their own indulgences for more breathing room and open space. It wasn't a land grab; they paid for their bungalows in cash. But they were insisting on more—more food, more space, landscapes that were mountainous and vistas of open skies, and yes, more laughter, too.

I spent summers among these people, but I didn't exactly know it. My parents were Holocaust survivors—concentration camp survivors both. During the school year for most of my childhood we lived in Washington Heights, in the northern end of Manhattan. It was all congested and dirty and, oddly enough, given the already thick Teutonic shadow that hovered over the world like a modern day Hindenburg filled with the hot air of the Master Race, Washington Heights was an enclave populated by many German Jews who spoke German and felt German and couldn't do anything to rid themselves of their Germanic stigma, not that they much wanted to anyway.

But we summered in the Catskills where Yiddish was the preferred language and pinochle the preferred game. For eight straight years we rented a bungalow in Kiamesha Lake. And even though I was only a small boy, I knew that my parents were different from the other Jews who were our neighbors at the colony. Yes, they were also Jews. And, yes, many were born in Europe. But none of them were refugees from the Jewish dead of World War II. My parents stood out, for all the reasons that the dead would normally call attention to themselves among the living.

It actually never dawned on me that my parents were not alone in the Catskills, that other refugees were spending their summers the very same way and doing the very same things. My parents never spoke of their experiences in the Holocaust, and they didn't have many friends among the survivor community. I somehow naively thought that my parents, of all the people among those who had escaped from Hitler's killing machine, had taken the brave step of plunging into the frolic and frivolity of other happy Jewish campers—in a very different kind of camp, surrounded by people who had no knowledge that other camps, those devoted to death, existed at all. I wouldn't have guessed that other survivors lived in neighboring bungalow colonies. And I would have never imagined that there were actually hotels and bungalow colonies that catered exclusively, and especially welcomed, the refugees of the fallen Europe.

And that's why, nearly three decades later, I had to actually imagine it. I published a novel-in-stories entitled, *Elijah Visible*, the tales of Adam Posner, a child of Holocaust survivors who learns the lessons of the Nazis by proxy—simply by being raised by two of their tragic victims. Each story is set in a different location, and the names of Adam's parents change with each tale, and so do their circumstances, but the one immutable plot line that serves as the spine of the book is that each of the Adams live with the unspoken knowledge that he is the first man born into this new post-Auschwitz world, and he doesn't like what he sees. In this fractured post-Holocaust world, the Prophet Elijah finally becomes visible, and yet there is still no messianic return or deliverance.

One of the stories, "Bingo by the Bungalow," is set in Sullivan County. And Adam, unlike his creator (not that creator but rather the novelist), does live among Holocaust survivors in his summer bungalow colony. In fact, the entire colony is comprised of Jewish refugees, and Adam has the unfortunate responsibility of being the only child among them. All that collective fear and tag-team smothering is, understandably, projected onto him. And as both a coda and as temporary relief from all the crushing pains and memories that this colony is forced to endure, they are rewarded each summer with an annual and strangely lucrative Labor Day bingo game. Yes, bingo as a psychic balm, with all those random numbers that match the ones on their arms, and those wooden balls indiscriminately let out from their cage, which wasn't that much unlike how the survivors themselves managed, miraculously, to make it all the way to the Catskills on a transport that was originally bound for Auschwitz and Treblinka.

Ironically, at the time I didn't know there were such places. I somehow imagined that my parents were pioneers in the fledgling and still improbable enterprise of Holocaust renewal. Who knew that there was such an establishment as the Four Seasons Lodge, and that it was filled with Holocaust survivors, and that they kept coming back, summer after summer, even after all the American born Jews had already left— for good? I thought I had invented it, that it could have only been imagined by a novelist or a magician, that nobody would really have believed it anyway. Holocaust survivors and their bingo games, trying to act like normal people? What are the odds of that?

Much better than you'd think. The biggest miracle of the Holocaust was not that there were survivors—although that alone makes the Jewish highlight reel along with the parting of the Red Sea and Mt. Sinai's burning bush. Greater still in the universe of the absurd is not just that they survived, but that so many—most actually—threw in their lot with the rest of humanity. You could almost hear them say: "Deal me back in. Given what I just escaped, I like my odds in any other game I'm allowed to play."

Holocaust renewal certainly sounds like a misnomer, but it actually comes with its own truth, follows its own logic, and possesses its own special poetry. The survivors surely know what these words mean. They merely have to wink at each other and the message is sent, a Yiddish-accented Morse Code among the Catskills set: "We're alive. Nobody gave us a chance, and nobody lent a hand. And here we are. You want to go for a swim?"

A Catskills Muse

Phil Brown

Between meals, Paul, the new busboy mostly stayed in his room writing short stories that he believed reflected a mixture of Isaac Bashevis Singer, Gabriel Garcia Marquez, and Jorge Luis Borges. Since those literary role models used three names, so did Paul—he always signed his work Paul Alexander Feldman. A string of successes in the high school literary magazine brought Paul to Brooklyn College with a strong faith that he could conquer the college literature journal and then move on to professional publications. In his sophomore year he had already published one piece in Brooklyn College's magazine, and the summer promised an atmosphere ripe for material. Paul's father had a friend who often stayed at a South Fallsburg hotel, and that connection got Paul the job. The Eastern European accents, joining with various New York dialects, offered endless possibilities for brisk dialogue. The hustling, bargaining, and frenetic pace of hotel life provided easy access to subplots, intrigues, and outrageous situations. What more could he ask for?

"Hey, Paul, how about some basketball?" asked Bill, the main organizer of staff pick-up games and Bill's roommate. The court adjoined the pool, and the staff games attracted some guest attention. Lots of the waiters and busboys liked this opportunity to parade their skills to the teenage daughters of the New Valley Lodge's clientele.

"Sorry, Bill, I'm writing."

"You're always writing! Don't you want to get some excitement between lunch and dinner?"

"This is excitement to me. I love writing in the room after everyone changes for swimming or whatever. The whole staff house gets quiet, and I hear only the muted sounds from down below."

Paul was in no way an airhead. Nor was he a pasty-faced writer, nor an unattractive young man. Indeed, Paul had a good assortment of friends, dated a lot, and played basketball and softball as well as any typical Jewish kid from Flatbush. But he loved to write, and that was his passion for now. The fellows respected that passion by and large, and their teasing was no more extreme than any other hotel staff *kibbitzing*.

"Paul, you don't want to get flabby. The girls'll be uninterested in you if all you pick up is a pen."

"Come on, you don't think lugging busboxes all day builds you up? I get in better shape here in the summer than any time. I'll play ball in a couple of days, after I get this story line a little more solid."

"You guy, stuck in the books. Listen, that new girl at table twelve is going to be right by the court. Her family got a couple of chaises on that side of the pool. Everyone wants to get her to give a look."

"I know. My station's right next to her table, so I'll get a chance. I might slip her an extra dessert from my waiter's tray."

"She can get all the dessert she wants. She's a guest."

"Yeah, but Manny's her waiter, and by the time that slowpoke serves dessert, the rest of the dining room will be empty and the waiters will be setting up for breakfast."

"Well, you might be right about that. Anyway, I'm off to play. Hope you get your story going. See you later."

The door shut, and Paul easily made the transition to his current story. He didn't mind the bantering and friendly harranging. He very much liked working at New Valley, and the jibing just provided new material for his fiction.

Abe Schwartz, the social director, flapped his arms at the dining room entranceway about fifteen minutes into lunch.

"Hubba, hubba, hubba!" Abe yelled, his signature attention-getter and filler chat that accompanied his arm flapping. "In two days it's Thursday, and you know what that means. Talent Night at New Valley Lodge. It's the time when our dear little community gets to see the future stars, the soon-to-be has-beens, and the grandparents' great *mechias*. I want lots of volunteers for this great event. We're doing auditions at three o'clock in the Playhouse. Who's going to provide the marvelous talent for this week?"

"Yeah, it's great talent because Mrs. Greenwald doesn't have to book an act. It's a no-cost show," yelled a guest at a nearby table.

"You sir, for that comment, will be the first act. Tell me what talent you have," retorted Abe.

"Me, my talent is telling it like it is. But I'm not going on any stage."

"OK, you are the one and only exception. Next person opens their mouth gets star billing in the New Valley Playhouse. I might even call in the booking agent to look you over." Abe glanced toward Jack, the maître d'. "Oh, oh, Mister Jack is looking my way. I better get out of the aisle before the waiters spill soup on me. Better they should spill it on the guests." Abe did a back-and-forth shuffle, spun around, and followed up with a Charlie Chaplin walk. "I'm back to my table for lunch. I want bodies in the Playhouse at three. Hubba, hubba, hubba." Abe flapped his way back to the staff table to join the head counselor, the band, the book-keeper, and the lifeguard.

From his sidestand, where he was stacking dirty soup bowls and underliners in the busbox, Paul took in Abe's challenge. He would read his latest story this coming Talent Night. It would push him to finish it early, and he thought the audience response would be very useful. He had never read a story out loud before, and this excited him no end.

⤙ ⤚

When the last guest left his station, Paul saw that Abe was still lingering over coffee, while prepping the band on the kind of music they should do that night for Champagne Hour. Loosening his shirt button and letting his bowtie hang on one side of his collar, Paul walked over and pulled up a chair backwards, sitting with his arms resting on the rounded top of the brown wood.

"Mr. Schwartz, I'd like to volunteer for Thursday night."

"Ah, a new busboy, perhaps hired for his extra talent at Verdi arias. What will you offer us?"

"I will read my newest story, '*Shtetl* in South Fallsburg.'"

"What! Read a story! And such a name for a story! We need singers, comics, dancers, musicians, maybe dramatic actors doing Yiddish knockoffs of Shakespeare scenes. But in all my years here we never had someone get up and just read a story, especially a busboy who wrote it. When did you write this story, between soup and appetizers?" Abe could never slip out of the tummler mode, but it didn't bother anyone. The whole hotel expected this kind of banter.

"I did write it between meals, and it's a good story. It's about a hotel very much like this."

"Hoo, boy! Juicy stuff, then, *shtup* and go traffic in the woods?"

"Well, I don't know about that. But there's lots of good dialogue, and you won't really recognize people; I've disguised them a lot, done composites, included snippets from other hotels. Mr. Schwartz, I really think the guests will enjoy this."

"Listen, my boy, I have been a social macher in the Mountains for years, and in this dear hotel for nearly ten of them. Catskills guests do not like to listen to people reading books and stories to them."

"Mr. Schwartz, they did listen. At places like Maud's Summer-Ray and Chaits and Chesters, at a lot of places. Years ago, I. B. Singer himself read aloud after dinner, at Green Fields just a few miles down the road. It was a big part of the whole Catskills scene."

"OK, sonny, what's your name?"

"Paul."

"Paul; call me Abe. We'll try it. Worse comes to worse, Mrs. Greenwald yells at me and fires you. Maybe your guests cut your tip in half. But you're persuasive. We'll try it. Just don't make it too long."

"Thanks, Abe. I'll do a great job. Thanks a lot." Paul returned to his station to clear the dishes, and as he did so, the girl at table twelve passed him, looking delicious in her white shorts and forest green shirt, brown hair bouncing with her lively step. Sure enough, Manny had gotten so behind that day that his guests were the last ones left in the dining room. Paul gave a smile, and said hi, and she said hi back as she continued past him.

After the setting up for dinner was done, Paul began to get nervous about the reading. Would he really be doing something that the guests wouldn't appreciate? Was Abe's sarcastic tummling the highest degree of culture that prevailed in this setting? At any rate, Paul didn't have the story finished, and it would be hard to carry on at rehearsal. He would just have to say a few words about the theme, run through some of the characters, and promise a final product in a few days.

Instead of exiting through the kitchen, Paul walked into the lobby, which Mrs. Greenwald didn't like. The girl was sitting alone on a chair near the picture window to the left of the main entrance. Paul remembered the friendly hi, and was amazed that some of his co-workers had not yet found her there. As he was about to walk up to her, Mrs. Greenwald appeared out of nowhere, her specialty.

"Paul, I know this is your first year here, but remember what I told you about coming into the lobby in your work clothes. You need to go out though the kitchen."

He had no choice, but he shot a quick glance toward the girl and hoped she caught it. Out the back door and up the hill to the staff quarters, Paul couldn't take his mind off the girl, even as he was still nervous about the Talent Night rehearsal. He changed into shorts and a t-shirt, grabbed his notebook with the story in progress, and found a quiet lawn chair under a maple tree along the front driveway. That would provide a pleasant location to polish up some flaws in the story. Soon he was lost in the pages, oblivious to the hotel murmurings around him.

"You're so busy writing. You must be working hard on something."

Paul looked up to see the girl standing in front of him. "That's usually the kind of line we guys come up with." He was surprised to hear himself say this, but she didn't flinch.

"Well, that's probably true, but I wasn't trying to pick you up. I saw you writing in a notebook and figured it wasn't a letter, and maybe you were a writer. I say that because I write, and I use those kind of spiral notebooks too."

"You're kidding? I thought that was my own quirky thing."

"No, all us writers are in the same boat." She looked toward Paul's notebook and asked, "What are you working on?"

"I'll tell you, but first, I'm Paul Feldman. Who are you?"

"Janet Lemberg. Glad to meet you."

"Well, Janet, this is a story I am going to read Thursday night at the Talent Show. It's the thing that the MC was yelling about at lunch. Will you come to it?"

"I'm sure I will, especially if you tell me what the story is about."

"In truth," Paul replied, "I don't want to give away the whole element of surprise. I'd rather you hear it on stage the first time, but I'll give you some general ideas. It's called 'Shtetl in South Fallsburg,' and it's about a group of guests at a South Fallsburg hotel—five or six families. They just have this sort of magical friendship—hanging around together, helping each other out with the little things in life like driving kids into town, sharing problems and hopes. But mainly, it's about how they stay in contact when they get home after Labor Day. They keep in touch over decades, and figure in each other's lives in many ways. So, the whole idea is that they are recreating a Jewish community like in the old country."

"I really like the concept, Paul," Janet said. "I definitely will be there Thursday."

"How about tonight? I can't wait till Thursday. Will you join me for a soda after I finish dinner."

"I'd like that. Where should I meet you?"

"Outside the front entrance. The boss tries to keep us out of the lobby."

"I know. I saw her chase you away before."

Paul got a little flustered, but managed to get out, "I was hoping you'd see me. I really wanted to meet you. Listen, you didn't tell me what kind of things you write."

"Now, I'm mainly working on science fiction. But sometimes I write comedy travel logs about trips through Brooklyn. I did this one piece on the ailanthus trees along the Franklin Avenue Shuttle."

"Have you got anything published yet?"

"I did get a sci-fi piece in a small fanzine. I even got $50 for it. Made me feel like a pro in the making."

"Congratulations," Paul said. "I've only made the college lit mag, and they sure as hell don't pay anything. I'm hoping to get lots of material this summer, and come out of it with at least two or three stories that I can send around. Did you bring any of your work with you?"

"I did. I'll bring it tonight after dinner, though the coffee shop may not be the easiest place to read, with the dim light and the noise."

Listening to that, Paul had fantasies about bringing her back to his room where, he would tell her, it would be quiet. But as he began to run those thoughts through his head, one of the band members passed by and yelled, "Hey, Paul, it's almost time for rehearsal." Paul told Janet he was sorry to run off but was looking forward to seeing her later.

Paul couldn't tell if he was more excited at getting a date with the girl everyone was looking at, or at meeting a girl who shared his writing fervor. It didn't matter which, he told himself, it's just going to be wonderful. If only he didn't get too nervous and drop a busbox while rushing to finish quicker than usual. Paul thought he would ask Dan, his waiter, if he, Dan, would bring out his set-up plates himself, and clean the sidestand. That would save ten minutes or more.

❦

At the rehearsal, people were not overly excited by the idea of a story reading, but they were polite enough, since their own acts were not necessarily going to be very professional. Paul listened to three singers, covering the range from Peter, Paul, and Mary songs to "Sunrise, Sunset" to a medley of Broadway show tunes. He heard a guest do a Myron Cohen routine, and another act with two teenage brothers recreating a Marx Brothers *shtick*. A waiter sat at the piano and ran through a jazz tune he worked out from listening to Brubeck records. That was six other performances, and Paul worried that he would be given too little time. Worse, the show could go on too long, and he'd be at the end when everybody was drifting out. Paul was last to go on, and he only read a couple of pages to show the tone he would take. Abe, the social director, cautioned him that he had only fifteen minutes, and to make sure not to run over. As expected, Paul would go last.

Abe clapped his hands over his head. "Well, everybody, this was great! We are going to give them some show on Thursday. Dress up like a real act would. If you want to borrow some costumes, I've got a trunk full of things. Everyone be sure to be behind the stage by 8:30, and we'll start at 9 after the band plays a few numbers for dancing."

Alan, the waiter who played jazz piano, glanced at Paul and said, "We better get dressed in a hurry. It's time to get to the dining room." Was it possible that so much time had passed in such a short while—first the conversation with the most attractive looking young woman he'd seen at the hotel that season, then the rehearsal. Paul joined Alan to trot up the hill to quickly take the second shave of the day, a firm request of Mrs. Greenwald, transmitted through Jack, the maître d'.

Dinner was smooth, though not perfect. Dan speculated poorly on soup, and Paul was forced to make an extra run into the kitchen to beg a couple of cups of vegetable soup and plain consommé. Then Dan was short two chicken fricassee appetizers, requiring Paul to go back to sneak two off the counter. Both extra runs caused the dirty dishes on the table to pile up. The maître d' noticed this, and gave him a little nudge. By mains, the meal shaped up quite nicely. Dan got on the main line very early, and nobody returned steaks for "more fire." Very few requests for seconds were made, and there were no special orders to fill. Paul got to the urns quickly to fill the round silver coffee and hot water pots, before the urns ran out and more coffee would have to be made. He offered to help serve the desserts, since Dan was going to let him out early. This was against policy, but both hoped that the maître d' would not notice. Mrs. Greenwald, they knew, was in the office, dealing with some problem the room clerk had fetched her about in the middle of the meal.

Paul was amazed how great it felt to leave the dining room while every other waiter and busboy was still working. Dan had done him a great favor by helping him get out to meet Janet. Running at full speed up the hill, Paul hummed happily all the way through his shower. He got back to the outside of the main lobby only fifteen minutes after he left the dining room, dressed in clean tan chinos and a short-sleeved chambray shirt. Janet was sitting on the concrete ledge alongside the stairway, reading a paperback. She looked luscious in a casual yellow dress with pleats, a string of dark beads around her neck. Next to her was a small book bag with her notebooks. Janet looked up and asked, "How did you get out so early? Some guests are still inside eating."

"My waiter was a good guy and let me out early. Waiters aren't always terrible to their busboys. I'm surprised you're here already. Your waiter is always late with every course."

"I skipped out on dessert. There was plenty to eat already. Well, I've got my stuff to show you. But first tell me how rehearsal went."

They walked toward the coffee shop, and Paul filled Janet in on the rehearsal, adding his fear of reading to an emptying house.

"I know you think this is too easy to say, but, don't worry. I can hear the passion you have for this story. I know you can convey that to them. I'll pass the word to my parents' friends to make sure to stay. Once you start, you can keep the audience going."

"Thanks for your confidence. But you hardly know me, and I haven't even shown you the story."

"I know that, but I can tell you have something special. And you will be telling them about their own lives, about the hotels they've gone to for years. It's going to be unlike other things they see at the Playhouse."

"Only another writer could tell me all this."

"Maybe."

They walked into the coffee shop, side by side with the Playhouse. Some young adolescents were enmeshed in the pinball machines, the jukebox blared its usual favorite selections, and a few staff members sat around having snacks. The off-duty bellhops always hung out there, playing endless gin games for money. The lifeguard often watched, preferring to save his money rather than gamble it. Behind the counter, Mike rested with both hands on the seltzer and water spigots that rose like chrome swans over the soda fountain. His fresh apron awaited an active evening of dishing out egg creams, ice cream sodas, sundaes, bagels, and coffee.

"Here, let's sit here," Paul said to Janet, as they grabbed a table away from the others. "What can I get you?"

"An egg cream would be great. Thanks."

Paul walked up to the counter. "Hey, Mike. A couple of egg creams, please. Put it on my bill."

"Boy, you got here early. How'd you do that?"

"Just hustling. I'm a fast busboy these days."

"You're not kidding," Mike replied, looking toward Janet.

He busied himself with making the egg creams. Mike's special touch was keeping milk containers in the ice cream freezer, wrapped in a towel. The freezer kept the milk nicely chilled but the towel prevented it from freezing; it made for the coldest and creamiest milk shakes, malteds, ice cream sodas, and egg creams anywhere. Mike worked the seltzer tap like a delicate mechanic, titrating the flow and angle of the carbonated water to get the maximum froth on the egg cream, rarely spilling any over the edge of the flared glass. He pushed them across the counter to Paul.

"Enjoy."

"Thanks, Mike."

Placing the egg creams on the table, Paul said, "A writer's best thinking food."

"Looks great," Janet said. "I always love these." She took one delicate sip of the foam, then tilted the glass to get to the liquid. "Wonderful. I love it. So, here is my latest sci-fi piece, a very short thing I am hoping to get brave enough to send to Isaac Asimov's Magazine."

Paul busied himself reading the typescript. It was the story of a janitor in his mid twenties, working in the NASA launch site. The janitor loved the whole aura of the place, and felt that his little task there was a significant part of the space program. He had begun to engage the scientists about their plans for a moon landing, and despite his lack of any college, he somehow seemed to understand their equations for getting the craft into orbit. After a touchy launch incident, where astronauts dangerously lost power, the janitor ran to one of the consoles, pushed away a NASA specialist, and rapidly reprogrammed the launch rocket's trajectory. The chief scientist, NASA brass, and senior technicians were amazed at the brashness of this act, and were floored that it worked. When they stopped talking about it to each other, they looked for the janitor, but he was gone. All day they searched for him, without success. As the days went by, people began to forget that there ever was a janitor who performed the rescue effort. In a few weeks, no one even recalled the nature of the original problem. The space mission crew, however, found an additional member of their entourage who simply appeared. Somehow they knew he was responsible for the mission's rescue, and they never told anyone about his presence. During the flight, he was extremely helpful in various tricky situations. When they landed, the janitor was long gone.

"This is a great story. They'll love it at the magazine. I'm not going to push the symbolism, but there clearly is a link to me in this story. I mean, the new guy in the show, calling the shots."

"You're perceptive, Paul. That's why I have faith in your reading this coming Thursday."

"Janet, did you just write this, or did you bring it with you from the City?"

"I'll make you a deal. I won't tell you now, any more than you'll read your story to me before Thursday. But I'll make sure you know Thursday night after the show."

They got off that topic, and refreshed with more egg creams, they rambled for a long time about their writing styles and habits, their parents' responses to their writing, their dissatisfaction with their college writing courses where they got no special encouragement. Janet's parents, unlike Paul's, were very down on her writing. They worried that she shirked her freshman year's courses, that she stayed home too much writing, and that she was preparing herself for a life of poverty.

Between meals and after dinner, Paul and Janet were together constantly the next two days. Initially afraid of losing time to finish his story, Paul found that he was piecing together the final parts while engaged in discussion with her about style, character, and Yiddish expressions. Late at night they lay on a chaise by the darkened pool, kissing and hugging. Paul had no idea where the writers' collegiality ended and the romance started, but it felt absolutely thrilling to him. His mind raced along with his heart, ideas and emotions churning into exciting mixes that would go into his story and that reverberated between the two of them.

⟶ð℈⟵

Finally, Thursday night came. Paul rushed through his table clearing, bringing out the dishes, and washing the silverware. He pawned off his side job of linen sorting, agreeing to take another busboy's place at it later in the week. Leaving his station, Paul slowed at Janet's table, where she stroked his arm and whispered, "Break a leg. I know it's going to be great."

"Thanks, Janet," he replied. "I'll be looking for you in the crowd."

Paul darted up the hill to the staff house, took a quick shower, and put on his good black dress pants, a fresh white shirt, and a necktie. He got backstage only a few minutes after the 8:30 curtain call, nervous, but full of confidence from Janet. Despite his earlier reluctance to let her see the story, Janet had come to help shape it, and she now knew it as well as he did.

Nine o'clock came, and the band finished their last cha-cha, "Poco Pelo." They segued into their theme song, and Abe Schwartz swept aside the side of the curtain, side-stepping onto the stage while flipping a straw hat on his head.

"Ladies and Gentlemen of the New Valley Lodge. Welcome to our wonderful Talent Night. I'll bet you never knew what talent we had here at this glorious resort. The guests at your table and the staff that serve you are here tonight to entertain you with songs, comedy, and whatnot. Unfortunately, I'm not exactly sure what the whatnot is, but we will soon find out. You're about to see acts that either will turn up at the Concord and Las Vegas, or wind up getting me fired for putting on such lowbrow material. But who cares? We're all in it for the fun. That is, unless anyone tries to do an imitation of me, in which case I yank them off the stage with my trusty umbrella and make them eat the rest of their meals in the children's dining room. But let's not let that sort of thing get in way. On with the show!"

Abe introduced the acts, one by one, and each did a creditable enough job for a Catskills Talent Night. The audience enjoyed seeing people they knew up on the stage, and gave them as much applause as if it were a Saturday night show with a comic and singer brought in from Todah, the booking agent. Paul took it all in from backstage, and finally it was his chance. Abe brought him on stage, put his arm around his shoulder, and stepped up to the microphone.

"I've saved for the closing act tonight our new busboy, Paul Alexander Feldman. This young man, from the wilds of Brooklyn, will read to you a short story based on Catskill hotel themes. It's called 'Shtetl in South Fallsburg.' Give him a warm welcome, ladies and gentlemen."

—◦—

"Good evening, guests, fellow staff, and Mrs. Greenwald, if you're here."

At that, people chuckled, since Mrs. Greenwald always appeared unannounced to surprise guests and staff alike.

"I thank you for this opportunity. With all due respect to our wonderful social director, Abe Schwartz, I must say that he was a bit taken aback by my request to read my fiction to you. He is, after all, used to the kinds of shows that we have here and at most other Mountain resorts. And so are you, so are you. But there was a time, and I'll tell you about that time, when Isaac Bashevis Singer spoke in Yiddish at Grine Felder, Green Fields not far from here, giving the guests a taste of what soon became some of the best Jewish fiction in the world. And at countless other hotels, in the teens and twenties, Yiddish was very widely spoken. Except for the few huge hotels, the resorts in those days didn't have big shows. People made do with their own devices, which often meant Yiddish poetry, fiction, and commentary read informally in the lobby after dinner.

"So, to place my story in its proper context, I want to take you back tonight to the humble beginnings of our beloved Catskills, when the lilting Yiddish, redolent with rich rhythm and subtle, creative meanings, put our Jewish souls in this new vacation world. And I'll take you to some other times as well. For some of you this will be your own time, for others, the time of your parents' visits here, and, for some others still, the days of your grandparents. It's likely that a bunch of you bridge all these generations in your Catskills presence. In all the generations of the Mountains, we are one with our heritage. In all the memories of working and staying here, we are united in the incredible stories, romances, jokes, and tears that have been fashioned here.

"Close your eyes, and dwell on these images: It's 1906; Moishe and Sarah, with their three children, live on 2nd Avenue and 7th Street, walking up three flights to a small railroad flat. They toil in women's wear shops in the Garment District, their only vacation being a subway ride for a long day and evening in Coney Island. Sarah has been doing odd jobs at night, sewing and altering for people on the block. Every penny she puts away. After a year, she takes this, along with the money she gets from selling one of the few pieces of family silver that came over from Poland with her deceased parents in the 1880s. This small bankroll will buy the family a week in a boarding house in Ferndale, owned by a neighbor's relative. A week before, she and her husband will have the regular summer break when their shops close. Sarah lights the *Shabbos* candles with a little more bounce than usual in her *benchlicht*. After the family passes around the *challah* for each to take a communal bite, she breaks the good news.

"'Children, Papa, our blessings of wine, bread, and food are joined by fresh air. I have gotten us a room in Mr. and Mrs. Kleinman's boarding house in the country. We'll take the train and the farmer will meet us at the station with the wagon. There is a wonderful river to swim in, hayrides in the wagon at night, and gorgeous stars to look up at night. The children can catch frogs in the pond, and maybe help out milking cows. Imagine to learn where the milk comes from.'

"'Mama, you mean it?' screams one of the children.

"'We're really going to the country?' another bellows out. They are gaping at her. Could their mama really do this for them?

"'Saraleh' Moishe asks, 'How could we afford this?'

"'Moishe, you see me sewing at night and on Sunday. For a long time I have put away bit by bit to do this. The children have never been to the country to just play and live in the clean air. And you and I, in the work-room all the time. Don't we deserve a real vacation?'

"No way will she tell him about pawning the silver as well. Instead she says that she will pay off an extra bit to Kleinman in the coming months, from new night work. Kleinman is a landsman of her father, even though she herself only recently met Mrs. Kleinman when she came to New York to recruit guests. The family bursts with excitement, as Sarah ticks off the things they need to bring with them. She instructs Moishe about getting train tickets ahead of time.

"In walk-ups all along the Lower East Side, other Moishes and Sarahs and their children are figuring out how to get such a vacation. For some, the landmanschaften has a connection to a cheap kuchalein or boarding house. Professional people and successful businessmen more easily arrange for vacations at small hotels. The burning hot New York summer that sends people to the roofs and fire escapes will not imprison all the Jews of the East Side.

"They are going to the Catskills. They are doing what the Americans do, because they are no longer greenhorns. But they are doing it with their fellow Jews, in common language, culture, and tradition. They are basking in each other's company in a magical place of green grass, singing birds, and breezy evenings. They are staying with farmers who coax from the land a living in chickens and eggs and milk, with some boarders to even out the accounts, in houses that will one day become hotels. They are picking wildflowers to make bouquets for the silly mock weddings that they will put on to entertain themselves. They are picking berries that the farmer's wife will make into pies for them. They are taking wrapped up lunches to the banks of the Neversink where they will eat with their feet in the ripples of the spritely river. They are counting stars they never knew existed. They are going to the Mountains."

Paul bowed his head a drop, took a deep breath, raised his face again, and continued. The audience was completely focused on him, as he stood in a spotlight-targeted position in center stage.

"Now, another image, it's forty years later. Berel and Sadie Feher have come to New York on one of the first ships to leave post-war Europe. Liberated from the camps, nursed back to health in a DP camp, they were then given a comfortable room with a middle-aged couple in London who wanted to help survivors. Hungarian Jews had been among the last victims of the Holocaust, and many remained in relative liberty until midway into 1944. Berel and Sadie, married only a year before, worked on a farm in a remote village. Ghettoization and then deportation to Auschwitz had been very recent, and they were able to stay alive. When the Allied forces opened the gates, Berel and Sadie quickly found each other and thanked God for their lives. But they sobbed at the dead and near-dead surrounding them, and they still sobbed at various times when they slept in their safe London bed.

"In New York, the Hebrew Immigrant Aid Society welcomes the young couple, and one of the volunteers tells them that there is a beautiful countryside a couple of hours away, where they can get jobs in a small Jewish hotel. Morris Pankowitz has asked HIAS to send him the refugees. He has lost many relatives, and has seen the trauma that other relatives and friends live with. So he tries to do his small part at Pankowitz's Parkside Resort in South Fallsburg. Sadie will work at the salad counter, making cole slaw, dishing out fruit, cottage cheese, and cream, slicing lox and putting it up on attractive plates with lettuce, tomato, parsley, and an olive. For Berel, a waiter's job. Morris figures that they will come away with a good summer bankbook, and no need to look for an apartment for a while. Further, he calculates, his guests and other staff will provide leads for jobs and apartments, as they come to know each other over the intimate summer of a Catskills community.

"The young couple feel like the hotel is their protection against the world. Yiddish is not a forbidden language, some people speak Hungarian, and they are improving the English they learned in London. At night, after work, they hold each other in the brisk air of June 1946. Moonlight is no longer a luxury. They are not alone with the blue numbers; some other workers and guests as well bear the mark. The survivors and the lucky Americans together will reconstitute a life, a culture. Throughout the Catskills, others like Sadie and Berel get this chance. And through them, all the Jews get their chance."

Paul paused again, relaxed his tense arms that had been embellishing his narrative. His face was gleaming with sweat but he didn't even pause to wipe it off.

"One more image, please. Focus with me. It is now only twenty years later, almost our present time. Marty Belkin is washing his goblets at the glasswasher's sink, placing them rim down on the used cloth napkins covering his tray. He already has his table set for breakfast, his sidestand is clean, and he is ready to check out with the maître d'. Laura Berenbaum has gotten rid of her day campers a half hour ago, and relishes her luck in not having night patrol this evening. With a little lead on Marty, she has had time to change into fresh clothes. Laura comes by Marty's room and sits on one of the beds while he shaves and changes. She and Marty are going to hear Jay and the Americans at the Eldorado, a treat they have been looking forward to all week. These rock and roll shows are one of the Catskills staff's favorite nights out, and Marty and Laura love this group. Afterwards they will probably go to Herbie's in Loch Sheldrake for a late snack, and maybe even to the little bar down the street afterward for a beer. They don't even think about how late they'll get to bed, knowing that they'll somehow muster the energy to rise early and work yet another day in the seven-day week that goes on for two months.

"Driving to Loch Sheldrake, Laura snuggles next to Marty as he drives, smiling as the oldies station plays the Mello Kings singing

'Tonight, Tonight.' It's the perfect song for the moment, and she can't think of anything better than this evening, a clear night in the Mountains, hanging out with this guy she's crazy about. They met before the season, working Passover, and fell into a very comfortable relationship. Back in the city they saw each other a lot, and were very eager to be away on their own in the Mountains for the summer. After Labor Day, both will go away to start different colleges, and no matter how wonderful things are now, they know that the separation may keep them from getting back to this degree of closeness. So they are packing into this summer a life of friendship and passion, even though their lives are still so young.

"Down Route 52 to Woodbourne, then left on 42 to South Falls-burg, Laura and Marty sing along with the radio. A thousand other cars with young men and women are traversing Catskill roads after work, on their way to rock shows, the track in Monticello, bars, delis, and parking spots for making out on the shores of Swan Lake. In the Catskills night they will sing, eat, drink, make love, and plant the memories to fill their futures. This generation of high school and college students is stamped with the work, romance, and money of the Catskills summer. These baby boomers who will leave their mark on the culture of the whole country are themselves fashioned out of the *Yiddishkeit* of this summer Eden. Are these your kids? Are they all of our kids? Their bowties and their whistles on lanyards frame their faces that we will all kiss and stroke for all the years of our lives."

Paul sighed deeply as he finished his last image.

"That's the background," he said. "I didn't know how long it would take. The story will have to wait for another time." And he slowly panned his head to take in every face that watched his.

⟶ ⟵

No one knew what had hit them. Listening to Paul, some people were propelled back to hotel nights in the 1950s, others were reminded of the days right after World War II ended, and others reveled in romantic nights in the 1920s and 1930s when hayrides were a major form of enter-tainment. Everyone was enmeshed in their own memories of Catskills vacations. Their spouses, dead and alive, danced in their minds. Their children, now grown, had given them grandchildren who at this moment sat at tables in the children's dining room eating raucous meals. A few people felt their bodies jiggle like when they rode the farmer's cart at the *kuchalein* a half century before. Mrs. Greenwald watched her late husband and her parents greeting guests in the lobby on a Friday afternoon. Abe Schwartz felt as if he was strapping on the cummerbund he wore as a waiter in Loch Sheldrake the years that the survivors began to show up regularly.

It took a while for the applause to taper off. Besides clapping, many people were yelling: "Oy, such a *shayne* kind," "*Gevalt*," "Unbelievable." Paul shifted his gaze to Janet's seat, smiling at her as her own smile penetrated the half-darkened room. She had given him the support to make this appearance, and she had cuddled and kissed him after their hours of writing talk. He almost wanted to call her up for a bow. Abe Schwartz trotted out, animated and pleased, clapping a hand on Paul's shoulder. "Ladies and Gentleman. Who knew what a genius we had here at the New Valley Lodge! Paul Feldman, ladies and gentlemen, our busboy author." The applause returned, and Paul turned back toward Janet, but she was no longer in the same place. He scanned the room but found no sign of her. He figured she was waiting for him outside, for a strong hug and congratulations. It took a while to get through the crowd of well-wishers. His own guests gave him the strongest congratulations. Mrs. Greenwald pecked him on the cheek. His dining room comrades pumped his hand.

But Janet was not outside. Paul could not figure where she had gone to. He stayed in front of the Playhouse for a half-hour, chatting with Dan and some others. Finally, the exhaustion of the evening caught up with him, and he trundled off to bed.

In the morning, Janet was not sitting at table twelve anymore, nor were her parents. Paul asked Dan if he had seen her, but he said he didn't quite remember a girl sitting there. Nor did others in the dining room, including the maître d'.

"Bill, everyone was talking about this girl. You wanted me to play basketball so she could admire me. How could you not remember her?" Paul asked of his roommate.

"Paul, there are lots of girls at the hotel all the time. We're always talking about one or the other of them. Why are you hung up on this one, especially since no one is sure who you mean?"

❧

After lunch on Sunday, there was always a large checkout. Today's was particularly big, since many guests on four-week specials were leaving. The dining room staff huddled by their own sidestands, handling the tips that came in Sunday afternoon. By custom, even guests who were still staying gave the week's tips at that time. Counting the money was always a private affair, though in a few minutes they would all be comparing notes and bragging about how well they had done. Paul joined a group of waiters and busboys sitting on the side porch, joshing about money, planning the night's staff poker game, making other plans for the night.

On a path next to them, an old woman of about seventy slowly walked by. She slowed when she neared the group, and with her eyes and a slight flick of the hand motioned to Paul so clearly that he knew he should get up and go to her. The woman looked familiar, he thought; she sat at the window station by the front of the dining room, but he'd never talked to her. Paul approached, and she gave a warm smile, extending her hand to gently touch his.

"I'm checking out now, but I wanted to make sure I told you how much I enjoyed your reading at the talent show a few nights ago. Your story reminded me of one I wrote many years ago when I was about your age. It's a very sweet story, dear, and it makes me remember so many wonderful summers in the Mountains."

July 10, 1997

Reflections on
"A Catskills Muse"

Phil Brown

Writing *Catskill Culture: A Mountain Rat's Memories of the Great Jewish Resort Area,* I was able to combine my memories with the more than one hundred interviews I conducted, visits to all the hotels and one bungalow colony where my parents and I had worked, and travels to many other locations around the Catskills. It was a privilege and a luxury to convey the Catskills life in a book where daily routines of waiters, counselors, guests, and owners could spill off my pages. It was part of my larger work—starting the Catskills Institute, assembling a huge archive, helping others do research and write, and running annual History of the Catskills Conferences for thirteen years.

I also gave myself the freedom to write five short stories including "A Catskills Muse," four of them in 1997 and another in 2000, all in a magical realist vein, that tone an attempt to convey the mysteries of the Catskills experience. While I have read my stories at events and conferences, none have been published until now. The stories gave me the opportunity to stretch the limits of how we remember Catskills life, and in fact, the stories are all about *re-creating* that life. Of course, the word "recreation" that denotes vacationing is based on "re-creating," i.e., giving a chance to create anew, to renew oneself. I was clearly trying to re-create the recreation taken by Jews over the twentieth century. At the same time I was indulging my fantasies of what a good life in the Catskills could mean, and inventing people who I wished had populated it. I was creating a universe of characters to do my bidding.

One of the themes of this book is nostalgia. We know we can never return to the place of our earlier life, but nostalgia allows us to visit for a while. During those visits, we can change things, rearrange life, re-invent characters, play with our identity. In this way, nostalgia is such a powerful, encompassing, and sensual emotion that it creates a kind of magic. Thus, the luxury I write of—being able to retell the Catskills experience—is being able to set aside the mundane realities of the present to dwell in the power and sensuality of nostalgia. Nostalgia here is communal, as I gather the Ulster-Sullivan tribe whose members are co-creating this nostalgic world as they attend conferences, donate post-cards, write memoirs, hold Catskills nights at *shuls* and Jewish Community Centers. Being in this community that shares this particular nostalgic shape is an additional luxury—to not be alone but to be accompanied by others and buttressed by their own longing.

At the same time, I was on my own personal search for roots. From birth in 1949 to 1971, I spent three months each year in the Catskills, and returned through the late 1970s to visit my parents who were still working there (my father died in his coffee shop there in 1972, and my mother was a chef until 1978). When my mother died in 1991 I began a search to understand my past, which increasingly felt to me like it was deeply tied to the Catskills. For instance, why were we such wandering Jews who had to leave our home in Florida each year to go work in the Catskills? Besides such mundane things, I was also looking for the secrets of the past, especially the reason that my parents kept hidden the story of their loss of the Brown's Hotel Royal that they owned from 1946-1952 before losing it to foreclosure, and whose sequence of subsequent owners kept it running through all those years up till the present. Even when we were near it, they refused to acknowledge it still existed and thus I never saw it. I was searching at the same time for my never-known half sister Marilyn, child of my father's first marriage, a journey I embarked on after my mother died. There, too, memory had been erased—my father never breathed a word to me, and when my mother told me about Marilyn when I was twenty in 1969, she swore me to secrecy. Only after she died did the pressure to forget that history collapse. Both journeys to the past were pilgrimages that intersected, and finally the first photo I located of Marilyn was at my paternal grandparents' fiftieth anniversary at Liebowitz's Pine View in Fallsburg. Surely this was a sign that both voyages of discovery were connected.

During my annual return to the Catskills in 1998, I slept in my parents' hotel, the Brown's Hotel Royal, now run as the Bradstan Country Inn, a surprising survival over so many decades when most small hotels crumbled or burned. This was an attempt to revisit my early childhood years there, to inhale some of the spirit remaining there, wondering which relative might have possibly slept in the same room. As I pondered how hard it was to convey the history of Catskills life, even to those who lived it, I wrote an essay "Sleeping in my Parents' Catskills Hotel" that I published in my second Catskills book, *In the Catskills: A Century of the Jewish Experience in "The Mountains,"*[1] in which I considered my mission:

> I come back to roam country roads in search of abandoned hotels to record on film for people, many of whom will never quite understand how a million people each summer came to relax in hotels and bungalow colonies, or how their doctors, professors, doctors' parents, and professors' parents came to work their way through the first generation of college.

This mission was largely the discovery of abandoned buildings, vine-covered handball courts, and swimming pools with trees and bushes. It was a series of encounters with ghosts of the past. And so I wrote:

> My camera records *dybbuks* grazing in the fallen timbers of old kitchens, hotel spirits lurking in the half-moon facades of "Catskills mission" architecture. My tape recorder picks up from overgrown weeds the murmurs of requests for pickled lox, embraces in the staff quarters, cha-chas from champagne night in the casino.

---

1   Phil Brown, *In the Catskills: A Century Of The Jewish Experience In "The Mountains"* (New York: Columbia University Press, 2002).

I wrote some years ago that I felt I had been called to bring back the Catskills characters who populated my real world and the world that circled my own. One impetus for this feeling was the set of coincidences alerting me to the fact that a small group of people were considering a Catskills history conference. A new colleague in my sociology department when I taught at Brown came from another university, where her colleague there was brother of a Catskills maître d' who was a member of this group who sought to hold the conference. One of them shortly thereafter showed up for a visiting research fellowship at a campus library that holds an important colonial Jewish collection, and this cemented my connection to the organizers.

A second impetus was that I kept running into people from diverse connections—grandparent-age hotelkeepers who knew my parents and remembered me from my baby years though they had not seen me since; people who had stayed at my parents' hotel; the musician from a key hotel in my life who contacted me decades after I last saw him.

A third impetus was that I felt like I was channeling things, as in the situation where one of my short stories conjured up an unknown hotel with a bridge to a pavilion on the Neversink River, only to later hear from someone that such a place existed. I think I was picking up on such *beshert* (fated) connections, and perhaps conflating the real with the imaginary. To a large extent, "fate" is less supernatural, and more a particular way that we interpret events, especially when they have interesting confluences. Yet the feeling that it comes from "outside" allows us to see it as a commanding presence. Indeed, the Catskills had commanded my life: its seasonal pressure made us go there in May to prepare for the season and even for my parents to seek a new job some years, and to return only after *Rosh Hashanah* and *Yom Kippur*. This interesting universe brought a chance to be older before my teenage years, the opportunity to work at a young age and make good money, and by age sixteen to work in a hotel away from my parents with my own car and vast freedom. I got to hang around musicians of the hotel band, play piano in a hotel lounge bar, go to the harness races at Monticello Raceway, and have a very independent life. This fast-paced world was so out of the ordinary for me, and friends back in Florida thought it was exotic. I thought so too, though I also realized the contradictory nature of this summer world. After all, the Catskills calendar uprooted me from school and friends each year, as I transferred into a Monticello or Ellenville school to finish the year and then was sent home alone before my parents finished for the Holidays, to stay each year with different relatives or family friends so I could at least start school without transferring. It kept us living in a different apartment each year for much of my life, and kept my parents from stable jobs or small businesses back home in Florida. Perhaps I was striking back, taking command of that legacy through studying it in its complexity. Yet rather than tame the seemingly magical nature of the summer Eden, I entered into a new kind of magical thinking—my stories of magical realism allowed me to hang on to the romanticization of the most special parts of Catskills life; they allowed me to return to successful and fortunate experiences, without experiencing the downsides.

My excursions back into my Catskills past have been punctuated by key books. In between the first and second History of the Catskills Conference that I organized, starting in 1995, I read Jack Kugelmass, *The Miracle of Intervale Avenue: The Story of a Jewish Congregation in the South Bronx*.[2] Like me, Kugelmass is an ethnographer who merged his personal quest with his research topic, as he recounted the tale of a dying congregation held together by lay leader Moishe Sacks. An English film company did a documentary on that *shul*, and Kugelmass went to London for the premier since Sacks was too frail. Kugelmass asked Sacks what he should say, to which Sacks replied: "I'll tell you what you can say. Tell them we should all thank God that we have lived to see this day." "You mean I should say the prayer *shekhiyanu*?" Kugelmass asked. "Yes, say *shekhiyanu*," Sacks replied. I was very struck by this, and it resonated with my feeling of gratefulness for reaching the second conference of remembrance. I shared this with our audience, and I said the *shekhiyanu* aloud, since it seemed continually appropriate. Given that I felt I had been called upon as a voice of the Catskills Jewish memory, I had to fulfill that role in its liturgical sense as well. I had come to see the Catskills

---

2   Jack Kugelmass, *The Miracle of Intervale Avenue: The Story of a Jewish Congregation in the South Bronx* (New York: Schocken Books, 1986).

as sacred ground, a place where Jews could live in safety and celebrate their history, a place where they built exquisite little *shuls* to cement their community. Maybe like lay leader Moishe Sacks, I was the lay leader of a congregation of Catskills veterans who sought to make it to this day and sanctify the arrival.

Shortly after deciding to work on this book, I read Tatiana de Rosnay's wonderful novel *Sarah's Key*[3] about an American journalist, long living in Paris, who searches for a woman who as young girl was rounded up by French police at the *Vel d'Hiv* (*Velodrome d' Hiver*), then escaped en route to Auschwitz. The emotional turmoil of this book stirred in me a frequent feeling that Jews must continue to remember the Holocaust in as many ways as possible. I've always felt this, and in light of rising anti-Semitism in Europe and elsewhere, the "Never again" mantra that always resounded for me picks up additional steam. As well, I've had a longstanding interest in history and literature about the Holocaust, and I considered that my writing had some role to play in memorializing the Holocaust in light of the Catskills milieu. De Rosnay's fictional adventures came at the right time, to solidify the urge to do my part in further preserving the Holocaust memories for all time.

No matter how much I know about the Catskills and how often I convey it in writings, lectures, and archival work, I remain unsatisfied about my ability to represent this multifaceted universe. For that reason, the turn to the imaginary helps because it transcends the normal boundaries of the mechanisms that I can use to share this world. It's a world too big for itself, and it requires fantastic fiction. But there is more to it—this fantastic fiction is a way for me to return to the Catskills, and my fiction was about characters who stood in for me as they were magically transported back: a local girl walking into a deserted hotel, or a mysterious hack (low-cost limousine that transported people to the Catskills) picking up a Brooklyn man and delivering him to work in the dining room.

My stories' characters experienced gains from these mysterious visits: emotional renewal following a difficult life event; an encounter

---

3   Tatiana de Rosnay, *Sarah's Key* (New York: St. Martin's Griffin, 2008).

with a guest who rescued a hotel owner who was losing his faith and connection; a young girl's satisfying fantasy-play. So these mysteries of the Catskills, besides ghosts and *dybbuks*, were miracles, and I often close my public talks with the following:

> Miracles! The Catskills is full of miracles. Turning little boarding houses into hotels and bungalow colonies is a miracle. Making a place for the Jewish working class to get some fresh air is a miracle. Building a summer Eden that stretched for two counties' worth of eternity is a miracle. Think of the plea-sure experienced by any one of New York's millions who first stepped onto the grounds of the *kuchalayn*, bungalow colony, or hotel, and saw the cannas in the garden, smelled the fresh-mown grass, heard the gurgle of the stream, smelled the brisket in the oven and the *rugelach* on the table. Think of the pride of ownership among hotel and bungalow colony proprietors who tended their family-style summer havens. Think of the waiters, busboys, counselors, and musicians who were so pleased to support themselves through college, and the fun they had while doing it.

There needs to be a logic for why an era was central to the journey to the "*Shtetl* in South Fallsburg," as Paul titles his story. The storyteller has to find emblematic periods of Catskills history for his cameos of people's lives there. The Holocaust had to be one of these, for several reasons.

First, I knew the Holocaust was important in the Catskills, from what I knew through living this history my whole childhood in the Mountains, where people talked about it. Despite many who experi-enced a lack of discussion of the Holocaust, I remember it as very present. Like me, Irwin Richman in *Borscht Belt Bungalows*, his combi-nation memoir and history of bungalow colonies, remembers how often entertainers in the Catskills sang *Vi Ahin Zol Ich Geyn*, a ballad of destruction in the years of pogroms and Holocaust ("Tell me where can I go") that finally resolve in the creation of Israel ("Now I know where to go"). Leon Uris' *Exodus* (Doubleday & Co., 1958) told the same story as well, and its 1958 publication when I was nine left the whole Seven Gables Hotel population talking about the book as they shared copies with each other. Having not started Hebrew School till twelve, with barely a year to prepare for my *bar mitzvah*, I certainly didn't learn about the Holocaust before then in any formal way. The Mountains was my Jewish education, and that included the tales of the Holocaust.

Second, the first person I interviewed for my book had been delivered to the redemptive safety of South Fallsburg by the Hebrew Immigrant Aid Society (HIAS) upon landing in New York in 1946. I felt that beginning of my research quest was a special entry into my journey, and so it triggers a significant element of this story.

Third, the very wealth of literature that we bring together in this book attests to the impact of the Holocaust, and the years immediately following demonstrates the significance of this period for the key writers who made the Catskills their subject matter.

I have been trying for over two decades to salvage memories of this great piece of our history and culture, so I invented a writer who was trying to do the same thing. Paul tells the Talent Show audience: "So, to place my story in its proper context, I want to take you back tonight to the humble beginnings of our beloved Catskills, when the lilting Yiddish, redolent with rich rhythm and subtle, creative meanings, put our Jewish souls in this new vacation world. And I'll take you to some other times as well. For some of you this will be your own time, for others the time of your parents' visits here, and for some others still, the days of your grandparents." Paul affirms that "In all the generations of the Mountains, we are one with our heritage. In all the memories of working and staying here, we are united in the incredible stories, romances, jokes, and tears that have been fashioned here."

So the story is about the Holocaust experience only when he frames the second era of context-setting. But there could be no other context-eras without this Holocaust era.

Our very same HIAS brings up Berel and Sadie Feher right after the war, forty years after the first era of Paul's story. In Paul's recounting, "The young couple feel like the hotel is their protection against the world. Yiddish is not a forbidden language, some people speak Hungarian, and they are improving the English they learned in London. At night, after work, they hold each other in the brisk air of June 1946. Moonlight is no longer a luxury. They are not alone with the blue numbers; some other workers and guests as well bear the mark. The survivors and the lucky Americans together will reconstitute a life, a culture. Throughout the Catskills, others like Sadie and Berel get this chance. And through them, all the Jews get their chance."

For Paul, and for me, all the Jews in the Catskills were getting their chance, but this was really the most important one.

Bibliography

Brown, Phil. *In the Catskills: A Century Of The Jewish Experience In "The Mountains."* New York: Columbia University Press, 2002.

De Rosnay, Tatiana. *Sarah's Key.* New York: St. Martin's Griffin, 2008.

Kugelmass, Jack. *The Miracle of Intervale Avenue: The Story of a Jewish Congregation in the South Bronx.* New York: Schocken Books, 1986.

From *Displaced Persons: Growing Up American After the Holocaust*

Joseph Berger

Those who didn't experience them cannot fully appreciate what the bungalow colonies were. But they deserve some historical footnote because they formed a distinct and colorful world with an all-too-short lifespan. They came into being early in the century as tenement Jews craved summertime relief from soggy apartments and steamy asphalt; by the late 1970s the plebeian Jewish culture that had nurtured them was all but extinct. Until they were lamented nostalgically, the bungalows were scorned as second-rate even by their habitués. What they didn't get enough credit for was that for people of pinched means—people who could not afford the gaudy Catskills hotels, let alone such lofty realms as the Hamptons—they provided a basic respite of pine-scented air, bracing lake water, and merciful shade.

Most families arrived at the bungalows in cars. My mother improvised our way up. She, Josh, and I, carrying or dragging baby Evelyn, hauled two laundry bags stuffed with ten weeks' worth of clothes and sundries onto a subway train heading toward the Forty-second Street bus terminal. From there we boarded a Short Line bus and spent three bumpy, airless hours until we reached the foothills of the Catskills and my mother nagged or sweet-talked the driver into letting us off right in front of the colony we had chosen that summer. Once the bus had vanished from sight, my mother rested the bags on the ground, took a deep whiff of the country air, and proclaimed, "Aaah, the air is like Otwock." Her remark had the same ceremonious effect as a champagne bottle smashed on the hull of a new boat. Our summer was launched.

The colonies we summered in, with names like Broadlawn Acres, Silver Crest, and Jay's, were essentially alike. Each had a necklace of two-room cottages arrayed around a broad lawn shaded here and there with oaks, elms, and maples that concealed a few reclining Adirondack chairs. The cottages were built on short, squat stilts and each had a screened porch for evening idling. The rooms were cramped and the tiny kitchenette intended for feeding anorexic pygmies, not the outer-borough *fressers* who usually inhabited the bungalows. The colony's heart was the casino, a barnlike social hall where on rainy days children played Ping-Pong and knock-hockey, and at nights the men connived and kibitzed over nickel-and-dime poker and the women gossiped over the clacking of mah-jongg tiles. Occasionally, the casino became the cinema for an outdated, flickering movie, although if the night was balmy the film was projected on the colony's handball court, where the guests, gauzily highlighted by a mix of screen-glow and moonglow, could watch transfixed from their fold-up lawn chairs.

On Saturday nights, the casino had a drawing card, a comedian, magician, or singer whose shopworn outfits and shopworn numbers corroborated what we all sensed: within a few years these entertainers would flame out. Why else would they be playing a bungalow colony? Still, the jokes they told were often lewd and laced with Yiddish bodily humiliations, so the grown-ups, wanting to laugh freely and heartily, would send the children off to bed early. How wonderful it was a few hours later to hear the laughter of our mother and father as they stole into the bungalow trying unsuccessfully not to wake us up. From their whis-perings it seemed like the tensions of the week had melted away, and we could reassure ourselves that there was still enough affection between them to hold our family together for another year.

Much of the time was spent near water. We went up to the colonies for three summers with another refugee family, the Coopermans and their two sons, Sol and Charlie, and the four boys raced one another at the pool in a variety of strokes and distances in what we fantasized as our own Olympics. One of the luminous moments of my life until then—outmatching the thrill of acceptance to Bronx Science—came on the day that I set out before dawn to fish. I pushed the rowboat out onto the glass-smooth lake, rose-tinted in the early morning light, and with the warble and chirp of foraging birds providing a tranquil background score, I cast my rod at the edges of weeds and lily pads. While blinking away the stabbing light of the rising sun, I landed a bass, then another, then a third, in such swift succession that I was ready to return before my mother had even started making breakfast. Docking my rowboat, I took the long way around to our bungalow, making sure I showed off to whomever I could those shimmering, stupefied carcasses dangling from a chain. This city boy had versed himself in a country thing or two.

In the bungalows—how did the name of these thatched-roof cottages spawned in colonial India become so familiar to the greenhorns that it entered their Yiddish lexicon?—the wives and children would stay up all week while the men toiled alone in the city. But the men would show up on weekends, an infusion of bottled-up sexual energy that could be felt in the otherwise indolent Friday-afternoon air. By Sunday morning, after reestablishing themselves with their families and reveling in the merriment of Saturday night at the casino, many of the men—mostly the Americans—were ready to play a pickup game of baseball, with youngsters like Josh and me taking in their antics.

My father worked Saturday mornings and so showed up late Saturday afternoons for his abbreviated weekend, bumming a ride from some other hapless stiff who worked Saturdays. He was elated to see us, his wavy black hair setting off a smile so radiant he might have just returned from a two-month trip to the Khyber Pass. On Sunday, he didn't play baseball. He didn't even come to watch. But he was up early, decked out in Bermuda shorts—a pair of worn chinos my mother had neatly lopped off—black stretch socks that contoured over his veined, bony calves, and well-shined black dress shoes. Not owning a pair of sneakers or sandals, he was trying as best he could to look summery. I would sometimes wince at the unfashionable sight of him, particularly those shoes and black socks, but he seemed pleased with the world, ambling through a grove of pines and brushing his hand against the needles as if he needed to test them for sharpness or inspecting the mushrooms at woods' edge for edibility in a habit that must have reached back to his country childhood. For him, this burst of freedom in the Catskills, this break from the unrelenting six-day cycle of predawn risings, obstacle-course commutes, and the evening daze of exhaustion, was all he could have asked for. A vacation for two on the Riviera could not have made him happier. Retreating to a patch of dappled shade, he and the just-as-reticent Mr. Cooperman would attempt a conversation. A great dialogue of Western man they did not have. But eventually their chattier wives relieved them of the obligation to talk, and the two couples whiled away the afternoon warding off the enervating sunshine in the kindness of the shade.

These were people, don't forget, who all the year round never allowed themselves a meal in a restaurant, a take-out lunch, a daily newspaper, a taxi cab to a doctor, a second week of vacation. Six months might go by before they took in a movie. Except for a single shot of vodka when company came, they never drank. Even their splurging on the bungalow colonies—was it $300 for the summer?—was a sacrifice made for their children. But since the children were up here anyway, they could indulge in the colony's cheap pleasures.

Clustered together under an ample tree, they recounted in Yiddish the pathos of their Polish hometowns, exulted over the achievements of their children, and quibbled over the merits of this or that. Mrs. Cooperman liked the tidy modernity of Queens, where she lived, my mother the theatrical liveliness of Manhattan. My mother liked movies with Burt Lancaster; Mrs. Cooperman adored Gregory Peck. Once or twice the conversation got so heated they did not talk to each other for a few days. But stranded together as greenhorns on this bungalow island, they were in no position to sustain a lengthy quarrel.

Sometimes, when the breeze and the shade were just right and she and Mrs. Cooperman had reached an amicable truce, my mother would clear her vocal passages, lean back, and burst into song. She had a full-throated, rich soprano that had never had a day of real training, but everyone who listened knew she was a gifted songbird. She would start off with an American standard like "Autumn Leaves," and you felt in the drifting leaves of red and gold and the memories of a lover's sunburnt hands that she was mourning things lost long ago.

"But I miss you most of all, my darling," she ended the song, her voice cracking with emotion. "When autumn leaves start to fall."

There had never been a lover that we knew of, but in the shattered Otwock of her childhood, there had been autumn leaves of chestnuts and oaks and a father, stepmother, brothers, and sisters, and she let us feel the rueful absence of a place and people we had never seen. When she felt especially comfortable with her audience, her eyes would twinkle merrily and she would follow up with the plaintive Yiddish melodies of her childhood, songs by wives of penniless scholars too engrossed in Talmud volumes to grasp their families' hunger, songs by young girls trying to assay the virtues of their betrothed, songs by emaciated boys peddling single cigarettes along teeming urban streets. Whatever complicated feelings one had toward my mother, her singing would disarm everyone.

Sometimes my parents and the Coopermans would venture into the lake, my mother executing a decorous breaststroke, my father slashing at the water and twisting his head to breathe in the terrified agony of a drowning man. No one had ever taught these people to swim. No wonder my brother and I felt we had to make up for their shortcomings by developing skillful swim strokes.

We went with the Coopermans each summer because my mother figured that Josh and I would have parallel playmates, Sol and Charlie, and she would have someone to talk with. The way it worked out, however, was that I hung around with Charlie, Sol's younger brother, and Sol hung around with Josh. Charlie and I took long walks while I introduced him to Pall Malls and gave him the benefit of the wisdom I had gathered from the three extra years I had lived. Sol and I, having been infected by our mothers' rivalry, seemed to spend our time together competing. We would try to outdo each other at swimming and baseball and making the bungalow gang laugh at ribald jokes. In the evenings we would compete for girls. One year Sol ended up with the prettiest girl in the colony, and I ended up with someone less so but adventurous, in her own way. Lorraine told me her boyfriend in Brooklyn had a gun and would shoot her if she was unfaithful. But toward the middle of the summer she decided to live dangerously, by the standards of that time. The next year Sol ended up with a plainer girl and I paired off with a girl who lived two miles up the Concourse. In the evenings, Barbara and I would dance in the casino to an old phonograph that came with some rock records, slow songs like "Oh, Donna" and "Blue Velvet," and I would feel her curves and inhale the cloying smells of lipstick and hair spray and long for some forbidden extra. But this was 1960 and we sensed the bounds of our gropings. I didn't deeply care for the girls I ended up with. Both, I felt with adolescent snobbishness, knew little more than the confines of their own neighborhood while I, in my inflated imagination, was on the verge of becoming a rakish boulevardier. These were not the deeply experienced girls I deserved. These romances, I sensed, would end when my parents took me home. And they did.

Resuming Life After the War: Survivors in the Catskills

Joseph Berger

The Catskills were a place where my parents were mostly at ease and happy. Given their frantic pace much of the workweek and throughout the colder seasons, the feeling there among the bungalows and tree-shaded lawns was ambrosial, and I wanted to write about that, to capture them in a setting I felt they deserved after all the losses they had suffered and the hard toil they put in to reestablish themselves in America.

That the Catskills were full of Holocaust refugees like them was not just incidental to my choice to include a Catskills chapter in my book; I always felt that my parents' lives embraced much of the postwar experience of the survivors, and their time in the Catskills reflected an essential part of the refugee experience—the impulse to resume life, even enjoy it as best they could, after so much suffering. Sure, I was drawn to writing about the flavor of their lives, not sketching a sociological portrait of a subculture. Still, I was pleased that much of what they went through in the Catskills happened to encapsulate some larger themes. How seldom did I see my parents take the time to smell the freshly-cut grass, idle in the shade, smell the honeysuckle, lie back on the plastic webbing of an aluminum chaise, laugh at the bawdy jokes of second-rate casino comedians. The two of them were always running, trying to build a new world for themselves because the world of their youth had been torn away from them. They were always scrambling to make sure they could keep a roof over their children's heads, put food on the table, and maybe have something left over for a small splurge. In the Catskills, they could catch their breath. I also wanted to write about my brother and sister and our friends. As children we too needed the relief not just from the city's hot asphalt but the often-desperate edge to our parents' daily lives. Yes, in those bungalow colonies, there were indeed many more times than back in "the city" when we saw our parents laugh and joke and even frolic in cooling lake waters.

Yet, as I look back, I realize how present the Holocaust and their lost European villages always were. Once at ease, my parents had the leisure to remember, and memory often included their slaughtered parents, brothers, and sisters. My mother could not breathe in the crisp sweet air of our bungalow colony without remarking: "It smells like Otwock," her shattered hometown outside Warsaw. She could not help but remember the summers she spent with her dead mother's parents in Parisow. In writing about my mother singing "Autumn Leaves," I was sure the song brought her back to autumns long ago in Otwock.

Though he rarely talked about it, my father, who grew up on a farm in the Galician village of Borinya in southeastern Poland (now Ukraine) probably could not help but remember the hayfields and meadows of his childhood and the six sisters who helped raise him but never lived long enough to enjoy a vacation like we were having. I remember how along a country road he passed a vegetable patch that to me looked like a collection of generic leafy plants. He pulled one of them out to show me a carrot and another to show me a beet. This textile machinist really had been a farmer before the Germans invaded.

To be sure there were many more thoroughly American families in the three colonies we went to in my teenage years. Most were descendants of the Lower East Side generation that immigrated before or just after the turn of the century; a few of them were not even Jewish. Yet, the survivors stayed among one another, seldom mixing with the

"Amerikaners." Who else could they talk with about their *shtetls* and ghettoes, about the concentration camps or Russian work camps, about the indelible grief that was buried in their souls and the memory snapshots of those they had lost? So the Catskills, Jewish as they were, always had for me a more particularized subtext—that of refugees of a catastrophe hoping to find some consolement and pleasure. Even something as conventional as swimming in the bungalow colony's lake was tinged by my parents' European experience. In describing their clumsy strokes in the chapter, I realized no one had ever taught these people to swim properly; heading off to camps were not what children in Otwock and Borinya did during the summer.

In writing about those summers, I was not aware that I was contributing anything to the literature of the Catskills; I was just detailing another chapter of my family's life. But I realize now that the refugees— and there were many of them—marked out a different story than the clichéd Catskills images captured in movies like *Dirty Dancing* (Vestron Pictures, 1987). For example, the refugees, who mostly could afford the bungalows not the hotels, would not have been wealthy, savvy, or brash enough to tear a hundred dollar bill in half, give one half to a waiter, and tell him he gets the rest if he provides good service for the week. They did not go to places expensive enough to feature Catskills stars like Jerry Lewis or Danny Kaye; that caliber of humor they would have to appreciate on television. And they did not have the same lumpen panache of the classic Catskills denizens who might smoke cigars, drive streamlined Buicks, dance the rhumba in the nightclubs. They didn't even dress right for the Catskills; as I said in the book, my father—and he was not alone—wore black socks and leather shoes with his Bermuda shorts, not sneakers or sandals. Nevertheless, the refugees too reveled in the chance to breathe a cooler, grass-scented air and be surrounded by forests and lakes, to pick forest mushrooms just as they had done in Poland, to see Jewish children—their children—scampering across a field just as their lost little brothers and sisters had done before the war.

I did not intentionally hold anything back about that experience, but there are things I probably did not remember during the writing or emphasize sufficiently. After seeing the film *A Walk on the Moon* about bungalow life in the summer of both Woodstock and the first moon-walk, I realized there was much more of a sexual charge to the bungalows, especially when women were separated from their working husbands for weeks at a time or on weekends when the men would come up from the city to the colonies to reunite with their wives. Still, I can't say I remember any of the wives acting on their impulses while their husbands were away in the city—as the wife does in the film. Sure, men and women still vigorous in their thirties and forties were suddenly surrounded by other men and women in exceptionally casual dress—swimming suits and tight shorts and halters—so I can imagine that the refugees might also have been stirred. I remember the appreciative comments my mother would make about the men in the colony's casino who were good dancers. I remember an Italian-American man named Romeo who had a certain confident, cool style that drew glances from the Jewish ladies. I remember a young woman or two who ignited a teenager's lust. Obviously, the casual vacations heightened whatever sparks might have been felt had we stayed in the workaday world of the Bronx where I grew up.

For the sons and daughters of the refugees, the bungalow colonies, even more than public schools, were a chance to wade into the American mainstream, to test themselves with girls or boys who came from "American" homes, to do "American" things like go canoeing, put on a day-camp musical of *South Pacific*, dance close and slow to songs like "Earth Angel," play poker. Without that exposure, we might not have been prepared to take on the social challenges of college and careers.

With the widespread and deeper knowledge Americans now have of the Holocaust, I can look back to the Catskills chapter in *Displaced Persons*, and feel gratified that I might have given readers a sense of the distinctive refugee niche in the mountains and how the refugees' families gradually integrated themselves into this new country that their horrific experiences forced them to adapt to. Their memories would never be erased, or even eased, but the Catskills was another place where they could carve out new lives for themselves and their children that were some odd combination of the harrowing past and a more benevolent future.

The Catskills (or What Was, Was, and Is No More) from *A Jew Grows in Brooklyn*

Jake Ehrenreich

To look backward for a while is to refresh the eye, to restore it, and to render it
more fit for its prime function of looking forward.
—Margaret Fairless Barber

I've always been fascinated by what happens when things that seem
permanent go away—like vinyl records or abandoned castles or
unused rail lines. They always carry something sad about them, and in
the case of places, they seem to retain an emotional "feeling" about
them—almost an echo or a remnant of their former glory that can still
be sensed. One of the truly important and formative places in my life,
both personally and professionally, has come to have that air about it.

The breathtaking Catskill Mountains in Upstate New York played a
monumental role in all aspects of my life. Featured in movies like *Dirty
Dancing* and *A Walk on the Moon*, the Borscht Belt (as this part of the
Catskill Mountain range was often referred to) was a lush, mountainous
resort area about 100 miles north of New York City. The area was home
to some of the world's most famous hotels and dozens of smaller hotels

and bungalow colonies. In its heyday of the fifties and sixties, the Catskills featured such performers as Jerry Lewis, Eddie Fisher, and Sammy Davis Jr., as well as sports stars like Rocky Graziano and later Wilt Chamberlain and Oscar Robertson. Many famous entertainers got their start in the Catskills, including Sid Caesar, Danny Kaye, Mel Brooks, and many, many others.

But there was another Catskills that was very important to me and to my family: the bungalow colonies where we spent every summer when I was a kid. My family was never wealthy enough to afford hotels, but the bungalow colonies were well within reach.

Near the end of the school year, the anticipation of going to the mountains would start to build. The summer seemed like an eternity then, and I looked forward to the experiences of a whole lifetime away from the city. On July Fourth weekend, we'd load up our car, tie a few old lawn chairs from the garage on top, and head up to our bungalow in the Catskills. The sense of joy and excitement began in the car on the ride up. In the old days, we traveled old Route 17, a single-lane highway that was the only way upstate, along with about a billion other cars. It was like the exodus of Moses leading the Jews out of Egypt. About halfway up was The Red Apple Rest, where everyone stopped to pee. This was the signal that we were halfway to paradise. After being surrounded by brick and concrete all year long, the idea of playing in the grass, going swimming and boating, seeing my summer "cousins," and being next to nature was the most exciting thing imaginable.

When we first started going, we stayed at a very small place called Roshvalbs in Greenfield Park, near Ellenville. I was just an infant, but I still have the fifty-dollar US savings bond my father bought for me that first summer of 1957. Roshvalbs was a *kochaleyn*, which in Yiddish literally means "cook alone" or "cook by yourself." It was a small cluster of old summer shacks and a main house with rooms for rent. The recreation was swimming in the nearby creek where we used tire inner tubes as floats. We were new immigrants with very little money, but my father always said that those were the best times of our lives.

Later, we graduated to full-fledged bungalow colonies, which carried names like the White House Bungalows or Paradise Estates. A bungalow colony was still just a bunch of non-air-conditioned shacks, but they weren't shy about their names. The names of these places reflected what they represented, not the décor of the buildings. These "fancier" bungalow colonies featured a swimming pool, a concession where you could buy lunch, and eventually even a "casino" with entertainment on Saturday nights. I'm not sure why they called these places casinos, since there was certainly no gambling. The only gambling occurred at the concession where you took your chances when ordering a hamburger.

Years later when I was dating Miss North Carolina, I made the mistake of telling her my family rented a bungalow for the summer. She perked up. I could tell she was picturing something out of *The Great Gatsby*. I tried to calm her excitement by explaining these bungalows were in Monticello. That only made things worse—she thought I was referring to Thomas Jefferson's historic estate. I made a mental note to stop mentioning bungalow colonies to my non-Jewish girlfriends.

We always went to the bungalow colonies with other immigrant families ("green-eh" families, which is Yiddish for "greenhorn"). Each family rented a bungalow for the entire summer. Like my family, the moms and kids stayed all season, and the men worked in the city during the week and came up on the weekends. Bungalow colonies were the perfect place for all types of families with children. They were an escape from the hot, noisy city where the kids would be safe and occupied, and the parents could enjoy some genuine "off" time. But this was especially true for our Holocaust-survivor families.

Here was a place where our parents were able to relax together with people like themselves and really let their guards down. They played cards, spoke in Yiddish or Polish, and even hit a soccer ball or two. It was a special treat to see my parents as well as my friends' parents, who had had so much tragedy in their lives, forget their troubles and just enjoy themselves. Sometimes, it seemed as if they hadn't a care in the world, and that made us feel better too. For short periods during those fabulous youthful summers, it almost seemed as if we could just be normal.

We always rented bungalows together in a cluster. At Ryke Inn Colony in Kiamesha Lake—where I have most of my memories—we rented up on the hill. Up the hill was our own little world where I personally felt most like everyone else. This was a place where the residents could roll up their sleeves and if they had a number on their arm, nobody looked twice. We were more like family than friends; in fact, we often referred to each other as cousins and relatives to fill in for those lost in the "milkhome" (the war).

All the parents on the hill had heavy accents and names like Shmulek and Mendel, which made Yonkee seem as American as if I'd arrived on the Mayflower. My best friends name was "Keevy." I think if someone had shouted "John" or "Mary" at the tops of their lungs, one of us probably would have called the cops.

We kids played outside all day long, catching frogs and playing baseball, dodge ball, basketball, Ping Pong, volleyball—every outdoor game imaginable. Of course we played with the "American" kids too, and we were all considered equal. But when we went in for the night, it was back up the hill to our little self-imposed *shtetl* (town). Despite feeling very much a part of survivor-based Jewish life in the Catskills, we were still outsiders. I envied those kids with regular American parents and regular American lives who stayed down the hill. I didn't yet understand that they had their own sets of problems, too.

I used to take hikes with my dad, and we'd pick berries or even go boating. When we went boating, though, he made us stay close to shore because he couldn't swim. I used to love the outfit he wore—a white tank top with red bathing trunks that partially covered a pair of spindly legs and a pair of shiny black dress shoes and socks.

I learned to swim early on, but I was the only one in my family who ever did. If I ate anything at all, even a crumb, my mom wouldn't let me go in the water for at least an hour. She said I'd get a cramp and drown. I would always shave a few minutes off the time and then have terrible guilt thinking what would happen if I drowned after all.

When we got a little older, many of us went to day camp at another bungalow colony just up the road. The grandfather from the family-owned Lakeside Villa (bungalow colonies were almost always family owned and operated) would make numerous trips back and forth in his station wagon to bring us kids to camp. We must have had thirty kids each trip—we rode on the roof, hanging off the back, and on the hood.

No one ever fell off, but Jeffrey Mermelfein threw up in the backseat once. I think he just had food poisoning from the concession.

Even though I liked camp, waking up so early was a drag. To my utter horror, every morning, bright and early, the PA system at the bungalow colony would blare "Wake Up Little Suzy." It wouldn't actually wake me up, but it was a cue to my mother that it was time to rouse me from my deep, comfortable sleep.

Waking up the kids was the main use for the PA system along with notifying the whole colony anytime someone got a phone call or to announce the arrival of Ruby, the knish man. But no other announcements were ever as early or as loud as "Wake Up Little Suzy." I still know all the words to that song by heart, and I can only assume that every family in our colony had a kid in camp, because I can't recall any murders ever being reported on account of it.

One morning, my mother decided to let me sleep late. Unfortunately, she chose the day of the BIG miniature golf trip. I was so disappointed, but also conflicted. I knew my mom was trying to do something nice for me and I saw how sad my disappointment made her. It was really hard to be mad at her. I ended up spending the day catching frogs down by the stream near the handball court where the handyman lived. He had one glass eye that always looked in a different direction, and I never knew for sure who he was talking to. I always wondered if that's what it was like talking to Sammy Davis Jr. up close.

My whole family seemed to thrive in the Catskills. Somehow the fresh air and the freedom of the setting made everything and everybody just seem happier—more joyful and carefree. It was a time when the nightmares of the war years were somehow put aside for another day. We were less dysfunctional there, and I will always reserve a very special place in my heart for those times and those places.

My family stopped going to bungalow colonies when I got my first gig in the Catskills as a musician. I was so young that half the summer I played drums in a band, and half the summer I went to sleep-away camp! I worked for an agent named Sammy Maslin. If you asked Sammy how much the gig paid, he would say, "Hey, there's gonna be girls there!" (And there were.)

That first gig paid thirty-five dollars per week, and in retrospect, I should have paid Sammy for the incredible training I began that summer. I was conscientious and talented, but I was still very young. The Catskills were the greatest training ground in the world. We were kids, but there were so many hotels that they needed as many musicians as they could get. The bigger hotels could afford the more experienced professionals, but the small places could only afford kids. And we really learned. It was the kind of place where, if you made a mistake, you kept your job . . . even if you made mistake after mistake, you still kept your job. There's no place like that today . . . well, maybe the Oval Office.

The Catskills had some of the world's most lavish hotels, and the finest entertainment as well—it was like Las Vegas without the gambling. The non-famous acts would often play several shows in an evening and move from the big fancy hotels for the early show, all the way down to the small hotels and bungalow colonies for the late show. Because of that system, we'd get to play with fairly good acts, even in the tiny places. Sometimes we couldn't play their music or "charts," even with a long rehearsal. Upon realizing this, the act would calmly collect the music, then ask, "Do you know 'You're Nobody Till Somebody Loves You' in B flat?" They'd end up putting together a whole "fake" show on the spot.

Periodically, we even messed up during the actual show. One singer turned to the band and stopped us right in the middle of a song. She faced the audience and explained that we were in fact excellent musicians (we were maybe fourteen years old) and that we had seen the music for the first time just that afternoon. She turned back to us and said, "Okay, fellas, let's try it again from letter B."

All of this made a huge impression on me, and I learned so much from watching these performers. As time went on, I perfected my craft and got into the really great hotels with the best musicians and performers—this all stood me in good stead for the rest of my career from nightclubs to touring to Broadway, both as a musician and a performer. No matter what kind of gigs I've done, I could never replace the training I got in the Catskills.

I grew up socially in the Catskills as well. Not only with peers of my own age, but also with much older people. As I moved to the larger hotels, my bandmates tended to be adults, and I also got friendly with some of the acts. I became particularly friendly with an African American singer at one of the hotels who told me he would knock out the next guest who told him he looked just like "Sydney Belafonte" or "Harry Portier." We both laughed.

Sometimes, this age difference thing didn't go as smoothly as one would have hoped. The bandleader/pianist at the Stevensville Hotel was Jack Kahn, a nice guy probably in his late sixties at the time. I was a young wiseass kid, but we liked each other. The bone of contention between Jack and me was that I was always late. Not *really* late, but just enough to raise his blood pressure; I would frequently show up at the last possible minute before we were to begin playing. Jack warned me many times, but he had finally had enough. He took me aside one day and told me he had to let me go. He said he had genuine affection for me and that I was very talented, but he had a weak heart and he feared for his health. Still, they weren't about to let a good young musician get away in those days. Jack arranged for my agent to switch me to another hotel that featured a younger bandleader with good blood work.

My memories of the Catskills are very precious to me, and although I arrived in the Catskills significantly after its heyday of the 1950s and 60s, I was still in time to witness the last of the glory days and experience that excitement. It was simply a dream come true in every way imaginable, and I had the time of my life.

Toward the end of my stay, the decline of the area picked up pace. I was moving on to greener pastures for my own reasons, but there was no denying what was happening to my beloved Catskills. For years, there had been talk of gambling coming to rescue the area and its hotels. At each turn, the dream faded. Cheap airline travel to exotic places, Atlantic City, and the breakdown of the nuclear family all contributed to the demise of the Catskills.

Not long ago, I again returned to my old haunts in the Catskills for a documentary that is being filmed based around my show. Almost all of the big hotels have been torn down. Others are boarded up. I stood on the stage of the nightclub at Kutshers where I had performed many years earlier as a young drummer in the show band (Kutshers Country Club is still alive and looking grand, albeit only seasonally). It was pretty eerie. Even though I'd been in this room on an empty afternoon getting ready for rehearsals many times in the past, there had always been an expectation in the air . . . a feeling that something exciting was about to happen. Now the room felt used up—as if the spirit was willing, but the body couldn't give anymore. This room, which had seen so many exciting nights, heard so many songs, and been part of so much laughter, was like a grand old southern matron who had lost her wealth, but still held on to her dignity.

After we left, I drove by the Concord and the Laurels. Gone. I stopped by the Pines Hotel in South Fallsburg where Speedy Garfin held sway in the lounge. The heavy steel chain across the front entrance couldn't block out the broken windows and overgrown grounds. The sign still sported the words GATEWAY TO YOUR FABULOUS VACATION. On my journey home, I passed by the decaying and now condemned Red Apple Rest, the place which for decades told generations of vacationers they were indeed halfway to paradise.

I can't help feeling nostalgic and sad for those places and those days, but I know all things pass. People, places, things . . . they all have their time and then make way for the new. It is a bittersweet reality that none of us would change, even if given the choice. *Vos geven iz geven un nito* (What was, was—and is no more.) This is the apt title of a famous Yiddish song.

What I can't totally comprehend is what happens to the love, the joy, the laughter, and the emotions that happened in these places. Where do they go? Are they in the walls or in the air where the buildings stood? Are they still occurring in some alternate universe right next to where I'm standing? I know that the emotions and memories still live inside those of us who experienced them—but is that all? Can walls talk? It felt like they could when I stood on stage in the empty nightclub at Kutshers.

Several times in the last few years, when on the site of one of these ruined old hotels or bungalow colonies, I've experienced a strange feeling. As I watch the wind blow across the overgrown fields and ruffle the torn curtains through the broken windows, I imagine I can almost hear the faint sounds of music and laughter, and I feel at peace.

Reflections on
A Jew Grows in Brooklyn

Jake Ehrenreich

Following an evening performance of my Off-Broadway musical *A Jew Grows in Brooklyn*, which tells my tale as a first-generation American, a smart-looking young woman approached me in the lobby.

"Would you like to write a book?" she asked. I took her business card and didn't call for six months. I was afraid they wanted a "tell all" book, which I was unwilling to write. When I finally did call, at my wife's urging, she went on to explain that she was an acquiring editor for the publisher of the popular *Chicken Soup for the Soul* series and felt that my story of rising above the challenges of being raised in a Holocaust-survivor family would fit into the publisher's mission to spread hope and healing.

After some thoughtful reflection, I agreed to write the book. As I did in the musical, I found myself focusing significant attention on the Holocaust and the Catskills—each having played a pivotal role in my family's life as well as in the lives of many other survivor families.

At the time I wrote my show and then my book, I believed I had fully acknowledged the profound impact our time in the Catskills had on all of us. However, an incident a few years back greatly expanded my conscious awareness, and my appreciation of those times suddenly became much deeper.

During an interview with a friend—also a child of survivors—for an upcoming film, we began reminiscing about the Catskills. He told me how he'd grown up listening to his father cry every night behind the locked bathroom door in their Bronx home, but when the summers came, he'd watch the same man laugh with the comedians in the hotel nightclubs.

His words momentarily stunned me. As an adult, I'd come to deeply appreciate the therapeutic effects of the fresh air and the freedom of bungalow-colony life on my family. Amazingly, however, I had taken for granted the laughter during those precious summers—that ubiquitous laughter, which permeated each molecule of the Catskills air every bit as much as the scent of freshly cut grass and lilacs in bloom. Although I intuitively incorporated it into my work and felt it in the very fiber of my being, I hadn't actually acknowledged or articulated it.

My friend's words again reminded me of the incredible healing power of laughter and how profoundly it had affected our survivor families with its transformative power. While the Catskills culture was all-inclusive, the comedians seem to make a point of speaking directly to us, instilling a sense of camaraderie and safety. In his wonderful book, *The Amorous Busboy of Decatur Avenue* (Touchstone, 2006), comedian Robert Klein bemoans the fact that, when he was in the Catskills trying to learn the ropes, half the punch lines were delivered in Yiddish! In Billy Crystal's nostalgic film *Mr. Saturday Night*, the Borscht Belt comedian comes triumphantly off stage and declares, "I hit them with a little Rumania . . ." referring to the ever-present, comic, romantic, and slightly suggestive Yiddish song made famous by Aaron Lebedeff.

The singers and other entertainers catered to the survivors as well. Classic staples like *A Yiddishe Mame* or *Vi Ahin Zol Ich Geyn* ("Tell me where shall I go, all the doors are closed to me") were always received with appreciation, longing, and deep understanding. While the laughter set us free, the music soothed our pain.

The first song I ever sounded out on the piano was the theme from the film *Exodus* (Carlyle, 1960), which was about a ship of Holocaust survivors and the birth of the modern State of Israel. I now find this choice fascinating, since as a kid, I wanted to be and do everything "American." At roughly the same time I was making Freudians happy by plunking out this theme song, my prepubescent friends and I at the colony would spend some of our afternoons exploring an abandoned farmhouse just across a huge empty field from our bungalows. We were told not to go there, but what kids with good sense would stay away from an irresistible haunted house? Even at that age, bungalow colony life was pretty free . . . and what kind of *putz* listened to their parents anyway?

One day my friends and I found some Nazi paraphernalia in one of the upstairs rooms. I can still feel the chilling, yet oddly fascinating feelings that erupted in my body—like being a voyeur of some nightmare time capsule in a *Twilight Zone* episode. It really freaked us out, because we finally stayed away from that old farmhouse after that. Presumably we were more afraid of Nazis than we were of ghosts. In retrospect, I'm pretty sure none of us told our parents about it. Even at a very young age, we survivor kids had a sense of having to protect our parents from certain things. Of course, our parents tried to protect us as well, so I guess everyone was attempting to protect everyone else, all at the same time.

When I began writing about the Catskills (or, more accurately, the "Borscht Belt"—the Jewish Catskills), I knew I would be paying homage to an experience that could not be recreated today. Although I faced some resistance from the non-initiated regarding its commercial potential ("But *we* spent our summers in Connecticut"), I deeply believed in the importance of what that time in our lives represented: rebirth, renewal, and getting comfortable with one's place in the world. I knew these themes and the lush comic/tragic setting in which they played out would be relevant to a wider audience. But, I had no idea there would ever be an actual body of work on the subject. Nor did I fully realize how these two parts of my life—spending summers in the Catskills and being a child of survivors—intersected to form a truly unique narrative.

My feelings regarding the relevance of this work have been corroborated many times—in the numerous theater and book reviews that go out of their way to point out the universal accessibility of our story and in the real-life situations people share with me. For instance, a non-Jewish woman from India proclaimed to me, "I have had the same life as your father!" She explained that she had come to America with nothing but her name, and like me, her kids wanted to be all-American. The same way I didn't want to be called by my name *Yankele* because I thought it "branded me" as an immigrant Jewish kid, they didn't want to be called by their Indian names either. In another case, a Catholic man about my age told me he hadn't previously understood why the Holocaust was still relevant before seeing my show. However, hearing about it from an American peer—*sans accent*—and about the ongoing effect it has had on my family and me had changed his mind. Then there was the rabbi in Kansas City who recounted how she had grown up hearing about New York's Catskill Mountains, but thought it was just a place with corny jokes. Now she began to understand the incredible importance this unique place had for the survivors and the role it played in their healing and integration into American society.

Some things about my experience growing up as a child of Holocaust survivors were deeply personal, and I tread a fine line deciding which to include in my work. The night before the galleys to my book were to be printed for the media, I had an intense interaction with my editor Carol Killman Rosenberg, in which I expressed my deep discomfort over some of the material I'd shared. She graciously let me edit out select passages at the last moment, and it took us until 2 AM, which she ribs me about to this day. However, I had a good reason for keeping her up late: my family and others had endured the most intense fear, loss, and stress imaginable. And while it is a miracle and a testament to the human spirit that any of them found the courage and fortitude to rebuild lives and families, none of them came through without scars. The deepest scars are mostly what I chose to leave out.

In my family's case, the stress, loneliness, and dysfunction that grew out of the survivor life ultimately proved too much for my mother and two sisters. Each in turn developed early-onset Alzheimer's disease: my mom in her late fifties (she passed at age sixty-two), my sister Joanie in her late forties (she passed at age fifty-five), and my sister Wanda in her early sixties. (Wanda passed during this writing, one day after her

Sisters. Courtesy of Jake Ehrenreich.

Parents and Survivor friends. Courtesy of Jake Ehrenreich.

seventieth birthday.) It is my belief that neither my mother nor my sisters were emotionally well during the course of their lives and that the way they handled—or didn't handle—their stress and sadness contributed to their illness. I haven't conducted a study, but anecdotally, it seems to me that the incidence of dementia in Holocaust survivors is extremely high. I am certain that the experience with my family's dementia has driven my journey to find empowering outlets for dealing with stress in my own life.

My family adored going to the Catskills for a myriad of reasons, but I think most of all because it was a place where our family's emotional diffi-culties surfaced less frequently and with less intensity. And we laughed. Boy, did we laugh. The joyful atmosphere that enveloped us fertilized any roots of optimism we still had about the world. We were with people who understood our experience and that helped us feel safe. We were happier and more stable during those summers. The air was vibrant with the vigor of youth and freedom, family and new beginnings.

And, of course, there was young love. Perhaps it was a combination of people at leisure, summertime heat, bathing suits, and adolescent hormones, but there seemed to be an abundance of sexual tension in the air—at least that's how it felt to me. I had my first real kiss at Schachts bungalow colony in Kiamesha Lake. I had no interest in this girl, and I don't think she had much interest in me either, but somehow it seemed that the atmosphere warranted it. It was more about being at the right time and place. As fate would have it, time and place turned out to be the defining factor in my first real intimate experience as well.

I was working as a drummer at the Melbourne Hotel in Greenfield Park outside of Ellenville. I was about fifteen years old. The band was sitting around the lobby after the show, and it was pretty late. One of the female guests had started hanging around with us; perhaps you could call her our groupie—let's call her Lori. We got on the topic of sex, as usual, and she admitted to being nineteen and a virgin. After much considered deliberation, the group decided the correct age for a girl to take the plunge was—wait for it . . . nineteen! What a coincidence. Unbelievably, Lori agreed! Doug Frank, the bandleader and keyboardist, being the oldest and most experienced at twenty, was the obvious choice for the job (Doug grew up to be head of music at Warner Brothers Pictures—lots of stories like that from the Catskills). To everyone's surprise, Lori exclaimed "No . . . I won't go with him . . . but I'll go with him," and she pointed directly at me. I almost fell off my chair. I felt flat-tered and kind of special, but it definitely took me by surprise. I hemmed and hawed a bit, but there was no way of getting out of this with my manhood in tact if I refused. I didn't want the guys to know I was a virgin too. Doug, a handsome and experienced "ladies man," seemed glad to be off the hook, and even provided the proper protection. The night desk clerk, who had been a part of this entire conversation, gave us the key to a vacant guest room, and off we went. I was nervous, but also really excited—this was it! I don't recall much, other than I'm pretty sure the logistics of it could not have been pretty. I do remember it being very sweet, though, and I recall I knew enough to be gentle. When it was over, the moment was so intimate that I was inspired to bare my soul and tell her the naked truth (pun intended). As we lay there in the afterglow, I whispered in her ear, "It's my first time too." She shot straight up in bed and promptly proceeded to freak out. "What?!" she yelled. "What do you mean, your first time." The anger on her face shouted even louder than the voice inside my head yelling "SCHMUCK!" and I knew I had made a huge mistake. She couldn't bear the thought that her first time wasn't with an experienced man.

Watching those Catskills performers must have rubbed off, because I was quick on my feet and made one of *the* great saves of all time: "My first time with a virgin, I mean."

"Oh! Your first time with a virg—I understand." She let out a huge sigh of relief, settled down, and was quite content once again.

Interestingly, I never had a girlfriend who was a child of survivors. Dating a girl with American parents (Jewish or non-Jewish) seemed like a powerful way of fitting in to the American mainstream. And perhaps I just thought there would be too much of the same *michigas* (craziness) for one family. Still, I would have appreciated in-laws with that great Eastern European accent, which was a never-ending source of humor and warmth, and which I now search out every chance I get. I particularly love when I ask someone with a heavy Eastern European Jewish accent, "So, where are you from?" and they respond, "The Bronx."

I get a kick out of that response, but the sad truth is, I know they're intuitively protecting themselves. And amazingly, the accent that brings me so much security, joy, and pride is actually an embarrassment to some Jews. I periodically sense a *sotto voce* intimation of superiority from some long-ago landed American Jews that makes my parents accents seem cheap and suggests that our survivor immigrant society is some-thing to be ashamed of. I also sense a version of this from some

Israelis—that we, children of Holocaust survivors, are part of a Ghetto culture, emblematic of the weak, oppressed Jew.

You say perhaps this hits too close to home? Wasn't I embarrassed by my parents' accents as a kid? Sure, but this is different—it doesn't feel like a kid's issue; it feels like a class issue. Ultimately, I know I'm extremely fortunate to have had a father who made me aware of the great heroism that took place in our community, the idealism, and the amazing accomplishments in literature, science, art, and so much more that this murdered culture spawned.

Today, we Americans have our own survivor story. After the Twin Towers fell, the talking heads on television centered much of their conversation on how we'd felt safe and secure before 9/11, but no longer. I can't swear to it, but I'm pretty sure I did a double take. They'd felt safe? Huh? Were they not aware, as I was, that civilization is held together by the most tenuous of threads? That our agreement of society could break down and everything we accept as true can disappear—ownership, justice, safety, freedom? Did they not viscerally understand that the proverbial—or literal—knock at the door could come at any time?

And then I realized, no, they probably did not. Perhaps this is what I unconsciously envied in my American friends and their families as a kid. This was new territory for them, but not for me. These feelings, unwittingly transmitted to me through my parents' experience, were so much a part of my being that I was not even aware that I had them—emotions that could debilitate some, but through which others manage to live joyful, fulfilled, and heroic lives. This is because, in the end, it is our reaction to events that define us—not the events themselves.

The Catskills of my youth were indeed a unique time and place, and I count myself fortunate to have personally experienced the tail end of this era. Much continues to change in the Catskills since the writing of my book: some good, some not so good. But when I review my thoughts, some things have remained the same for me.

I still give enormous credit to our Holocaust survivor parents for intuitively understanding the importance of extended relationships for us kids and for trying hard to give us the benefit of those relationships.

I'm sure they didn't read a parenting book to figure this out; they just knew, and gratefully I'm still in touch with some of those families today.

I still visit the Catskills, albeit infrequently now, but those times continue to be characterized by an unfulfilled longing and bittersweet nostalgia. I remain faithful in pointing out obscure details to my some-what bewildered family: "That's where the Heiden Hotel used to stand—I turned down a job there because they didn't have an indoor pool, so I got a gig at the Olympic." Or, "We played color war there, before that Home Depot was built—actually it was originally a Jamesway." And I still wow my wife and son with the story of how many kids would pile inside and on top of the old station wagon that took us to day camp. It's possible they are not entirely "wowed," but they humor me.

And perhaps I'll forever wonder if the energy of the old emotions that were felt in this special place—the laughter, the loves, the tears—still linger somehow. Maybe they are swirling in the vast atomic emptiness between nucleus and electron—or maybe just inside of us. The way I imagine my wedding ring still holds the energy of my wedding day or my son's hobbyhorse retains a kinetic memory of his youthful innocence.

My wedding day is one of the things that is new about the Catskills for me—I was married there. Imagine the irony: I started going to the Catskills as an infant, only to be married there years later. (You might say my life began . . . and ended in the Catskills.) We were married at a small inn, which originally served as the summer residence for the Catholic Cardinal of New York. It was mid July, and we planned a beautiful outdoor dusk to evening ceremony, lit only by dozens of torches. As fate would have it, Hurricane Bertha chose that day for a visit as well. The weather was touch and go, but ultimately it cleared just long enough for us to be outside as planned. During the ceremony, we invited all of our relatives who had passed to "join us": my mother, grandparents, aunts, uncles, and children lost in the *Shoah*, and Lisa's mother and family too. The sky was filled with eerie and haunting clouds as the innkeeper and his staff watched from the roof of the old Victorian mansion. He told us later that they could feel the spirits in the air surrounding us, and they were frightened. Lisa and I felt them too, but we welcomed them. And I found I was not overly surprised by their presence. The Catskills had always been a place of spirits for me. Later I came to understand that roaming through the Catskills evoked emotions similar to what I felt when I visited Poland, or the way I feel when I think about Yiddish—a sort of cloudy, remote sadness. In each there is a sense of a time or a place that has passed and is gone forever. There are differences to be sure, but in both physical places the ether seems filled with spirits. Of course, the spirits in the Catskills feel wistful and nostalgic, bittersweet yet joyful; in Poland, not so much.

When all is said and done, what's been corroborated most profoundly since the development of my work is the similarity of the experiences we all share as human beings. Certainly the Holocaust and the Catskills and their relationship to each other are unique, but in a much larger sense they helped me understand that our mutual journey with all the attendant feelings of alienation, loss, and the need to belong is truly universal. Ultimately, we are each a spark of spirit that is materially manifest, seemingly separated, but in reality part of the entirety of all things at every moment. It is in our shared challenge to find joy and love and meaning, regardless of our individual circumstances, that we learn and experience empathy and compassion.

There is a beautiful poem in the memorial service on Yom Kippur: "Life is a journey and death a destination." I imagine that this is our ultimate connection.

I am supremely grateful for my experience. For me, the tragedy of the Holocaust and the safety of the Catskills informed my life with a diverse range of deeply felt emotions from an early age. These elements define me, despite my periodic protestations, in ways I am still learning about—first as a son, now as a husband and a father—and in everything I do.

From *Dreaming in the Ninth*

Ezra Cappell

"I just want to know."

"Already, I told you. There is not much to tell. Nothing, really. It was very hard. It was very bad. I survived. And here we and Mummy are. Then we had your father and your uncles and aunts. It's a beautiful, sunny day. You shouldn't know from such things."

As they walked on the well-worn path in the Catskills, Ephie thought he could hear the sound of the great falls—Kaaterskill Falls—growing closer. Still several miles out, Ephie couldn't possibly be hearing that great rush of two-fisted water, but his overwrought mind told him otherwise. They walked on in silence for a good twenty minutes when his grandfather, looking up into the leafy canopy, stopped beneath the most enormous tree Ephraim had ever seen.

With his index finger pointing way up towards the sky where one hundred and fifty feet off the ground the top of the tree twisted and swayed above them, Grandpa said: "This one here is a hemlock." Grandpa pulled off some needles and crushed them in his enormous, rock-hard palm before absently placing the broken pieces into Ephie's sweaty hand.

"Stupid people think this is what the Greeks made the poison from to kill the greatest thinker that ever lived."

"Huh?"

"For telling stories to the boys of Athens. Now you know why I cannot tell you about Breendonk."

"But those are made-up stories—I want to know the truth—"

"True, made-up, what's the difference? A story is a story."

"Why stupid people?"

"Huh?"

"You said stupid people think it's the Greek poison."

Instead of answering, Grandpa pulled a Victorian engraved sterling-silver folding knife from his pocket. Ephie watched as he deftly, much like paring an apple, carved off a small piece of hemlock bark and, ceremoniously, placed it in Ephie's small hand.

"This is the true poison with this tree—not the leaves, not the needles. It's poison for the tree, not for us."

By now Ephie, who thought he was going to hear about Breendonk, was totally confused. Botany? I didn't come way out here to learn about the fucking trees.

As Ephie feigned interest, Grandpa continued to talk about how centuries before the Dutch settled this area, the Indians called the Catskills "the blue mountains" because of the millions of hemlock trees that filled the forests. From a distance, say coming up the Hudson River in the *Half Moon*, the hemlocks seemed to give the mountains a blue glow, particularly at sunset. Grandpa explained how in the nineteenth century, just a few miles from where they walked, Zadock Pratt began what would become the largest tannery in the world. With iron pokers and scrapers the tanners would peel the bark from these hemlock trees to extract the tannins needed to soften the animal hides that would be manufactured into the leather products used by all the fancy people of New York City.

"By the time they were done, Pratt had clear-cut millions of these beautiful hemlock trees, stripped the bark and just let the wood—good, beautiful wood—sit and rot. The hemlock was even better than the oak tree, which in Europe is what we all used to tan leather."

Grandpa took off the binoculars from around his neck, encased in a beautifully tooled leather case and handed it to Ephie. "See, this leather, made in Germany by the Leica factory, is brown—tanned with oak tannins. Most of the leather coming from the hemlock tanneries came out a reddish color—quite beautiful, soft leather. I have some at home—I will show you later."

Ephie handed the binoculars back to his grandfather.

"The many tanneries that operated here destroyed all the forest for hundreds of miles around. To the Hudson River east of us, to the Allegheny Mountains on the west, the Adirondacks up north, even all the way down south towards New York City. When those tanners were done, there were only a few stragglers left. Ephie, this hemlock," and here Grandpa patted the tree like an old friend, "is one of the few that somehow escaped."

Instead of explaining about Socrates and the confusion between the poison hemlock bush and the grandeur of the evergreen hemlock tree, Grandpa reached down towards the passing stream and plucked a long slender piece of grass. Carefully splitting the blade of grass down its center and pulling it taught between forefingers and thumbs, Grandpa brought his hands to his mouth. When he vigorously blew through his hands, a long duck call emanated and, for the first time that day, laughter danced through Grandpa's face. "I had forgotten about that one! That trick, she still works!"

"Show me, show me," said Ephie. Grandpa carefully selected another long grass stalk and making a small surgical incision he carefully split it down the middle. Cupping Ephie's hands in his own he showed his grandson how to make the grass speak.

"Now blow."

Ephie did as he was commanded.

"Gurnischt," said Grandpa. "Hard, you must blow hard."

Ephie did and a sad, little sound came out like a half-suppressed burp.

"*Atto zoy*. Good. Keep at it. Now you will have something to teach your sisters and cousins."

The two walked on in silence, an occasional duck call from Ephie's hands shattering, splitting the still air. Finally, Ephie worked himself up to ask his Grandfather the question again.

"Grandpa?"

"Yes, my child."

"I just don't understand why they put you in there."

At first Ephie didn't think his grandfather would answer. They walked on for several minutes in silence. When Grandpa finally spoke it was in a strange, almost dead voice. Without inflection, it was like he was reading an instruction manual and not speaking about the mysteries of Ephie's universe.

"Why? Because I was, I am, a Jew—you, my child, are a Jew too—if you were there, you would have been in Breendonk also—then you would know what it is . . ." Almost as an after-thought, Grandpa added: "and then you wouldn't need to ask me."

Ephie was silent trying to picture what that would be like, but no image came before his eyes.

"During those years the Nazis were searching for each of us Jews, like they were, like they were diamonds. The Gestapo wouldn't stop until they had us all. So eventually they found us all and they put us, I mean they put me, in Breendonk. But, *Boruch Hashem,* Mummy and me eventually came to America and now everything is beautiful. You see even today these beautiful hemlock trees."

Not sure if he should just let it go at that or continue, from somewhere Ephie found the courage, perhaps the stupidity, to ask again:

"OK. Yes, but what happened at Breendonk?"

"What happened was that I did not die, OK? I have been trying all of these days with you here in Tannersville, in this beautiful, peaceful place, to not come out with the real stuff, Ephie. I have been, I am always working very hard at this, not to come out with the real stuff. I don't know maybe this is a mistake." He paused on the well-worn path—laid down centuries ago so Zadock Pratt could rape the land, destroy the old-growth forests, and turn a legal profit in America.

"I don't know, you are almost a *bar-mitzvah* soon, maybe, *shoyn,* you should know about such things. I do not know which is right, but since you want to know—now you will know. But remember once heard there is no unremembering of such things."

The old tanners' path was wide enough for two to walk abreast and Ephie could see his grandfather looking straight ahead as he spoke, his eyes focused on the distant falls looming ahead and not on the boy striding beside him step for step. Ephie listened hard and thought he could almost feel the spray from the falls wet his face. They both held their elaborately carved walking sticks made the previous afternoon. After their military-style workout, and after Grandpa had taught Ephie and his cousins how to do one-handed push-ups, Grandpa had led a wood-carving workshop for all the children. This had been the premise for this outing: to break-in their new hand-carved walking sticks. Only Ephie had volunteered to accompany Grandpa on this walk. Now, Ephie noticed the whiteness of Grandpa's knuckles—he held on so tight it seemed he might split the wood in his enormous hands caked hard by decades old labor and filth.

Ephie watched as Grandpa composed his face into a hard mask before continuing. Ephie was certain he could hear that mad dash of water in the distance. Finally Grandpa began to speak:

"There was a moat—I dug that moat. In my mind Ephraim, I am going back over that moat." Grandpa paused fighting some untold emotion back down. "No, no, Ephraim, I do not go back. I do not cross the moat back into Fort Breendonk—I am there already.

"When you get into Fort Breendonk, it was a Tuesday in July of 1943, you were made to stand up against a wall and no one is allowed to move. Not to twitch, not to scratch, nothing. *Farshteisht?*"

Ephie nodded. He was so excited he could hardly contain himself. After years of asking, he was finally going to get the "real stuff," as Grandpa called it.

As Grandpa told Ephie about his arrival at Breendonk, perhaps without realizing it, he stopped walking and stood entirely still waiting for Ephie to nod his understanding.

"Nothing. If you moved you were punished—"

"How?"

"Usually beatings. Whippings. All the Nazis and Kapos had these truncheons—long wood sticks and they would beat you with these things. So nobody moved."

"What if you needed to go to the bathroom?"

"There was no bathroom until you were processed into the camp—and then only for a few minutes once a day. We arrived in the evening and they kept us like that until the following afternoon.

"Commandant Philip Schmitt also had this enormous German Shepherd dog that he used to have bite us poor Jews. Anyone who moved got a clop on the head, and the dog—what was his name, that *shwantz*, Lump! Lump, was its name and when he was done with you—believe me you had lumps everywhere . . ." Grandpa managed a quick, sad smile. Ephie did not laugh. As an afterthought, Grandpa added: "We were relatively lucky. One transport was kept like that for 36 hours. We weren't even made to stand a full day. People did their business where they stood. If you had to go, you had to go. You had no *breirah*—what could you do?" Grandpa seemed to ask this question of no one in particular. "Finally, after many hours, they came for me and they took me down a long, dark hallway leading down, down, down, further into the center of the complex. Sloped stone and brick—as if we were walking into the pit of hell itself. Breendonk was shaped like a giant crab—built right in the center of civilized Europe. I walked down this long hallway and the guard, a young, very dapper looking Flemish SS Nazi, who had previously shackled my hands behind my back, escorted me down this hallway. I can see his smile now—he said to me with a big grin: 'Now 552 you will see what it is.' I didn't know what he meant. As we walked in the near darkness we soon came to a room with a large sign over the door: BUSINESS ROOM. What kind of business is done in this place I could not say. From the ceiling in this place hung an enormous iron hook dangling and twisting from the ceiling. Lieutenant Praust was already sitting in a chair, and in front of him was a long wooden table covered with an enormous Nazi flag. Behind Praust was a tremendous photograph of Heinrich Himmler. You know who he was?"

Ephie had no idea but he couldn't speak—his mind was a riot of questions—none of which he could ask. Instead, he just mechanically walked beside his grandfather. He had become a listening ear—nothing more.

Grandpa continued: "Praust sat at his table smiling benevolently at me. He said, 'Prisoner 552, you really don't look too neat. That must have been quite a journey. You have nothing to worry about, however. We'll take good care of you. We'll clean you up a bit.'

"I remember thinking, 'What could they need such a hook for?' It wasn't long before I found out. Praust stood up and came around from behind where I stood. He took hold of that enormous hook and put it through the chain on the shackles behind my back. This hook was attached to a, *mistumah,* a wheel, a winch on the floor, and he began to turn this wheel on the floor and in so doing he raised me off the floor until my arms were going up behind my back and my toes were barely touching the ground. Soon the only sound in the room was my gasping for air trying to keep my toes on the ground because my arms were being twisted up behind my back. *Forshteyst?*"

Ephie nodded. All he heard now was the sound of rushing water mingling with the beating of his heart. Not satisfied that he understood, Grandpa stopped walking. He reached behind his grandson, and he put Ephie's hands behind him and began to pull them up to demonstrate.

"You see it is hard to keep your arms in such a position. Like this, in this position, they asked me questions."

Somehow, Ephie managed to ask: "What kind of questions?"

"You know, about my work with the Zionists, my work with the resistance—with Cyril Vedar and Pierre Carnawal. I had nothing I wished to share with these people."

Grandpa paused, as if not certain he should continue. He looked long at Ephie—thinking for the both of them—before continuing.

"So they continued to turn this wheel and as they raised it, at first I jumped up and held myself up with my arms straight down behind me—you know like they do in gymnastics, in the Olympics, but Ephie, you may have noticed I am not exactly a gymnast. And so after a few moments or so my arms grew very tired."

"So then what happened?"

"Well what happened was that I soon heard a terrible sound of ripping, a sound of tearing—I still hear it now—that was the sound of my muscles and ligaments in my shoulders and my back being ripped into pieces from the weight of my body. Soon I was hanging from rubbery arms. Just hanging. Dangling. Twisting from this iron hook—gasping for air like some giant fish—some leviathan that those Nazis had hooked."

Ephie heard the tearing sound emanating from the Business Room of Breendonk—the sounds seared his brain. He tried to think of the worst sounds he could to replace the sounds of the Business Room at Breendonk—the old men at the Y putting on their Velcro shoes, Rav Munk's fingernails hitting the chalkboard at school, Jan's dead baby sister, born with a hole in her heart, howling all night long—all, no doubt, horrible sounds, and not any of them sufficing. Tearing sinew and bone? He couldn't comprehend it. As he walked, dazed, down the old tanning path, all he could see were hooks, hundreds and hundreds of hooks reaching down from the sky to grab him. That image would not fade. Ephie closed his eyes. He could hear tearing human flesh, sinew, and crackling bone. Why had he pressed his grandfather? This was not what he had imagined learning.

"So then, I must have passed out, because they were throwing water on me to rouse me. Next I see Lieutenant Praust with that metal poker like from a fireplace and he is running it back and forth over my head brushing my hair with this razor sharp metal poker saying, 'You don't look so neat. You're a big mess, let's clean you up a bit.' This part I couldn't see too well because all of the blood was getting in my eyes and my face. Then they threw more water on me. That's when the horsewhip made its first appearance. Again with the water—many times like this."

For weeks Ephie had been after his grandfather to tell him about Breendonk. When Ari had been bragging about how tough his father Shimshon was: "He was in the fucking Israeli Navy—his father was the strongman of Aden and my father was born in the back of an IDF jeep for Christ's sake." They all had to admit this was impressive, manly stuff. Simcha then talked about his grandfather walking from Frankfurt-Am-Mainz to Shanghai saving his wife and baby daughter (Simcha's mother) from the fucking Nazis. He didn't know where Frankfurt-

Am-Mainz was, but it sounded like a long walk. Nonetheless, Ephie had said: "that's all bullshit—my grandfather survived the camps." When they protested, he added: "And he killed Nazis . . ."

Ari had asked, "What camp?" and Ephie said, nervously, realizing this was probably something he should know: "How the fuck should I know? It was somewhere in Belgium—it was awful."

Since that conversation with his friends, Ephie had been after his grandfather to tell him the full story of just what he had survived in Europe. At first he was nervous about asking him. Ephie would watch that vacant look come over his grandfather—as if he was clearing out memories—erasing type and leaving blank pages in his brain. Now, he could hardly believe that his grandfather was actually speaking about the camps. And now, when he finally was getting what he wanted, Ephie wished, he actually prayed for the first time since Jan's death, that Grandpa would stop speaking. He had heard enough. Actually, he realized he had heard way too much. That dog, Lump. That whip. How much more could he take? When he looked up at the green canopy above him, every curved, leafless branch seemed like a snare, come to take him away. But where? To Breendonk? To Cedarhurst? To Fat Joey? This couldn't really be happening.

"Well, what the fuck does that mean? He survived what?"

In his brain Ephie kept replaying Ari's question, over and over again. During *shemona esrai*, the endlessly long and silent meditation at *minyan* three times a day, as he waited deep in leftfield beside the brook for a fly ball to reach him, Ephie would hear his friends' question: "Survived what?"

Beside the great falls of Kaaterskill, Ephie knew he had heard enough, but now that Grandpa had begun, he did not appear to be able to stop. The words issued forth in a great roaring rush making Ephie as dizzy as after a beating from Fat Joey—a legendary Tannersville delinquent—whose greatest joy was knocking yarmulka-wearing boys off their summer bicycles. Every Fat Joey encounter ended for Ephie and his friends with a queasy feeling of humiliation and shame, and with pain in every sharp edge of their bodies. If you were Jewish, an encounter with Fat Joey usually ended on a blisteringly hot patch of sun-baked asphalt picking pebbles out of your bloody elbows and knees. After their last encounter with Fat Joey, Ari, Simcha, and Ephraim, so filled with their powerlessness and shame, could not even look at one another. They each silently wandered off in different directions up Tomkins, Main Street, and South Main towards their families' rented summer cottages.

Ephie looked beseechingly at his grandfather's flushed face for a sign of comprehension—his eyes attempting to mime: "Enough, please. There are children here," but if Grandpa had noticed any sign appearing in Ephie's incredulous eyes, he made no mention of it in his monologue that flowed swiftly along. As they approached the falls, gnarled roots of huge trees made the path almost impossible to continue. It had recently rained, so the path was wet and slippery; they needed to use their hands as well as their feet to make any progress on this well-worn tanners' path deep in these northeastern woods. Pulling themselves up a small incline, they finally got their first unobstructed view of the great falls just a few hundred yards in the distance.

It was a glorious sight—swelled with rainwater, the two cascades of Kaaterskill Falls flowed from high out of the sky. Maybe it was the contrast with the uninterrupted horror of his grandfather's testimony, but Ephie had never seen anything so magical. They were drawn in silence towards the falls. The mist from the great falls filled the surrounding air and a small rainbow filled the cavernous region around the falls as the sunlight from high above prismed through the trees and lit the double falls.

"Let's begin our climb. I'll tell you more when we stop at the center of the falls. There is even a pool there. Thousands of years old. Maybe we can swim."

He wasn't sure what or where he was headed with his grandfather, but he pulled himself up the last two hundred vertical feet by sheer will alone. His arms were so tired he didn't know where he got the strength; Ephie focused on the roots and dirt in front of him and not the gigantic iron hook that he imagined hung right in front of his line of vision. Since Grandpa had mentioned the Business Room and told him about Lieutenant Praust, the apparition of Breendonk's hook appeared before Ephie as a perpetual afterimage—as each stray branch clawed his hands.

Using roots, grass, and branches, they pulled themselves forward, scrambling up the side of the mountain to where there was an enormous cavern—the amphitheater—behind the center of the falls. Breathing heavily they looked down into the precipice and it seemed to Ephie that they were in some giant creature's mouth and that they, along with everything else in existence, would be swallowed down into the great emptiness beyond.

"All creation Ephie! We can see all creation from here! All the beauty and all the ugliness. There are no Nazis here in the Catskills. But here," and Grandpa pointed to the side of his head, "Praust remains. Out there," Grandpa pointed toward the west, "is Slide Mountain, the highest peak in the entire Catskills range. Maybe we'll take your cousins and we'll all go hiking there next week. And behind us used to be the Catskill Mountain House right here at the top of the falls—this is where every US President would come to take in the sights and to swim at the twin lakes. Yes Ephie, while I was twisting, breaking in the Business Room at Breendonk, your American President was enjoying a *schnapps* on the Greek Revival verandah. *Ach.* It makes me sick to think about."

Grandpa pulled his Ernst Leitz binoculars from their hand-tooled leather pouch and scanned the distant horizon.

"As I said, there is Slide Mountain, there is Overlook, and over there, over there is . . . look Ephie! You can see Fawn's Leap—where A. B. Durand painted that big picture I showed you *chol hamoed Pesach* at the library—*Kindred Spirits*—remember?"

"The one on the stairway leading up to that big room?"

"Precisely the one. In the picture Thomas Cole and William Cullen Bryant are looking out to where we are standing."

Lost in thought Grandpa put a tired but hard hand on his grandson's shoulder pointing towards the stone promenade in the distance.

"Yes, I think I see it Grandpa. Yes, there it is." Ephie couldn't really see much of anything through those old binoculars. All he saw was lots of green interrupted by more green, but he knew it meant something to his grandfather who had lugged those heavy old German binoculars on this hike, so he made the effort.

"Let us make a *bracha* first and then I will tell you the rest of the story."

"What *bracha*—we didn't bring any lunch."

"Not food for our bodies, but nourishment for our souls—even more important. Ephraim, repeat after me: *Barush atah adonai eloheini melech haoylam*—"

Ephie repeated without all the "*oys*" and "*ees*."

"*Baruch atah adonai eloheanu melech haolam*—"

"*Haoyseh maasey beresysheyt.*"

"*Haoseh maaseh bereshet.*"

Grandpa added a good strong "*Umean.*" It was strange to Ephie how, although they were speaking the same language, their Hebrew was so different. The Hebrew he learned in yeshiva in Long Island was like a whole different language from the European variety his grandfather spoke with different vowels, sayings, for all Ephie knew, maybe even different meanings as well.

Grandpa was speaking again—the hook! thought Ephie, but no, he was just translating the blessing for his ignorant American (read: Long Island) grandson.

"Blessed is *Hashem*, king of the universe, who creates the world from the very beginning of time."

"*Ani yodeah et mah atah omer, lamah atah lo meavin sheani midabere ivrit meah achuz?*"

Grandpa put his hand out and stroked Ephie's cheek, said something unintelligible to Ephie in Yiddish, before gazing into the distance of Round Top Mountain.

Ephie knew that in researching his latest article for *The Algemeiner Journale* on the Revisionist Zionist Ze'ev Jabotinsky's death in Hunter, NY, Grandpa had been taking the train daily into Grand Central and reading all he could at the New York Public Library about the Catskills. He had even taken Ephie in with him one day during the intermediary days of Passover that past spring, but despite this knowledge, Ephie was amazed at how much his Grandfather seemed to have learned about the region. Ephie had been coming to these mountains since he was a baby and he couldn't tell you the name of the mountain Tannersville was situated upon (South Mountain) or what kind of tree he and Ari had built their tree-house in (Beech) a few summers before.

"You know my article about Jabotinsky, I've told you he died on the mountaintop, but did I show you the pictures I took of the Betar Youth Zionist Camp he was visiting?"

"Yes, about twenty times—we picked them up together at McManus Pharmacy remember? Your Leica pictures?"

To this, Grandpa didn't reply. He continued to speak in that far-away lecturing type of voice. He had spent months researching this area—last spring it had all seemed important to flesh out the Jabotinsky piece. Why did the Zionist Congress meet in Tannersville in 1906? What was Jabotinsky searching for on the mountaintop in the summer of 1940?

"Ephie, this gorge was formed 15,000 years ago when the last ice age ended. The big thaw thousands of years ago formed this whole area—*glaciation*—the geologists say. What can I tell you my child? The pain was what it was. What else can I tell you? I am sorry to tell you these things. You are almost a *bar-mitzvah* now. You can know, perhaps you need to know, such things exist in this world too."

Grandpa then looked down into the great maw of the falls collecting in the pool hundreds of feet below. He turned to look behind, where he knew, but could not see, the two great lakes, North and South, collected rain water and mountaintop snow melt—a place where his grandchildren, including Ephie, had spent the best days of their American childhoods, hooklessly swimming and splashing in the lake and listening to calm lake water lapping on the shore as many a beautiful Catskill summer day came to a dusky close.

"If I told you that the lash of each whip felt like a flame singeing my skin. Or, that the iron poker Praust used to comb my hair was like the slow flaying of Rabbi Akiva and the *asarah harugei malchut*—your Yeshiva teach you about these martyrs killed by the Romans?" Ephie nodded again . . . "—all I would be doing was substituting one useless expression for another, one story of horror for another, mere words. To have you fully understand . . . I don't know how I could do that exactly."

Grandpa remained silent for several minutes during which time Ephie just stared down into the great rush of water disappearing beneath them. He felt like the ancient rock holding him in place would also give way in that great rush of water and memory. Finally Grandpa continued.

"I guess it would require you to undergo what had been done to me. I think this would be the only way." He paused for several minutes deep in thought before continuing. "Yes, there is no other way. That would be it. But this would make me standing here with you, my American grandson, on this rock, scoured by retreating ice fifteen thousand years ago, into a Nazi." Ephie was vigorously shaking his head.

"Of course not Grandpa!"

Undeterred, Grandpa continued, ". . . and we already said Ephie that there are no Nazis in these beautiful Catskills. *Forshteysht*? There is no Praust here. There, in Breendonk, there was no why. Here, in the Catskills there is no Nazis—only the remains of ancient hemlock trees that somehow avoided Mr. Pratt's ax, and a few scattered Jews here and there." Grandpa smiled and gently placed his hand, on Ephie's shoulder.

"So what can I say to you my child? So eager to learn about the Nazis. You want to impress your friends with your brave grandfather?"

Ephie shook his head slowly back and forth.

"It's OK, Ephraim, I too was young once. I remember how it was. That is my problem, our curse, really: no matter how hard I try, I cannot forget anything. We in our family have this type of memory.

"Yes. The pain was what it was. That is all. Believe me Ephie. You haven't heard it all. You haven't heard that much. *Baruch Hashem* you don't know a thing about Isa, about loss. About loss that drives you crazy. About not being able to scream or forget. About a stomach as empty as a frog in winter. Ay. Maybe this was all a mistake. But for today anyway, it is enough. *Shoyn dayenu*."

There was so much Ephie wanted to say to his grandfather. Yet he remained silent, staring off into the distant ravine where the mountain-top's snow melt gathered in that pool and where, thousands of years before the Third Reich was imagined, native peoples of the Mahicans, Munsees, and the Lenni Lanape meditated.

"The Indians felt the souls of their ancestors gather here in this amphitheater. This has been a holy place for thousands of years. Maybe not to us Jews, but if you know how to read the stones—you can see history took place here. Look at all those marks, Ephie." Grandpa pointed to long striations and gouges in the granite they were sitting upon.

"Were those marks carved by the Indians?"

"No, Ephie, not by Indians, but by ice! Retreating ice carved up these stones. Time and pressure—that is all it takes to leave a mark."

That and an iron hook, thought Ephie—though he said nothing. Instead he moved closer to inspect the rocks.

"Maybe it is time for a *niggun* Ephie. You know when I was a boy I would sit in my grandfather's lap, the Modzitzer Rebbe's lap—can you imagine that!—you are named after him: Rabbi Ephraim Yedidyah Taub."

"I know. I know—he composed many of his most important *niggunim* when you were a baby playing in his lap."

"Yes—he would look at me with my blond hair and my blue eyes and he would gently tug on my *peyos* and he would start to *shuckle* back and forth, and soon a *dveykus niggun* would appear, note by note—as if by magic."

"What's *dveykus*?"

"You said they taught you Hebrew, excuse me, 'Ivrit' at that 'Yeshiva' you go to on the beach in Long Island, no?"

"Yes, but I never heard that word before."

"Sure you did, look at the *shoyresh: dalad-vuv-kuf—davek*."

"Oh—glue! He made a song about glue?"

"*L'davek*—to cling. A metaphor—a twisting, a turning of language. Use your brain a little bit, it helps once in a while. A *dveykus* song helps a Jew to cling to *Hashem Yisborach*. Let us sit here beside the Kaaterskill Falls, in this holy place and sing the Modzitzer *dveykus niggun*. My grandfather's *niggun*—your great-great-grandfather's *niggun*, Ephie. I will sing it once and then you join in with me."

"OK Grandpa, but Rabbi Luzzato says the only thing my voice is good for is scaring away the frogs in Rip Van Winkle Lake."

"Nonsense—I have heard you *layn* your *bar-mitzvah parsha*—you're getting much better. You will soon make us all proud. Remember, you are a Modzitzer—you were born into a great musical tradition."

Slowly Grandpa began *shuckling* as if engaged in prayer. He came so close to the edge of the giant precipice where the water frothed that Ephie worried at first that he might go over the falls as well. Slowly he began chanting, wordlessly humming what seemed like stray notes. Slowly, very slowly, he began with the first words. *Kol haolam kulo. Gesher tzar meod. Gesher tzar meod*—all of the world in its entirety is a narrow path. He motioned for Ephie to join in and he did.

The entire world is a narrow path—they sang it low, but soon, little by little, without their having noticed, their voices began to rise and soon their singing echoed through the ancient amphitheater filling the great gash in the wall of Manitou that the Dutch had named Kaaterskill Clove.

There was a second part to this Modzitzere *dveykus niggun* and Ephie's grandfather was not about to stop midway.

"Repeat after me: *v'haeykar, v'haeykar lo l'phachaid, lo l'phachaid klal*—and the key point is not to fear anything. Ephie, fear can do many things to a grown man or a *bar-mitzvah* boy. God has a plan for us. We may not be smart enough to see it right away, but there is a plan—make no mistake about that."

They sang the song together loudly, strongly, like the marching song of the *Palmach* Grandpa had taught him and all of his cousins the previous week. Their voices echoed and repercussed, returning to them with the idea that the world was the home to both Nazis and Dutch cloves. Still, they had a voice and an ancestral Modzitz tune in which to sing.

Finally, after a half hour of singing, their voices slowly came to a halt. "Come on, Ephie, we should be getting back—Mummy will be worried." And with that they began the hike back towards the Bonneville waiting for them in an empty parking lot on route 23a. The parking lot stood guard over the famous spot where William Cullen Bryant and Thomas Cole supposedly had stood admiring the deep cut in the mountain wall leading southeast towards the Hudson River and Kaaterskill Falls in the distance. A. B. Durand's fantasy—these two great nineteenth century Americans never really having stood together on that particular spot. Yet a large and beautiful painting guarding the entrance to the reading room of The New York Public Library commemorated this event that never took place. When Ephie first beheld that painting, he looked closely at the three Catskill eagles flittering about the picture, and he thought he could discern in the shadows of a blasted hemlock tree a lone Indian boy peeking out from behind a rock watching those two white Americans enjoying their summer stroll.

That night Ephie had visions of hooks dangling high above his bed, but what truly haunted his dreams was a vision of a wooden box, as large as a small child's coffin. When Ephie would open the lid, he could see the box was empty save for one sepia-toned photograph. Standing above the box he could see the picture was of a beautiful woman, but when he stepped into the box and held the picture in his hand, her features faded into the background.

Ephie knew there was no vessel to contain the memory of Isa—this woman whose love and loss led his grandfather to the depths of despair, to the brink of insanity on *Tisha B'Av*, during that brutally hot Belgian summer of 1944. He wasn't sure why, but Ephie believed that his destiny was somehow inextricably tied to this woman. He knew that before his grandparents left Tannersville and traveled back to New York City, he needed to find out all he could about her—he needed to put a face back on that fading photograph.

Balm of Gilead:
Haunted in the Catskills

Ezra Cappell

. . . and there is a Catskill eagle in some souls that can alike dive down into the
blackest gorges, and soar out of them again and become invisible in the sunny
spaces. And even if he forever flies within the gorge, that gorge is in the mountains; so that even in his lowest swoop the mountain eagle is still higher than the
other birds upon the plain, even though they soar.

—Herman Melville[1]

Is there no balm in Gilead? Is there no physician there? Why then has not the
health of the daughter of my people been restored?

—*Jeremiah*, 8:22

Since 1983 was both the summer that Fat Joey was released from
reform school in Troy and came back home to his familiar winding
and narrow streets of Tannersville, and since it was also the summer that
my grandparents, survivors of the Holocaust, came up that troped and
twisted mountain gorge path to fitfully watch over us for most of that

---

1   Herman Melville, *Moby-Dick* (New York: Barnes & Noble Books, 1994), 425.

historically hot July, it would be hard to say which of the two events haunted my twelve-year-old nights more. Both would, by *Rosh Hashanah* (through the strange fates of our lunar existence, falling early that year), come together in surprising and furious violence—a violence that is at the heart of the Catskills story. That story begins with the "benevolent hand of God," as if by a miracle clearing millions of acres of the most beautiful land of the North American continent, and thereby creating a haven for white men. This, in actuality, meant removing by force the thousands of native tribes—the Iroquois, Mohican, Munsees, and Lenni Lenape—who had made their home in this region for thousands of years, since the last ice age melted away, to make room for the coming Dutch settlers and untold fortunes and glory. It was also the summer I came into possession of the dark, twisted history my grandfather bequeathed to me beside the roar of Kaaterskill Falls, which for generations had guarded the ancestral spirit of Native Americans, and nothing was quite the same after he told me about the hook he had hung from high in the Business Room deep within the long hallway's embrace of Fort Breendonk.

⤙❧

To a young boy, almost a *bar-mitzvah,* which is worse: the threat of a hand raised in violence or the aftermath of that repercussioning sound echoing in one's bloody ears? The high-pitched notes of pain and humiliation held at a constant, as if suspended in amber, forever and forever. Or is it neither? Is it the knowledge of past violence committed against dearly loved grandparents or is it the commensurate understanding of complete and utter powerlessness to alter any of the awful facts of our shared European history?

I have often thought that Ephie, my protagonist from *Dreaming in the Ninth,* bears more than a passing resemblance to the tiny Indian painted into Thomas Cole's masterpiece, *Falls of The Kaaterskill*—placed in the painting almost as an afterthought.

The Native American Indian forlornly looks down from the center of the great falls where his ancestors' spirits, going back fifteen thousand

Thomas Cole, *Falls of the Kaaterskill*, 1826. Oil on canvas, 43 x 36 inches. The Warner Collection of American Fine and Decorative Arts, Gulf States Paper Corporation, Tuscaloosa, AL. Image courtesy of The Thomas Cole National Historic Site.

years to the end of the last ice age, perpetually reside. Not visible in the painting is what that lone Native American man would have actually seen from that spot at the time of Cole's composition: he might have discerned a scraggly old white man sitting beside a sign that shouted to the thousands of tourists staying at The Laurel House, The Hotel Kaaterskill, and The Catskill Mountain House: "25c to Turn on Falls." This blatant commercialization and exploitation of the falls and the ecological devastation of the region during the nineteenth century reveal a portrait of the Catskills quite different from the image depicted in the natural and sublime landscapes of Thomas Cole, Asher B. Durand, and the many other Hudson River School painters who chose to romanticize the clove and the wider Catskills region.[2]

⁓ჟ℮

---

2   I am indebted to Alf Evers' book, *The Catskills: From Wilderness to Woodstock* (Garden City: Doubleday, 1972), a comprehensive history of the region.

The Catskill region is so filled with magic and wonder that by the time my grandfather had come to visit us in the summer of 1983, its tragic myth was almost as old as the mountains and streams that fed the Hudson River and the fertile valley thousands of feet below. But before Fat Joey more fully enters our narrative, let me set the scene. Perhaps American literature gets started in the backyard of Congregation Anshei Hashoran—Tannersville's wood-frame Orthodox synagogue founded in the nineteenth century. Almost in the shadow of this *shul,* James Fenimore Cooper placed his hero, Natty Bumpo, who gazes off into the distance of the Catskill Mountains and says that "all creation"[3] is visible from that spot. And indeed, nearly two centuries after Cooper published his first novel, despite all the unfettered development this leather-stocking region has been subjected to (the tanning industry, bluestone quarrying), Natty's words still ring true. Tannersville is blessed with numerous lakes, brooks, and rivers: the sound of flowing water is a backdrop to almost all of the town's activities, including the

---

3   In a key scene in James Fenimore Cooper's *The Pioneers,* Natty Bumpo describes the view from Pine Orchard near North and South Lake. He then goes on to describe Kaaterskill Falls and the breathtaking view from the top of the falls:

"There's a place in them hills that I used to climb to, when I wanted to see the carryings on of the world, . . . You know the Catskills, lad, for you must have seen them on your left, as you followed the river up from York, looking as blue as a piece of clear sky, and holding the clouds on their tops, as the smoke curls over the head of an Indian chief at the council fire. Well, there's the High-peak and the Round-top, which lay back, like a father and mother among their children, seeing they are far above all the other hills.". . .

"What see you when you get there?" asked Edwards.

"Creation!" said Natty, dropping the end of his rod into the water, and sweeping one hand around him in a circle—"all creation, lad. . . .

"Why, there's a fall in the hills where the water of two little ponds that lie near each other breaks out of their bounds, and runs over the rocks into the valley. The stream is, maybe, such a one as would turn a mill, if so useless thing was wanted in the wilderness. But the hand that made that 'Leap' never made a mill! There the water comes crooking and winding among the rocks, first so slow that a trout could swim in it, and then starting and running like a critter that wanted to make a far spring, till it gets to where the mountain divides, like the cleft hoof of a deer, leaving a deep hollow for the brook to tumble into. The first pitch is nigh two hundred feet, and the water looks like flakes of driven snow, afore it touches the bottom; and there the stream gathers together again for a new start, and maybe flutters over fifty feet of flat-rock, before it falls for another hundred, when it jumps about from shelf to shelf, first turning this-away and then turning that-away, striving to get out of the hollow, till it finally comes to the plain." (James Cooper Fenimore, *The Pioneers* [New York: Oxford University Press, 1991], 292-294).

singing of *Modzitzer niggunim* loud and clear on a perfect summer *shabbos* morning in Congregation Anshei HaShoran, the watery backdrop to the Jewish voices resounding over Rip Van Winkle Lake.

Throughout the nineteenth century, the high peaks of the Catskills, the setting for *Dreaming in the Ninth*, inspired many of America's leading artists and writers. In "The Try-Works," a key chapter in *Moby-Dick*, Herman Melville turns to a Catskill eagle to help explain the importance of a proper perspective if one is to lead a life not wholly subjected to darkness and depression. As Melville writes: "The sun hides not the ocean, which is the dark side of this earth, and which is two thirds of this earth" (424). Despite this somber observation, Melville suggests that Ishmael will not succumb to complete darkness—unlike Captain Ahab, who is subsumed by his madness. The chapter concludes with a stirring American metaphor of a Catskill eagle used to lend perspective to Ishmael's difficult journey, as quoted in the epigraph of this essay.

As Larry Reynolds forcefully argues, in turning to a Catskill eagle to make Ishmael's perspective visible to his readers, Melville was clearly inspired by the famous painting, *Kindred Spirits*, by Asher B. Durand.

Asher Brown Durand, *Kindred Spirits*, 1849. Oil on canvas, 44 x 36 inches. Crystal Bridges Museum of American Art, Bentonville, Arkansas. Photography by The Metropolitan Museum of Art.

As I discuss in the chapter excerpted from *Dreaming in the Ninth*, the painting depicts William Cullen Bryant and Thomas Cole looking out towards Kaaterskill Clove in the midst of the Catskill high peaks. Bryant had recently eulogized his close friend Thomas Cole, and Durand, who was commissioned by Jonathan Sturgis (who was a patron of both Bryant and Cole), created his masterpiece *Kindred Spirits* to honor Bryant and to memorialize Cole.[4] In his article, Reynolds locates the three eagles from the painting and connects them to Melville's chapter "The Try-Works" in *Moby-Dick*. While I agree with Reynolds, I would go even further and suggest that in addition to his making allegorical use of the three Catskill eagles depicted in Durand's painting (an homage to Cole who often painted in the allegorical mode),[5] Melville acknowledges his debt to *Kindred Spirits* by placing strategically the key word "kindred" in this chapter.

As he stands watch at the helm of the *Pequod*, Ishmael says: "The continual sight of the fiend shapes before me, capering half in smoke and half in fire, these at last begat kindred visions in my soul."[6] As Reynolds, Wolf, and many others have pointed out, Melville uses this scene to depict the differences between Ishmael, who has been much affected by woe, and his fully-mad Captain, Ahab, who has allowed his darkness to overtake all. As Melville writes: "There is a wisdom that is woe; but there is a woe that is madness."[7]

In setting my chapter in this famous Kaaterskill Clove, a place that has inspired so many writers and artists for centuries, I am well aware of the possibility of allowing a tragedy such as the Holocaust and the torture experienced by Ephie's grandfather to turn my characters towards irrevocable madness. Because Grandpa tells an innocent young boy of his torture under the Nazis, some readers might view the grandfather's narrative itself as a form of madness—of his darkness overtaking all and clouding his vision as a grandfather who should above all be

---

4   James, T. Callow, *Kindred Spirits: Knickerbocker Writers and American Artists, 1807-1855* (Durham: The University of North Carolina Press, 1967), 67.

5   See, for example, Thomas Cole's *The Voyage of Life,* a four-part series of allegorical paintings.

6   Melville, *Moby-Dick*, 423.

7   Melville, *Moby-Dick*, 425.

protecting his impressionable grandson from these images of horror. Yet, I believe the grandfather's narrative reveals an Ishmael-like under-standing of the universe—his is a vision fully aware of the two-thirds of darkness that covers the earth. However, there remains a third space for sunlight, and there is even a place within Kaaterskill Clove for song—for a *Modzitzer niggun*, which fills the scene with the true lamp of the natural sun.[8] My aim in this scene was to steer these characters just short of the madness Ishmael warns us about, allowing them, both the grandfather and grandson, to relive the torture of the Nazis, and to swoop low into the blackest gorges, but all the while to maintain their proper perspective on this famous Catskill mountaintop. Through their song, they come to realize that even in their "lowest swoop," much like the mountain eagle, they remain "still higher than other birds upon the plain though they soar."[9]

My novel, *Dreaming in the Ninth*, therefore begins with an evocation of the natural beauty of the mountaintop: "There is a place where the road curves steep and sharp, where the trees touch branches high above the pavement forming a canopy of leaves beneath which all who wish to enter the home of love and death, dreams and reality, must pass; these travelers are soused by the spray from the great falls, the spirits of ancestors blow the wind that whips the leaves high above, and their ears are filled from the haunting sound of falling mountain streams that collect nearly five hundred feet below. These summer pilgrims quickly pass, oblivious to all, save that they must slow down on Platte Clove Mountain's horseshoe curve or they, too, will be carried away in the awesome rush of water, water, water."

It is also a place that holds the mystery of existence within its cloves and streams. It is a place where the mornings break cold and clear, even in July, and the late afternoon air is heavy with the scent of clover, aster, and the beating of insect wings. It is a place where, as their *challahs* rise in their rented kitchens, *Yecha* survivors of the Holocaust walk the country lanes on Friday afternoons picking wildflowers, which they will artfully arrange to sanctify their *shabbos* tables for their

---

8   Melville, *Moby-Dick*, 424.
9   Melville, *Moby-Dick*, 425.

husbands returning to the mountaintop from their workweek in the city. The many Jewish families of Tannersville reunited in *kabbalat shabbos*—the queenly emanations of the *shabbos* glory flittering from cottage to cottage up Park Lane and down Spring Street—leading all Jews to the enormous oak doors of Anshei HaShoran standing guard for the prayers and songs emanating within.

—⁊⁊—

At sixteen years old, Fat Joey was simply enormous. To us he seemed as large as the occasional old-growth hemlock tree that somehow, miraculously, survived the saw of the tanners seeking the magical ingredients contained within that would transform high fashion downriver in New York City, decimate the natural beauty of the region, and forever associate Tannersville with this less-than-holy American enterprise, the leather-industry, that gave this hamlet its workaday name.

He was well over six feet tall and weighed in at close to two hundred and fifty pounds. We, in contrast, not quite yet *bar-mitzvahed*, were not even responsible for our own sins—the rabbis teaching that our sins belonged to our parents and grandparents until we were called to the *Torah* at age thirteen, a full year away. We were just big enough to be fully conscious of our lack of stature in the grown-up world, yet barely weighed enough to keep our corporeal bodies anchored to the ground, as if with one missed meal we might just fly away like a lonely child's balloon floating high above Central Park.

More than any other crime or mischief, Fat Joey, best of all, loved knocking Jewish boys and girls off of their bicycles. Even trained killer whales, who for years abide with giving rides to their trainers for a pound of herring, will, after docile decades, revert back to their ancient instincts and bite their trainer's hand. Can you blame these tremendous beasts? It is just their nature. So, too, with Fat Joey. Yes there was the marijuana dealing down at Rip Van Winkle Lake, there was the joyful Saturday nights of punching out car windows on Main Street, and even, it was rumored, an occasional rape, but make no mistake: Fat Joey was born to push Jewish children off bicycles. It is simply the natural order of things. There was something almost beautiful in watching Fat Joey stalk his next prey. Everything about him was adapted for these instinctual behaviors. In your entire life, you never saw such glee as when Fat Joey sent a Lichtenstein boy to the hospital or bloodied the nose of one of the Goldman girls—her white tights shredded in the potholes of Tompkins Street.

So, how could I (how could you?!) really blame Fat Joey for doing what came natural to him? My mistake was in trying to invert the laws of the universe, which even Jewish physics will tell you are incontrovertible (if relative . . .). My mistake was trying to outrun him. When I saw him on his moped, which although quite large, seemed like a toy beneath his enormous flanks, I should have just taken my beating like the other Jews—accepted my American fate of being somehow reviled and scorned while the object of other hyphenated Americans' unending rage and jealousy. I must confess. I did not meekly accept this fate. Stupidly, I calculated that I could outrun Fat Joey. There he stood next to his parked moped beside the firehouse not twenty feet from Main Street. To get to my house and avoid a beating by Joey, I would have to somehow avoid him right at the very beginning of Main Street and manage to out pedal him on my ten-speed Schwinn (he had a motorized bike, you idiot!) and furiously race all the way up Park Lane, past Willie the handyman's house, past our old rented little red cabin (which, I might have made . . .) all the way to where the road quickly turns west towards Spring Street and the Hudson River beyond—where the virgin forest still grew on the last undeveloped plot of Park Lane—to our newly-rented railroad-flat cabin over a half mile away. Stupid, I know. Nature is nature. There is no outrunning it.

What really spooked me was that Fat Joey held in his hand what looked like a long truncheon of some sort. It might have been a broken-off broom-handle or, from my father's childhood in the Bronx, perhaps an old, long-discarded regulation stickball bat. Whatever it was, it freaked me out and, upshifting at the top of the hill, I began to peddle as fast as I could. I could see Jim Burns polishing the fire engine through the large plate glass window of the Tannersville-Hunter Volunteer firehouse, but I had already made my decision. I was going to be the first to outrun Fat

Joey. In his special theory of relativity, Einstein said that one time in a billion the laws that govern our universe will shift. I was and remain a dreamer in the ghetto of my own mind.

Joey looked so happy to see my yarmulke that, as I sped past, he seemed to shed a tear, almost in sympathy. I, of course, had the lead until well past the Helmreich house. I could hear his moped starting up into gear and the high wail of those 49 ccs gaining on me. I can only imagine the scene I must have made as I whirled past the bespectacled and bow-tied Bert Schwartzbach out on his porch to water his prize rose-bushes sprouting along his Victorian wrap-around porch. I could hear Fat Joey yelling something at me, some sort of war cry that sounded like "Ju, Jew you, Jujitsu . . ." as he gained ground. I turned to see him not ten paces behind as the road entered that one undeveloped plot that a local Jewish builder had his eye on for a low-income condominium—busing welfare recipients up from Starrett City and the Bronx projects. Joey was laughing now and was waving that long stick towards me menacingly. Soon he was beside me and Joey wore a look of beatitude—it was a look of someone accomplishing their life's mission, a look of utter joy, almost serene, other than the fact that he was howling something in my face. That was the last thing I saw. That and Fat Joey standing over me as I was in a semi-conscious daze as he swiftly kicked me twice in the balls and spat the biggest grape-scented luggie I ever saw or smelled right into my bloodied face.

"That's what you get for running, you Jew-Bastard-Christ-Killing-Son-of-a-Fucking-Bitch."

I rolled over and vomited up some bile and blood from my mouth. I thought I had an even chance of having knocked out a few teeth as my face hit the pavement. Joey then laughed and mumbled something about being "The Mountain-Top Jew-Jitsu Black Belt Champion." He let out one more high-pitched rebel-yell, then got back on his moped and calmly sped away back towards the volunteer firehouse.

Not fifty yards from my front porch, I tried to get up and assess the damage. I couldn't. I spit some more blood out from my mouth. Only then did I notice that both my elbows had been skinned pretty badly, almost down to the bone on the left side, which was steadily bleeding.

My right elbow was not bleeding nearly as much, but it was already swelling up—I could hardly move either arm. My legs, as well, were bloody messes, and my lip had been split where it had hit the pavement and I had, apparently, loosened several teeth. I crawled on the side of the road through the high grass towards our front porch. My grandfather was the first to see me.

"*Oy veih*! What happened, my child?"

My adrenaline flowing, I couldn't quite yet speak, but fell onto the steps of the small porch. When my father came running to see what the commotion was, all I said to his panicked, "What happened?" were two words: "Fat Joey."

My father ran to the shed in back of the house to retrieve the ax we used to chop down some wood poles for the rustic *succah* we were building for the Feast of Tabernacles. *Succot* arrived so early that year we would be able to celebrate it in Tannersville instead of "the city," which meant the horrible little cicada-filled hamlet of hell we lived in on Long Island's South Shore—oh Gatsby, how right you were.

My grandfather, who, forty years earlier, had been torqued and twisted and broken in the Business Room of Breendonk spoke up immediately.

"Raoul, this is not the way. I will come, and we will speak to this boy's parents and be reasonable. He will apologize for this."

"He is no boy—he is an animal," said my fury-filled father.

Nonetheless, we all three got into my grandfather's blue Pontiac Bonneville (I tried not to bleed onto the elegantly upholstered backseat) and drove down beside Rip Van Winkle Lake (wishing that I, too, could go to sleep for the next twenty years like that good old Dutchman . . .) the known residence and hang-out of Fat Joey. He could often be seen lakeside blasting a boom box when not eagerly waiting for his prey in the Jewish streets of Tannersville.

—⚜—

So, to the lake we drove, with Grandpa having put on his jacket and straw hat, me bleeding in the backseat, and my father clutching Bertram

Schwartzbach's ancient-looking ax, borrowed for our *succah* making expedition. When we got to the lake, I saw Joey's moped parked in the dirt and gravel driveway of the trailer home sitting beside Rip Van Winkle Lake.

We walked to the front door—Grandpa knocked loudly, determinedly. It wasn't Joey who answered, but rather an even more enormous man of indeterminate age who came to the door. The man wore a cut-off t-shirt, his enormous muscles bulging as he grasped a Genesee beer can in one fist. He didn't say anything—he only stared incredulously at Grandpa and then slowly looked to me and then to my father who now had Bert's ax raised and resting on his left shoulder. This local's expression seemed to suggest he hadn't been expecting a visit from a bleeding kid, his European accented grandfather, and a Jewish Paul Bunyan with a modified pompadour on this particularly squalid early September day.

"Good afternoon," said Grandpa.

"Yeah, what of it," said the man—he looked at my father's fingers twitching on the ax.

"You have a boy here. I am certain he is basically a good boy, but he has done something bad to another child," and with the mention of child he pulled me in front of him as exhibit A, or J—as the case may be.

"Look I don't know what in God's name you're all talkin' about but that motherfucker better get the fuck off my property holding that ax up or he better know how to fucking use it."

My father snorted. "Your scumbag of a son, I assume he's your son, knocked my son off his bike. Now I'm gonna knock in some of his teeth—yours too if you don't bring him out here."

Grandpa put his hand up towards my father as if warding off an imaginary blow. "No, no, no," there will be no more hitting and fighting today. Enough already. All we want is your son to come out here and apologize—children sometimes don't always realize what they are doing and the consequences of their actions. I know what I speak of. I have seen enough violence in my lifetime. Please, where is your boy?"

"Joey! Some crazy people here to see you. Get your ass over here."

I could feel the blood rush to my face as I heard his voice coming from an interior room of the double-wide: "What the fuck now?"

In another moment, there was Joey staring at us through the torn screen door.

"Please. Come outside here. We would like to speak with you."

"Not until that son-of-a-bitch puts down that ax—he ain't coming out." This would be where I might have chimed in: "Chicken shit Fat Joey you motherfucking piece of shit! Not so tough now are you, you little fucking coward!" Instead, I looked down at my blue Puma suede sneakers. I noticed a few drops of blood polka-dotting the yellow swirl.

My father lowered Bert's ax and the two locals exchanged some words inside the trailer before finally emerging out to the street.

The father figure in this rural tableau, still holding his Genesee, spoke first.

"Look, I'm sorry your boy is hurt, but Joey says it was him who started the trouble—wanting to race. Your boy just fell off his bike is all. Happens sometimes with beginners. You should teach your boy to ride better, he wouldn't fall off, he wouldn't get hurt so much."

My father, through clenched teeth said in a low animal-like voice: "Your reform-school delinquent goes around town knocking kids half his size off their bikes. He stuck a stick in my kid's spokes. Does that sound like an accident to you?"

"Look—I don't have time for this right now. I need to go get paid at Legg's. I wasn't fucking there so I don't know what all the fuck happened. Joey, tell them what you just told me."

"That little cry-baby wanted to race so I raced him."

I finally found my voice. "Liar! I was trying to get away from you! What kind of a race is a bike against a moped? You stuck a stick in my spokes then spit on me and kicked me. You called me a dirty Jew bastard." I was crying now, trying to look at the ground so they wouldn't see.

"Well you got to admit you are dirty—look at you all filthied up," the father said laughing.

"Come, come." My grandfather said, as if convening a board of synagogue directors and not talking to two anti-Semites. This little UN peace-seeking mission clearly wasn't going all that well.

"Saying ugly things does no good. Please come here and shake hands you two. I'll shake his hand. I know where such speaking leads.

Children should be nice to one another—you may someday regret such things as this. Come here now children and shake hands. When I was a boy many such terrible things like this happened."

Joey sauntered up to me and said: "No hard feelings. Next time just try to stay on your bike."

I shook his hand and, with that, our new best friends turned and went back into their double-wide.

My father stood there incredulous. "Detty, what good did that do? Couple of knocks to the head with the blunt side of this ax and he wouldn't be so fast to knock kids off their bikes."

"You will not teach these people this way." We all climbed back into the car, my father driving this time. Through the rear-view mirror my father looked at my reflection, disgusted and disappointed at how things were, at how it all turns out. He smacked the steering wheel, loudly cursed, and then added, "Detty—I should have hit that kid in the mouth."

There was no response from anyone until we had turned back onto Park Lane. My grandfather finally broke the silence as we were pulling into our driveway.

"Nothing good will come of that—only more blood." Turning towards me in the backseat: "Believe me, I know what it is. Ezra, my child, your cuts will heal. Hatred is everywhere. Do not swallow it down." He waited for me to get out of the backseat, then he kissed the top of my head and, though it was nowhere near *shabbos*, holding my head in his hard palms, he slowly recited the priestly benediction. I watched him wipe a tear from his cheek before disappearing back inside the cabin to report it all to Grandma. My father glaring at us both, silently walked to the back of the house to continue his work building our rustic *succah*—a reminder of the transient state of *olam hazeh*, this profane and fallen world we inhabit.

—❧—

I recall this little scene of horror from my childhood because it bears more than a passing import to the chapter excerpted from *Dreaming in the Ninth*. Writing these words from the comfort of 2014 it is hard to remember just how persistent and malevolent anti-Semitism was in the America of my childhood. Both in my summer haven in the Catskills, where we Jews were almost universally reviled by the locals, and in our year-round Long Island "Five Towns" North Shore community, the state of inter-ethnic understanding and tolerance wasn't all that different from a hundred and fifty miles upstate. Three times in my Long Island childhood we had rocks thrown through the large plate-glass windows of our home. Halloween wasn't a time to dress up in fancy rented costumes and come home late with bags of chocolate and candy. For me, growing up Jewish in Cedarhurst, Halloween consisted of my standing ineffectual guard on our front porch—supposedly to scare off any would be neighborhood Jew-haters from our friendly Long Island community. The aftermath of Halloween was consumed with cleaning up the stinking mess left on our house and cars. Annually, my father would come home late from his evening job teaching and Americanizing Southeast Asian immigrants to discover egg slowly dripping down our home's stucco façade.

In Cedarhurst, when I was bored out of my mind, I was occasionally stupid enough to venture down to the local playground by the public school just down the block from our home—at least I would, until the time I was cursed and spit on to the taunts of the older kids screaming "Christ Killer" in my face. If, on a special occasion, I was taken into the city to see a Knicks game, of course, like all the other kids in my yeshiva, I was instructed to take off my yarmulke (with a gentle sweep of the hand over the head and into the trousers' front pocket went the ethnic marker), or face taunts and insults from other upstanding (and long-suffering) Knicks fans. These were the realities of my childhood in the 1970s and 1980s in and around NYC. How much different a place America was thirty years ago.

The Catskills, to me, seemed like a refuge, but it was also a place of danger and violence as we Jewish children faced different forms of anti-Semitism and the locals' lingering hatreds lent a melancholy tinge to even the most beautiful summer day. To combat these ancient hatreds, we children were weekly instructed in how to make ourselves less Jewy Jew to the "goyim"—chief among these rules was to never, under any circumstances, wear a *tallit* in the street as you walked to *shul* on *shabbos*. Somehow the sight of a prayer shawl would so enflame the local population that, if you believed the *Yecha gabbai* of the *shul*, it would immediately lead to a full-fledged mountaintop pogrom.

But for centuries before Hebrew resounded through the Dutch cloves of Tannersville, the Catskills had been a setting for far worse violence perpetrated against the numerous Native American tribes hundreds of years before a yarmulke made its first appearance in the Catskills. In retrospect, the highest Catskill mountain peaks where I spent my childhood summers would seem an appropriate setting for the Holocaust witnessing that is described in this excerpt from *Dreaming in the Ninth*. The devastation and loss that lone Native American Indian witnessed in Thomas Cole's painting could possibly frame the Holocaust witnessing my young protagonist endures. Given its tortured history, the Catskill region lends an appropriate perspective to my novel.

In the preface to his last novel, *The Marble Faun*, Nathaniel Hawthorne discusses his rationale for the European setting of his book. Hawthorne says that, unlike America, Italy afforded him "a sort of poetic or fairy precinct." Hawthorne writes: "No author, without a trial, can conceive of the difficulty of writing a romance about a country where there is no shadow, no antiquity, no mystery, no picturesque and gloomy wrong, nor anything but a commonplace prosperity, in broad and simple daylight, as is happily the case with my dear native land."[10]

A century and a half after Hawthorne's conception of an innocent and carefree America, I began writing this key chapter excerpted from *Dreaming in the Ninth*, and as I researched the Native American history in the Catskills, I uncovered "gloomy wrong" and not "simple daylight."[11] The more I explored the sedimentation of geological, environmental, and cultural history of the Catskills, Kaaterskill Clove asserted itself as the only place such difficult witnessing could possibly be contained.

---

10   Nathaniel Hawthorne, *The Marble Faun*, iv.
11   Hawthorne, *The Marble Faun*, iv.

Bibliography

Callow, James, T. *Kindred Spirits: Knickerbocker Writers and American Artists, 1807-1855.* Durham: The University of North Carolina Press, 1967.

Cole, Thomas. *Falls of the Kaaterskill.* 1826. Oil on canvas. The Westervelt-Warner Museum of American Art, Tuscaloosa, Alabama.

Cooper, James Fenimore. *The Pioneers.* New York: Oxford University Press, 1991.

Durand, Asher B. *Kindred Spirits.* 1849. Oil on canvas. Crystal Bridges Museum of American Art, Bentonville, Arkansas.

Evers, Alf. *The Catskills: From Wilderness to Woodstock.* Garden City: Doubleday, 1972.

Hawthorne, Nathaniel. *The Marble Faun.* New York: Penguin, 1987.

Irving, Washington. "Rip Van Winkle." In *Norton Anthology of American Literature, Shorter Fourth Edition,* 401-413. New York: W.W. Norton, 1995.

Melville, Herman. *Moby-Dick.* New York: Barnes & Noble Books, 1994.

Reynolds, Larry J. "Melville's Catskill Eagle." Melville Society Extracts (MSEx) November 1985; 64: 11-12.

Wolf, Bryan. "When is a Painting Most Like a Whale?: Ishmael, Moby Dick, and the Sublime." In *Herman Melville: A Collection of Critical Essays.* Englewood Cliffs, NJ: Prentice Hall, 1994.

New Imaginings
and
Last Days

The Four Seasons Lodge:
Survivors in the Bungalow Colony

Andrew Jacobs

They were refugees, in a manner of speaking, overworked, disillusioned city folk whose thick accents betrayed their recent arrival to the United States. Tailors, butchers, rag dealers, and cobblers, they looked north of the fetid, sweltering metropolis and saw an irresistible expanse of farms and forest with sweet air and the promise of redemption.

The year was 1837 when these German, Austrian, and French Jews sought to establish an agrarian utopia in the Catskills, a sparsely settled offshoot of the Appalachian Mountains that had more recently been home to itinerant tribes of Monsee and Mohican Indians. The Society of Zeire Hazon, as the pioneers called themselves, settled on a patch of land above the Neversink River, 120 miles and two days rough travel from Manhattan. There, on nearly 500 acres, a dozen families set out to create *Sholem*, Hebrew for peace.[1]

---

1   Stefan Kanfer, *A Summer World: The Attempt to Build a Jewish Eden in the Catskills, From the Days of the Ghetto to the Rise and Decline of the Borscht Belt* (Toronto: Collins Publishers, 1989).

According to the scant records that survive, the colonists built houses, a synagogue, and a general store that served tea and hosted free-wheeling discussions. When the rocky soil failed to sustain them, they stitched beaver pelts into hats and fashioned goose feathers into writing quills, shipping the finished goods back to the city.

Within five years, however, the experiment was winding down, the pioneers defeated by the inhospitable winters and the parsimonious soil. In debt and disillusioned, the settlers abandoned their colony and returned to New York.

Little more than a century later, another tribe of Jewish immigrants would head north from New York City seeking fresh air, greenery, and an escape from the difficulty of their workaday lives. They, too, had heavy accents and modest professions. Unlike the earlier group of émigrés, they were bona fide refugees, having survived the unspeakable atrocities of Hitler's homicidal war on the Jews.

Their bucolic Shangri-La, however, would endure for three decades.

They chose as their sanctuary Excelsior Lodge, forty acres of maple and clipped lawn that had once been a thriving hotel and children's summer camp. As the crow flies, it was eight miles from the place where the founders of Zeire Hazon had built their failed utopia.

By the late 1970s, when the decline of the Catskills as a summer resort was apparent to all, the survivors—55 couples—poured their savings into this dog-eared collection of wood-plank structures. They repaired the pool, built a dozen new bungalows, and made earth-tone curtains for "the casino," a ubiquitous Borscht Belt reference to the building that housed evening entertainment. A section of the hotel's kitchen was rechristened as a synagogue with homemade stained-glass windows. They formed a cooperative system of governance and called the place Four Seasons Lodge.

Carl Potok, a Krakow-born house painter who became the colony's vice president, explains why they gave this modest assemblage of buildings such a glitzy name, and it had nothing to do with pretension. "We wanted the place to be used all the seasons, not just during the summer," he said.

As it happens, the planned winterization of the bungalows never came to be. In the early years, a few Lodgers tried coming up for the leafy splendor of autumn or the luminous greenery of late March, but as Helga Grunberg, one of the original residents put it, the empty card room and darkened casino on Saturday night provoked unease.

"We always wanted to be together, to share noisy poker games and laughter," she said. "We are not the kind of people who would be alone with nature." She paused and then added, "I don't think we like the quiet because it leaves us alone with our bad memories."

By the time I discovered the place in 2005—I was writing a series of stories for *The New York Times* about Catskills summer life—Four Seasons Lodge was one of the few Borscht Belt resorts that had survived the new millennium. Of the 1,100 hotels, bungalow colonies, and boarding houses that once dotted the region, where in the 1950s and 1960s up to a million Jews spent their summers, only a few dozen survived.

> *Our little granddaughter was five years or six years old when she noticed my number. And she says, "Grandma, what kind of number do you have here?" I wouldn't tell her "it's a telephone number" like other people I know did. I couldn't say this.*
>
> *I told her bad people didn't like my name, and they wanted to give me a number.*
>
> *And that's it. She never asked anymore.*
>
> *—Regina, survivor of the Krakow Ghetto and*
> *five camps including Auschwitz & Theresienstadt.*

Legendary hotels like Grossinger's and the Concord had long since been abandoned, and the colonies that remained had been taken over by Orthodox Jews, many of them black-hat Hassidim whose idea of a satisfying Saturday night involved prayer, not the big band entertainment and ribald comedians who had put the Borscht Belt on the map.

That summer I ended up writing a short article about Four Seasons Lodge, but 600 words buried inside a newspaper felt like an insult to this remarkable place and its residents. The frustration—and a sense of urgency—were magnified when I found out the following summer would be their last. I contemplated a longer article or perhaps even a book but questioned whether the written word, or at least those written by me, could bring to life the subject at hand. I asked myself: Would I want to read a book about a group of aging Holocaust survivors? The answer: Probably not. But at that time, I thought only a film could capture these compelling characters and the unique world they inhabited. The only problem is that I had never made a film, although in the end, I got an abundance of help, including cinematography assistance from Albert Maysles, the legendary documentarian who made *Grey Gardens* and *Gimme Shelter*.

> *. . . Then we saw our losses, we missed our parents, saw that so many people didn't return. Only then we found out what they did to all those people in camps and crematoriums. . . . Knowing this, there we waited in DP camps, waiting for visas to emigrate.*
>
> —*Ester, survivor of Lodz Ghetto, Auschwitz & Bregen-Belsen*

Like the founders of Zeire Hazon, who sought to build an idealized society of shared values—one guided by their Jewish faith and free from the anti-Semitism of the outside world—the members of Four Seasons Lodge created a place where they could be themselves, with their bad memories and without judgment from outsiders, including other Jews who didn't share their wartime traumas.

The Lodgers rarely articulated such sentiments, and one might encounter some defensiveness when the question was raised. One night, over a raucous mah-jongg game in the card room, Linda Mandelbaum volunteered her thoughts on how 100 survivors ended up together, both as married couples and as a community of Landshaftsmen. "A lot of American Jews are not comfortable being around us, perhaps because we talk about the Holocaust so much," she said. "And maybe we are a little bit bitter because none of them lifted a finger to help us when we were in hell."

These days there is something melancholy about the region, with once bustling towns like South Fallsburg, Loch Sheldrake, and Woodbourne decidedly forlorn, even more so off season, when many Main Streets become a ghostly succession of vacant storefronts. Although astoundingly beautiful, the fields and meadows that spread out along winding back roads are flecked with abandoned cottages and crumbing wooden hotel buildings, picturesque but also heart-rending.

The decline of the Catskills has been blamed on changing tastes and the mass production of cheap air conditioners and color televisions that made August in the city bearable. But the region's bigger enemy was perhaps the dawn of the jet age, which provided affordable vacation alternatives to middle class Jews, who as the 1960s progressed, discovered that the brazen anti-Semitism that barred them from many venues was largely fading.

It is a tribute to their tightly bonded friendships, and their determination to keep their Catskills *shtetl*, that Four Seasons Lodge survived until 2008. (It's worth noting that a few other survivor-dominated colonies endured nearly as long, but as Anita Skorecky, one longtime resident put it: "The others don't compare. We're the A Number One.")

Most of the Lodgers were Catskills veterans, having started "coming up to The Mountains," as they call it, in the late 1940s and early 1950s, soon after arriving in the United States from the Displaced Persons camps of Europe. With few exceptions, they were orphans, having survived the camps as teenagers and emerged as adults in their early twenties. Despite a smattering of Hungarians, Austrians, and Romanians, this was a Polish crowd, one that freely mixed Yiddish, English, and Polish.

Their demographic is notable for one other reason: they are the last cohort of Holocaust survivors, the final living witnesses to an appalling chapter in modern history.

There were other things that they shared. To a person, they were deprived of higher educations, having spent a crucial chunk of their schooling years in ghettos, concentration camps, and then refugee centers. Once in the United States, English had to be learned and before long, other smaller mouths had to be fed. Faced with the immediate need to earn a living, they gravitated to semi-skilled professions that, back then, often rewarded hard work with decent wages.

Before long, many of them had settled within walking distance of each other, in a leafy swath of working-class Queens with bucolic names like Forest Hills, Kew Gardens, and Rego Park. Off-season in the city, their social lives, not surprisingly, revolved around one another, with regular card games or a never-ending string of *bar* and *bat mitzvahs*, weddings, and more recently, funerals.

In the early days, they spent the summers in rented bungalows, switching locales en masse when a better deal could be had. For years, the group took a liking to Cutler's Cottages in South Fallsburg, one of the largest colonies and where a season's rent, at $500, was hard to beat. The crowd, a mix of American and European-born Jews, was mostly women and children during the week. On Fridays, the men would drive up, haggard from the week, and join their families for two frenzied days of leisure before heading back to the city on Sunday night.

In 1979, when word spread that the owners of Cutler's might sell the place to religious Jews, the crowd with the thick accents and the tattooed forearms decided to look for a place of their own. "We realized we couldn't keep renting forever," Carl said.

An elegant hand-written sign graced the wall of the casino, just to the left of the stage, right beside the headshots of the entertainers who would return year after year. Entitled "The Ten Commandments," it listed the rules by which the Lodgers should aim to live, at least while sharing a semi-communal existence in the woods of Ulster County.

There were exhortations against sloppy living—"Don't look for any janitors, you are your own super"—and feel-good reminders like "Surround this colony with a fence of happiness." But perhaps the most telling commandments, Number 8 and 9, were prohibitions against playing favorites: "Let us live like one family. Do not establish cliques" (#8) and "Don't make preferences sitting or playing at the table. The person who sits next to you is as worthy as you are" (#9).

These commandments were a reaction to life at the other colonies, where running card games would coalesce each night on bungalow porches or at kitchen tables, effectively atomizing the social energy of the place. As Hymie Abramowitz, the Lodge president and author of "The Ten Commandments" explained, there would invariably be a handful of people left out of the action, forced to pass their evenings alone. "We just want that everybody should be together at night, that no one should have to sit in their bungalow alone," he said. "During the day, the people can do what they want, they can even play card games in their bungalows or on the lawn, but at night everybody should be together."

> Between uncles, aunts, cousins nieces, I would say we were about 300. . . . After the war, I was the only one left. . . . And now I am a free man with a big pool.
>
> —Hyman TK

Life at the Four Seasons was intensely social, with rituals pegged to a few anchor activities: the nightly card games in the social hall, the Saturday evening party in the casino, and for the devout, prayers in the *shul*, although on many days the men might struggle to attract the required *minyan* of ten people.

In between there were decidedly non-aerobic walks down Geiger Road or group marketing expeditions to the Shoprite in Ellenville. In the afternoon, there was always someone at the pool complaining about the frigid water. ("Hymie and Carl don't want to spend the money," was the typical refrain. Hymie and Carl's predictable riposte: "You people never go in the water so why should we waste the money.")

On some Saturday afternoons, the men would go to the horse track in Monticello while the women gave their hair its weekly lift at the local beauty parlor. By late afternoon a rotating crew of a half dozen women—plus Carl, who specialized in deboning the metallic gold smoked whitefish—would head to the communal kitchen, where the Saturday night meal was fashioned amid a hubbub of shouted orders and off-color jokes.

The menu was simple and predictable. On alternate weeks, dinner was either meat (cold cuts) or dairy (bagels and smoked salmon) and although nothing was cooked, everything had to be elaborately sliced, displayed, and garnished according to the dictates of the women, few of whom could agree on how to best layer a plate of bright pink fish. One weekly staple, besides the fully stocked bar, was the pickled herring appetizer orchestrated by Rose Ashkenazy, who became affectionately known as the Herring Queen.

Upon completion, the trays would be carried out to an old wooden door lain across the back of a golf cart. Then, with everything piled atop the door, the feast would be slowly rolled across the lawn, driven by Hymie, to the casino. On the receiving end, another team of women who had been charged with setting up the casino would be waiting to deliver the trays to the numbered tables.

In his nostalgia-laden book, *In the Catskills*, the sociologist Phil Brown explores how the Borscht Belt helped European-born Jews adapt to the prevailing culture. "Jews could have a proper vacation like regular Americans, but they could do it in Yiddish if they wished, and with kosher food, varying degrees of religious observance, a vibrant culture of humor, theater, and song," he wrote in the introduction. "Through the small and large communities they built, the Jews created in the Catskills a cultural location that symbolized their transformations into Americans: their growth in the middle class, their ability to replace some anxiety with relaxation, their particular way of secularizing their religion while preserving some religious attachment and ethnic identification."[2]

This melding of cultures was most apparent on Saturdays in the casino, where the house band led by Harvey Schneider might start off with a Polish waltz, circa 1925, pour out a string of Big Band classics and fox trots from the 1940s, and then end with the Macarena or Gloria Gaynor's "I Will Survive." The parties were not for spectators and the dance floor was always crowded with couples or widowed women who would partner with one another.

The headline entertainment, a kaleidoscope of performers whose best days were behind them, offered up salty comic routines in between schmaltzy renditions of Broadway show tunes or Jewish classics like *Hava Naghila*.

The crowd was extremely zealous and on some nights, Hymie would have to flash the casino's lights to coax everyone home. Fortified with flashlights and steadied by the arm of another, they would edge their way through the darkness accompanied by the thrum of crickets. After arriving home and carefully hanging up their evening wear, they would shout a goodnight through the screen window and flip off the lights.

I used to come up Thursday night after work, after I went out to Bernstein's Restaurant on the East Side, for a good dinner. I'd eat, then drive up. It was dark, peaceful, nobody on the road, and you went flying. It was nice . . . you look forward to coming here to relax, then we'd leave Monday, early in the morning and come back into work.

—*Sol, survivor of six camps including Plaszow,*
Buchenwald & Theresienstadt

In the morning, after a breakfast of cantaloupe and cottage cheese, they might gather on the lawn and recall the previous night's one-liners with a laugh or complain about the consistency of the potato salad. It was during these quiet moments, beneath the expansive oaks, that talk of their former lives in Europe would seep out.

During those first years in America, when the past was too raw to be exhumed, it was enough to be in the company of others who implicitly understood why you screamed in your sleep or why your daughter's *bat mitzvah* had so few guests.

Looking back, a few children of the Lodgers say their parents seemed to do everything with far more intensity. The parties went on until 2 am and the empty vodka bottles would pile up, although as Marty Potok, Carl's son put it, "no one got stinking drunk. They just got happy."

Miriam Handler, who survived Auschwitz with her mother, explained why she never told her daughters the details of those years. "We were trying to shield our children from these horrible things," she said. "Why should they know how much their parents had suffered?" Still, compared to some survivors, who surrounded themselves with American-born friends or wore long sleeves to cover their tattoos, this was not a group trying to run away from the past.

As they grew older, many of the Lodgers found themselves reminiscing about the war more frequently. Talk of Mengele's selections at

Auschwitz would carry across a game of rummy. Sometimes the men would trade horrifying stories about hunger, luck, and violence that sounded like competitive sparring. ("You think the Warsaw ghetto was bad, in Lodz people died like flies. . . .")

It is hard to say why the stories came out more readily in their later years. Perhaps the pain had lost some of its sting. Or maybe there was an unconscious realization that such memories had a shelf limit, especially as their numbers began to thin in the 1990s. Some seemed to be pushed by grandchildren clamoring for details of their past or driven by the rise of Mahmoud *Ahmadinejad*, the Iranian leader, who has called the Holocaust a myth.

⤙⤚

By the time our camera crew arrived, many of the Lodgers seemed desperate to share their tales. In those first few weeks, they accosted us in the card room or invited us for coffee in their kitchens, their recollections leaving them emotionally exhausted but relieved knowing someone had recorded them. Some clammed up until the end or provided generalities, skirting over personal experiences that were still too horrifying to voice. "My past is not a good one," Hymie would say again and again when asked why he never wanted to talk about his childhood. "I have only bad memories, and they're better left unsaid."

Over the course of three years, we shot over 300 hours, much of it personal accounts of loss and survival. One of my abiding regrets is that the finished documentary was only an hour and a half, leaving so many vital stories unused on the cutting room floor.

For the Lodgers, seeing the finished product provoked mixed reactions. After a screening of the film in the casino that final August 2008, some of the Lodgers slipped out as soon as the lights came on. A few were emotionally jarred; some said we should have left out scenes that focused on the physical decline of their friends.

More than one Lodger later complained about having been left out of the movie. "I talked to you for hours and hours and I barely saw myself," Joe Fox, a feisty Polish partisan with an incredible story to tell, later admitted. Hearing such disappointments was painful.

For most, however, the documentary was a source of pride, a validation of their accomplishments and a tribute to the community they had created. Even if they were sometimes depicted unflatteringly, Carl and Hymie reveled in the prodigious attention they received at the festival screenings and public events. The premiere of our theatrical run at the IFC Center in Manhattan was a thrill for the dozens of Lodgers who came with their families. Dressed in their finest, they reveled in the standing ovation and danced the night away at the opening night gala.

Even if I came away with a sobering pile of debt, the project was extremely rewarding. The critics were generous, festivals clamored for the film, and audiences were visibly moved. But more importantly, I believe we had created a tribute to an amazing group of people and a valuable document for future generations. We had shown Holocaust survivors not as embittered victims but as ordinary people who had survived the unspeakable and then gone on to lead largely normal lives. They had found love, created families, and built an extraordinary community in the mountains of New York state. They had found a way to move past the trauma—to laugh, to dance, and to celebrate life.

> *I have been married fifty-eight years. I had a wonderful, wonderful husband. We were very, very happy. We never went by ourselves, we always went together and I love him dearly till today, even though he is ninety and sick, and I have to nobody to communicate with. We had a beautiful beautiful life together. He gave me the world when he could. And I tried to do the best, to whatever I can make him comfortable, too. I would give him my life when I could.*
>
> *—Anita TK*

Four Seasons Lodge outlived so many other Catskill resorts, but, in the end, the residents could not avoid the inevitable. By 2005, more than half the original tenants had passed away, the vast majority of them men. Asked why he was clamoring to sell the place, Hymie pointed to a row of sixteen bungalows on the far side of Geiger Road and said "Over there, everybody is widow," he said, flashing a well-practiced flash of exasperation. "Every time a light bulb goes out, they call me. Every time the toilet doesn't flush, they call me. I can't take it no more."

That summer, the co-op board's leaders waged a persuasive campaign to convince the shareholders to sell. They reminded everyone that Carl and Hymie, the patriarchs and resident repairmen, were too old to keep tending to a crumbling infrastructure. And they also repeated the previous summer's tangle with the Ellenville health department, which had forced the colony to install a chlorination system for the water supply, costing $20,000 and nearly depleting the colony's maintenance funds.

Beyond his status as the colony treasurer, Hymie was a retired stockbroker and as the only Lodger who had worked in an office, he knew his way around a profit and loss ledger. With his charisma, biting wit, and the philosophizing skills of a rabbi, he also knew how to work the crowd. "People, we have to face reality," he said again and again. "We're not getting any younger. This place has turned into a nursing home."

When a referendum was held in late August, a slim majority voted to sell, with one caveat: they be allowed to come back for one final summer. If they were angry with their fellow Lodgers, those on the losing side did not express it. Resignation settled over the colony as they packed up and went back to the city after Labor Day.

During that winter, a number of residents, among them a forceful woman named Regina Peterseil, fretted, stewed, and rehashed the vote that would mean an end to their summer world. "What are we going to do, sit and sweat in Florida?" she said. "People don't even realize what they voted for. They just did what Hymie told them."

Not long after the Lodgers arrived for their final seasons, a small rebellion began to take hold, encouraged by Regina and a handful of others who had voted against the sale the previous autumn. It didn't hurt that the film crew traipsing around the Lodge that summer was enchanted by Four Seasons and its inhabitants. In retrospect, our mere presence must have influenced the resistance, which gained steam with a plea to cancel the sale. By the end, the call to action was summed up by accusations of perfidy. "It was stolen from us," Regina said one day on the lawn.

The only problem from a legal point of view is that Hymie and Carl, acting on behalf of the colony, had already signed a contract with a new buyer, a community of Orthodox Jews from the city.

One Sunday in August, the Lodgers poured into the card room for another meeting. There was shouting, applause, and then a vote: this time on whether to hire a lawyer who would do what lawyers do and try to thwart the sale by any means necessary. The majority raised their hands and the fight was on. "They'll have to take us out of here in hand-cuffs!" Charles Swietarski, one of the leading voices against the sale shouted out only half in jest.

The battle lasted two years, tying the sale up in court and effectively allowing the Lodgers to return to their beloved colony until the fall of 2008. In the end, the majority came to see that Hymie and Carl, well into their eighties and frequently at wits end, could no longer run a resort that was often held together with duct tape. But there was another force at play, which Helga Grunberg gave voice to the day she was packing up her bungalow for the last time. "It's better we leave this place while the memories are good, when people can still laugh and dance," she said.

But the last chapter has yet to be written. As the new owners, a group of religious Jews from Brooklyn, began renovating the Lodge in 2009, transforming the casino into a large prayer hall and adding new bunga-lows for their growing numbers, two dozen of the former Lodgers set out to find another home. They didn't have to travel far, migrating to a neigh-boring colony, Silver Gate, where they remain to this day, playing cards six nights a week. On the seventh night, Saturday, they throw a party in the casino.

I'm walking down the road here every morning. I hear two men walking and hear them talking how it was at the camp and the ghetto.
I'm not together with them, and can't really hear them, but I still hear them.
—Regina, survivor of the Krakow Ghetto and five camps including
Auschwitz & Theresienstadt.

Bibliography

Brown, Phil. *In the Catskills: A Century of the Jewish Experience in "The Mountains."* New York: Columbia University Press, 2002.

Kanfer, Stefan. *A Summer World: The Attempt to Build a Jewish Eden in the Catskills, From the Days of the Ghetto to the Rise and Decline of the Borscht Belt.* Toronto: Collins Publishers, 1989.

Prize-Winning Essays:
Fiction

Catskill Dreams and Pumpernickel

Bonnie Shusterman Eizikovitz

Summer in the Catskills. The ramshackle bungalows, now faded shrines to a lost world, were once teeming with life for two brief months of respite from the city's heat. I was a small soldier in that army of people who invaded the area for eight weeks, to conquer that Paradise. I have a story to tell.

It is the sounds more than anything else that brings it all back to me now. They are sweet, these sounds that I hear in my dreams, even today, fifty years later. As I burst out of the door of the bungalow, all suntan, ices, and energy, the sound is behind me; the weathered screen door hits the frame with a comforting smack. It is as familiar to me as anything else I am sure of in my life. There is the clicking of the mah-jongg tiles in the efficient hands of the mothers. Even the melodies of the birds here are unique, different from the ones that wake me up at home. The rhythmic thump of the little blue rubber ball, catapulting off the paddle racquets as the men wail away on the asphalt paddleball court comforts me too. The weekend warriors take aim at the commanding white wall, a monument with the name of our bungalow colony, Happy Acres, painted in black across the top. It validates the place.

It is the first thing I see as we approach the colony's grounds at the end of June, once school has let out for the summer, and our old Buick turns off Harris Road into the parking lot. My little sister and I are wedged into the back seat of the sedan, surrounded by heaps of clothes, toys, pots, and dishes. And shoes. My mother's shoes are tied together in their boxes, carefully labeled so she can locate them when she dresses for the festive evening activities. They wait patiently to be released from under my feet. Our brother, the self-appointed co-pilot, is crammed in between our parents in the front seat. The journey from Brooklyn is too long for us, as we anticipate what lies ahead. We have counted all the piers that dot the West Side Highway, played "License Plates" a dozen times, and eaten everything our mother has packed for the long drive up to "the Mountains." The mountains don't need a name. They are the only mountains that mean anything to us.

We can barely contain our excitement as we burst out of the car. Like clowns in the circus, we and our belongings tumble from the vehicle with noise, unbridled joy, and enthusiasm.

For us, city kids, summer in the Catskills means freedom. It means we can run, or ride our bikes, the equivalent of city blocks by ourselves, all day, every day, without our mothers' cautions ringing in our ears. It means unbridled adventures—salamander hunting, berry picking, forest walks, and just plain imagining under a tree if we want. The very air we breathe is different. It is crisp and cool in the morning, as the promise of a new day unfolds. The midday heat brings us in for lunch, and an imposed rest hour, so we do not to tempt the water gods who prey on children daring to swim with full tummies. The swimming pool, once it is permitted to us, beckons all afternoon, until early evening, when the sun goes behind the main house, and the waterfront is engulfed in shade. That, and our chattering teeth and blue lips, are our signals to come in for dinner, much needed baths, and the evening's activity of movies, energetic card-playing, and on weekends, live entertainment, tantalizing and forbidden to children.

I am a chubby child; nicknamed "Pumpernickel" by Mrs. Greenspan, because I am "round and brown." I don't mind the moniker, because I love the woman who has bestowed it upon me. She is an exotic creature, different from my mother and the other women in the bungalow colony. Delicate, and almost birdlike, she has beautiful red hair, which she keeps on top of her head in a bun. Sometimes her hair will break free from the confines of that tight structure and cascade down her back in a river of red waves. She boasts a trim figure and a heavy European accent. She is my mother's age, but she sounds more like my Bubby, left behind in the city to help my widowed aunt and her small children. For two months, Helen Greenspan becomes my surrogate grandmother. Her laughter is genuine and infectious. She plies me with honey cookies and entertains me with songs from the old country. She teaches me to swim. She makes me feel so special when I am the beneficiary of her attention and affection.

She takes me to dance lessons, taught by a landsman, a countryman of hers, Alex Birnbaum. Dance class is one morning a week, on the sprawling lawn in front of the main house in the bright sunshine. It is probably the only place where the Latin *Mambo* and the Israeli *Mayim* make sense on the same bill. Alex Birnbaum and his accordion accompany our attempts to master the classics as well as the latest dances. He is a congenial, pixie-like character. Often, when he wants to demonstrate a new step, he will put down his accordion, extend his hand gracefully to Helen to join him in the center of the circle, and afford everyone the chance to see how the dance should be done. They are so graceful together. I like him, even though he teases me, because he makes my friend Helen happy, and I think she deserves happiness in her life. I can sense, despite my inexperience, that she has seen an awful lot of sorrow. There is something about her eyes; at times, she seems so far away from this world of ours. But on the dance floor, she comes alive. Her dancing is a pure expression of joy and freedom. Her smile is so genuine, and her eyes crinkle with pure delight.

I always avoid dance, embarrassed at my adolescent awkwardness, until Helen beckons me to partner with her one day. "Come, my delicious Pumpernickel," she calls out to me. Most of my friends sleep till almost noon anyway, so until they join me for our afternoon adventures or in the pool for hours of Marco Polo, Helen is my companion. My mother and her friends partake in the dance class as well, but I am Helen's regular partner, at least until her husband returns on Fridays with the other men from the city. I have come to love to dance; my gracious partner compliments me on my proficiency and growing talent. I just revel in the attention she gives me. Her hugs come so easily; she is so caring and giving. I feel tall and graceful, like the tiger lilies that dot the path to the main house, blooming under her sun.

I think the Greenspans are the most interesting people in the bungalow colony. They are a striking couple, and the only ones here who have no children. Marvin Greenspan is tall, handsome, and good-natured, with a great laugh that accompanies him wherever he goes. He does not have the same heavy accent as his wife, having the good fortune to be born in New York City, years before the winds of war swept through his wife's beloved Poland.

Helen and Marvin Greenspan met after the war decimated most of the Jewish population of Europe. He was a GI, helping the American army restore order to the chaos brought about by displaced untold numbers of people who survived. Rumors about how they met abound. One account was that he rescued her from Auschwitz during the liberation of the death camp—literally scooping her up and whisking her away to America and the promise of a new life. Another romantic tale was that he pulled her off a boat docked at the coast of Italy, bound for Palestine, and, unable to take his eyes off the red-haired beauty, insisted that she marry him then and there, as soon as a rabbi and a *chuppah* could be dispatched.

The truth is that Helen Wyzshniaki worked in an office of the HIAS in Poland after the war. Marvin Greenspan came in one day to get information about European family members who might have survived. They spent many hours together combing through whatever information was available. In the end, they never uncovered the mystery of what became of his family, but a fine friendship and mutual respect blossomed between them. The young woman was so lonely, so needy, so beautiful, and the handsome GI was soon taken with a new personal mission; to right the wrongs of the past, and give this girl everything she deserved. The new Mrs. Greenspan was honest with her young husband. She confessed that she wasn't in love with him; that she would always be grateful to him for saving her from the wretched, lonely life that awaited her if she stayed in Poland, and that she was excited to come with him to America and be the best wife she could be. She meant it, and that was enough for him.

Marvin Greenspan is a mechanic. All the boys love to hang around him when he comes up on weekends and watch as he tinkers with his car, a mint green convertible. It stands out among the drab sedans that are lined up like soldiers in the bungalow parking lot. He indulges the children when they want to take a drive to the ice cream parlor in town, or take a motorboat out onto the algae ridden lake, trying to catch the elusive fish hiding in its murky depths. He is never too tired for a catch on the dusty baseball field, or a game of Rummy on the Adirondack chairs that dot the front of everyone's bungalow. He is probably the most popular man in the colony. He can fix almost anything and is happy to oblige almost anyone's request, never seeing it as an imposition. There are always bikes, radios, and fans that need attention. Because the Greenspans have no young family with its obligations tugging at them, they are both more than willing to spend time with everyone else's.

Not surprisingly, no one's parents mind one bit. Anything and anyone that keeps us occupied and out of our parents' way is welcome. This is our parents' vacation, as they are very quick to remind us. Now, I am hard-pressed to understand why my mother needs a vacation. My father is a different story; he works hard at his factory job, and the three days that comprise the summer weekends in the country are well deserved. Our mother doesn't have a job. She is a housewife, as are most of the women I know. Now that my baby sister goes to school, my mom has many glorious hours of freedom until we kids return, tired and needy. I imagine she has wiled away the day without us. So the summer should be no different than the rest of the year for her. But it is.

My parents talk about "The Mountains" all year. As far as they are concerned, it is a taste of the World to Come. The friendships they have made and fostered here in the Catskills are so precious to them. Each couple is like an aunt and uncle to me, their children almost cousins. The stories they relate of summer incidents are as sacred to me as tales from the Bible. I never get tired of them. I can see the gleam in my father's eye when I beg him to tell the story of how he and his pals hid all the furniture from the main house one day when the owner was in his office. I laugh uproariously at the account, as I do every time. The legends of the Mock Weddings, the Talent Shows (which should have been called Lack of Talent Shows!), sneaking into the big hotels for the biggest shows of the year, all comprise a crazy quilt that, joined together, define summer in the Catskills for me. These stories have a special place in our family lore. I hear them, chapter and verse, all year long. They are like bedtime tales that children never tire of hearing over and over again.

The Catskills to my parents are a dream, an escape from the daily grind of the real world, with its responsibilities and burdens. Here there are no aging, demanding parents, no inflexible bosses to be accommodated, no snow to shovel, no homework to oversee, no bills to pay, and no home with its inherent needs. It is one big playground. And boy, do they play. The moment my father's sneaker-shod feet hit the pavement after his long trip on Thursday evening, his big voice booms "Anyone out for handball?" This embarrasses my adolescent sensibility terribly. And thereafter, until the Monday morning trip back to the city in the early morning darkness (to beat the traffic; of course), his weekend is full of activity.

The Greenspans are outsiders. Everyone gets along fine when, on the weekends, Marvin is around. He is an athlete, a great card player and "tumbler," and fits right in with the men. But during the week, Helen Greenspan stands outside of my mother's clique of friends. They are civil, but standoffish. At times she is clearly the object of their ridicule, as she is different. They make fun of her heavy accent, her gold teeth, and her taste in clothing. One Sunday, when she announced she was going to the A & P—did anyone need anything there?—one of the women retorted, "Well, why not the Y and shit?" to the delight of the assembled crowd, my mother among them, roared with laughter.

Helen looks quizzical, shrugs, not getting the joke, and turns on her heel to her husband's waiting car. My face is ablaze with shame, as I am old enough to understand what has happened here. The disrespect stings me like the bee that found its way to my brother's instep the first week of the summer, bringing him to his knees in pain. I am so hurt for my friend; I cannot believe that my own mother would be part of the public humiliation of the woman about whom I care so much. What bothers me even more than that public display is that Helen Greenspan is unable, or perhaps, and even worse, unwilling to defend herself against the barbs and taunts that come her way on a regular basis.

I turn to face my mother and her friends in defiance, a ten-year-old's fury rising like bitter bile in my throat. Somehow I find the courage to shout at them. "How could you be so mean to her?" I cry. "Why do you have to treat her like that?" I expect contrition. I expect that heads would be hung in shame. Instead, I am greeted with even more jocularity. "Oh, come on, don't be so sensitive," they coo. "We're just having fun here." "She doesn't care." "What's the problem, honey?" are the retorts that come back to me.

I am horrified. This is not going well. How am I to avenge my friend's honor if the offenses against her are not taken seriously?

This hangs very heavily on me for the duration of the week. Helen, on the other hand, seems unaffected by the women's disrespect. I am so embarrassed I can barely meet her gaze all week long, but her behavior towards me is unchanged. She is as nonchalant as can be. I am at a loss to understand this. What I do not realize is that a small and petty act on the part of foolish women could not possibly have any place in her life. She has seen so much real tragedy and has lost so much, that she appreciates what she has now with fervor; a fine husband, a nice home, and the affection of the children of the bungalow colony that she has adopted for the summer as her own. We fill a void in her life that these women could never, even if they were inclined to do so.

I cannot wait for my father to return from the city so I can unburden myself to him. Surely he, a man of reason and sensitivity, will see the folly in the women's behavior and reprimand my mother and her friends. Yes, justice will be served. I imagine the whole scene in front of me, like the television shows that consume me during the year (there is no television in the bungalow, as one is meant to spend as much time as possible outdoors in the summer). The whole thing would wrap up in less than half an hour, with no commercial interruption.

There is very little time to corner my father alone on the weekend. Somehow, I manage to get his attention for a few minutes on *Shabbos*. After our lunch, I tell him that I need to talk to him about something important. I bare my soul and relate what happened with Helen Greenspan and the other ladies. He does not give it the importance that I think it deserves. He admonishes me to be a good girl and listen to my mother when he is not there during the week. It is very hard for her to take care of us three kids without him, he reminds me, and as the most responsible of the children, I am being counted on to be of great help. He hugs me tight, his Aramis cologne reminding me who he is; he kisses my forehead, and heads off to bed for his *Shabbos* afternoon nap.

I am so disappointed. I cannot believe my efforts to obtain justice have been summarily shot down, dismissed without another thought. There is no one with whom to share these feelings, except Helen. But her bungalow door is closed, a sure sign that she and Marvin are enjoying some private time together. Bungalow doors are usually open; a closed door is the equivalent of a Do Not Disturb sign on the guest rooms of the many hotels that dot the area.

I am so hurt for my friend that I cannot think of anything else all day. The shabby way my mother and her friends treated Helen has been eating at me all week. I had been hoping for the wrong to be righted and it was not to be. Friends beckon me to join them in their *Shabbos* activities; card playing, swinging a leg over a pink Spalding ball to a sing-song melody conjuring up the alphabet, or jump rope, but I have no interest in anything but moping around.

With nightfall, our little world comes alive. The lights of the casino burn brightly, and music is in the air. A lively band is playing the popular tunes of the day, and the men and women of the bungalow colony are dressed in all their finery. The men are in dinner jackets, and some of the ladies even sport mink stoles, warding off the chill of the evening air. Children are allowed to join in the festivities for this part of the program.

I watch in awe at the beautiful couples dancing to the music. My parents are great dancers, and even though I am consumed with anger at my mother, I am proud of her in spite of her behavior.

The Greenspans join the others on the dance floor. They are quite a striking couple. The music seems to have transported her to another place and time, her eyes focusing on something very far away, as usual. She is dancing with her husband, but does not seem to be completely with him. Then the music changes, and a lively folk tune is the next selection. It heralds a dance that we have been practicing all summer long with Alex Birnbaum, who has joined us for the evening. I am shy to show my parents what I have learned, and Helen has been chosen to dance with our intrepid dance instructor anyway, so I find a good seat to watch them.

They seem to have the dance floor to themselves. What follow are a stunning display of dancing, athleticism, and something else I don't quite understand yet, sexuality. It is disturbing to me.

Mrs. Greenspan seems bewitched by the music. Her eyes are closed most of the time, and when she opens them, they sparkle with enthusiasm, confidence, and desire. She seems captivated by her dance partner. Alex is capable of enchanting her; he is a small man, but very masculine. They move beautifully; together, apart, and together again. Her hair has come undone, splaying across her back in a wild tangle. Her skin glows with a sheen of perspiration, like the morning dew on the flowerbeds in front of the casino. I have never seen her as alive as on this night when she dances with such abandon. She has become someone I do not recognize.

Finally, mercifully, it is over. Alex bows to his partner in a courtly, Old World manner. She curtsies back to him, and they both bow to the crowd. The room has erupted with applause in appreciation for the show to which they have just been treated. The women of the bungalow colony grudgingly accept that Helen Greenspan is quite a talented dancer, and nod their approval as she passes them, as Alex escorts her back to her husband. He is so proud of her and tells her so. She basks in his affection, but more important to her is the approval and acceptance of the group of women of which, it has become clear, she is truly desperate to be a part. I now realize how much that means to her. I always thought she was indifferent to their lack of attention and friendship towards her. I am so happy for her! For now, a wrong has been righted. But that acceptance is fickle; it fades quickly, and soon things are back to the way they were before.

Helen spends most of her time during the week teaching the bungalow kids to swim, walking the grounds, reading or knitting on her porch. She is never invited to join the other ladies in the mah-jongg and canasta fests. She seems to genuinely enjoy our dance time together, and invites me and my friends to go blueberry picking with her. We happily tote our pails, anticipating the wonderful blueberry pies and muffins she will bake for us with the spoils of our pillaging. She is an excellent cook and an even better baker.

As we hike, Helen regales us kids with tales of the old country. Not the Nazi stories. She tells us about when she was a girl in Poland, with long red braids down her back. We learn about her town and the people who lived there, about her family's store. She tells us how she loved books, and read anything she could get her hands on. Even though her family was quite provincial, they appreciated how smart she was, that she was stifled in her small town. When she graduated Gymnasia, they sent her to the University of Warsaw, in the big city, so her gifts would be fostered. She studied engineering and dreamed of being an architect. She loved the humanities classes as well, studied poetry and literature. The world was open to all kinds of possibilities, she told us, until things went dark. At this point, she changes the subject, preferring not to delve into the parts of her history that are troubling to her.

We only have a hint as to what she is referring. We are Americans, progeny of American born parents. Our fathers are proud members of the Greatest Generation, having served in the United States Army in World War II. They reap the benefits of the GI bill that sent some of them to college, and furnished mortgages for their first houses. Our understanding of the catastrophic events that swallowed our people whole like Jonah's Great Whale is limited. We do not appreciate how fortuitous it was that our grandparents arrived safely to the Golden Door of Ellis Island in the early part of the twentieth century, thusly saved from annihilation at Hitler's hand. We are spared the burden of being survivors' children. We are a much more carefree generation, real Americans. Occasionally there would be news of a distant relative who would find his way to a doorstep here from that lost world, telling tales that defied belief.

Our parents were very quick to divest themselves of any semblance of the world their parents had known soon as they could. "Greeners" or "Mockies," as European refugees are derisively known, are uncomfortable and embarrassing to be around. They are a reminder of our grandparents and everything they left behind in Europe: old clothes and old ways. While it is true that every generation thinks it is better off than the one preceding it, privileged first-born Americans in particular, in an effort to establish themselves on solid footing, embrace everything the United States has to offer, throwing off the shackles of Europe. Often that includes religious observance as well, although my parents enjoy being Orthodox, while most of their friends have discarded religious observance as they would a tattered pair of shoes.

Helen Greenspan is a real life link to that lost world. And to her, the Catskills Mountains symbolize all that she has lost. She enjoys nature; she often takes walks by herself, savoring the morning air, the sun breaking through the mist, lifting the fog that floats around the hills like tulle. She imagines she is back home with her family. The comparisons are plentiful; the fresh milk, the clear skies, and the beautiful flowers like those in her garden, the small wooden dwellings like those in her village. In the Catskills, she can lose herself, wistfully pretending that nothing has changed.

She surrounds herself with the children of the bungalow colony in an effort to replace the scores of young friends whose lives were cut short by Hitler's fury, and the children of her own she might have had if a Nazi doctor had not cruelly denied her that possibility. And since the women of our place have no use for her except as the object of their ridicule, or as a non-entity to be ignored, we are easy, natural, and pleasant companions. It is clear that she loves children. We are never a burden; we are a nice diversion from the long, lonely days and nights, until her husband returns from the city.

I love the time I get to spend with her. She listens to me when I share my adolescent baggage. She takes my concerns about growing up seriously, and she doesn't regard my sibling discord as foolish and petty. She, of course, has no need to reprimand or discipline me. Our relationship is pure. I feel totally validated when I'm with her, sure of myself and confident in what lies ahead for me. It's a great feeling, and I believe her utterly and completely when she tells me that I'm pretty, that I'll soon be a great beauty, and that boys will vie to be with me one day. My mother, on the other hand, tells me I need to watch what I eat so I don't get fat, and that I will need a nose job when I turn sixteen. She has the doctor picked out already; he's a congenial, Jewish surgeon who has already done the twins in Bungalow D; their younger sister will be on the operating table at the end of August.

Helen has befriended one couple who spends the week here. A literature teacher at Brooklyn College, Harvey Bloom is the only man here who has the summer off, and indulges in the midweek activities of the Catskills Mountains. Mrs. Bloom, known to all as Dee, and her husband are avid tennis players. As we have no tennis court, the Blooms, their children happily ensconced in a nearby sleep-away camp, frequent the local Concord Hotel each morning. They partake in tennis lessons and occasional matches, arranged courtesy of the hotel pro Gary White. The Blooms play well, and the wise tennis director takes advantage, utilizing them to make good mixed doubles matches with discerning hotel guests. They look very glamorous in their tennis whites when they leave for the hotel each morning. After all, they do not want to look like bungalow *shnorrers* when they unpack their racquets, readying themselves for play at the immaculate tennis courts of the Concord.

The Blooms, in a way, are outsiders too, but are never the object of scorn or derision. Instead, they are envied. A golden couple, they are college educated; most of the people here can only boast of finishing high school. The Blooms seem in a different class. They are friendly people, not snobs at all, and enjoy the revelry and raucousness that provide homemade entertainment in the bungalow colony. But somehow, they seem more cosmopolitan than the rest of the bungalow couples. There seems to be an air of refinement about them. Harvey Bloom has deep history with some of the men here, as far back as *cheder*, or Hebrew school, in their old neighborhood of Williamsburg, Brooklyn. He has the distinction of having "married well," as his wife is a supermarket heiress. He was fortunate, after returning from military service, not to have to go straight to the workforce. Supported as newlyweds by Dee's parents, Harvey went to college and graduate school. Nevertheless, they are accepted as part of the crowd, although often teased, good-naturedly, about their wealth. But it is clear that neither Harvey, nor the rest of the fellows, have forgotten where they came from, and the old friends enjoy carefree summers in the bungalow together. It is a well-known joke here that, in discussions about summer plans, Harvey's colleagues assume his "bungalow" is a multi-room structure a la Newport, Rhode Island, with a pool, sports facilities, and many acres of landscaped grounds. He has done nothing to discourage that idea, and if anything, has fun with it. Yes, he tells them, there are many bedrooms, a basketball court, ball fields, an Olympic size pool, and acres and acres of land! People howl with laughter at his account of the conversation with his fellow professors. To the people who summer here, their tiny bungalows are no less valuable than if it were the most beautiful, rambling estates.

The midweek afternoons find the Blooms and Helen Greenspan together at the pool. Dee is a sharp mah-jongg player and is sought after at the poolside games. Helen and Harvey can usually be found side by side, having animated discussions about politics, books, and poetry, smoking cigarettes and sunning themselves on the white wooden lounge chairs that dot the pool landscape. Harvey and his wife are gracious to Helen; Harvey genuinely enjoys their lively chats. I don't understand a thing they talk about, but I am proud of my friend when she keeps that kind of company. To me, they epitomize the upper class, and I think Helen fits right in with them.

They often invite her to join them Monday nights at the Raleigh hotel for *Mambo* Night. I'm not sure what that is, but I know my mother goes there too, and I also know I'm not supposed to wake her up early on Tuesday mornings. I am charged with getting my sister dressed, making sure she eats breakfast, and is ready for the nursery group at day camp by

10 am. For this I get 25 cents to spend as I please at the canteen, which is our snack shop and soda fountain adjacent to the casino. There's another quarter in it for me if I make my brother breakfast too.

So the weeks pass, with their particular routine. They are a blur of beautiful July days, with all the activity we can pack into them, the hot sun high over our heads. But there is always something out of the ordinary that shatters the calm of the summer. One of my mother's friends, Clara Einhorn, unexpectedly goes home for a week. That is unheard of, unless someone has to sit *shiva* for a parent who has passed away. Her kids come to stay with us, packing our already crowded quarters. We think this is just great, and have so much fun with the Einhorn kids all week.

There is a lot of whispering, and serious looks pass between the women. I try to make sense out of the conversations, desperate to garner some sliver of information. "She had no business getting herself knocked up at her age."

"It's a good thing Robbie found somebody who could take care of this."

"What was she thinking?" When Clara comes back for the weekend with her husband, she looks peaked and wan. The path that leads to her bungalow is well trod by the women of the bungalow colony, who are laden with all manner of nourishment for the family. There is no privacy; in this place, life is an open book; there are no secrets in the Catskills.

I turn to my friend Helen for an explanation. I know I can count on her to be honest and forthcoming. I go straight to her bungalow, and find her door open. Of course I walk right in. To my surprise, I find her sitting at her kitchen table, her head in her hands, her eyes closed. She has been crying. She looks up when she hears me come in. "Oh, my little Pumpernickel," she sighs. "People are so foolish, so selfish." I don't understand what she means. I'm impatient, and I ask her to explain what's been going on with Clara Einhorn. She looks up at me; her eyes fill with such sadness and longing. She is silent. She is not going to share her wisdom with me this time. My eyes brim with tears. I feel her sadness, even though I don't understand. I just know in the depth of my being that something very wrong has happened, some major transgression, and Helen Greenspan has been affected by it uncommonly. It wasn't until years later that I put the pieces of the puzzle together and finally understood what had taken place, and that an abortion of a Jewish baby in America was something a Holocaust survivor could not fathom or tolerate.

The weather changes in August. By the second week, I need a jacket when I go out in the morning. I hate that. Even the sun responds to the cue, hitting the earth differently, as it filters through the trees that dot the acres of landscape. The leaves already have touches of red and gold in their tips, heralding the approaching High Holidays in a few weeks. The days grow shorter by mere moments each day, but the effect is palpable. I savor the precious days of freedom left, before the inevitable return to school and the year-round routine, with its stifling lack of freedom.

Helen has an interesting habit this time of year. Sundays, in *Elul*, the month before *Rosh Hashanah*, my father blows the *shofar* at the end of *Shacharis*, the morning services, at the neighboring bungalow colony. It is a time-honored ritual throughout the Jewish world, setting the mood for the coming days of repentance. She walks in the early morning to the little *shul* down the road, to hear the capable, melodic, and mournful tones of my father's *shofar*. She dons her husband's faded plaid jacket against the morning chill, and ties a kerchief around her beautiful red hair. I find this odd, as she otherwise observes no other religious rituals, as far as I can tell, except for lighting candles Friday night. What is it about the *shofar* that draws her? Curiosity gets the better of me, and, one rainy afternoon, I gather up the courage to ask her.

I find her in her bungalow, reading a novel, the four burners on her stovetop all ablaze in an effort to ward off the August chill. She hangs up my wet slicker. I sit down on a kitchen chair next to her; a cup of hot chocolate finds its way to my cold hands, and she proceeds to enlighten me.

She has my full attention as she sets the stage. It is prewar Poland. She is a young girl, a few years older than I am. It is summer, she is back from the university, and her village is alive with activity. It is a tiny town, with vibrant Jewish life. She and her friends enjoy the freedom that summer brings very much the way I do, playing with friends, reading, swimming in the nearby lake, and playing card games. It is carefree and idyllic. Her parents hope she will find a *shidduch*, a marriageable partner this summer, but she is not interested. She is enjoying her casual friendships for now. She has ambition beyond marriage.

Her parents are respected and active members of the Jewish community. Her father has a small dry goods shop that her mother helps him run. He takes time out of his busy day to study *Torah* with other men of the town, and performs many acts of *chesed*, or kindness, throughout the year. But the one thing he is renowned for, besides his capability as a *ba'al tefilah*, one who leads the prayer services, is his proficiency at *shofar* blowing. He is a master. His tones are clear, not sputtering like the sexton's, and inspiring. Young Helen, or *Shprintse* as she is known, enjoys hearing him practice for the High Holidays, which he begins in earnest in August. It is the most reassuring sound in the world to her in its consistency.

At this point Helen's voice takes on a whole different tenor. Her hands tremble as she continues her story.

Their world begins to change. A dark wind blows through Poland, bringing restriction and unsettled feelings. People of their village are fearful, walk with their heads down. The carefree days are no more. *Shprintse* gets sent back from school. Jews are not allowed at the university any longer. One by one, their property, businesses, and freedoms are taken away. Then people are rounded up. Helen spares me the details, but what I gather is that her family was sent to Auschwitz, and, forcibly separated from them, she never saw them again.

She thankfully spares me the details of her incarceration, and instead focuses the story on her survival. She is determined to live. She tells me she did whatever it took to stay alive, but doesn't elaborate. Since she was never a big eater, it is easy for her to subsist on very little. The girls who were fat had a much harder time with the imposed starvation. I swallow hard.

One year, before *Rosh Hashanah*, there is a rumor that someone has smuggled a *shofar* into the camp, and with it, hope has come to Auschwitz. To *Shprintse*, the *shofar* reminds her of good days that will return once the war is over. Someone in her bunk has been keeping track of the calendar, and lets *Shprintse* know when she should be mindful, in case the miraculous *shofar* blowing is going to take place.

She listens for it ardently on the appointed day. Late in the morning, she finds herself drawn to the men's section of the camp, and waits. She is suddenly aware of a long, mournful sound. It is coming from very far away, but there is no mistaking the distinct long note, and then the clipped ones, of which she is more than familiar. She vows then and there that if she survives, she will never miss the chance to hear the *shofar* again, in memory of her father. That is why she avails herself of the opportunity before her now; to savor my own father's beautiful, powerful *shofar* blasts, quietly remembering what was lost.

An uncomfortable silence surrounds us. I don't know what I'm supposed to do now. Should I say I'm sorry? Should I hug her? I instinctively reach out and just take her hand; it is small, the same size as mine. We sit in silence like this for what seems like a long time, the cuckoo clock on the wall keeping time; it's the only other sound besides the insistent, driving rain pelting the bungalow roof, and my own pulse pounding in my head.

I hear my mother calling me for dinner, and I rise to leave. Helen takes both my hands in her hands, squeezing them tightly. Not a word passes between us. I feel so close to her right at this moment. She nods her head that it is alright for me to leave her.

I return to my bungalow lost in thought, consumed with all I have learned this afternoon. My head is swimming and it hurts. My mother sees my face and asks me what's wrong. She feels my head and puts me straight to bed with two aspirins and a wet washcloth on my forehead. I promptly fall into a restless, dream-laden sleep.

I dream that our bungalow colony has become a work camp, surrounded by barbed wire, patrolled by Nazi dogs. The casino, the source of so much fun and revelry all summer, becomes a factory where we are forced to work on munitions and small parts for the Nazi war effort. Our bungalows have been gutted and the furniture replaced with wooden bunks lined up in rows. We are all wearing tattered, ragged clothing and worn shoes.

I wake with a start. My heart is pounding. It is very dark. It takes me a moment to remember where I am, and to realize that everyone I love is safe, and I promptly crawl into my mother's bed, seeking solace and security. I smell the remnants of her *Bal de Versailles* perfume that she wears every day, and I am immediately comforted. She doesn't have to say a word. She puts her arm around me and kisses my forehead. I drift back to sleep until the morning.

Everything looks brighter in the daytime, my mother reassures me. She is right. The sun is shining through the gingham curtains in the kitchen window, and it just glorious. . . . I feel much better about things today. I have not shared the details of the previous day, nor the nightmare with my mother, but she senses I was troubled about something serious, but doesn't pry. She lets me know she's available if I want to talk. I don't. My friends, up unusually early for them, come to call for me, and the day beckons with endless opportunities for fun, sports, and mischief. The wet weather has brought out tons of salamanders and frogs, and we spend the better part of the morning catching them, and putting them into the camp house's glass tank allocated for this purpose. We have furnished it with lots of leaves, twigs, and added some water. We feed our captives flies from the sticky tape that hangs from the ceiling of the camp house porch. It's a perfect bungalow day.

The afternoon finds us all at the pool, enjoying an uncommonly hot day for mid August. Everyone is there. Our handsome lifeguard, Jesse, is seated in his perch high above us, with his pork-pie hat, his nose covered in zinc oxide. Our mothers are entranced by the mah-jongg tiles in front of them, and Harvey Bloom and Helen Greenspan are, as usual, discussing something I don't understand. All is right with our little world.

The topic of discussion around the pool is the big show in the casino this weekend. There is always music of course, provided by the Happy Acres Orchestra. The children will be allowed to stay for the music, as usual. But the late show will feature a comedian, and something else that is also off limits to anyone under twenty-one. My curiosity and that of my friends is peaked.

We are remanded, after the music, to our bungalows and the care of the day camp counselors, who have Night Patrol duty. They circulate through the colony at regular intervals throughout the night, making a cursory check of the bungalows, certain the children are in their beds, and not crying or otherwise in need of assistance. Most of the times the counselors congregate on one central porch, listening to Cousin Brucie spin the latest hits on someone's transistor radio.

We have got to find out what is going on in the casino! My friends have hatched a plan. It's a good one. We wait until the counselors have passed our units, and rig our beds to look as if we're sleeping in them, just in case a zealous counselor decides to take his job seriously. We sneak out the back bedroom windows, meeting at the old well as we had planned. Then we go down the hill, behind the bungalows, and find our way into the casino through its back door. The room is engulfed in total darkness, which assists us in our mission. We sneak behind the long bar in back of the room and stay so very quiet, watching the show, only our eyes peeking above the counter.

The comedian is in the middle of his act. The crowd laughs uproariously at his jokes. He is very funny, and very profane. He delivers many punch lines in Yiddish, which none of us understand. My parents are having a great time, smoking, drinking, and enjoying the show.

We have the surprise of our lives at the next portion of the program. A stripper takes the stage! She is all spangles and fringes. The music accompanies her bawdy routine, and, as she takes off most of what she is wearing with great flourish, the crowd goes wild. She singles out men in the front rows whom she thinks will be receptive to her charms, sits on their laps, kisses their bald heads, and musses up what little hair they do have. Their wives are overcome with laughter.

I am horrified, embarrassed, and fascinated at the same time. I have never seen anything like this before. And I don't understand why a wife would allow a woman like that to flirt with her husband like that, and right in front of her! The boys in our little group are amazed, and rendered speechless. They almost cannot believe their good fortune. Seeing a nearly naked woman is more than they could have hoped for.

Once she is completely undressed, save some strategic bits of cloth, the music reaches a crescendo, and wild applause and whistles ensue. It is a good time to make tracks for our bungalows before the show breaks. We exit the same way we came in, stealthily making our way back up the hill behind the bungalows. It is hard to stay quiet, but we know we must.

We dare not get caught. We see that the counselors are still huddled on a neighbor's porch, and we disperse, ready to climb through the back bedroom windows of our respective bungalows that previously served as our escape hatches.

It is then that I recognize Helen Greenspan, who is behind her bungalow, her face lit by the cigarette she is smoking. She doesn't see me in the pitch darkness. She is with someone who is not her husband; this man is too short. It's hard for me to see, but as I get closer, I can hear the unmistakable husky voice of Alex Birnbaum. He is holding both of her shoulders, and talking in a very serious tone. She is pleading with him. I can't understand what she's saying; she's speaking Polish. But I know he is being very insistent and wants her to do something she doesn't want to do. He pulls her close, and to my shock, he kisses her, full on the lips. She doesn't resist, and soon begins to respond to his advances. She laces her arms around his neck, her body as close to his as it can be.

At that moment, I spot my parents coming up the path leading to the front door of our bungalow. I run as fast as my legs will carry me, climb in the back window to my room, and quickly get under my covers. I feign sleep. My mother comes to check on me before retiring. I smell the whiskey and cigarettes on her breath, and do my best not to react, lest my transgression be discovered.

I'm so confused. My mind is racing! What is going on here in our little community? I have seen too much tonight. And I don't know what to think about it, or worse, what to do. Should I tell someone? Should I confront Helen and demand an explanation? Or should I just keep quiet and hope she comes to her senses? Did I completely misunderstand what I saw? No, I know what I saw. Alex is not married, but she sure is. And she has no business locked in that kind of embrace with a man who is not her husband. This much I do know.

I feign a bad headache when dance class comes around this week and stay in bed. I tell my mother to apologize to Helen, but no, I cannot possibly be her partner this week. I just can't face her, after witnessing her indiscretion. I skip our swimming lesson too. I do everything I can to avoid her. I can't meet her gaze. When she finally spots me later in the week at the pool, she asks me how I'm feeling and tells me how much she misses me. I mumble some apology and run off to be with my friends. She seems perplexed by my behavior, as I am usually so affectionate with her, but doesn't say anything.

I can't share the awful thoughts running around in my head with anyone. I don't even have the words for it. I feel more than disappointment; I feel disgusted and betrayed. I try to clear my brain and concentrate on punchball, tetherball, anything other than that scene that is burned into my consciousness. In the pool, I stay underwater as long as possible, trying to blot out what I know. I am unsuccessful. My friends tease me that I need to come back to Earth, that I seem like I'm on another planet. I tell them I've been visiting the planet Yuck. That's just how I feel.

Our days here are growing shorter. I feel so uneasy in this place now. I almost want to go home already.

The next few days pass quickly. I do my best to avoid Helen at every opportunity.

Sunday morning heralds another glorious, sunny day. I push my baby sister grudgingly on the swings. Helen comes back from her usual routine of going to *Shacharis* services and hearing my father blow the *shofar*.

I see her going back to her bungalow. Suddenly we hear shouts coming from the paddleball court. People come running to get Helen from her bungalow, take her by both arms, and run with her down the hill in the direction of the court. Soon the wail of an ambulance shatters the peaceful Sunday morning. A sea of people seems to become aware of the excitement and file quickly out of their bungalows. I am becoming more and more curious, and make my way down there, my sister in tow.

The scene before me on the paddleball court is like a movie set. Our little community seems bathed in light. A ring of humanity surrounds several men drenched in sweat. Paddle racquets and balls are scattered all about. Several men hold back the crowd as the ambulance crew works frantically on Marvin Greenspan, who is lying on the ground, motionless, eyes closed, his face very gray. Helen is next to him, holding his motionless, limp hand. She is very quiet, and she is shaking.

This is all very surreal to me. Everything seems to be moving in slow motion. The emergency technicians are trying their best to hold back the *Malach haMaves*, the Angel of Death. But it soon appears their efforts are for naught. One of the crew shakes his head, stops his ministrations, and quietly leans over to Helen, saying a few words to her.

She is silent. Her eyes close briefly as she absorbs what he is saying to her. Most of the women and a few of the men begin to weep. It is clear that a catastrophe, much worse than what happened to Clara Einhorn, has shaken our world to its core.

Marvin is put on a gurney, loaded into the ambulance, with Helen right there with him, not letting go of his lifeless hand. Her face is a mask of resignation. She is no stranger to tragedy, and this is just another body blow to her already battered soul. The ambulance pulls away; its siren seems to pierce the August sky. Everyone left behind slowly make their way to their bungalows, heads down.

The next few hours are a blur. Women come and go from the Greenspan bungalow. They help pack it up. My mother locates Helen's phone book and calls her rabbi. He will help make the arrangements. The Blooms drive her back to Brooklyn to face the *Shiva* week and what lies afterwards. I can only imagine what her life will be like now. She is really, truly, all alone.

It is unanimously decided that everyone will just go home at this point in the summer. Since Labor Day is almost upon us anyway, and everyone's summer has pretty much come to an end with Marvin Greenspan's death, there seems to be no point in staying. A hasty pack-up seems to be the order of the day. Goodbyes are said, promises to keep in touch and blessings for the New Year exchanged.

I do not go to the funeral or the *shiva*. My mother dispatches the three of us to our Bubby's house, which turns out to be fun, as our cousins are there too. Bubby makes us a great dinner, parks us on the couch for the night, where we can watch our favorite shows on her big TV until we fall asleep.

I do not think about Helen or any of the things that happened at the end of the summer, until my mother informs me that she has invited Helen to spend *Rosh Hashanah* with us, and that she will be sharing my room with me! I am amazed at my mother's generosity, and at the same time, fearful.

The beginning of school is a welcome distraction. I am happy to see all my friends again. I like my teachers and the newness of it all. I am excited about getting new clothes and shoes for the High Holidays. My mother takes me after school downtown to Martin's Department Store. I feel very grown up suddenly. The truth is, I have grown up this summer.

Before I know it, *Rosh Hashanah* is upon us. My mother has been cooking up a storm in preparing the house for our guest's arrival, seemingly preparing everything she knows how to. Then the doorbell rings. Helen is here! My mother begs me to answer the door, her hands busy assembling a cake, the phone, as usual, pressed between her shoulder and her ear.

I nervously open the door. There stands Helen Greenspan, her blue suitcase at her side, and a gift in her hands. She seems even smaller to me than I remember. Was it only two weeks ago that I saw her last? It seems like an eternity. So much has happened since then. I beckon her to come inside, show her up to my room where she will spend the next two days with my family. "My pumpernickel," she says quietly. "I'm so happy to be here with you and your family. It was so kind of your mother to include me for the holiday."

I am numb. I finally find my voice. "*Gutyur*," I say to her, the traditional Yiddish greeting for a good year. "*Gutyur*," she wishes me back. And we hug. The ice is broken.

We spend most of the next two days in *shul*. My parents procure an extra seat at services for Helen, and she sits next to me. My sister gets kind of restless, so we are sent outside for a break, admonished to return in time for *shofar* blowing. We play jacks and cards with the other kids similarly dispatched, and then we are summoned into the sanctuary for the anticipated highlight of the services. My father stands at the ready on the *bimah*, the platform that is the stage, the focal point, his beautiful *shofar* poised at his lips. The congregation stands, waiting.

Helen is standing next to me, her presence so frail. I almost feel I should put my arm around her waist to hold her up. Suddenly, she steels herself, as if making herself ready for the firing squad. She squares her shoulders and stands tall. The first, beautiful, clear tone of my father's *shofar* is always a shock. Everyone jumps. Once the first blast has sounded, the congregation in unison silently sighs and relaxes. It has come.

After services, we return home for a wonderful, festive lunch. Helen and I take over the kitchen afterwards, so my mother can have a break, and between us we polish off the dishes. The house has quieted down, and it's just Helen and me at the sink. I have always been able to talk to her, and I decide that I'm going to ask her about that Saturday night behind her bungalow. I tell her what I saw. I tell her it's the reason I was so aloof and didn't want to be with her after that, and I say that I'm sorry for that. I start to cry and tell her how sad I am that her husband died.

She puts down her dishtowel, makes us both a cup of tea and beckons me to the kitchen table. "You must understand, and I know you are very young, but I think I can tell you this. I loved Marvin with all my heart. He saved me. I was a good wife to him. But he couldn't understand me the way Alex did. We were both damaged people. We had seen things in the war that no one should ever see. We were like the same person. So what you saw was kind of like reassuring each other that we were alive, that we had survived. It wasn't love. Not romance. And it never was more than what you saw. Do you understand that?

"I told Alex the next day that there could be no more between us. Oh, he wanted more. He wanted me to go away with him. But Marvin was my whole life, my whole world, and I would never do anything to hurt him. I owed him too much. I never told Marvin. I could never. He didn't deserve that. And before he died, he did know how much I loved him and how grateful I was for every minute of my life with him. I didn't know, of course, that I was going to lose him so soon after that. Something made me tell him that, and brought me close to him in those last beautiful days. People from the war have the feeling that every single moment of our lives now is so important. You can't waste a single minute.

"I know you're so young, and it's hard for you to understand all this. There is just something about the Mountains that brings me back to the best time in my life. The air is so clear, the green land just goes on and on, and the days, so carefree. And the dancing. The dancing! It makes me feel so alive, so young, like nothing will ever be wrong again. Something happens to me when I am there. It's like I can pretend all the bad things, the terrible things never happened.

"So remember to think about good things like the best days in the bungalow, Bonnie, and always be confident that things will work out for you. You will make that happen. You are like Wonder Woman, my young friend. You can do anything."

I told her I understood. And we never spoke about it again.

Helen goes home after the holiday, hugging and kissing all of us and wishing us a good year. My mother asks her what her plans were. She tells us that she is going to go back to school. Harvey Bloom has made it possible for her to continue her studies at Brooklyn College, picking up where she left off all those years ago. She will get her degree in early childhood education, and become a pre-school teacher. It is the beginning of a new life for her.

She never went back to the bungalow.

The following summer finds my family home in the city. It is the year of my brother's *bar mitzvah*, and the celebration has left my parents short of cash, so we stay home, joining the neighborhood swim club. It's a fun summer, but different. We are not as free to roam the city streets as we are in the Catskills, with its endless, safe green vistas.

After that, we three kids are old enough to go to sleep-away camp, my father gets a promotion and takes my mother to a hotel for the summer. My parents take up tennis and golf. Many of their old friends have joined them here, anticipating making wonderful memories.

Epilogue

With the exception of the summer I stayed in the city, I have spent and continue to spend every summer in the Catskills. My husband and I joined a group of friends years ago in a bungalow colony not far from where I spent my childhood summers. My children grew up there. Now my grandchildren love to spend weekends at their Bubby's bungalow.

My summers here mirror those of my parents' during my childhood. We have had wonderful years. And we have lost friends tragically. We hold each other up. The Catskills for me, as it was for Helen, has always been a refuge. The Mountains is like the "home base" of my childhood games, where one goes to be safe, home free.

Your Dovid

Rita Calderon

Mama swiped her sweaty forehead with the white dishtowel and didn't even bother looking up from the worktable. "If I see one spot of chicken grease on the pictures your head vill go to the silver platter."

As I scooped up the photo album, I kept the page open and pointed to a glossy black-and-white snapshot of Papa with his two brothers. Its white border was scalloped, only the upper right edge was torn, so that it was missing one curlicue.

"Mama look, don't Papa and Dovid look like twins?"

Mama, who stood just over five feet, reached on her toes for a bowl from the cupboard. Its bare wood, exposed through peeling white paint, looked naked.

"Papa is one year older, for your ducky information." Her tone of voice mirrored the day, leavened with a dank heaviness as the rain refused to let up.

"And how come only uncle Dovid is wearing a straw hat?"

Mama started kneading dough. "I should remember? Dat was a long time ago." Her heart-shaped face was powdered with white flour. "Boater hat," she muttered to the soft mound of dough. "That's what they called them."

A breathless waiting shaped that summer of 1938, for me and for all of us, since others were in the same boat, with parts of families left behind all over Europe's map. The anticipation was excruciating—soon I would have an uncle, aunt, and two girl cousins!—yet we followed the same routine, fulfilling our roles per usual: me, Mama's kitchen slave at thirteen. Mama, the chief cook, going all out for Shabbas dinner in addition to daily cooking for the guests and workers of the small summer hotel in the mountains. Papa coming up by train on weekends, plus summer vacations, from our Bronx apartment and his tailor job at the sweltering shop.

Rain pounded the rooftop all day, that first Thursday of July. Papa, starting his vacation, would meet uncle Dovid's ship Friday morning in Manhattan. Mama was making pot roast for Thursday's dinner, just to have the succulent leftover beef, better the second day, for *kreplach* soup on Friday. Also per usual, I got called away from reading *Little Women* to wash carrots and celery. Friday we would mash up the leftovers and stuff them into the dough, then shape them into half-moon dumplings. Sophie, Mama's best friend from the old days when they lived in Paris, assisted. All day guests and workers, the two populations being somewhat interchangeable—the same lefty bunch of union shop tailors, teachers, shoemakers, and out-of-work intellectuals from the city—poked their heads into the kitchen. While at dinner dissonance reined with opinions flying across the table, now we were as one, all salivating from the wafting aromas of Mama's dumplings, which floated in her scintillating chicken consommé like little buoys out in the river where we swam.

Sophie checked the oven, her blouse and apron stuck to her midriff from the damp heat. She attacked her frizzy red hair with both hands and knotted it in back, sweat beading her neck. As I left the kitchen with the album under my arm I pouted and mumbled, "Well anyway uncle Dovid's a dreamboat."

Sophie swatted me playfully on the backside as I passed her. "Dollink, you're man-crazy. Better you should pull your head out of your books and go swimming with the nice boys your age." Her lilting voice, which made me think of nightingales, even when scolding never rose above the volume of best friends sharing secrets at a corner table. Like sisters, they were, in spirit if not in looks. Mama's slender frame, soft chestnut hair (which I inherited), a mountain range apart from Sophie's brazen orange mane and hazel eyes, her curvy figure hovering over Mama in a way that always seemed protective. Although, petite as she was, Mama needed no help protecting herself. And if Sophie was Mama's sister in spirit then she was my aunt, plus big sister, friend, confidante. We always shared a tiny bedroom at the hotel. Back home in the Bronx, it was Sophie's lap I ran to all through the years, with crises of wardrobe or boys, or anything at all really.

At some point Friday morning Mama told me to get lost as I was all butterfingers in the kitchen, dropping silverware left and right. So out I ran to the porch and took solace in my diary, which next to Sophie was the most forgiving presence in my life. Mama always repeated, "What can happen that's so exciting for all that writing?" Papa would say, "Maybe she writes for us a book, Chaya." I wrote that down too. If Papa's obsession was reading the Yiddish newspaper *Forwerts*, ears glued to the radio—news every hour on the hour, throughout his life—mine was listening to live words. Let the other kids throw horse-shoes; my preferred pastime was spying on the world of grown-ups and getting it down in my secret shorthand. How else was I going to under-stand the craziness of the times, or my weirdly tiny family (it was just the three of us)?

Being too excited to write or read I went back upstairs and picked out my best blouse with the lace collar and set it out, along with my first pair of heels, which I had to practice walking in even though they were barely two inches. Then I ran back outside, letting the front screen door slam, and down the sloped emerald lawn to pick black-eyed susans for the vase. I scanned the landscape, scheming which path I would lead my European family on to pick blackberries. Our part of the Catskills was the gently rolling mountains in New York State, not the taller peaks to the north. Still, I couldn't wait to show off my personal corner of heaven. These were *my* mountains; *my* trails; *my* mushrooms. Often I'd hike alone, then stagger up the broad porch steps and sink low down in the Adirondack chair to read, or write in my diary, interrupted only by the buzzing of insects. At night we'd mingle on the porch after dinner, slurping juicy peaches, often singing songs, always swatting flies.

Uncle Dovid arrived at the front door with Papa in the late afternoon. He marched right up and swooped me off the ground in a bear hug. "So, this is the young lady I sailed the Atlantic to meet!" My cheeks caught fire. He smelled of aftershave and cigarette smoke, only a different flavor than Papa's Pall Malls. His gray jacket was badly wrinkled from the trip. Still, standing so near his tall presence felt like the Fourth of July. Maybe they were like twins in the pictures, but not so in person. They shared the same wavy sandy hair, but Papa's blue eyes were a calm lake, while Dovid's eyes twinkled like the ocean on a bright day, when the sun makes sparkling diamonds on the water's surface, the glistening gems protecting darker waters below.

"Chaya, where are you!" Papa called in a voice louder than usual.

Mama came out in her lilac dress with the modestly ruffled bodice. Dark waves draped her rosy cheeks. She caught her breath, something she did often, being mildly asthmatic. "Hello, Dovid," she said in a rehearsed English. "Velcome to the Ketskills."

He took Mama's hands in his and held them there, then gave her a gentle hug.

"Aah, Chaya," he said, "so many years! *Baruch hashem*, tell me I'm not dreaming. And the little lady here, she's beautiful too." He winked at me. I thought I would die on the spot.

Finally I focused on the empty space surrounding Dovid. Where was my aunt Gerty, my cousins Mindy and Bertha? Later, I learned that Dovid had been holding out hope the visas for the rest of them would come through at the last minute, but that did not happen. Papa had called from the station and told Mama, who said she was too busy all day to tell me. Although disappointed, everyone seemed to take the news in stride. For a while I fought gravity as the corners of my mouth turned a downward trajectory and I struggled to right them; if I wanted to live in the adult world, acceptance was a skill I had to learn, and here was my training.

Shabbas dinner was sumptuous. Everyone promised to keep an eye out for work for Dovid, scarce as jobs were. Already he had some rudimentary English. He would shine shoes, anything he said, to live here. "Ay, Amerika!" he boomed over a second round of schnapps. All eyes around the table were fixed on Dovid. What news of France? What about his family? Don't worry, the visas are imminent, and like so many other immigrants he would pave the way and save up for their passage. And the third "baby" brother, Manny the journalist, what of him? Avrum had already explained to them all, so Dovid just added clucking his tongue, "He'll be the last holdout. Actually still believes in Leon Blum's Liberal Front, can you imagine," he said looking around the table and acknowledging nodding, smiling heads. "All the Yiddish papers are shutting down, his will too, but he's a stubborn ass." And what of old friends?

"You remember Max, from the federation?"

"The button maker," Papa said. "Remember when we first moved to Paris, and Mama—your grandmother, Racheleh—when we met Max and translated the name of his street, Rue des Enfants Rouge, Mama joked, 'The babies are red?—these Parisians are so immoral they even make their children winos!'"

Dovid continued. "And I joked that I'd move to that street and later when I got married we would dress our tots in red coats and tell them the street was named for them." Everyone laughed and Dovid turned to me: "The name comes from centuries ago, Rachel, when the children of an orphanage on that street wore red uniforms."

I pondered that as I ate my soup, picturing Dovid's children, and those children so long ago, in the time of castles, all wearing the same red coats, and it seemed like something out of one of my fiction books, something fantastical. Sophie, sitting next to me, nudged me and smiled at Dovid: "She's in her own world sometimes. Dollink your uncle's addressing you."

I sat up straight and said, "It'd be like cousins Mindy and Bertha paying tribute to the children who had no family; like lighting a Yahrzeit candle."

Mrs. Gershon, the lumpy loudmouth from Brooklyn whom I never much cared for, was still laughing at Dovid's remarks, but stopped abruptly and shot me a frown: "Ay, Racheleh, always turning funny things into serious things."

Dovid turned straight to me and said it was a lovely sentiment. I loved him for understanding me, I loved him for dismissing the sourpuss Mrs. Gershon, and for calling me by my proper name instead of tacking on the infantilizing, diminutive "eh" at the end. And those were only some of my reasons.

"It didn't matter that he abandoned the socialist movement; already long ago he quit the federation," Dovid waved his hand and continued. "A few months ago he was shot dead on the street outside the grocery on Rue Lamarck. Now they attack Jews wherever, random beatings, killings."

I gasped and put my hand over my mouth.

Mr. Brunbaum the hatmaker from Jerome Avenue said timidly, "There's kids here . . ."

Papa shushed him. "Our little Racheleh reads adult books," to which Mr. Brunbaum said that books were one thing, real life was another.

Dovid followed both men with that bemused twinkle in his eyes I was becoming familiar with and said, "Never mind adult books. She thinks serious thoughts. Real life thoughts."

After a sobering pause, Papa asked about Max's defection, remembering him as a staunch believer back in 1920. Dovid shrugged his shoulders: "A man marries, has children, gets a promotion, and starts to view life differently."

Mama half smiled and muttered, almost to herself, "Love and politics, and so the world goes round." I recorded those words in my head and later in my diary, sensing strongly that, although I didn't quite get her meaning, and no matter how low the volume, they bore a weighty meaning.

The other mystery in my mind I actually articulated: "Why do Hitler and all those Nazis hate our people?" Answers bombarded me from all points at the table. Some acted like the world was coming to an end for Jews. Like another world war (G-d forbid! I thought) would break out any day. Others poo-poohed them and insisted that lunatic Hitler would not get his left toe inside France; western Europe, Britain, all the strong and sane hearts and minds of the world would soon topple him.

All this time Mama was up and down from the table, feeding everyone in the dining room with the soft green-painted walls. Dovid wolfed down whole kreplachs at a time. The room fell quiet as katydids serenaded us through the open screened windows. The only other sound was Dovid's faintly audible sipping of chicken soup in which Mama's dumplings bobbed. Suddenly he looked up, surprised by the hush. Everyone's gaze fell on him. They were looking at Dovid, but I came to think they were seeing their own brothers, husbands, fathers, cousins, whom they had left behind. One guest dabbed at her eyes with her napkin.

Dovid looked around the room. All he could do was to spoon one last dumpling into his mouth and slowly chew it. Then he wiped his full lips with his napkin and pronounced in a deep, authoritative voice: "Such exquisite kreplach soup one cannot find in all of Paris since 1921. Since Chaya and my *bruder* left." The brothers' eyes met for a fleeting moment before Dovid set his large soup spoon down on the table.

That night we settled as always into the hodge-podge assortment of chairs on the wide porch, only uncle Dovid's presence made it special. Even the way he smoked was different. Most of the men and some women, like Sophie but not Mama, lit up cigarettes. While the other men held their cigarettes between the thumb and index finger, Papa cupping his hands, Dovid held his between his index and middle fingers, which extended straight up like sticks. It was more like a women's way, only he was in no way feminine! I concluded it was a French thing to do. Mama and Sophie passed around fruits and cinnamon rugaluh, and the adults smoked and eventually we all sang our songs, drowning out the crickets. They were mostly union songs and Yiddish songs they brought over from the old country. For my parents and Sophie it was the old-old country, as they were immigrants twice over—from Poland to Paris to New York. From all the foreign tongues represented at the hotel, deciphering their butchered English was a full-time enterprise. If it weren't for Yiddish, I was convinced the whole motley bunch would be deaf and dumb to one another.

It was lucky for me that I spoke Yiddish, which was my first language, truth to tell (not something I admitted in school), even though I was born in New York two years after they came here. You'd think after all these years immigrants would be fluent and not keep reverting back. They'd start a sentence in English and by the time they got to the end of it you had been dragged across Russia, Poland, Germany, Palestine, France, and the Bronx. It was as if they simply could not decide where their loyalties lay. And while this bothered me to no end at times, Dovid's being there seemed to shine a narrow shaft of light on my parents. The way he smoked, holding those two fingers so straight, the way he peppered his talk with French words, made him seem suave. Yet his voice and his Yiddish had a different sound than all the others: it sounded *older*. As if his two fingers holding the cigarette resided in glamorous Paris, but the rest of him never left Poland, where I heard people still got around muddy streets in horse and wagon. To make matters more confusing, here he sat throwing out modern English words, sitting tall with crossed knees, like a Hollywood movie star. As I pondered this about Dovid and immigrants like my parents that summer, I wondered if you were born somewhere else, maybe in your heart and your mind you just always lived in more than one place at a time. And although I could not fathom why, sitting on the porch that first night on the floorboards near Dovid who I insisted sit in my favorite Adirondack chair, Mama's words from dinner popped into to my mind. *Love and politics, and so the world goes round.*

—✦—

Like everyone else, Dovid fell under summer's enchantment as the days passed. At the river one day, Papa and Dovid took a long swim. Others splashed about near the shore or lay on the scratchy, army-green woolen blanket. I sat just off the blanket in the grass watching Papa and Dovid swim out to the raft and back. They raced feverishly. It was moving toward late afternoon but the brassy sun was still high. Everyone went back to the hotel except us. Papa and Dovid came back to the blanket and plopped themselves down, water droplets glistening on their sunburnt shoulders.

The brothers lit up Pall Malls and peered out at the river. Papa worried that the authorities could send them all back to Poland if the visas failed. I casually picked up my diary and started writing, looking up at the trees so if they looked my way they'd see an inspired girl writer pondering nature's wonders.

"The visas are promised. Anyway, we are French citizens." Dovid took a long pull on his cigarette.

"You are *immigrant* citizens," Papa shot back with an uncharacteristic brittleness. "You'll never be a French Jew, name change and all."

Dovid added quickly, "You're one to talk, Avrum. I notice they call you Abe here—like Lincoln!"

"Dovid, David, call yourself what you want. Speak *haute francaise*, eat ham—which nearly gave Mama a heart attack, remember? To the French you're a foreign Jew—an undesirable."

What bickering children, I jotted down. And bringing their mother into it, how low of Papa!

Dovid kept looking at the water and lit up another cigarette; my uncle smoked like Detroit at peak production. "We were kids when we moved to that stinking hovel on rue de Belleville with no plumbing, remember? Since what, 1912? Hey, remember sneaking into the Eldorado?" Suddenly he laughed. "The dancing girls kicking their naked legs in the air? Remember the girl who came up to us later, she thought we were twins and she—"

Papa shushed him and glanced around at me, where I sat looking seriously detached, writing furiously now. Dovid dropped his voice and swiveled his lowered head like a snake in the grass, toward me and back to Papa: ". . . and she proposed a *ménage a trois* and you said what's that, and then your eyes popped out? Remember?" They cackled, shoulders shaking, like nervous boys telling smutty jokes in the schoolyard.

Dovid turned serious. "I feel as French as I do Polish. Manny works around the clock on the paper for France, while we—"

"The French call it subversive literature."

"A legitimate Yiddish paper—you forget you rallied with us in the Place de la Republique—while we sit here in America, in comfort . . ." His eyes moved slowly across the postcard-perfect setting and there seemed to be a hint of pain in his face, mixed with amusement. ". . . arguing in the mountains."

A mute stillness seeped through the trees, broken only when a fish jumped out of the water, causing a faint ripple. With the sun now partially blocked by the mountains, there was a chill in the air. We started folding the blankets.

Papa said, "Well, I guess you have to argue somewhere."

I had never heard my mild-mannered father talk in such tones, or seem angry one minute and laughing the next. Worse, I sensed a new tension in the air between the brothers, and those changes began to steal something away from my paradise.

Feeling a little mopey next day, I declined when a few of the hotel's teenagers asked me to join them on a hike to pick berries. As I sat on the porch struggling to focus on *Little Women*, Dovid strolled out, the *Forwerts* under his arm. We'd fallen into a routine of going through the *Forward* together, me giving him the English word for the Yiddish, and him sometimes giving me the French. But suddenly "berry picking!" popped into my head—and my mood miraculously restored, I asked if he would like to come along to see the woods. "Vunderful!" he said. I ran inside to get a pail, and we caught up to the others.

Dovid and I followed closely behind down the narrow dirt trail amid the tall oak, poplar, and pine. He kept stopping to pick and rub leaves between his fingers, snapping twigs and sniffing loud and long, breathing the whole forest deep into his lungs. I always thought I was the only one who inhaled the woods, and even then demurely, as I thought befitting a girl, keeping my pleasure in the moist, earthy scents to myself. But here was my uncle, sniffing every living organism with no shame—the charming Parisian at our dinner table transformed into a camping dog.

He stopped by a tall, straight tree with compact leaves. "We have those trees too, in the Bois de Vincennes. In English?"

One of the hikers, a bona-fide camper, turned and said it was a beech tree. Dovid's eyebrows scrunched up. "Beach? But isn't that like the Coney Island?"

The others giggled. "Shush!" I scolded them. I informed him that it was spelled differently, I would write it down when we got back. Then I asked if he took his family to the beach in Paris.

"We don't have a beach. Although once I jumped into the Seine on a dare by your Papa." I could just see Dovid taking the dare, but I had to stretch to picture my serious father being so playful.

Farther on, still trailing the others, I took a short skip and reached for Dovid's hand as we hiked. His fingers enclosed mine briefly in a gentle squeeze, and I noticed then that I was no longer comparing him to Papa. His hand was the only hand.

"Tell me about Paris. Mama and Papa never talk about the old days. Did Papa and you and Manny fight?"

"Like the boxers in a ring, no. But cats and dogs, as you say. Manny liked one political party, your Papa liked the other, and me, I changed my mind sometimes. That's all. But all us brothers, we loved each other. That's what to remember, *ma cherie*." He smiled and with a flick of his fingers, fast as a magician, tickled my ear and pinched my cheek in one smooth movement.

"What's ma sheree?" I blurted and took a skip.

"It's like dollink, a term of endearment like your Mama calls you."

"But only Mama calls me that, never Papa. You are so different but you look like twins!"

He laughed, and I fluttered. A future boyfriend or husband, would need to be exactly like my uncle, only much younger of course. It was a secret pact I made with myself.

We walked in silence for a while. The sun kept flickering in my eyes through the branches. Suddenly Dovid stopped short: "Aha, look, scouts," he boomed. "Berries!"

I loved hiking in the woods as much as swimming. The air, its bonus gift of perfume, was damp even though you were dry. Even on a hot day you could feel cool. And strangely, while you could be tromping along with others, singing songs and laughing, you could also feel alone. Sometimes that was a welcome feeling, and sometimes just lonely. I felt as if I knew the trees; one by one they were good friends, and the forest as a whole was like a second, sheltering home. And now, by my side, uncle

Dovid identified trees as if he lived there too, instead of so far away in a once beautiful but now dangerous land. Of all those heavenly summers in the Catskills woods, there was never, ever another hike like the hikes we took that summer.

—◦◦—

When Papa's vacation was over he took Dovid with him to the Bronx. That night I cried in bed. For the rest of the summer I lived for Fridays.

After breakfast Mama said don't worry, he'll be back soon.

"That's if they don't kill each other, Mama! You should've seen them at the river. Papa was so mad at uncle Dovid about Paris."

"Never mind about that. Come dollink, today ve go to the market. Go find Sophie." Go fetch. I was the family dog we never had. But today this puppy kept yipping.

"Mama, wait. Papa said they could send the whole family back to Poland. Does that mean they might not come here?"

Mama stopped wiping the table and gave me a dead stare. She went to the back screen door, opened it, and shook out toast crumbs from the dishcloth into the fresh, floral scented air. She wore a blank expression I had never seen before.

—◦◦—

An expression I had never seen before would forever attach itself in my mind to a tone I had never heard. I was reading on the porch one day, thankful for the quiet while everyone was at the river. Mama must have thought I had gone too. Suddenly I heard voices inside the screen door.

"Oh! I thought you went with the others." Mama sounded startled.

"I had letters to write. To Gerty." There was a silence, and then, "I think you know we met after you left, at the next federation meeting. I proposed to her the following week."

"One week, you knew her? You fall in love easily—"

He broke in. "It didn't matter anymore."

"—and often!" Their voices overlapped each other.

There was another pause. When they next spoke, their voices sounded different, muffled.

"No, Chaya. I fell in love only once."

I held my breath. Their voices got lower, and I heard from Mama again one of those mild gasps that I never knew was from asthma or from surprise.

"Please, Dovid."

There was a silence then, during which I heard, or sensed, it was nearly inaudible, a shifting, like shoes shuffling.

"We are grownups, Dovid. We live with our choices. You made yours." And then, softer, "Don't forget that."

"Oh, Chaya. There never goes a day I don't remember that."

Mama's voice was all trembly, it sounded on the verge of tears. Dovid's was husky and solemn. My heart thumped, and my stomach sank into a queasiness. The words on the page dissolved as I sat there feeling shame for eavesdropping, but also shame for something else that frightened and confused me.

For the first time ever, I refused to help Mama in the kitchen that day. Later that night when we all retired to sleep, behind closed doors in the room I shared with Sophie, I demanded my right to know adult things.

"What happened in Paris, tanta Sophie?"

"So your Papa was the oldest of the three brothers. In 1918 we just finished with the deadliest war, the Great War, so bad it's called the War to End All Wars. After, we were even poorer. Manny got a job at a small Yiddish newspaper, writing articles about politics and workers' conditions, how to get better jobs and strengthen the unions, like they do here, dollink." She took the hairbrush from the dresser, sat by my side on the edge of my bed and brushed my hair, now grown to shoulder-length. "Dovid and your Papa helped with distribution, even after long hours at the tailor shops.

"We all met at those political meetings, we belonged to a federation, and we'd do all sorts of things, even serve soup on the soup lines, can you imagine, poor as we were we helped the newer immigrants. But we had to relax sometimes too, dollink, and at one of the federation socials one night Dovid asked your Mama to dance. They danced so gracefully, and though your Mama was shy, she was a beauty in her quiet way, and you could see her eyes alight in his arms.

"Suddenly Manny burst into the hall. He wanted to get a special bulletin out before dawn. There was great upheaval in those days, thousands of people so poor and nervous, they were leaving their homelands for a better life. We lived in chaos. Which leader you followed—we kept our eyes on Eastern Europe too—who won, who lost, these things dollink could touch you personally, where you'd live, what language you'd speak. Politics fractured families worse than a broken leg; sometimes brothers and sisters didn't speak to each other. Your uncles and their friends were passionate messengers."

Suddenly, Sophie laughed. "Poor Dovid was torn this way and that. Take an arm! he said—Manny pulling him to work, Avrum pulling him to stay and enjoy the social. But underlying that was a bigger tug of war. Manny was an idealist, he believed in France. Avrum said the future was in America. And to make matters worse, their parents went back to Poland; sometimes I think they left because they couldn't stand the brothers fighting."

"But what about Uncle Dovid!" I said.

"Ay-ay, you're obsessed with that man. So being Saturday night, imagine, dollink, Manny wasn't getting many takers to help him with the paper distribution. Avrum refused, but Dovid rarely denied Manny anything. He told Avrum keep Chaya busy, dance with her till I get back he said, so at least nobody else horns in, but remember now, she's mine! One hour of his time and no more, that's what Dovid promised Manny. Avrum protested; he didn't dance, he didn't know her, he was shy whereas Dovid was quite the ladies man. Dovid laughed it off, Tell her you're me, we look like twins, she'll never know the difference. Papa called him completely meshuggah. But he did it. The brothers, they were loyal to each other. Well, Chaya accepted the dance, we all watched, my beau and I laughing on the sidelines."

"Did she catch the switch?"

"Is your Mama stupid? One minute she's being twirled around the dance floor by a dashing charmer, and now she's having her feet nearly stepped on. Not to mention, these brilliant revolutionary brothers who were going to change the world never considered they were dressed differently?" Sophie slapped her thigh and we both giggled like little girls. I jumped up for my hairbrush and pins and Sophie started brushing and pinning up my hair on the bed.

"One thing led to another; she actually liked Avrum's gentle ways, his plain talk. Things got bollixed up after that. Dovid was so arrogant he figured he'd charmed the skirts off Chaya, you should pardon, and was shocked that his brother won a date with her. They came to blows over Chaya. Two brothers loving the same woman was worse than locking horns over politics. For a while they weren't speaking."

"So who'd she go with?" I blurted.

"Stop chewing your cheek," she said. "Chaya and Avrum started to formally 'keep company.' He would arrange a Saturday night rendez-vous. Meanwhile Dovid wiggled his way into her heart. He brought Chaya over to the newspaper, and she was so impressed she volunteered to help out along with the brothers—they would distribute, run errands. Somehow Dovid found time to spend with Chaya. But Avrum being the oldest was working like a dog and contributing money to the household; he didn't have as much free time."

I bolted upright. "Oh no, didn't that make Papa furious? Wooing Mama right under Papa's nose!"

"Well, don't feel too sorry for your Papa. After all, he won your Mama."

"How did she finally choose?" I sat on my haunches and hugged the pillow to my chest as Sophie curled my hair. A horsefly circled frantically overhead. Sophie grabbed a fly swatter and whacked out its miserable life, then got up to shut the crooked window since the screen had holes in it.

She paused and lowered her voice. "She didn't. Don't ever bring this up with your Mama. Finally Dovid thought he found a way to keep the family peace. He stayed in Paris to make Manny happy. He sort of felt responsible for Manny, being the youngest brother, and . . . well, he had his sad moods, Manny. He gave up Chaya to make Avrum happy. It killed him inside; but he had his activism, whereas he felt Avrum really just had Chaya. Avrum proposed to Chaya and started looking for a steamship to America. I already had family here, and we all made arrangements to leave. But believe you me, your Mama was in agony just like Dovid. It was like Chaya was Dovid's farewell present to Avrum. It's funny; Dovid was always the most generous. I actually saw that man skip meals to feed a friend."

I frowned. It didn't all make sense to me, but it answered a mystery: so that's how Dovid was practical in 1921. Sophie got up from the bed and sighed deeply, brushed her own hair and put the brush on the dresser. "Like I said, dollink. Those days were very complicated."

One sunny morning after breakfast Mama reminded Papa about the chickens. It was Papa's job to walk up the road to Trovitsky's chicken farm and bring back fresh-killed chickens, and this day Dovid went with him. Mama, Sophie, and I would spend the afternoon preparing the birds, holding them upside down over the stove while plucking and singeing off any remaining feathers, which process Mama claimed also killed bacteria; so we were killing two birds with one stone, so to speak. But until then, I had free time. Mama said don't waste a divine sunny morning, go down to the river and swim with the other kids, and per usual I declined, taking my book and diary to the porch. Later, from the corner of my eye I saw Papa and Dovid walking back from the farm, their arms full of chickens. As they came closer, I saw something that nearly popped my eyes out onto my lap. Papa was carrying a large bundle of poultry, but Dovid was holding, his arm stretched out from his body, a live bird by the neck.

They were walking apart, looking none too friendly, toward the outbuildings in back of the hotel. I discreetly walked the wraparound porch toward the back and then out near the shed. Their voices grew louder and angry as I hung back but stayed in hearing range, behind a leafy, fat oak. I heard the clanging of tools and saw Dovid sharpening an ax on a boulder with one hand while securing the squawking bird with the other. Papa was fuming, and I swear to this day I could see the veins pulsing on his red face.

"You're hallucinating, we never did this in Belleville, nor the Marais," said Papa.

"You forget Pinchov Poultry. You forget all about the days before," Dovid quipped.

"It was his slaughterhouse; Pinchov killed them. We didn't know how, we were city people. You live in a world of fantasy. You always did."

Dovid raised his eyebrows, then the ax, and looked at the scrawny bird. "Fantasy?" he sneered. "You forget who was the practical one in 1921, when you left." The sneer disappeared. "Anyway, in Poland, for sure we did it. When we were boys. Mama taught us. *You* forget."

Swack! The deed was done. I shuddered, Papa jumped back a bit. Dovid stood looking down at the bird, a pained expression in his face, which lost its normal robust glow and now appeared slack. Blood splattered his shirt. What bothered me more than witnessing the slaughter was Dovid's comment. It was the second time he mentioned 1921; the other time was shabbas dinner, when he said you can't find such exquisite *kreplach* in Paris since Chaya left. Once again, I was confused.

I caught up with the brothers at the back screen door to the kitchen.

Mama looked curiously at the gory chicken. Dovid gave her a shy smile and said, "They're cheaper you know, if you kill them yourself."

Mama just stared at the bird, then up at Papa. He winced, dropped his bundle into the deep tub sink, washed his hands, and went back outside. I kept myself small, practically tiptoeing to the sink, and put on an apron to start washing the poultry. I might've been confused about all these strange goings-on, but I knew by heart how to perform my kitchen tasks. Mama's little helper now felt squirmy inside, and not only about the slaughter. The queasiness was mixed with a guilty thrill, seeing Mama and Dovid alone.

Dovid spoke tenderly. "Let me help you, Chaya, with the one I killed since it's dirtier."

Mama answered all businesslike: "I'll manage, thank you. And since when do men stay in the kitchen?"

Dovid squinted, smiling. "What about the soup kitchen?" And turning to me he said, "Rachel, we ladled out soup for hundreds of people in Paris."

Mama gave a short laugh and shook her head. "Ay-ayay. The poor feeding the poor."

Dovid looked at her. "I hope you haven't stood on soup lines your-selves. I know about the American Depression, even if Avrum never wrote to complain."

"We get by. Better off I should've been in Paris?" she said in a near-mumble. I saw her bite her bottom lip and very slightly shake her head, as if regretting the words.

He finished cleaning up the bloody bird. After washing and drying his hands he walked slowly, with a swagger though a subtle one, not at all show-offy, toward the door. As he passed Mama at the counter, he leaned his head close to hers and almost whispered, with a very faint smile, "If only."

⇥⇤

The next trip to the post office finally produced news. Gerty's letter circu-lated on the porch after dinner. Dovid's family would not be coming to the mountains. They would not be coming to New York. They would not be coming to America. The visas were denied; preliminary approvals apparently were overturned.

Mrs. Gershon jumped up from the chair and gasped, fanning her flushed face frantically with her hands: "Oy vey I'm going to faint! Where is justice, where is God *mein got*!" Mostly everyone stood shocked in silence. But then heads gradually started to nod in acceptance, as though the news was inevitable. I was the only one who remained in the dark. My world was crumbling.

Dovid chain-smoked and paced for a while, not looking up. Papa went inside and brought out a bottle of whiskey with glasses. They all sat down, clustered their chairs tightly around Papa and Dovid, and weighed in. The man would surely want to return to be with his family—that was a given. But then speculations took flight like jittery gnats after a down-pour. Everyone spoke at once: You could wait it out with us. The Nazis will be crushed, Europe won't put up with such grotesque aggression. Then Gerty will come. Hey, it's not like they're in a repressive totalitarian state. It's France, land of the Revolution—*Liberté, Egalité, Fraternité*—they emancipated the Jews for crissakes!. That was two goddamn centuries ago, someone else snapped. But they elected a Jewish prime minister! Look, you can return to Paris—just not now, with things so uncertain. Manny with his connections, they'll protect Gerty and the girls. Then, exhausted of ideas, they fell silent. Only the crickets kept up their racket. But crickets go on gabbing night after night, and always will, indifferent to our troubles.

Mama told me it was way past my bedtime, but I insisted on helping wash the glasses; I had to find out how it ended. Did she think Dovid would stay here and wait for Gerty and my new cousins? In the kindest tone she asked, if I were his daughter, wouldn't I want my Papa to come home?

It was a trick question. An attack of meanness crept over me like poison ivy and I put my hand on my hip and smirked: "And if you were his wife and don't you wish you were, you'd want him home too."

Mama turned pale, wide-eyed. Seeing her like that, I erupted in tears, my lips quivering. "But Mama! He can wait here, they'll come here, the news even said the Nazis will go away."

I was supposed to answer a simple Yes, I would want my father home. Mama never had use for tears; her back stiffened as she soaped the glasses. She had an infuriating way of answering questions with Yiddish witticisms. Only this one she delivered as a somber pronouncement. "The Nazis leave? *Az di kats zol leygen eyer, volt zi geven a hun.*" If a cat laid eggs, she would be a hen.

I couldn't sleep that night. When I finally dozed off, I slept till noon and never heard Dovid packing his suitcase.

⊰⊱

After World War II broke out, I stopped badgering Mama and Papa about letters from Paris. When I did ask they answered irritably; everyone was on edge, and in any case I was a teenager, and eventually my attention drifted elsewhere. Yet I too was affected by the dark and heavy air that hung over our whole section of the Bronx. For a long time I suffered from headaches and depression, which were blamed variously on school pressures, later boyfriend miseries. Mama kept her mind and hands busy cooking, mending clothes, volunteering at the Workmen's Circle, but the warm light in her eyes had dimmed. Papa sat by the radio even in the postwar years, through the Glenn Miller years, and into the Ed Sullivan era, whom Mama called Ed Solomon. She could crack jokes, but Papa was serious, always serious, his head buried in the *Forward*, radio news on the hour, every hour, as though waiting for something. *News bulletin: your brothers did not go to the gas chambers.* He never spoke of his brothers again. We all have two minds: one rational, fact-knowing, and the other inhabiting a world that we paint with colors we ourselves mix. In that world Papa was waiting. I know this because I waited with him.

Maybe there had been letters, maybe not. Until I found a metal box many years later while cleaning their apartment, I never knew. But our rational minds, of course, knew the facts. Nearly 13,000 Jews, Papa's brothers and family included, were rounded up over two days in July 1942 by the French police, from their homes and streets. From their homes and streets to transit camps, and from those camps to the death camps. Dovid, his wife and children, and Manny, to Auschwitz. In the Catskills there were hushed words in fragmented sentences among the numbed, unbelieving families. We sat fanning ourselves in the Adirondack chairs, sitting low to the floorboards. As if the wood planks, the sympathetic porch, the sloping lawn, and the purple clover would absorb our incurable grief.

$\vartheta\varepsilon$

Love and politics make the world go round, that's what Mama used to say. One day in my Manhattan apartment, when Mama and Papa were well on in years, I asked her how she chose between Papa and Dovid, loving them both; because that was a given. As we all aged, Mama had mellowed and I gained more entrée into her heart. Maybe I filled a void for her since Sophie had passed, not more than a year before. We were making dinner and I spoke in low tones; Papa was in the living room watching the 6:00 news. I spoke quickly, before the news ended when we would call him in for the ritual schnapps toast. I asked if it was the events of the times, and the promise of America, that drove her from France with Papa, more than love. Mama held the green ceramic bowl steady while I whisked olive oil briskly into the egg yolks. She smiled ruefully into the bowl. "Find me the oil. Find me the eggs. You can't; it's already mayonnaise—you mix and mix, and finally you can't separate them."

Once I discovered the letters, I read them over and over, and kept them with the pictures, and the picture with the torn edge. Other things too, I put into the metal box. Leaves we picked on our hikes that I had dried and kept all those years. Things like that. I kept them and the pictures in acid-free paper, which at some point I bought at an art supply store.

Paris, August 1940

Dear Avrum,

I hope this reaches you, circuitously via a neighbor who was going to Portugal and promised to mail it from there. I didn't join the mass exodus from Paris to the South. I begged Manny to come with us, but he's adamant to work even harder. Some think we're crazy to stay. Gerty seems to walk as if in a fog, while the girls simply pray for a normal day. Of course we'd be on foot like thousands of Parisians walking, bicycling alongside cars, families and children carrying their possessions on their backs. We wouldn't get far with Gerty's arthritis. I was torn between going and staying. Remember the last time I was crippled by indecision? But decide I did, and Gerty has been a wonderful wife and given me two lovely daughters; since they were born here, their citizenship should protect them.

I try to keep up my hopes and support Manny, whose fits of melancholia are overridden these days by our work with a growing number of resisters. Risky, but they're out to destroy all us Jews anyway; not to fight back is unthinkable. Keep appealing to the immigration aid society on your end. Whatever the outcome, I got to see you and Chaya again and that memory alone sustains me—the thought and prayer that some day we might again toast schnapps in the Catskills. Give Chaya and Rachel a big hug for me.

Your Dovid

Prize-Winning Essay:
Non-Fiction

Forgiving God in the Catskills[1]

Michael Kirschenbaum

Dad is wheezing as he goes through his morning rituals, shaving, cleaning his dentures. He sits down to put on his pants. He is ninety, and we are sharing a hotel room in the Catskills for *Rosh Hashanah*. I pretend to sleep as he readies himself for morning prayers. He likes to get there early to reserve seats for the family in the Stardust Room. My brother and my nephew are in the room next door. It is just the boys. My father and I are widowers. Mom and Ronnie are dead. My brother Ben is in the midst of a divorce. Ben and I both have girlfriends who are not

---

1 "Forgiving God in the Catskills" is a chapter from my forthcoming memoir tentatively titled *A Jewish Chicken Farmer's Son*. I was born in Munich, Germany, but my memories start as a four-year-old on our chicken farm near Lakewood, NJ. My parents were refugees, survivors. They were Polish Jews who lost their families in the well-ordered madness of genocide and the chaos of war. My mother, Bronia, fought with the Jewish resistance. My father, Godel, an inmate at Auschwitz, was an Orthodox Jew with a number tattooed on his forearm. His parents, his brother, his sisters, his nephew were all victims of the Holocaust. My father often told us stories about his life in Europe. They were tales that wandered from the small town where he was raised, to his war years in the ghetto and at Auschwitz, and sometimes his postwar years in Munich. He taught his family to see suffering clearly, but he also taught us to try to live life with joy. "Forgiving God in the Catskills" focuses on a family visit to the Catskills to celebrate the Jewish New Year.

Jewish. My nephew's girlfriend is Jewish; a Russian immigrant who grew up without religion and never missed it. None of the women were tempted by religious holidays in the Catskills.

I can smell Dad's cologne. He takes pride in the clean new shirt and fresh tie he has for day two of the holiday. The older crew at the Catskill resort is pretty well turned out, but, even here, some of the older folks have trouble keeping food or drool off of their shirtfronts. I am in my late fifties, and I feel just a little guilty about how being among the truly aged makes me feel young.

Dad picks up his *tallis* and heads for the Stardust nightclub. The room is a large indoor amphitheater whose blue walls are decorated with stars and galaxies. A dark horsehead shadow peeks up from one of the nebulae. Most nights the room hosts the cabaret; today it is doing double duty: *Rosh Hashanah* services in the morning and a stand-up comic at night. We are at Kutsher's, an aging resort, one of the few left that serves kosher food and has a *Rosh Hashanah* program. This is the Borscht Belt. In its heyday, names like Buddy Hackett, Danny Kaye, and Joan Rivers headlined. There is a poster in one corner for an upcoming "Polka Fest," which triggers TV memories of the Lawrence Welk Show (my mother loved the show). She thought Welk was Polish because he had a Polka band. Wikipedia tells me he is Russian, from German stock. For me, all accordion players bring Polkas to mind, or is it the other way around—that all Polkas remind me of accordions? Before Dad leaves he makes sure I'm awake.

"Don't be too late! They blow the *shofar* today."

The ancient ram's horn is somehow part of our covenant with God. Bob Dylan comes to mind. "God said to Abraham 'kill me a son.' Abe said, 'God you must be putting me on.'" When I first read Genesis as a child, I asked my father, "How could someone tie up his child and kill him?" My father explained that Abraham knew God was just testing him and was not really going to let him burn his son on a mountaintop altar. God does relent and the *shofar* harkens back to the ram that Abraham sacrificed instead of his son, Isaac.

My father's faith has been tested by a God that did not relent, a God that took his whole family as sacrifice, burnt offerings in Nazi crematoriums. I know he sees his own survival as a miracle. For him and most of his *Greeneh* friends, the survivors, the post-WWII immigrants, holding on to the religion, to the traditions meant, at least in part, not giving their enemies the satisfaction of completely destroying their community.

"Dad, are you going down for coffee first?"

"No, it's too far. I'll be okay."

Yesterday, I brought him coffee on a whim and he drank it gratefully during the rabbi's sermon. He still gets around pretty well, but the dining room and the Stardust lounge are at opposite ends of the property. The 1,000 yards of extra walking is more than he will endure for a cup of coffee.

"Ok. Coffee and a roll or a piece of cake. Not too much. And, please, this time put it in a bag."

Even though he and others are worshipping in a nightclub, seated at tables that rise up in tiers surrounding a round stage, Dad's sense of decorum remains. It is violated by eating his food at prayers. Or perhaps he does not want to offend others who have not had their coffee and might look longingly at his bagel.

I struggle out of bed, grateful for the thin sheet of plywood between the bed and the mattress that keeps the mattress from being concave. I cannot find a new razor blade and on a whim use Dad's Norelco. I pop off the top and empty the grey-white beard trimmings. The three floating heads prove surprisingly comfortable and effective, better than my fancy European electric shaver. When I clean the shaver I notice that my beard trimmings are almost the same color as Dad's.

Sitting next to my father in the Stardust Room as the cantor leads the morning prayers, I think about our rabbi in the old farmers' *shul* in New Jersey. He drank too much and his beard was tobacco stained. He was a gambler and played poker till all hours of the night. There were rumors that he had a mistress in his younger years, but when he prayed on the High Holidays and the tears ran down his cheeks staining his robe and the congregation joined him wailing as he recited the *Unetaneh Tokef* prayer, he became my archetype of a rabbi. The *Unetaneh Tokef* is a dark prayer with a dark history composed by a rabbi who was tortured and killed in the eleventh century for refusing to give up his faith. "Come let us declare our faith as we pass before the lord to be judged, who shall live and who shall die, who by sword or plague, by water or fire, by stoning. . . ." Those assembled had seen whole cities destroyed, generations murdered as they watched. They lost fathers and mothers, sons and daughters, husbands and wives, sisters and brothers. In that New Jersey *shul*, the dead were gathered among us, a tangible presence. No one was unscarred and even the children trembled. A coda ending the prayer told us that repentance, prayer, and charity reduced the harshness of the decree. They asked for forgiveness, but I marveled that they had kept their faith, that they had forgiven God for what he had done to them.

Here in the Catskills my father is not the only one with a number tattooed on his forearm. The Holocaust left marks on many in the crowd. The survivors and their families carry the same burdens.

Dad was from Wyszogrod (*Vish- e- grod*) along the Vistula River in Poland where Jews are mentioned as early as the fifteenth century and a famous synagogue was built of stone in the eighteen century and stood for two hundred years. He spoke with awe of the place with its Baroque architecture, the biggest building he ever saw in all his youth. The Nazis destroyed it in 1939.

As we sit in the Stardust Room, he asks me if I will be fasting on *Yom Kippur*, the Day of Atonement that marks the closure of prayers for the New Year. This tenth day of the New Year is the final settling of accounts with God. It is a traditional fast day, one in which you take neither food nor drink. I ask him if I should fast, knowing he will say yes. Getting him to say it out loud somehow makes it another *mitzvah* I could do for him. He tells me about fasting on *Yom Kippur* at Auschwitz, how the first year was very hard, and he thought he would pass out during his work detail, how the thirst was worse than the hunger. The second year was easier because he was assigned to work nights, and so he could sleep in the day. He hid his soup and crust of bread under his bunk and it sat waiting for him, waiting for the fast to end.

Rosh Hashanah is not a fast day. And after prayers we join the crowd heading for the dining room. It is a vast space. The numbered tables, plates gleaming, seem to extend to the horizon. Gefilte fish, chopped liver, kugel, herring, challah, and bagels are already in place as people find the seats. The holiday feast brings back memories of the "glory days." The resort was built in 1907. Next year it will be a hundred years old. The dining room can seat over a thousand. Eddy is our waiter, a small man who looks like a teenager until you get closer to his hands and eyes. He and his bus person, Andrea, are from Brazil. Both have been working in the Catskills for fifteen years. You can usually judge seniority by how far away the waiters are from the kitchen. Eddy is not one of the oldest hands, but there are newer crews walking past Eddy's station into the deep recesses of the dining room. They carry platters with fifteen entrees balanced on their shoulders.

"It's not like it once was." Andrea in a slightly accented voice bemoans the decline. "Now it's just the old folks."

Last night as we sat around the table, it seemed the dead reached out to us. We reminisced about the Concord, a more upscale resort, near Kiamesha Lake, where our family had once gathered for the Jewish holidays—until the resort closed down. We were trying to recall what year that was. 1997? Or was it 1998? Our timeline was measured by who was still with us and who was not.

"Did Ronnie come to Kutsher's?"

"Yes. Remember, she helped Mom walk to the dining room."

"Yes, Mom was still walking then."

Before lunch today, we had paused in one of the lobbies near a wheelchair elevator. Dad was resting, although still on his own two feet, holding hands with my brother and me as we walked.

"Dad, are you thinking of Mom?" Dad, a little teary, looks at an elderly woman wheeling away from the lift. "We took her just like that. . . . She didn't like to be in the chair."

"But, thank God for wheelchairs." My brother reminds us of the painful year when Mom insisted on hobbling about, taking ages to get from place to place, a two-person escort required at every stage.

Mom always showed up at meals especially when there was a Jewish menu.

"Wow, they have gefilte fish."

"But it's not like Mom's."

"Oh, look there's honey cake."

"Not as good as hers."

My nephew Rickie has been looking forward to some honey cake. He loved Mom's. But, he has some allergies that make eating at the resort challenging. It is a long list, including milk products. Today, it is the nuts that keep him from eating the cake. Mom's cake did not have nuts. Hers was dense, chewy, dripping with honey. Think of fudge brownies. She made something like fudge honey cake. Almost every time I visit my old college friend, Claire, she tells me that of her biggest regrets was not getting Mom's recipe. "It was amazing. Somehow, instead of drying out it got moister over time."

Dad has taken on Mom's role, trying to make sure everyone eats. My brother Ben and I are good eaters. Tall mesomorphs, Mom claimed that we were finicky in our childhood eating, but we had blossomed. Dad watches us with satisfaction, but complains to Rickie that he hasn't eaten anything. Rick is tall too, but doesn't carry any extra weight on his narrow frame. His mother has struggled with weight, but her mom, a Lench, can still wear the size 4 gown she wore at her wedding sixty years ago. Dad would say, sometimes jokingly and sometimes not, that she looked starved or withered. Maybe I'm being harsh, and skinny is a better translation from the Yiddish.

Dad's at it again. "You don't eat like a Kirschenbaum. You eat like a Lench." Ben and I are doing our best to uphold the family honor, asking our waiter, Eddy, to bring out extra entrées, and some potato latkes and schmaltz and herring to try alongside our three egg omelets. Plates crowd the table. Ben and I sample them all, devouring, deracinating, digging through the offerings shamelessly. Rickie is more circumspect, dainty even, his plate half full, unmoved by the abundance. In my youth, I was embarrassed by the seeming gluttony of some my parents' friends. Were they beggars afraid that they would never see food again? Their plates looked like the tangled growth of dense tropical forests, tendrils of food hanging over the edges. The men and women moved past the smorgasbord, stuffing whatever cookies, bread, crackers they could scrounge into white linen table napkins for late night snacks.

Not limited to the Catskill's Jewish Alps, the same behavior was evident at a Jersey Shore resort where I worked one summer. I was similarly repulsed. Over the years, my attitude and abdomen have softened.

Nowadays I worry about Dad. We live three hundred miles apart, and I don't get to see him as often as I'd like. I know he's lonely. After all, he and Mom were together for over fifty years. But Dad's proud. And private. Later in the afternoon, after playing a round of golf with my brother, I return to our room energized by the fresh air; it had been overcast on the green, but still warm, warm enough to be comfortable in long sleeved jerseys.

Dad is already dressed for dinner. As I dress, I ask him how things are going with Krisha. She's the Polish woman whom my parents hired when my mother became ill and who stayed on as a live-in companion after Mom died. Krisha cooks for Dad and cleans the house. It is a great relief to Ben and me that Dad has someone to talk to, someone who makes it safe for him to live at home.

"How's Krisha?"

"She's good."

"She's always so happy to hear my voice when I call and she seems disappointed when you're not home."

My conversations with Krisha are restricted by her limited English and my nonexistent Polish.

"Father, not home. Play cards," she tells me.

Dad plays cards with the ladies now. There are not enough men left to play poker. They have all died.

"She likes you," Dad smiles. "She says you are one in a thousand."

"I told you more than once how great your sons are." I tease him. "But, what does she mean?"

He gets a more serious look on his face, still bemused, but not laughing.

"She means because you are not jealous, not bitter. She likes that you are quiet and don't get angry. She says if every man was like you there would be no war."

Dad recalls an old Jewish proverb about who is truly a rich man. A rich man is the man who is *Sah-mey-ach B'chelko*, someone who is happy with his portion. Ben walks in to see if we are ready to go eat again, and I miss a chance to push Dad on what he thinks. Jealous of whom? My brother, his wealth, his children?

Krisha is a deeply religious woman who goes to mass most days. One son lives nearby. He came on an education visa, and is probably an illegal immigrant by now. She calls home most days and talks to her husband, her daughter, and her daughter's husband, who all live in the same house in Poland. I think her mother-in-law is there too and perhaps others. Krisha has probably sent $50,000 back to her family in the few years that she has worked for my father, and in Poland that is a small fortune. They have bought land. I think they are building a new house.

It is easy to imagine why she might wonder at my not being bitter. My wife died a horrible death as the cancer choked her lungs, but I have worked hard to forgive the fates. My father likes to use the German expression: *Alles geht vorüber.* Everything goes by, and you can get past anything, but sometimes I think of another German expression: *Alles geht drunter und drüber.* Everything goes haywire, and it ties you in knots.

After dinner in the hotel dining room, people wander about in the lobbies socializing. There are couches and overstuffed chairs arranged so that families can lounge in the semi- comatose state brought on by sugary wine and generous portions of Borscht Belt food. To be honest, I have not seen any borscht, although we have been served chicken soup and beef *flanken* and *veal paprikash* . . . and . . . and . . .

Dad runs into some guys he knows. They are *Greeneh* too. Friends of friends, they were members of the "society" or the "organization," which usually refers to a Holocaust survivor group but it could be any Jewish organization.

I leave them to chat. The conversation often begins with an old person's Jewish Geography, asking about who is still alive and in what state of health, but moves on to children and grandchildren, business ventures, travel, politics, the state of the hotel.

I drift towards the Flying Saucer Café, a smaller companion to the Stardust Room. It is a bar/café halfway between the dining room and the larger amphitheater. There is music drifting out. As I walk by one of the larger family groups, a white-haired woman looks up at me and says, "It could be John Kerry." The others turn towards me and mostly nod. I smile. I have heard it before.

"I'm not sure whether that's a compliment."

They laugh and argue that he is a distinguished man. Their accents mark them as native New Yorkers. Yet apart from a young woman Rickie's age and her mother and father, the others belong to my parents' generation.

I complain that Kerry has always looked dour and that, even though I voted for him, I could not remember a single thing he had ever said or championed.

I break off and wander into the lounge. A woman with an amazing voice, of gravel and honey, is belting out rhythm and blues with some show tunes and rock and roll mixed in. There is a small dance floor. Two couples are dancing and several groups of women are sitting about. Ben joins me for a drink, "Ask one of the old ladies to dance and make her New Year happy!" He pokes me in the ribs, pushing me towards the dance floor. I do love swing dancing, and sometimes the older ladies display greater ballroom skills than the younger ones. One is tapping her foot, expensive shoes keeping a good beat; her outfit shimmers and she looks game. Shirley is her name, and I ask her to dance. She does pretty well twirling about, smiling when she gets the hang of the stop and goes. She is flushed and breathing hard. I slow down the tempo and let her collect herself as the song winds down. She goes back to her friends beaming.

Since Ronnie died, whenever I dance, the memory of holding her on the dance floor brings back a tumult of joy and loss. We got to be hot stuff when a band was rocking, but it didn't start out that way. Ballroom dance has gender-based roles. Feminism was in an intense phase when we started dancing. Men leading had implications of patriarchy and oppression. Radical feminism, consciousness raising, and women's liberation were a fire racing through the country and especially hot where we lived in Cambridge, Massachusetts. Ronnie was in the Boston Women's Graphics Collective that silk-screened feminist t-shirts and posters. One of my favorite photos shows a woman working at a construction site wearing one of their t-shirts. Shovel in hand, the t-shirt proclaims: "Women hold up half the sky"—one of Chairman Mao's proverbs.

Getting Ronnie to accept that I was leading on the dance floor was a problem. We had faced similar issues when we were learning about white water canoeing, sorting out who would choose direction and tactics for avoiding rocks in the fast water streams.

"Left!"

"Left?"

"No! Right!"

"Right?"

After swamping the canoe a few times in chilly New Hampshire streams, we learned to trust each other. I would steer from the stern when the water was calm, and Ronnie would call out directions from the bow when the water got choppy. The struggles over who leads on the dance floor, and what it means to feminist ideology seem a bit quaint now. Ronnie had spent almost the entire first ten years of our relationship in a t-shirt and jeans, but she swallowed her wardrobe dogma and bought some skirts and dresses for dancing. She had always been shy, very restrained in expressing sexuality, but dancing transformed her into someone that didn't mind being a center of attention. If the music had a good beat and we could find some space on the dance floor we would fly, her skirt rising in quick turns, her eyes shining, her smile beaming out at the cosmos, electricity passing between us as we moved to the music. Our dancing was a controlled mayhem, and if we lacked the precision of some of the best dancers, the joy and energy we generated often made us stand out on the dance floor.

At the Flying Saucer Café some of the "Kerry" gang had wandered in while I was on the dance floor. The young woman pushes her mother along. "Mom, ask him to dance! You'll have fun!" Her mother, Susan, hesitates, and I ask her if she wants to try. Susan may be just a bit younger than my first dancing partner, Shirley, although she wears the same fancy shoes, glittery dress and stiff hairdo. She's showing a little more cleavage, as well, and as we whirl about one of her straps threatens to slip off her shoulder. Ballroom dancing with a stranger begins with a dialogue, but usually no words are necessary: stance, grip, balance. The man's job is to lead and to showcase the woman.

Susan has gotten used to leading herself, but I make an argument for leading. Not a word is spoken, but we do have a conversation set to music (credit Arthur Murray). It may have been a long time since she danced with someone who could provide a strong lead, or who wanted to, but after a few missteps she starts to trust me and have fun. The band takes a break, and she goes off happy, sweating, and a little disheveled. I go to look for Dad.

The next morning I am carrying coffee and a bagel and a piece of cake to Dad, who is praying in the Stardust Room. It is almost 9:30 AM and he has been here for a couple of hours. He is glad to see me, and asks after Ben and Rickie. I am pretty sure they will get here in time to hear the *shofar*. We need to make an appearance or "people will talk." Dad worries that his buddies will tease him about his *yeshiva bochers*, the young unmarried men in his family, who might not attend *shul*. I remind him that there are few people left of his generation to pay attention to such things. He is off the hook. It's now my generation's job to worry about these things.

The congregation is reading from the *Torah* the chapter about Abraham, the ram, and Isaac (*Yitz-chak* in Hebrew: *He will make us rejoice*). Dad takes the bag of food I brought him and discretely walks out of the room to have his coffee in the lobby. I am left behind to guard our seats. This part of the service, the *Torah* reading, had always served as a break for most of the congregation. The kids and the smokers would make a beeline for the outdoors. As I have grown older and given up smoking, I've started to enjoy this segment more than the regular prayers, reading along in the biblical Hebrew that I learned in grade school and watching the parade of people called up to say blessings.

This is when the rabbi gives his sermon. The seats are filling as the time approaches for *musaf*, the prayer added on holidays. I look behind me and spot Susan, one of my dance partners in the large amphitheater, which rises in tiers. We exchange nods and nervous smiles. My other partners are also in the crowd, and it feels a bit like high school, furtive glances with hidden meanings.

Shirley's husband is sitting next to her and notices when we make eye contact. He may be eighty, but his eyes narrow, and his brow and lips add to the grimace and frown. It brings me back to the Bible. The chapter before the sacrifice of Isaac is about Abraham and Sarah when they lived in the Negev, near the kingdom of the Philistine, during the reign of Abimelech. Even though they are both old, Sarah is still a great beauty. Abraham asks Sarah to tell strangers that she is his sister so that men will not be tempted to kill Abraham and take Sarah as a wife. Shirley's husband is safe. I am not tempted.

After the service, a woman as old as Sarah in the story struggles to maneuver her wide walker down a narrow corridor into the main lobby. A small speed bump causes her to list to the left. She approaches the lift designed for those with wheelchairs and walkers, pushes the button, and waits. And she waits. I ask if I can help. She says, "It is okay, they will come and help me." And they do. One person carries the walker and the other takes her arm. When it becomes clear that even with help she is not able to climb the stairs, they sit her down in a chair and the two sturdy young men lift both her and the chair, carrying her up the stairs.

I walk out to the back patio overlooking the lake. The sky appears unsettled, and I hear the distant rumblings of thunder. In this moment before the storm, I turn and spot one of the young men who had carried the woman with the walker. He is telling his daughter about the woman. She is holding his hand. Her head is turned up, the tiny chin pointing just above his kneecap, her eyes, searchlights, probing. White leggings reach down to shiny patent leather shoes below her party dress. He bends down to tell her: "Honey, we try to help people. That's what we do."

I feel tears running down my cheeks as I remember one of my father's stories from Auschwitz about an inmate named Avrum. Avrum is a Yiddish variant for Abraham. Did the Bible story bring him to mind? Abraham was asked by God to sacrifice his son Isaac. Dad often referred to those who died in the camps as *korbanim*, slaughtered sacrifices, gassed and cremated. My father lost his parents, his brother, and four sisters to the Holocaust. We would have needed a very large table in Kutsher's dining room had they survived.

Dad managed to survive Auschwitz in part because he landed a job at the laundry. "This German Jew gave me the job in the laundry." My father is talking about a prisoner who served as a factotum for one of the guards. The laundry job was a blessing, because it was a warm place in the winter and it gave Dad the opportunity to steal clothes. A fellow inmate helped him trade the clothes for food. If you did not bend the rules, you did not survive.

"This German Jew, I don't remember his name, took care of one of the SS men and lived in a small room in the attic above the block where the prisoners slept. My partner and I would take rice or macaroni, and sugar to the attic and he would cook it for us.

"One time we were sitting looking out the window in the attic. Each of us had a plate with macaroni with a little sugar on it. One of the prisoners from the block came up behind us. He was a Polish Jew. Avrum was his name.

"It was a bad day for Avrum. The guards sometimes came through the bunks making selections of the people who could not work anymore. That day they had picked Avrum. Being selected was a death sentence. The next day he was supposed to be taken to the gas chamber. He came up behind us. He was in bad shape, skin and bones. He was staring at the floor, muttering over and over, 'It's my last Sunday, my last Sunday.' I tell you, the spoon would not go into my mouth."

He coughs, his throat closing again sixty-five years later.

"I couldn't look at him. I gave him my plate like this."

We were sitting in Dad's kitchen in New Jersey when he told me the story. He picked up a plate from the kitchen table and handed it back over his left shoulder.

"'It's my last Sunday' Avrum said."

My father shook his head slowly. A sad smile crept across his face before he spoke. "I couldn't eat anymore so I gave him my food."

It wasn't always possible, but even in the camps people tried to help each other.

I walked back into the hotel and stopped in to visit Ben and Rickie in their room. I watched Rickie go through a couple of bags of chips and most of a pint of avocado dip and realized he was not a dainty eater, but simply had tastes that Kutsher's kitchen could not satisfy on the High Holidays.

For most people, the kitchen and the dining room are the main reasons for coming to the resort. The rooms are "getting tired," or they were that *Rosh Hashanah* weekend. We put up with old carpets, sagging, lumpy mattresses, peeling paint, the occasional moldy bathroom, and hot water shortages. Ben had stepped into the shower and soaped himself up before realizing that the water was not getting any hotter. He was grumpy most of the morning, but cheered up at lunch. A comic at the hotel had joked, "Let me eat in the dining room and I'll sleep under the table."

The resorts were in decline when my mother was still alive. Even so, coming to the Catskills was still a celebration of life for my father and mother. And then there was always the memory of the glory days when places like Grossinger's, the Concord, and Kutsher's served kosher food and had comics that delivered punch lines in Yiddish. They were places where Jews could gather with their children and grandchildren for festivals that renewed old traditions. Some of the Jews had immigrated before WWII, but many had come after the Holocaust. They called themselves the *Greeneh*, the greenhorns. Now they were old people, but still thought of themselves as the new ones in the herd. The *Greeneh* were happy to mingle with the others who still embraced a Jewish culture with European roots. My parents and most of the survivors are gone. The hotels aged with them and most have passed away, but the memories still linger.

Index

CPSIA information can be obtained at www.ICGtesting.com
Printed in the USA
LVOW10s1932230616

493882LV00009B/18/P